SOCIAL WORK SKILLS AND

KNOWLEDGE

A PRACTICE HANDBOOK

Third Edition

SOCIAL WORK SKILLS AND

KNOWLEDGE

A PRACTICE HANDBOOK

Third Edition

Pamela Trevithick

 Open University Press

Open University Press
McGraw-Hill Education
McGraw-Hill House
Shoppenhangers Road
Maidenhead
Berkshire
England
SL6 2QL

email: enquiries@openup.co.uk
world wide web: www.openup.co.uk

and Two Penn Plaza, New York, NY 10121-2289, USA

First published 2000
Second edition 2005
Reprinted 2005, 2006, 2009
First published in this third edition 2012

A catalogue record of this book is available from the British Library

ISBN-13: 978-0-33-523807-1
ISBN-10: 0-33-523807-6
eISBN: 978-0-33-523808-8

Library of Congress Cataloging-in-Publication Data
CIP data applied for

Typeset by Aptara Inc., New Delhi, India
Printed in the UK by Bell & Bain Ltd, Glasgow

Fictitious names of companies, products, people, characters and/or data that may be
used herein (in case studies or in examples) are not intended to represent any real
individual, company, product or event.

MIX
Paper from
responsible sources
FSC
www.fsc.org
FSC® C007785

The McGraw·Hill Companies

For Charlie Beaton and our son, Tom Trevithick

PRAISE FOR THIS BOOK

"What a sensible book, a book born of much wisdom and practical experience. Pamela Trevithick takes the reader on a wonderfully clear but thorough journey of social work's knowledge, skills and values in which theories are elegantly put into practice. The whole enterprise is reassuringly held together by a strong commitment to organised thinking and the value of the social work relationship. For those who want to sharpen their ideas while keeping their practical feet firmly on the ground, this is the book for you."

Professor David Howe, University of East Anglia, UK

"This new edition is an excellent resource for practitioners, students and indeed managers in social work and social care who are committed to effective practice and service delivery . . . Trevithick provides a comprehensive knowledge and skills framework and excellent practice examples to enable the reader to apply the knowledge to undertaking skilled and effective practice. This is a clear, readily understandable and comprehensive text which also integrates the complexity of practising social work. I highly recommend it."

Professor Joyce Lishman, recently retired as Head of School of Applied Social Studies, Robert Gordon University, UK

"A fantastic guide to social work practice and one I would recommend for the bookshelf of any social work student. It has a user friendly style that presents issues in an accessible way."

Kate Grant, Social Work Student, University of Bristol, UK

"A brilliant MUST BUY book for all social workers. It covers an amazing range of issues which are easy to find using the index. I will use it constantly throughout my career."

Amanda Moorcroft, Social Work Practitioner, UK

CONTENTS

Acknowledgements   ix

PART 1: Theories and Theorists

1   Introduction   3

2   Theoretical knowledge   25

3   Factual knowledge   61

4   Practice knowledge   91

5   Understanding human beings   123

PART 2: Skills and Interventions

6   Communication, observation, listening, and
    assessment skills   153

7   Interviewing skills   185

8   Providing help, direction, and guidance   225

9   Empowerment, negotiation, and partnership skills   253

10 Professional competence and accountability   275

APPENDICES

Appendix 1: Behaviourist approaches   311

Appendix 2: Cognitive approaches   315

Appendix 3: Crisis intervention   319

Appendix 4: Ecological approach in social work   323

Appendix 5: Feminist perspectives in social work   329

Appendix 6: Motivational interviewing   333

Appendix 7: Person-centred approaches   337

Appendix 8: Psychological approaches   341

Appendix 9: Radical and activist perspectives in
social work   345

Appendix 10: Strengths perspectives   349

Appendix 11: Task-centred approaches   353

Appendix 12: Stages of change (or cycle of change)   357

References   361
Index   395

ACKNOWLEDGEMENTS

This book is a testament to the generosity of friends and colleagues who have taken time out from their busy lives to read and comment on different chapters. In particular, I would like to thank Alan Howe, Amanda Moorcroft, Andrew Whittaker, Bridget Brown, Bridget Powell, Charlie Beaton, Donald Branch, Jason Schaub, Madeleine Howe, Mary Taylor, Maureen Stanwell, Peter Dolman, Rachel Mirrlees, Robert French, Sally Richards, and Stuart Matthews. I would also like to pay tribute to the expertise and skill demonstrated by members of staff at Open University Press. I am especially grateful to my editor, Katherine Hartle, for the thoughtful and competent way that she has guided this book to publication and to Richard Townrow and Bryony Skelton, and particularly Claire Munce, for the editorial support they have given me.

I would like to offer my special thanks to Judy Golding. I would have withered in my efforts to send this book on its way without her encouragement, insightful comments and friendship. I am also grateful to Sophie Ainsworth and Peter Dolman who offered their considerable skills, often at short notice. In addition, I would like to acknowledge the people I have worked with over the years. Their stories, and courage in situations of adversity, have taught me so much and continue to fuel my belief that we can create a better and fairer world.

My greatest appreciation is reserved for Charlotte Paterson. I owe Charlotte more than I can say for everything she is – and for all she has given me. She has shared her knowledge and experience with generosity and in ways that have sustained me through unsettling periods of self-doubt and the suspicion that this book will never leave my hands.

Finally, while the ideas and experiences of many people have shaped this book, it is important to state that all errors are mine.

PART 1

THEORIES AND THEORISTS

1   INTRODUCTION

Social work has changed a great deal in recent years. Indeed, in relation to the UK it would be more accurate to say that social work *has been changed*, and *is still being changed*, largely in response to initiatives proposed by successive governments. Nevertheless, one fundamental feature remains the same, namely that social work involves working with some of the most complex problems and perplexing areas of human experience. For this reason, social work is – and has to be – a highly skilled and knowledgeable activity, for as Coulshed notes, *'there are no easy remedies in social work, especially when we are confronted daily with oppression and deprivation'* (1991: 3). The complexity of this task is highlighted in the definition of social work agreed in 2001 by the International Association of Schools of Social Work (IASSW) and the International Federation of Social Workers (IFSW):

> The social work profession promotes social change, problem-solving in human relationships and the empowerment and liberation of people to enhance well-being. Utilising theories of human behaviour and social systems, social work intervenes at the points where people interact with their environments. Principles of human rights and social justice are fundamental to social work.
>
> (IFSW/IASSW 2000)

This influential definition has been incorporated into the National Occupational Standards (TOPSS 2002: 12) and is featured in a number of important publications, such as the Code of Ethics of the British Association of Social Workers (BASW). However, this definition is currently under review and readers are advised to refer to the IASSW and IFSW websites to check for an updated version (website addresses provided at the end of the book).

The purpose of this text is to describe this knowledgeable and skilled activity and to identify how social work skills and interventions can be used in practice to enhance effectiveness and to help bring about the kind of changes, results, or outcomes that are being sought. It focuses in particular on 80 generalist skills and interventions commonly used in social work, but with greater coverage being given to some skills more than others, such as assessment skills. The first edition of this book, published in 2000, was written to bridge a gap that existed because, at that time, few texts focused specifically on social work skills and interventions. The extent of this gap was not confined to the UK as is evident from the fact that this text has been translated into Chinese, Japanese, Spanish, Swedish, and Korean. It is a gap that has also been highlighted in relation to social work education and training (Marsh and Triseliotis 1996; SWTF 2009a), a subject covered later in this text.

Perspectives that inform this text

Five main perspectives inform this third edition. First is the view that to be effective, social work practitioners must work from a sound knowledge and skills base. This must have 'utility' (Pawson *et al.* 2003: 40) in terms of its relevance to the issues and concerns regularly encountered in practice. A second perspective focuses on the central importance of communication in social work. A third recognizes the importance of a relationship-based approach in social work, which provides a foundation to enable us to 'understand and help other human beings' (Munro 2011a: 36). A relationship-based approach is linked closely to a fourth perspective that looks at the notion of 'capacity building' or 'capacity development' – and the role that social workers can play in terms of enhancing individual, family, group, organizational, and environmental capacities. A fifth perspective is a more personal account where I outline the assumptions that inform the way I think about human beings and human behaviour. Although these perspectives are described under separate headings, they overlap with one another. They indicate the kind of issues that I consider important within social work – issues that are central to the themes covered in this text. The following account describes these perspectives in greater detail.

1. The importance of a sound knowledge and skills base

For social workers, it is essential to acquire a sound knowledge and skills base from which to begin to understand people and their situations, and to formulate and negotiate plans of action appropriate to the circumstances encountered. This involves understanding how experiences are perceived, understood, and communicated by people, and how this impacts on behaviour and life situations, both positive and negative. To some extent, this understanding will always be incomplete, uneven, and sometimes baffling, because in the realm of human experience, life is unpredictable and some uncertainty is inevitable (Marris 1996). This complexity is acknowledged in regulations and requirements stipulated for social work and evident in a further extract from the IASSW and IFSW definition of social work:

> Social work in its various forms addresses the multiple, complex trans-actions between people and their environments. Its mission is to enable all people to develop their full potential, enrich their lives, and prevent dysfunction. Professional social work is focused on problem-solving and change. As such, social workers are change agents in society and in the lives of the individuals, families and communities they serve. Social work is an interrelated system of values, theory and practice.
>
> (IFSW/IASSW 2000)

From this knowledge and skills base, it is possible to locate a number of practice skills and interventions that can be used to address the complex issues regularly encountered in social work. However, attempting to bring about change, whether focused on people, their environments or both, can be a formidable task and an area where no profession or professional practice approach can claim complete success. This is largely because the detailed and in-depth understanding we have of the range of factors that give rise to certain problems has not been sufficiently developed in ways that reveal how to work alongside people to stabilize fraught situations or to facilitate change. This is particularly evident in the area of behaviour change, which is a 'field that remains relatively underdeveloped' (Halpern and Bates 2004: 67). We can continue to extend our knowledge through research but we still need to be able to integrate and use these findings and what we know in ways that are more effective. This involves better integrations of theory and practice – or knowledge and skills. In this text, the *Knowledge and Skills Framework* that I have developed is designed to achieve this aim. The importance of integrating knowledge and skills is also evident in the definition of an *intervention* put forward in this text, which constitutes *knowledge, skills, and values in action*. The purpose of a professional intervention is to affect change, whether targeted at an individual, family, group, community or in relation to a wider social and institutional aspect.

Does social work have a distinct knowledge and skills base?

The extent to which social work's knowledge and skills can be considered to be distinct when compared with the expertise claimed by other professions is a complex issue. The absence of a clear and distinct knowledge base can mean that social work is represented as being 'an activity which any reasonably competent person might carry out' (Sheppard 1995: 290). This difficulty is compounded when the terms *social work* and *social care* are used interchangeably when they refer to different types of practice. In *Options for Excellence*, which looked at the future development of the social care workforce, a distinction in the roles adopted by social care workers and social workers is clearly indicated:

> The term 'social workers' refers to those workers trained to assess and respond to people with complex personal and social needs. It is a protected title and can only be used to refer to those workers who are qualified and registered and hold a social work qualification recognized by the General Social Care Council (GSCC) . . . Social workers carry out a variety of tasks, including casework, acting as an advocate, risk assessment and working as a care manager. As a profession, social work promotes social change, problem solving in human relationships and the empowerment and liberation of people to enhance well-being.
>
> (Department of Health and Department for Education and Skills 2006: 9)

The above account stands in contrast to the definition of *social care* put forward by Skills for Care, where the importance of 'practical help' is highlighted:

> Social care work is about helping people with their lives. People who have physical or psychological problems often require practical help coping with the everyday business of living. Social care workers provide this practical support.
>
> (Skills for Care 2010)

Given the differences that are evident in these two definitions, it is important that social work and social care are not used interchangeably. Although in some situations a considerable overlap is evident, not least because the legal responsibilities and the professional accountability required of social workers differ markedly from the requirements of a care worker.

The extent to which social work's knowledge base is distinct compared with that of other disciplines and professions can be difficult to gauge. Marsh and Fisher (2005) argue that no area of social science can lay claim to an 'exclusive ownership of a knowledge base with fixed boundaries – indeed, it is a mark of a modern discipline that it draws on a wide range of appropriate knowledge' (p. 12). If any distinctiveness can be identified, this might not lie in social work's knowledge base but in the 'social analysis' that is undertaken and the extent to which this analysis informs the interventions used (Marsh and Fisher 2005: 12). For example, a central feature of this 'social analysis' is the fact that social work takes account of wider social and structural factors, such as the home situation, or what is happening within a particular neighbourhood or community. Also, a central feature of this 'social analysis' is the way that social work draws on the knowledge, skills, expertise, and experiences that service users, carers, and others bring to the encounter.

My view is that social work's particular contribution to the field of social welfare or human service provision could be considered to reside in two areas. First, we work with people from some of the most deprived and disadvantaged sectors of the population and, as a result, we have developed specific knowledge, skills, and expertise from the concentrated work we continue to undertake in this area. Perhaps more than any other profession, social work has a long history of working closely with disadvantaged groups – often with limited resources – in order to be helpful in some way. As mentioned earlier, a feature of this expertise includes the legislative powers that are invested in social workers. Also, the 'social analysis' that is central to social work means that our contact with service users is mainly not undertaken in the safety of a clinic or solely located in an agency. Instead, we place considerable importance on attempting to meet people in locations that facilitate easy contact, such as their own homes. Doing home visits offers other benefits because they provide an invaluable insight into people's lives and social surroundings – and an area of practice that requires social workers to develop a different range of skills.

Second, a central feature of the contribution we bring is evident in the way that social work ethics and values shape our work – a perspective that embraces the importance of social justice as embodied in the General Social Care Council (GSCC) *Codes of Practice for Social Care Workers and Employers*, which requires social workers to 'protect the rights and promote the interests of service users and carers' (GSCC 2002). The same emphasis on social justice can be found in the statement from the British Association of Social Workers' Code of Ethics, which states that as a profession, it is our responsibility to 'seek to change social structures which perpetuate inequalities and injustices, and whenever possible work to eliminate all violations of human rights' (BASW 2002). Or again, the Subject Benchmark Statement for Social Work, which sets out the requirements that need to be achieved for a degree in social work, states that 'social work is characterized by a distinctive focus on practice in complex social situations to promote and protect individual and collective well-being' (QAA 2008: 6). For some writers, it is social work values, and not our knowledge and skills base, that makes social work distinct as a profession: 'values ... are central to the profession; without them, there is no social work' (Bisman 2004: 120). This comment appears to suggest that our intentions are enough – the view that if we mean well, we will do well. How we treat and respond to service users is clearly important but there also has to be some substance – concrete knowledge and skills – embodied within that communication. (For an informative analysis of the codes of ethics adopted by different professional associations across the world, see Banks 2006.)

2. The central importance of communication skills in social work

A second perspective that runs throughout this text recognizes the vital role that communication skills play within social work (Koprowska 2010; Lishman 2009a; Moss 2008). Thus, communication skills constitute the primary skill of social work because it is through our capacity to communicate that we form assessments, undertake interviews, engage in problem-solving and decision-making activities, negotiate an implementation plan, and evaluate our effectiveness. The importance given to this subject is evident in the Department of Health requirements, which state that students must 'undertake specific learning' and that this should include 'communication skills with children, adults and those with particular communication needs' (Department of Health 2002: 4). Its significance becomes more obvious if we compare social work to, say, nursing or medicine where a number of clinical treatments or interventions often involve physical contact with patients (e.g. injections, dressing wounds, physical examinations). In contrast, social work does not involve physical contact with people in this way, except under special circumstances that are clearly defined. For example, we may be called upon to provide *therapeutic restraint* for young people (Gilligan 2001: 124) who need to be protected in a professionally appropriate way, or have physical contact with someone who is upset or bereaved – as a gesture of compassion and concern. However, it is almost always the case that our communication skills are concentrated on the use of verbal and non-verbal skills, although other areas of activity need to be included such as those involving the written word and the communication that can be interpreted in the actions we undertake.

Yet given its importance, it is perhaps surprising to note that the findings of a knowledge review, commissioned by the Social Care Institute for Excellence (SCIE), found very few publications that focused specifically on the learning and teaching methods used on social work training programmes in relation to communication skills, and even fewer publications that attempted to evaluate the effectiveness of this teaching (Trevithick *et al.* 2004: 34). The findings of this knowledge review suggest that the importance given to teaching social work skills has changed little since Marsh and Triseliotis (1996) published their landmark research that called for more teaching to be focused on social work skills, including communication skills.

It is important to note, however, that practice is also a location for learning. It is in practice that I learned most of the skills that I have acquired and describe in this text. It is where I came to realize that it is not possible to be an effective social work practitioner without being an effective communicator, and it is not possible to be an effective communicator without a sound theoretical understanding of people in their particular social context. However, the extent to which social workers are able to use the knowledge and skills at their disposal is increasingly under threat (Richards *et al.* 2005: 410). This concern is borne out in a workload survey of social workers' time, which noted 'the frustrations felt by social workers that they did not use the skills for which they were trained' (Baginsky *et al.* 2010: 95) – a theme we return to later in this book.

3. Social work as capacity building

A third perspective that underpins the knowledge and skills described in this text views social work as a *capacity-building activity*. This emphasizes the important role that social work practitioners can play to enhance 'human growth and development' (TOPPS 2002). This may focus on the capacity of individuals, families, groups, and communities to access and benefit from the resources and possibilities that are located around them, but it may also involve working alongside services users and carers – and others – to press for more and better resources. The notion of *capacity* is widely used within social welfare contexts yet rarely defined. It is derived from the Latin *capax*, meaning 'able to take in'; 'the ability to receive or contain; holding power' (*Oxford English Dictionary*), and is often used to describe the personal resources or abilities that people have at their disposal (Sheldon 1995: 126). However, the term capacity is not only an account of *what is* (actual and present abilities) but also what *can be* (potential and future abilities). It highlights the importance of working with people in ways that can help to maintain the capacities they have already developed but also highlights the *potential* for greater capacities to be developed or learned (French 1999). This may be evident in positive changes that occur in the way that people feel about themselves (feelings of self-esteem, self-worth, confidence), in relation to others (forming friendships, repairing broken relationships, being a successful group member), and how they relate to structures and organizations within society that have an impact on their lives (how to access help from appropriate organizations, learning how to be assertive when dealing with authority figures). However, the fact that capacities can change also means that existing skills or abilities can be lost through under-use or lack of practice, or through the impact of stress, fatigue, anxiety, low morale, trauma, or a sense of hopelessness and defeat. These are feelings that social workers can experience as well as service users and carers, what in professional circles is described as de-skilling (Dustin 2007).

The notion of *capacity* is central to the work of Winnicott, a paediatrician and psychoanalyst, whose work was influential in social work during the 1950s and 1960s (Winnicott 1958, 1965). Winnicott used the term to emphasize the importance of individual differences and also to highlight the range of 'stored possibilities' that people possess – possibilities that can be freed up when the external context provides a *'facilitating environment'*. In Winnicott's work, the capacity to relate is particularly important. Other examples include the capacity to manage anxiety, to be alone, to mourn, and to bear difficult feelings. In Winnicott's later writing, he described the capacity to play as a feature of health (Phillips 1988: 47). This includes the importance of playing with ideas and playing with different ways to embrace life and the challenges that we encounter as human beings. The perspective I adopt in this text sees social work as a *capacity-building activity*. Eraut, whose work is covered later, has proposed a comparable concept, the notion of *capability*, to describe current performance and also a person's 'potential to perform in the future' (Eraut 1994: 2000). Capability is a term that is being promoted by the UK Social Work Reform Board (SWRB 2010) and is defined by Stephenson as follows (original emphases):

> Capability is an integration of knowledge, skills, personal qualities and understanding *used appropriately* and *effectively* – not just in familiar and highly focused specialist contexts but in response to *new* and *changing* circumstances.
>
> (Stephenson 1998: 2)

Again, it is important to emphasize that these capacities or capabilities can change depending on individual situations, but particularly the extent to which they are promoted or inhibited by external factors, such as the culture of an organization.

For example, when attempting to analyse the capacities that lie within a particular situation it can be helpful to think of this concept from three different perspectives. First, it involves analysing the capacities, qualities, attributes, knowledge and skills, strengths and limitations that practitioners bring to the work. Second, it involves the capacities that service users, carers, and others bring to the situation. And since the capacities that practitioners and service users bring are influenced by wider organizational, cultural, and environmental capacities, these constitute the third range of capacities. In effect, such an analysis includes anyone or anything likely to influence, both positively and negatively, the direction and effectiveness of the work undertaken.

The capacities that service users and carers bring to the encounter

A commonly used term within social work is *coping capacity*, often used to describe the extent to which people are able to cope with particular problems (England 1986; Sheppard and Crocker 2008). One reason for an inability to cope is that the problems being faced are overwhelming, something all of us would find difficult if not impossible to bear. In my experience, some of the most painful, demoralizing, and overwhelming experiences are those that involve being treated unfairly. Another reason why some people are unable to cope is that they lack practical and emotional support, which can leave them feeling seriously depleted and without the energy required to 'take charge' and to bring about change. The capacity to cope can grow from positive experiences, or it can shrivel through the impact of negative experiences and neglect. From this perspective, every encounter carries the potential to be a growth-enhancing and capacity-building experience or one that weakens existing capacities – a weakening that may result in defensiveness and a reluctance to address the difficulties being experienced (Trevithick 2011a).

For example, when people are haunted by negative experiences, whether in the present or in the past, precious emotional, physical, and intellectual energy can be tied up trying to cope or to survive the internal and external conflicts, demands, and hurdles that life throws their way. When energy is tied up in this way, the capacity to change – the ability to embrace new experiences or ways of being – is often limited. In this situation, practical forms of help may be invaluable and a growth-enhancing opportunity. This may involve organizing help with household chores, childcare responsibilities or transport problems. In my experience, practical interventions of this kind are greatly valued by service users and carers and, in some circumstances, they can be more important than advanced, specialist or more costly interventions. However, the opportunity for social workers to provide the kind of help requested may not be possible where these tasks do not accord with agency policy and procedures or the way in which the role of a social worker is seen in a particular organization.

The capacities that social workers bring to the encounter

In relation to social work practitioners, the concept of capacities can help us to understand the resourcefulness – or lack thereof – that some practitioners and students of social work bring to their work (Collins *et al.* 2010). As a positive attribute, it describes the ability to think about others in ways that are flexible, creative, and courageous and that open up new possibilities (Gambrill 2006: 193). This can be evident in the capacity that some practitioners demonstrate in relation to working with conflict; being able to bear and contain others' anxiety and negativity; being curious about people, the work environment, and the world around us; being interested in exploring new ideas, new practice approaches or interventions; demonstrating the courage to work from a clear value base in adverse circumstances, and so forth. Hopefully, we have all encountered professionals of this calibre – and are moving in this direction ourselves. Further coverage of professionals' capacities is provided later in the book.

In contrast, we have no doubt encountered professionals for whom this kind of resourcefulness is beyond their reach. Instead, we encounter a range of limitations: people who are rigid and inflexible; who feel troubled if they are not in control; who feel seriously demeaned by people who question their decisions or authority; who struggle to take their gaze off themselves and their own needs, thereby failing to truly appreciate the plight of others. It is not my intention to be critical: we become the people we are through a range of experiences, some of which are not sought and often beyond our control. I mention these personal and professional capacities because they influence our work and the extent to which we can be creative and effective practitioners. As a general rule, a workforce that is stressed, de-skilled, overworked, and suffering from low morale is not well placed to provide for the needs of other people (SWTF 2009b: 29). The impact of the working environment on practitioners' capacity to be effective is crucial, making it important to look at the whole picture, rather than one aspect or any one individual.

Organizational, cultural, and environmental capacities

These capacities describe the resources, commitment, priorities, and so on that agencies and organizations bring to the work, and also capacities that are located in the local community or neighbourhood. In this regard, the culture and atmosphere adopted by different agencies is particularly important and can greatly influence the effectiveness of work undertaken. A positive environment could indicate the characteristics of a 'learning organization', that is, a culture that 'rejects a view of learning as being solely the inductive application to practice of knowledge or techniques' (Gould 2000: 586) but instead emphasizes the importance of learning from practice through a 'process of purposive engagement with practice'. On the other hand, some organizational cultures can inhibit practice effectiveness. For example, in the Climbié Report the organization of social work was described as indicating 'widespread organisational malaise' (Laming 2003: 4). Similar organizational concerns were highlighted in the report published on the tragic death of 'Baby P', where in particular 'concerns were raised about the morale of frontline social workers' (Laming 2009: 20).

From a wider perspective, a focus on capacities – and capacity building – can enable us to combine a systems or ecological perspective (see Appendix 4) with that of a strengths perspective (see Appendix 10). As Jack notes:

> Within an ecological perspective, developmental outcomes are understood to be dependent on the interplay between strengths and vulnerabilities in the various settings within which people live their lives, including their families, friendship networks, school or work situations, neighborhoods, and the wider communities of interest and the society to which they belong.
>
> (Jack 2012)

In this context, eco-maps can be helpful to aid communication among people from different backgrounds and to highlight the strengths and weaknesses within an individual's social network. Or again, *capacity building* links to the concept of *social capital* (Jack and Jack 2000: 96), which provides a framework from which to map what is present and absent in a given community or neighbourhood, such as the degree, range, and quality of social support networks that are or are not evident within a ṛ. locality.

4. The importance of a relationship-based perspective

A fourth perspective relates to the quality of the relationship we seek to build with service users and carers, and with other professionals and involved individuals. The following description captures the importance of the relationship we strive to create in social work:

> While it is true that people do not come to us looking for a relationship and while it is no substitute for practical support, nevertheless we are one of the few groups who recognize the value of relating to others in a way which recognizes their experience as fundamental to understanding and action.
>
> (Coulshed 1991: 2)

In the past, the client–worker relationship was considered to be at 'the heart of social work' (Collins and Collins 1981: 6) and an essential feature of good practice (Biestek 1961; Coulshed 1991). It tended to be associated with counselling, particularly the work of Carl Rogers (1951, 1961) and later followers. For some time, it was directly associated with psychosocial or psychodynamic approaches, particularly *casework* (Hollis 1964) or *social casework* (Hollis 1977; Howe 2002: 171). Then for a number of years its importance appeared to wane and to take up a 'confused and ambivalent' position in social work (Howe 1998: 45) until, more recently, when there has been a welcome resurgence of interest in the importance of the relationships that are created in social work (Ruch *et al.* 2010; Trevithick 2008; Wilson *et al.* 2008).

One way to see the relationship is as a 'communication bridge between people' (Kadushin and Kadushin 1997: 100). It can represent the medium through which services users and practitioners communicate and negotiate a pathway towards agreed and desired destinations. It can also provide a sense of connection where differences are identified, sorted out, and worked through. That is not to idealize the worker–client relationship or to suggest that the relationships we create always work out well or achieve positive results. Yet the quality of the interaction and the trust and understanding that are held within the relationship can act as a vital thread. It is a thread that can open up the possibility for defences to be lowered, for the truth to be faced, for doubts and fears to be worked through, and change to be integrated and embraced in ways that are not possible without this connection to another trustworthy and reliable human being. Some of the personal attributes that contribute to the development of a facilitative relationship, or a good 'working alliance', include the capacity to communicate a genuine feeling of warmth, compassion, and concern towards another human being (Koprowska 2010; Lishman 2009a).

The specific features of a facilitative relationship

In spite of the importance of this area, in many ways our knowledge is limited in terms of identifying the specific benefits that are a feature of a helpful, facilitative, or empowering relationship. This is partly because every relationship is unique and made up of intangible factors that are difficult to identify (Cheetham *et al*. 1992: 12). Yet the task of establishing sound working relationships is essential to many activities that we value. One centre that has researched and analysed the importance of relationships and relationship building is the Stone (Women's) Center in Boston, Massachusetts, a feminist organization that sees building relationships as central to empowerment and growth (Surrey 1991: 167). Within this theoretical framework, it is the experience of connection that leads to growth – a growth that is based on 'an interaction between two or more people that is mutually empathic and mutually empowering' (Miller and Stiver 1997: 26). The emphasis placed on 'connectedness' is a feature of the work of Folgheraiter, who describes how the 'relational attitude of social workers' can be used to enhance the social networks to which people belong (Folgheraiter 2004: 76). The benefits that can be derived from people feeling connected to others are also evident in the work of Jean Baker Miller, the founder of the Stone Center, who described the changes and psychological growth that positive relationships can lead to in terms of five observable phenomena (Miller 1986a: 3):

- feeling a greater sense of 'zest' (vitality and energy)
- feeling more able to act and being able to act
- acquiring a more accurate picture of herself/himself and of other people
- feeling a greater sense of worth
- feeling more connected to other people and 'a greater sense of motivation for connections with other people beyond those in the specific relationship'.

This description captures the heightened feelings of self-worth and sense of well-being that a good relationship can foster. It stresses the importance of relationships as a way to help people to 'achieve and maintain a sense of contact and connection' (Jordan 1991: 283) with other people and the importance of professional working in ways that help people to establish this sense of connection. The importance of this relational connection is highlighted in relation to teaching and learning. For example, Edwards and Richards (2002) draw on the work of the Stone Center to apply 'relational/cultural theory' to learning and teaching in social work education. They argue that how students are taught influences what they learn, and that this, in turn, influences how they use this knowledge and understanding in practice (p. 3).

The relationship should not be viewed as an end in itself

It is important to stress that forming and maintaining good relationships, or relationship-building, should not be seen in social work as an end in itself, but as a way of working that provides a foundation on which to build future work – that is, a 'good working relationship is a necessary but not sufficient condition for being an effective helper in this field' (Hudson and Sheldon 2000: 65). The concern is that if too great an emphasis is placed on creating and maintaining a good relationship with clients and services users, this can be at the expense of working from a sound knowledge and skills base. The capacity to take tough decisions is an essential social work skill – decisions that could lead to conflict and make it difficult to maintain a good working relationship. In such a situation, what constitutes the best interest of the service user has to be our professional priority, which may mean that the relationship has to change for progress to be made.

A different concern is that the relationship between a service user and practitioner could become highly individualized and lead to a 'privatized solution to public ills' (Pearson 1973). This could mean that contributing factors – for which the person in question is not responsible – can end up being ignored and divorced from wider social or political causes. As a result, the opportunity to link 'personal troubles' to 'public issues' could be lost (Mills 1959: 130), which in turn could mean that the opportunity to seek social solutions could also be lost. It is possible to avoid these pitfalls if we review our work from a critically reflective stance, use supervision effectively, and seek honest feedback and support from our colleagues, service users, and carers.

The impact of positive and negative experiences

The ethical or values perspective mentioned earlier is evident in the actions we take but also in the way that we communicate with service users, carers, and others. According to the status that certain groups hold within society or within a particular context, the right to social justice can be threatened and lead to prejudice and discrimination. These injustices can be based on an individual's class, race, gender, age, disabilities, sexual orientation, religion/spiritual beliefs, culture, health, and geographic location (such as the divisions that exist between the north and south of England) – or simply the fact that some people are poor or behave in ways that reveal the suffering they have experienced and their lack of life chances. Social work is not unique in its values perspective, but other professions may not have ascribed this issue the same importance, although the picture is changing. For example, in recent years there has been considerable coverage in the medical profession of the impact of poverty and health inequalities within the UK (Marmot Review 2010), coverage of which can be found in important publications, such as the *British Medical Journal* and the *Lancet*.

By developing relationships that take account of our importance to one another, and the reciprocal nature of our connection, we are attempting to avoid adding ourselves to the pile of disappointing experiences, failures, and 'let downs' that many service users and carers have experienced. By remaining within clear professional boundaries, being true to our word, keeping to the commitments we have made, never promising more than we can deliver, and responding as closely as possible within agency constraints to the needs identified by the individual, we are offering the possibility of a new and different experience. If all goes well, this can increase confidence and form a basis from which to explore other possibilities. Within the confines of inner city or rural neglect and decay, these possibilities may be few and difficult to identify but every experience – whether positive or negative – carries with it the possibility of influencing the next stage of a person's life (Salzberger-Wittenberg 1970: 162). The challenge here is a formidable one, namely how to sort out and work through the barriers that inhibit progress so that these experiences can be turned into opportunities for growth and change.

Positive experiences engender hope and trust, and convey a comforting sense of being understood and accepted. As human beings we have a deep-seated wish to be understood, accepted for who we are, and for our lives to have meaning and purpose (Howe 1996: 94). This desire is as true for people who come from deprived sectors of the population, who form the vast majority of social work service users, as it is for people who come from other, more advantaged sectors. Although at times this desire for meaning and understanding may elude us, most of us continue to yearn for someone who can bring this sense of understanding and meaning into our lives and with it the transformation that this offers. Some find this through religion, while others turn to their families or friends to fulfil this need. Another, smaller group are forced to look to professionals for this kind of understanding and meaning, perhaps because they have not had enough love or care, or enough positive experiences to be able to trust others. Or perhaps the capacity to adapt – or to give and take – which is central to the task of relating has broken down and needs to be addressed and *mended*.

On the other hand, negative experiences can reaffirm old suspicions and doubts, deepen mistrust, shatter hope, and produce even greater despair and defensiveness (Trevithick 2011a). Too often service users who are burdened by the load they carry are a bundle of negativity, with little belief in the possibilities that change can offer. Try as we may, we cannot avoid the fact that some service users pose a threat to themselves (Herbert 2008: 373–4; Huxley 2008: 55; Pritchard 2000b: 338–40) and/or to others (Harne and Radford 2008; Waterhouse 2008), whether intentionally or not (Pritchard 2000a: 309–10). All forms of risk need to be acknowledged in any assessment or evaluation process (Kemshall and Pritchard 1999). As far as possible, all judgements, whether positive or negative, should be backed by evidence. If, as practitioners, we can involve ourselves in the experience of relating to another human being, what we ourselves gain from this involvement is that we too can develop and learn from the encounter, about ourselves and about other people (Howe 1987: 113). That is our ultimate reward. To be invited to enter another person's world, if only for a brief time and in a limited way, can in itself be a mark of trust and hope and, from this place, so much can happen. The small gains that some service users achieve can feel to them, and to us, like major successes and act as a reminder that some people can travel a long way on a little, while others require much more to be able to move their lives forward. That is not to idealize poverty and the sense of shame and social exclusion that can haunt the lives of poor people, but it is important to remember that, as human beings, we are complex and unique individuals and always more than our suffering (Angelou 1994).

5. A personal account of the assumption that inform this text

The following fifth perspective is a more personal account of the assumptions that inform the way I think about human beings and the influences that shape this text. I have included this personal account because we almost always work from assumptions about other human beings – assumptions that influence what we observe and believe about people and also how we act in certain situations. For the most part, these assumptions are often not named or owned in ways that encourage an open discussion and debate, and the chance to be influenced by the views of others. Our beliefs and perspective on life shape our work and our 'philosophy of practice' (Bricker-Jenkins 1990; Gambrill 2006: 12–15).

The personal perspective that informs this book is influenced by a range of different authors and theories – particularly psychoanalytic theory – and includes the following overlapping and interweaving principles or beliefs:

- Early childhood experiences are important to the development of the personality. This perspective states that 'The poorer the quality of people's relationship history and social environment, the less robust will be their psychological make-up and ability to deal with other people, social situations and emotional demands' (Howe 1998: 175). Alongside earlier childhood experiences, throughout our lives we continue to be shaped by – and to shape – the social environment that we inhabit, the experiences we encounter, and the social relationships that we create.
- As human beings we are, by nature, social beings who need positive and nourishing relationships with other human beings for healthy psychological functioning and to feel that life is worthwhile and meaningful. 'Well being, then, is equivalent to being well with others' (Hoggett 2000: 6).

- A central feature of our humanness is our capacity to grow and change throughout life. Freud (1919/1924) described this tendency for growth and emotional development as an innate, 'instinctual propelling force' (p. 396) or a 'life force' that strives for personal growth, stimulation, and fulfillment. This is a view shared by many other writers, including those covered in Chapter 6 (Erikson 1965; Maslow 1954; Rogers 1951, 1961; Winnicott 1958, 1965).

- The existence of unconscious (unaware), preconscious (beyond immediate awareness but capable of being recalled), and conscious (aware) states has an enduring influence on our behaviour, thoughts, feelings, and the actions we take. This means that as human beings we can think and act rationally – that is, in well thought-out and reasoned ways – but also irrationally. Also, we can experience ambivalence, that is, we can feel two opposite or conflicting emotions or desires at the same time.

- All human beings have the capacity to behave defensively as a way to deal with assumed or real threats, or as a way to avoid having to deal with difficult feelings or conflict-ridden emotions (Trevithick 2011a). As well as protecting the individual from negative experiences, defences can inhibit the capacity to experience new and positive experiences. 'Defences are strategies which a person employs either knowingly or unknowingly, in order to avoid facing aspects of the self which are felt to be threatening' (Jacobs 2010: 110).

- A feeling of need and the desire for satisfaction is central to human motivation and is evident in the desire to know, to be understood, to belong, and to be accepted. For human beings to be able to use desire as a catalyst for change requires a degree of emotional and physical health, and a 'facilitative environment' (Winnicott 1965) or 'external circumstances' to converge in positive ways (Freud 1919/1924: 396). The features that indicate and lead to human growth and development include an innate curiosity, a need for stimulation, and a desire for fulfilment (Weick 1983). However, desire can be distorted or manipulated – such as through advertising – and lead to a situation where need can easily become confused with greed. In this book, *need* and *greed* are differentiated because the irrational and insatiable drive to acquire more (greed) does not in itself satisfy any fundamental developmental movement forward or moral purpose.

- As human beings, we have the capacity for 'good' and 'evil', that is, the capacity to be destructive towards ourselves and other people (Hoggett 2000: 14), as well as the capacity to love and cherish other human beings, including ourselves. This perspective states that the opposite of *love* is not *hate* but *indifference*, where love is the 'state in which the flourishing of one individual comes about through the flourishing of others' (Eagleton 2007: 166). From this perspective, one way to measure our progress as human beings and as a society should not be in terms of material goods but in relation to the extent to which we care for people who are sick, weak, poor financially or in spirit, or vulnerable in other ways. I also believe that as human beings we are diminished emotionally and spiritually if we do nothing to alleviate the suffering of others – if we allow the 'social ills' or the 'social evils' that we encounter go unchallenged.

It is clear from the above account that one of the major influences on my work has been psychoanalysis but this is a subject that I approach quite critically. At the same time, I also recognize that all theories and theorists have their limitations yet still say important things – and that a good idea in the wrong hands can easily go astray. For example, in a chapter that looked at the relationship between psychoanalysis and social class, I compared the therapeutic choices available to working-class men and women as follows:

> I often think of psychotherapy as a meal – an opportunity to be nourished. What this meal is made of will depend, to a large extent, on what is wanted, affordable and available – financially and emotionally – and whether we have the time, space and stomach to consume and digest all that is there ... Having money buys choice and the chance to be served quickly. It also buys the expectation that the money spent will purchase food of a particular quality. Those who cannot 'pay their way' must seek out other alternatives. For this group, what food there is may involve long queues, be limited to one menu, and served in a way that makes it virtually unpalatable. As a result, whilst having the appearance of being a nourishing and satisfying meal, it may provide neither: too often, it is a handout and that fact is not disguised. The picture that comes to mind is of one group heading for an expensive restaurant of their choice while another much more hungry group shuffle to the single menu soup kitchens of the NHS, craving for something, anything to 'fill the hole' as quickly as possible. If there is no food available – or it is placed tantalisingly beyond their reach or too rich for an empty stomach to digest – then they must, for lack of choice, do without. Doing without is not new for working class people – it is almost a class characteristic.
>
> (Trevithick 1998: 115)

In the extract above, I draw on a little known publication by Freud that calls for psychoanalysis to adapt its technique to meet the needs of what he called 'the poor man' (Freud 1919/1924: 401) – something that has largely not happened. The importance of any theory – in this case psychoanalysis – is only useful to the extent that it 'speaks truly to the human condition ... able to help others with their struggles to be real persons living meaningful lives' (Guntrip 1977: 44). Part of our 'human condition' is a toleration of oppression. Here, the work of Lerner (1972) reminds us that 'treating malaria victims in a mosquito-infested swamp' (p. 6) may be a heroic gesture yet can be futile if, in our efforts to help malaria victims, we fail to address the source of the infection – the swamp – so that we can prevent new infections. From this place, I see social action and social work to be inextricably linked.

Introduction to this third edition

My hope for you, the reader, is that you find this an enjoyable, stimulating, and informative text. Before reaching your hands, it has been read by a number of different people – service users, students, academics, people outside social work and from the world of publishing – who have added their voice to its contents. A particular concern has been to ensure that my writing is accessible, a difficult task because social work is becoming increasingly complex. In an attempt to unravel and to order this complexity, the themes covered in this text are located in terms of a *Knowledge and Skills Framework* that I have developed. This confronts a difficult challenge – namely, how to categorize and to integrate knowledge and skills, or theory and practice, in ways that are meaningful and can be related to contemporary social work practice.

I began my exploration of what constitutes *knowledge* in social work in the second edition of this book, *Social Work Skills*, published in 2005. I described the bewilderment I faced when writing this second edition in the following way:

> ... the more I read and wrote, the more confused and lost I became until I reached a point where I had to stop and to start again ... I felt compelled to understand more about what constitutes social work's knowledge base. In this process, I have waded through Schön's swampy lowlands (Schön 1991: 43) and stumbled through a landscape of dense, unclear and inapplicable theories, some with their own concepts and language – or knack of saying the same thing but in a different way. I have also found some wonderfully illuminating pieces of writing – publications that have been inspiring in their thoughtfulness and clarity. In some ways, I may have allowed myself to become lost and bewildered on purpose, perhaps thinking that if I can't find my way out of this jungle, how can practitioners or students manage this task? Of course, they may be more 'fit for purpose' or 'fit for practice' than me. Whichever way, at times it proved hard to find some of the paths or the markers that other authors have left behind.
>
> (Trevithick 2005: vii)

Much to my surprise, it became clear that I was not alone – that others shared my confusion about how best to conceptualize the subject of *knowledge*. I later developed my thinking further in an article entitled 'Revisiting the knowledge base of social work: a framework for practice', published in the *British Journal of Social Work*. Since that time, I have continued in my efforts to unravel and to order this complex subject – and this text marks my latest thinking on this topic – which accords with the comment by Howe on this topic:

> To travel at all is to hold ideas about the behavioural and social terrain over which we journey. To show no interest in theory is simply to travel blind. This is bad practice and unhelpful to clients.
>
> (Howe 1987: 9)

I have been aided in my efforts by a number of important publications but also by two organizations: the Social Care Institute for Excellence (SCIE) and the Social Work and Social Policy Subject Centre (SWAP). Much to to my regret, and the regret of many people in social work, SWAP has been disbanded by the UK Coalition Government. Having travelled abroad, where organizations of this calibre have not been set up, I have come to realize the important contribution SWAP has made to promote effective practice and to enhance the knowledge and skills base of social work. I hope this text will encourage you to explore the range of resources that continue to be available – free of charge – from SCIE and from the Higher Education Academy.

Outline of the text

This text differs from the two earlier editions in a number of ways. First, in this edition I draw on a wider range of different sources. As you would expect, I cite a number of recent texts but I have also included a considerable number of journal articles and web-based publications. I have done so to encourage you to read around a subject as widely as possible but also because some publications are more easily available than others. The stock of new publications held in academic libraries can be poor due to limited funding and, for this reason, journal articles can be a valuable source of information if these can be accessed free of charge. Again, the free publications available in social work are an important resource but sharing written material with other students and practitioners can help overcome the difficulties experience when publications are in short supply and costly.

A second difference is that in this edition, greater prominence is given to the importance of adopting a systemic and a structural approach in relation to our work. This approach has been promoted by several authors (Davis and Garrett 2004; Elliott 2008; Ferguson 2008; Ferguson and Woodward 2009; Mullaly 2007; Munro 2011a; 2011b) and is a theme that I cover in detail in Chapter 3 on Factual Knowledge, where I outline the important way that legislation, social policy, and agency policy impact on social work. In this chapter, I also stress structural factors that impact on people's lives, such as the impact of poverty and health inequalities, and explain why certain types of problems are likely to be encountered in social work.

Third, in this Introduction I have outlined in some detail the perspectives that inform my work and writing. I have done so to be clear in terms of where I locate myself in my understanding of human beings and human behaviour. I hope that this account will encourage you to explore the assumptions that you have and that you bring to your work.

Fourth, some new and some revised chapters have been included. For example, Part 1 includes four new chapters: Chapter 2 on Theoretical Knowledge, Chapter 3 on Factual Knowledge, Chapter 4 on Practice Knowledge, and Chapter 5 on Understanding Human Beings. These chapters place an emphasis on theories and theorists, including how psychology can illuminate our understanding of human behaviour. Part 2 focuses more explicitly on the subject of skills and interventions, and identifies 80 generalist skills and interventions that are used in social work on a regular basis. From the feedback I have received from a number of practitioners, it is clear that naming these skills has been important, and has led some social workers to realize that they are more skilled and skilful than they previously thought. This generalist list is not designed to cover all skills and interventions used in social work. For example, the range of specialist skills and interventions linked with specific practice approaches are not included in this text unless covered in the Appendices, but whenever possible I have tried to provide references to further reading. Similarly, it was not always possible to include the theories that underpin the different skills and interventions covered. Hopefully, such a text will one day be written.

The perspective I stress throughout this section, and the text as a whole, is that before we intervene we need to be clear about our intention and purpose – and that this should accord, whenever possible, with the purpose that service users and carers want to progress. If we fudge our intentions, role, and purpose at the outset, difficulties are likely to emerge at a later stage. This clarity on our part enables us to assess the appropriateness of specific social work practice methods, practice theories and approaches, values perspectives, skills and interventions in terms of their effectiveness in bringing about desired and agreed outcomes. It is in this area that the transferability of knowledge, skills, and values become possible. Within this process, I also stress the importance of intervening at a structural level, which involves directing our interventions at the organizational, social, and political structures that give rise to certain social or personal problems or that perpetuate discrimination and other forms of unjust treatment.

Fifth, the appendices included in previous editions have proved enormously popular and, in response to the feedback and requests I have received from students and practitioners, there are two additions: appendices on motivational interviewing and strength-based perspectives. These include references to further reading. As a *handbook*, as opposed to a more general text, an important goal of this book is to signpost readers to other relevant publications to encourage further in-depth exploration and reading. Also, the themes covered are ordered to enable readers to dip in and out of the text, which means that some key points tend to be repeated to ensure links can be made.

Some final points...

Some final points of clarification are worth noting. In the scenarios and practice examples referred to throughout this text, all names and other identifiable characteristics have been changed to protect people's identities. These examples are mainly drawn from my work with children and families and I am aware that these may seem less relevant to practitioners working in different areas of social work. This is a drawback that I acknowledge but it is not possible to focus in detail on a range of different contexts in a generalist text of this kind. However, the skills described are transferable, that is, some have features that can be generalized, theorized, and made relevant to other practice orientations, different settings, and similar problems encountered. Also, the skills and interventions described in the text could prove relevant when working with colleagues, managers, and other professionals – some of whom may need to be supported and challenged in ways that enable events to move forward.

In relation to the terms we use to describe *clients* or *service users*, after some deliberation I have decided to continue to use the term *service user* to describe those individuals who come within the remit of social work. This term is not ideal, but nor are any of the others – *client, customer, consumer, recipient of services, expert by experience* – not least because as far as I can tell, none of these terms have been coined by service users or clients. An unacceptable term that I encountered came, I believe, from the Department of Health in 2008 where some treasured human being suggested to SCIE that the term *service users* should be replaced with the term *people who use care services/carers* (PWUCS/C). This invitation was not taken up but I note that Skills for Care and the Care Quality Commission have adopted a version of this terminology – *people who use services* – but again, this is not a term that service users have asked us to adopt. Another even more worrying term that I recently encountered is the use of the abbreviation *cus*, used to describe a social work 'customer' (service user). It is clear that there can be no hard and fast rules in this area. For example, publications written outside the UK, such as in Australia and the United States, tend to use the term *client*. So, too, do some authors from the UK:

> We have chosen the term 'client' throughout this book since we think it better defines the ethical relationship which should exist between would-be helpers and might-be helped. Therefore, respectively, it confers more rights and requires more obligations than 'customer' or 'service user'.
>
> (Sheldon and Macdonald 2009: 4)

What this subject highlights is the importance of language and its limitations (McLaughlin 2009: 1114). Being critically reflective about the words we use is essential, but this in itself cannot fundamentally alter the stigma and oppression that travels with words and the way that language can be used in offensive ways to describe certain people, and the groups to which they belong. My concern is that an over-zealous concern for 'getting it right' in terms of language can mean that we fail to focus on the bigger picture, which involves being active in our efforts to address the discrimination that some groups continue to experience, on a daily basis, within society.

On a less contentious issue, this time in relation to spelling, a differentiation is made in this third edition between the verb *to practise* and the noun *practice*. In the USA, the word *practise* is rarely used but this is not the case in the UK, and in countries that have been influenced by UK English usage, although this situation is likely to change with spelling being increasingly dominated by Microsoft Word's spell check system. However, since competent or compassionate social work practice does not depend on an awareness of this grammatical distinction, I would not want this issue to be given more attention than it deserves. Finally, on occasion I have chosen to add the adverb *sic* to indicate the idiosyncratic, sexist, incorrect, dated, or potentially oppressive use of certain terms.

2   THEORETICAL KNOWLEDGE

This chapter looks at the knowledge base of social work. It begins with an account of how different interpretations can influence the way we approach our work, and how knowledge and theory have been conceptualized in social work. Of particular interest is how these more abstract subjects can be integrated and linked to the skills and interventions used in everyday social work practice. It is the ordering and integration of theory and practice, or *knowledge* and *skills*, that is a central theme of this chapter, and that theme is illustrated in the *Knowledge and Skills Framework* I have developed. The chapter ends with a discussion of the influence of ideology on social work and the uneasy marriage between theory and practice. An important feature when exploring the subject of knowledge involves attempting to identify – and to build on – the knowledge you have already acquired as a unique human being. Relating what we discover to our own experience – and the world around us – can be an unnerving experience if we find ourselves having to change what we think, feel, do, and believe but it can also be illuminating. To facilitate this exploration, whenever possible I have used practice examples to illustrate the use and importance of knowledge in social work. I hope this inspires you, the reader, to explore the subjects covered in greater depth.

Knowledge

The ability to draw on – and to use – knowledge is central to effective social work practice. This makes it important to understand what 'knowledge' means and to understand how knowledge shapes and informs the way we work in practice. For example, in the inquiry into the death of Victoria Climbié, an eight-year-old African child who in 2000 was murdered by her great-aunt and her aunt's lover, the inquiry Chairman, Lord Laming, stated: 'it may be that assumptions made about Victoria and her situation diverted caring people from noting and acting upon signs of neglect or ill-treatment' (Laming 2003: 16). The assumptions made in this case included 'misplaced assumptions about her [Victoria's] cultural circumstances' – assumptions that were not questioned by a whole range of professionals. In the report, it was noted that there were:

> ... no fewer than 12 key occasions when the relevant services had the opportunity to successfully intervene in the life of Victoria. As evidence to the Inquiry unfolded, several other opportunities emerged ... there can be no excuse for such sloppy and unprofessional performance.
>
> (Laming 2003: 3)

All assumptions should be open to question. As Lord Laming stated, 'the concept of "respectful uncertainty" should lie at the heart of the relationship between the social worker and the family' – an approach that needs to 'involve the critical evaluation of information that they are given' (Laming 2003: 205). What this example highlights is the importance of questioning all sources of information – of thinking carefully and critically about the information or data available to support our assumptions and the positions we adopt – whether this originates from our own personal experience, the professional knowledge that we and others have acquired, the teaching we have been given or the research findings we have read. This may not always lead to a clear picture because how people interpret and understand events or information can lead to different conclusions, and it is this tension that needs to be grappled with. A similar situation can be found in research findings where different research studies can arrive at very different if not contradictory findings. These complex issues are explored in this chapter and at different points throughout the book, especially the way that knowledge about a subject (*knowing that*) can be linked to practice concerns (*knowing how*) (Ryle 1949). Here it is important to note that in the conceptualization I am putting forward, research is not considered to be a source of knowledge in its own right but a method by which knowledge can be acquired and updated. This subject is covered at the end of this chapter under research skills.

How knowledge has been conceptualized

We seek and use knowledge to understand ourselves, others, and the world around us. A central aspect of this quest or exploration is the search for truth – the desire to know what constitutes reality or, as Karl Popper states, the shaping of reality through truth (Popper 1994). Thus, an exploration of what constitutes knowledge naturally leads to a discussion of what constitutes 'truth' or 'reality'. This in turn gives rise to an important dilemma, namely the difference between *subjective* and *objective* interpretations. What may be true or real for me may not be true or real for others. As a result, how people interpret events, and how they view their interaction with others and the world they inhabit, can vary greatly. It can lead to important differences in the way that people perceive events and the understanding and meaning they give to the experiences they have had, including the experiences they have witnessed. These issues can appear far removed from contemporary social work, yet what constitutes truth or reality lies at the heart of the assessment process and other aspects of our work. This highlights the multiple perspectives gathered from a range of different sources, as indicated in this second quotation taken from the IASSW and IFSW definition of social work, mentioned in the Introduction:

> Social work bases its methodology on a systematic body of evidence-based knowledge derived from research and practice evaluation, including local and indigenous knowledge specific to its context. It recognizes the complexity of interactions between human beings and their environment, and the capacity of people both to be affected by and to alter the multiple influences upon them including bio-psychosocial factors. The social work profession draws on theories of human development and behaviour and social systems to analyze complex situations and to facilitate individual, organizational, social and cultural changes.
>
> (IFSW/IASSW: 2000)

The reference to 'local and indigenous knowledge' is important because it highlights the knowledge that non-professionals bring to the encounter, particularly service users and carers. In social work, and in other professions, this source of knowledge has been seriously overlooked in the past (Coates *et al.* 2006: 381; Croft and Beresford 2008: 394), although in some areas this picture is changing. Indigenous knowledge is similar to the term *subjugated knowledge* (Hartman 1992), which describes knowledge that derives from people in their everyday contexts who have important personal, social, and cultural experiences to recount (Hafford-Letchfield 2010: 496–505; Penna 2000: 220). However, unlike professionals, they are not considered to be *experts* and, therefore, their knowledge runs the risk of being discounted or considered less relevant. Thus certain forms of knowledge are legitimated and 'privileged' over other forms of knowledge, a privileging that is highly contentious and contested. I experienced the way that power and status could be used to give credibility to professionals over non-professionals when I worked with women suffering from depression. This work revealed the extent to which women's personal, indigenous, lay or informal knowledge was at times discounted when they encountered professionals who adopted an 'expert' stance, and an inflexible interpretation of their role. For many women, being *pathologized*, that is, having their thoughts, feelings, and actions disregarded and reframed as a 'symptom' of mental illness, was a deeply upsetting and disempowering experience.

The attempt to identify what is 'real' or 'true' in a given situation often takes us to the realm of belief, which for some people carries much the same weight as 'truth'. In this context, *belief* is defined as: 'The acknowledgement that a proposition is true in the absence of demonstrable proof as required by scientific method' (Bullock and Trombley 1999: 72). Sheldon (1995: 153) describes beliefs as 'settled views of experience' that we seek to preserve and have confirmed. The notion of *proof* can be viewed as 'an attempt to convince people of the truth of what you are saying' (Bullock and Trombley 1999: 692). It is a situation that is often highly influenced by ideology – by ideas and assumptions that are dominant and that influence our thinking at a particular point (Howe 2008a: 88; Mullaly 1997: 31). 'Ideologies appear to be rational. They appear to be open to debate . . . This apparent rationality is how they win over adherents' (Barnett 1994: 188). It is a rationality that can be seen in the way that politicians state a particular belief or viewpoint as being self-evident and beyond question. On the other hand, the emphasis in the approach adopted by Popper is one where 'proposed proof' lies in its resilience and testability: 'proposed proof must be able to stand up to critical discussion' (Popper 1994b: 13). From this perspective, an assertion can be considered to be true 'if it corresponds to, or agrees with, the facts' (Popper 1994b: 174). The importance of testing hypotheses is given greater focus in Chapter 4 and we return to the subject of ideology towards the end of this chapter.

It is important to realize that we experience life through our histories but that these histories are always in the making. It is for this reason that we look for factors that can verify what we think, feel or believe – such as evidence, information, research findings – in the hope that these can point us in the right direction and help us to see what is 'true' or 'real' with some degree of accuracy. Yet we know from the work of Kuhn (1970) and others that the search for objective knowledge is problematic and highly influenced by human factors. It is for this reason that considerable emphasis is placed on critical thinking and reflection/reflexivity in social work, as a way to be able to identify the personal and ideological assumptions that we make and the extent to which our hypotheses are blinkered by the assumptions we bring to experiences.

It is this relationship between objective and subjective truth, and the role of belief, proof, and evidence, that remains complex and problematic in social work because, as already stated, it can be difficult to know what is real or true amid conflicting realities and people's differing understandings of events and experiences. But if what constitutes knowledge is a complex issue, so too is the task of applying that knowledge to contemporary social work practice. To address these complexities, the Social Care Institute for Excellence (SCIE) commissioned a knowledge review, entitled *Types and Quality of Knowledge in Social Care* (Pawson *et al.* 2003: 73). The remit of this review, which stretched beyond social work to include social care, was to 'consider what types of knowledge SCIE should draw on, and how to distinguish good quality knowledge from that which should not be relied on in policy making and practice' (Fisher 2003: vi). This proved to be a difficult task, as Pawson and his colleagues (2003: vii) noted, because of the 'diverse and fragmented' nature of social care knowledge and the different interpretations placed on what constitutes *knowledge*. To understand this tension, it is important to look in some detail at how social work knowledge, particularly social work theory, has been defined and conceptualized, so that we can draw a map of the territory that this subject covers and, in the process, provide some directions and signposts through this vast terrain.

How theory is defined

In everyday speech, Barker defines theory as: 'A group of related hypotheses, concepts, and constructs, based on facts and observations, that attempts to explain a particular phenomenon' (Barker 2003: 434). These theories may take the form of a 'single concept or idea' or attempt to explain 'interrelated concepts' (Fook 2002: 38). In this text, a *concept* is an abstract idea – with some concepts being linked to specific theories, while others tend to be more general. For example, *happiness* and *well-being* are concepts that are quite general, and not normally linked to a specific theory or discipline. However, the concept of *unconditional positive regard* is almost always linked to client/person-centred approaches. An important characteristic of a theory is that it goes beyond the descriptive to include *explanations* of why things (phenomena) happen. This can include a 'particular *interpretation* of whatever it seeks to explain, whether that be the plight of women in society, racism, schizophrenia, poverty, and so on' (Gray 2010: 96–7). Thus we use theory in an attempt to make sense of the world and/or particular events. Theories are also important because they can help us to predict what is likely to happen in a given situation, and thus offer a degree of choice in the action we can take 'in our danger-avoiding, satisfaction-seeking lives' (Sheldon and Macdonald 2009: 36). Sheldon sees this desire for predictability in evolutionary terms:

> ... it is psychologically impossible not to have theories about things. It is impossible at a basic perceptual level, at a cognitive and at an emotional level. The search for meaning, as a basis for predicting behavioural success and avoiding danger, appears to have been 'wired' into our brains by evolution.
>
> (Sheldon 1995: 8)

However, this search for meaning can shift and change. For this reason, the theories we formulate need to be seen as tentative, so that 'a theory always remains hypothetical, or conjectural. It always remains guesswork. And there is no theory that is not beset with problems' (Popper 1994b: 157). As such, it is essential to avoid seeing theory/theories in terms of *absolute notions* or as *knowledge set in stone*:

> Theories are not absolute notions of the way things really are, but, so long as they account for what appears to be happening in a particular way that satisfies the observer, they are retained. Theories provide

'workable definitions' of the world about us. They make it intelligible. In a very real way, theory-building is reality-building ... Our theories define what we see.

(Howe 1987: 10)

The notion of 'theory as explanation' places theories and theorizing at one end of a spectrum as something accessible: something that we all do, whether intentionally or not. This category could include *anecdotal experience* (Gambrill 2006: 80), *common-sense* notions (England 1986: 33; Gray and Webb 2009: 3) or *lay* theories (Rogers and Pilgrim 2010). All these terms describe learning or explanations that have been primarily gained from direct experience – sometimes described as an *experiential* learning or *experiential* sources of knowledge (Pawson *et al.* 2003: 13). A different way to describe this is in terms of *bottom-up* explanations, which in relation to social work means theories or explanations that are mainly generated from practice. This emphasis is often associated with the writing of Schön (1983: 1987). Developing bottom-up theories – or explanations – in this way is a form of *theory building* when it involves refining existing theories or formulating new ones. This form of theorizing falls under the heading 'practice knowledge', which is covered later in this chapter under the heading 'Theories relating to direct practice', and also comes within the *Practice Knowledge* domain, covered in Chapter 4.

At the other end of the spectrum from bottom-up explanations lies a more *top-down* test of applicability, which refers to the way that research findings or different theories are applied to practice situations. Top-down approaches tend to draw on theories that have been classified in terms of grand theory or middle-range theory. The term *grand theory* was used pejoratively by C. Wright Mills (1959) in *The Sociological Imagination* to attack conceptualizations formulated at a highly abstract level, sometimes referred to as 'grand narratives' (Fook 2002: 12), which purport to explain more or less everything in society (e.g. Marxism, psychoanalysis, feminism). Lesser claims are made under the heading *middle-range* theories, a term coined by Merton (1968) to explain only a limited range of phenomena, such as social inequalities or oppression. However, when middle-range theories are not developed directly from practice, they can present a bewildering array of explanations that do not sit easily together. Postmodern and poststructural 'discourses' have been criticized in this regard, yet their role has been important in challenging the status and validity of grand narratives or the 'universal truths' that have been put forward in the name of 'science' or 'reason'. Critics of grand narratives see these as 'a mass of conflicting ways of making sense of different experiences from different perspectives' where 'there is no one universal truth or reality, but instead "reality" is constructed out of a multiplicity of diverse and fragmented stories' (Fook 2002: 12). Postmodernism occupies an important position in the current evidence-based climate, although some authors question its value, calling it 'antithetical to social work itself' (Sheppard 2006: 78). Indeed, Sheldon (2001: 801) considers that a postmodern approach would be more appropriately phrased as indicating a 'post-rational' standpoint.

However, in the realm of theory and theorizing, it can be easy to be drawn into abstract conceptualizations and to lose sight of the fact that for any theory to be relevant it needs to be able to 'speak' to the dilemmas and complexities regularly encountered in social work practice, that is, any knowledge gained has to be capable of being *used*, a process sometimes described as 'knowledge utilization' (Fisher 2002: 42), 'utility' or 'fit for use' (Pawson *et al.* 2003: 39). In this regard, Howe (2008a: 88) identifies five key areas where the use of theory can illuminate our understanding of people and their circumstances:

1 *Observation*: it tells us what to see and what to look out for.
2 *Description*: it provides a conceptual vocabulary and framework within which observations can be arranged and organized.
3 *Explanation*: it suggests how different observations might be linked and connected; it offers possible causal relationships between one event and another.
4 *Prediction*: it indicates what might happen next.
5 *Intervention*: it suggests what might be done to bring about change.

Howe's description provides a clear general account of the way that the use of theory can help us to unravel what is happening and why. These five points are equally relevant and transferable in relation to assessments undertaken in social work practice. Whether general or specialist, the task of theory is to provide a framework to explain and understand what is happening and why, so that, as human beings and as professionals, we can take appropriate action. To do this well means that we need to draw on the perceptions, explanations, and understanding that all people bring to a particular encounter – especially the knowledge that service users and carers bring, as well as the explanations put forward by other individuals, such as family members, friends, neighbours, other workers, and professionals. It also involves learning how to communicate what we know – what constitutes our knowledge base – in ways that illuminate others' understanding so that we can avoid becoming lost in abstract theories or jargon, or avoid being lured off course or enticed down dead ends:

> . . . social work theory should never become an end in itself . . . It should provide some explanation for the complexities we observe in our practice so that out of apparent chaos we might expose the patterns and regularities in behaviour and situations; it should therefore help us to predict future behaviour . . . a truly useful theory would provide guidance towards a more effective practice, giving a measure of confidence so that we do not feel totally at the mercy of our working environment;

if we build on and record effective strategies and techniques, then we build transmittable knowledge by directing others to what is common and regularly occurring in human experience.

(Coulshed 1991: 8)

The notion of *transmittable knowledge* is similar to *transferability* of knowledge and skills, covered in Chapter 4. Figure 2.1 locates and integrates the definitions I have described in the *Knowledge and Skills Framework* I have put forward. Its purpose is to link theory and practice, or knowledge and skills, within a coherent structure.

Summary of the Knowledge and Skills Framework

The *framework* shows the integration of knowledge and skills and illustrates 'a users' map of the knowledge-base of professional practice' (Eraut 1994: 50) as it applies to social work. The first two domains of the *framework – on theoretical knowledge* and *factual knowledge* – focus more on how knowledge can be acquired. The *practice knowledge* domain indicates how we turn that knowledge into action. This emphasizes the importance of adapting our knowledge, skills, and interventions in the light of the knowledge we have gathered, including the knowledge that others bring to the encounter, particularly service users. Historically, the main interventions used in social work have tended to be grouped under the heading *communication skills*, although it would be more accurate to describe this subject in terms of *communication skills and interventions*. Our ability to communicate is the bridge that connects us to other human beings based on the rapport and relationships that we create. This includes an awareness of how we present ourselves as professional social workers, which is illustrated in Figure 2.1 by indicating that we shape the knowledge we present through our *professional use of self*. In this task, and depending on the context, we can apply or *use* knowledge in a straightforward and uncomplicated way, but we can also use knowledge *creatively*. When these different factors are integrated, it is possible to see that the skills we learn – and *interventions* we use – constitute knowledge, skills, and values in action. It is the creative acquisition and use of *theoretical, factual,* and *practice knowledge* – adapted by the work context and the knowledge that service users bring, and woven into the relationships we build – that leads to knowledge-based interventions that can inform the process of assessment, analysis, decision-making, and action.

To differentiate the conceptualizations I describe from those of other authors, I have opted to use the term *domain*, which merely refers to an item within a classification. As a conceptual tool, the purpose of this *framework* is to aid understanding in ways that underpin the processes involved in analysis, action, reflection, and evaluation by categorizing the range and type of knowledge commonly referred to in social work. The need for such a framework is not new – nor is this gap evident only in relation to the United

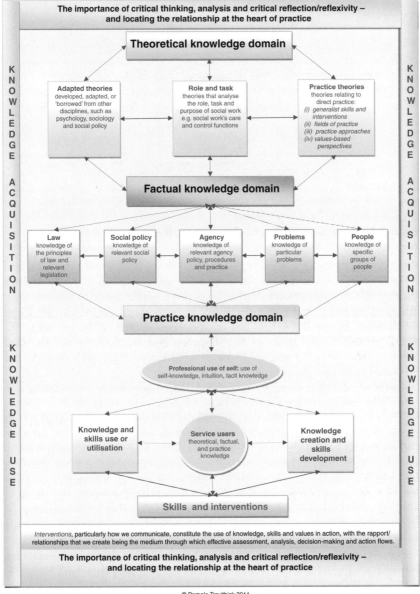

A knowledge and skills framework integrating theory and practice in social work

© Pamela Trevithick 2011

Figure 2.1 *Knowledge and Skills Framework* integrating theory and practice in social work

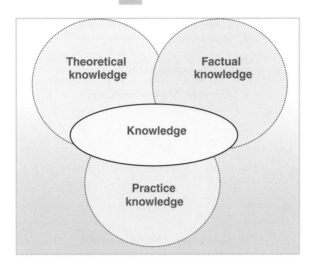

Figure 2.2 Three overlapping and interweaving domains of knowledge

Kingdom. For example, Reid noted in 1978 that 'innumerable theories' and conceptualizations have been put forward in social work in the United States but that 'little of this knowledge has been put together in the form of specific propositions to guide practice decisions. In other words, most knowledge at the disposal of social workers has not yet been shaped to the proper form' (Reid 1978: 378). A feature of this shapeless body of theory is the fact that 'there is no universally accepted idea of valid knowledge, skills or expertise for social workers' (Asquith *et al.* 2005: 2).

In Figure 2.1, the three knowledge domains appear as distinct and discrete, whereas in reality they overlap and interweave in complex ways, as indicated in Figure 2.2. Although the circles or domains are of equal size in Figure 2.2, in reality they are likely to differ in size, depending on the type and quality of knowledge that has been acquired. For example, students may well acquire considerable *theoretical* and *factual knowledge* from studying the range of subjects taught on their social work course. If they had no prior practice experience in social work before beginning their training, the area marked as *practice knowledge* is likely to cover a smaller surface compared with the other two areas. However, *practice knowledge* also encompasses the personal knowledge that all people acquire in everyday life and these experiences, and the meaning and understanding acquired, need to be taken into account (see Figure 2.3). This subject is covered in greater detail in Chapter 4.

Theoretical knowledge

This section on theoretical knowledge begins with an account of how theory has been conceptualized in different social work publications. This coverage

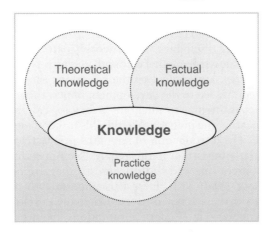

Figure 2.3 An example of how students' knowledge base might be represented

is designed to make these concepts and theories more accessible and, in this task, it is important to note that there is no fundamental difference between the terms *theoretical knowledge* and *theory*. The three categories that make up the *theoretical knowledge* domain are (see Figure 2.4):

- Theories that are developed, adapted, or 'borrowed' from other disciplines (e.g. psychology, sociology, etc.).
- Theories that analyse the task and purpose of social work (e.g. raising questions, such as: Should the focus of social work be 'revolution' or 'reform'?).
- Theories relating to direct practice, that identify the different fields of practice, practice approaches, values-based perspectives, and skills and interventions used in social work (e.g. client/person-centred, task-centred, etc.). It is in this realm that a more practice-oriented range of social work theories can be found.

Theories that are developed, adapted, or borrowed from other disciplines

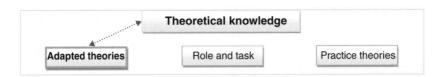

Figure 2.4 Theories that are developed, adapted, or borrowed from other disciplines

The first of three sub-headings looks at the extent to which social work has developed, adapted, and borrowed theories from rich and diverse sources that originate in other disciplines. Social work's particular contribution to this vast body of knowledge can be found in the way that key abstract concepts and theories are applied to the situations encountered in direct practice. This focus has led to the development of new theories such as practice approaches that attempt to integrate a sociological and psychological perspective by locating the individual within his or her wider social and cultural perspective. The introduction of strengths perspectives in social work has been particularly important in this regard (see Appendix 10). However, this wealth of sources can lead to difficulties if they are borrowed uncritically (Loewenberg 1984: 312). Here it is important to note that almost all the disciplines that we draw on were originally developed – and most continue to be framed – in Western assumptions about human behaviour and social relations. As such, the assumptions they embody, particularly when supported by prevailing ideology (Mullaly 1997), can limit our understanding of what it means to be a human being at any particular moment. For example, many theories tend to be *Eurocentric*, in that they 'undermine the importance of nondominant cultural patterns, beliefs and expectations' (Robinson 2000: 222): 'The root of "modern racism" is in a continuing Eurocentric philosophy that values mainstream (dominant culture) beliefs and attitudes more highly than culturally diverse belief systems' (Robinson 2007: 7). Attachment theory and other theories of growth and development have been criticized in this regard (Robinson 2009: 151). Also, some theories harbour patriarchal or gendered assumptions and some have been the focus of feminist scrutiny (Mullender 2008; Orme 2009; White 2006). However, fewer theories have been subjected to scrutiny in terms of the class assumptions that they carry.

A different problem can emerge if knowledge is drawn from too many diverse sources. This can lead to fragmentation, producing a 'knowledge pile' rather than a 'knowledge base' (Sheldon 1995: 6). In relation to how theories are presented, some accounts are located 'at a highly abstract level of analysis, quite speculative and fiercely contested' (Stepney 2000: 21) and, as a result, are not easy to apply to contemporary social work practice. Consequently, *transferability* can be lost, that is, 'the ability to remake knowledge for relevance across different contexts' (Fook 2002: 156). Some theories can be described or applied in ways that constitute an inaccurate representation. This problem is particularly evident in the manner that a client/person-centred approach has sometimes been presented. This approach has a very clearly defined theory base but one that was originally formulated for and applied to counselling practice. It is often confused with a relationship-based approach but it involves much more than this. For example, in situations where social workers are required to use their statutory powers, it is argued that a client/person-centred approach 'has no role' (Thorne 2002: 175).

This is because the use of statutory powers contradicts the principle of self-determination, which is a central feature of this approach. An incorrect theoretical interpretation is most often encountered when applying theories that have been developed outside social work.

The main disciplines that social work draws on include: psychology, sociology, law, social policy, organizational theory, politics, economics, medicine, and philosophy. Some, such as psychology, are more influential than others, but I would argue that a more sociological perspective is equally important because of the emphasis placed within this discipline on social and economic factors that affect people's day-to-day experience, and the wider context or system within which our work is located (Cunningham and Cunningham 2008). The privileged position given to psychology could be considered to promote a more individualized approach within social work.

1 *Psychology.* Psychology is 'the study of the nature, functions, and phenomena of behaviour and mental experience' (Colman 2009: 619). It is the most influential discipline in social work and one that embraces a number of 'schools' or perspectives, such as humanist, behaviourist, psychoanalytic, cognitive, biological, and cross-cultural perspectives. The first three of these perspectives are covered in greater detail in Chapter 5.

2 *Sociology.* Alongside psychology, sociology is an important academic discipline in social work because of the focus placed on the relationship between the individual and his or her social context or social world: 'of all the social sciences it is sociology that most closely scrutinizes change and conflict in the wider society' (Scott and Marshall 2009: 719). This subject includes, for example, coverage of social class, gender, race, and religion, but it can also include different 'schools', such as functionalism, positivism, and structuralism or classical theorists, such as Durkheim, Weber, or Marx.

3 *Principles of law/key legislation.* Social work is located within a framework of legislation, shaped by government policy: 'Law regulates social work practice, informs it, and provides a framework within which social workers operate. It suggests that the discretion and flexibility inherent within social work can be actively moderated *externally* through the courts and the legal system and *internally* through workers' awareness of human rights issues' (Munby 2008: 458).

4 *Social policy.* Social policy refers 'both to the process of developing and implementing measures to combat social problems in society, and to the academic study of these measures and their broader social context' (Alcock *et al.* 2002: 240). These measures, which include government policy on housing, health, education, social security, and social work (Spicker 1995), are covered in greater detail in Chapter 3 on *factual knowledge.*

5 *Organizational theory.* Organizational theory relates to the way that social services departments, community and voluntary agencies, and other organizations and institutions, are structured and run in terms of their culture, policies and procedures, and their approach to issues such as service delivery, the management of risk, accountability, performance, and quality assurance. Organizational theory could, for example, explore the particular features of managerialism or 'communities of practice' (Wenger 1998) or 'learning organizations' (Gould 2000).

6 *Politics.* Politics 'directly impacts on the responsibilities of social workers' (Jordan and Parton 2000: 258). Giddens (2001: 695) describes politics as: 'The means by which power is employed and contested to influence the nature and content of governmental activities. The sphere of the "political" includes the activities of those in government, but also the actions and competing interests of many other groups and individuals'.

7 *Economics.* Economics is the 'study of the production, distribution and consumption of wealth in human society' (Bannock *et al.* 2003: 122). Since the 1990s, the 'marketization' of social work has meant that market forces and *managerialism* dominate almost every aspect of health and social care provision (Hughes and Wearing 2007: 21). This is often represented as the three E's: effectiveness, economy, and efficiency. The impact of managerialism is addressed in Chapter 3.

8 *Medicine.* The influence of medicine, and the *medical model* or *biomedical model*, has become more pronounced in recent years, although its benefit is limited where illnesses fall outside a disease model (Wade and Halligan 2004). The medical/biomedical model is based on several assumptions that tend to neglect the importance of social and psychological factors (Nettleton 2006: 2). It is worth noting that more than a quarter of primary care patients in England present with unexplained chronic pain, irritable bowel syndrome or chronic fatigue, so-called medically unexplained symptoms (see Hatcher and Arroll 2008).

9 *Philosophy.* 'All men and all women are philosophers' (Popper 1994b: 179). This subject includes: the theory of knowledge and how knowledge is acquired and used (epistemology); the meaning communicated in language (semantics); how we come to 'be' and 'know' and to understand reality (metaphysics); the reasoning used in thought processes and decision-making (logic); and the professional and personal moral values that we adopt (ethics) (see Aymer and Okitikpi 2000).

To this list could be added other subjects, such as history and social anthropology. For example, the history of social work from Poor Law reform to the development of the welfare state makes fascinating reading. An interesting historical account can be found in Sheldon and Macdonald (2009). Similarly, according to Giddens (2001: 686), 'Culture is one of the most distinctive properties of human social association', and we need to recognize its impact on individual behaviour, interactions between individuals, and interpretations of meaning between them. Social and cultural anthropology can deepen our understanding of different cultures and how they view 'concepts of time, place and community' (Shaw 2007: 667).

Theories that analyse the task and purpose of social work

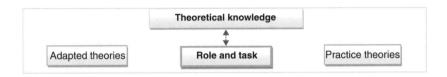

Figure 2.5 Theories that analyse the task and purpose of social work

The second sub-heading of the *theoretical knowledge* domain looks at the task and purpose of social work (see Figure 2.5). This is an area that is fraught with confusion, both for individual social workers and social work agencies – a situation that is not new and one where history can help to illuminate our understanding of more recent events.

The development of personal social services in England and Wales was embodied in post-war legislation that led to most services being organized in three separate departments: children, welfare, and health. Within this 'organizational specialization' (Stevenson 2005: 576) child care officers, welfare officers, and mental welfare officers tended to work from a more generalist knowledge and skills base. However, it became evident that there were gaps, duplication, and fragmentation in service provision and, as a result, the Seebohm Commission was set up to review service provision. The recommendations of Seebohm led to the establishment of 'generic' social services departments, and a more 'integrated approach' to service delivery (Seebohm Report 1968: 11). It also led to the setting up of the Central Council for Education and Training in Social Work (CCETSW) in 1971 – which was replaced in 2000 by the General Social Care Council (GSCC) as the regulatory body for social work education and training.

However, uncertainties and confusion began to emerge in the late 1970s, with social workers expressing an 'unease about what they should be doing and the way in which they are organized and deployed' (Barclay Report 1982: vii). In response, a working party was set up 'to review the role and tasks of social workers in local authority social services departments and related voluntary agencies in England and Wales' (Barclay Report 1982: vii). The recommendations of the Barclay Report included less bureaucratic approaches to service delivery, and devolved decision-making to team level. It also promoted a more self-help and community-based approach, as well as stressing the importance of providing counselling to help people 'manage the emotional and practical realities that face them' (Barclay Report 1982: 180).

This brief history is important because many of the same issues are still being aired in relation to how social work should be organized, whether it should be providing a generalist or a specialist service, and the extent to which the burden of bureaucracy hinders the provision of quality services. For example, a confusion about the role and task of social work has been described in terms of 'the challenges posed by . . . the diverse needs of those who use services, as well as the diversity and complexity of the workforce tasked to deliver them' (Blewett *et al.* 2007: 2). In a document published in 2008 by the GSCC, *Social Work at its Best: A Statement of Social Work Roles and Tasks for the 21st Century*, the following definition of social work was offered:

> Social work is an established professional discipline with a distinctive part to play in promoting and securing the wellbeing of children, adults, families and communities. It operates within a framework of legislation and government policy, set out in *Putting People First* and the *Children's Plan*, and contributes to the development of social policy, practice and service provision. It collaborates with other social care, health, education and related services to ensure people receive integrated support. It is a profession regulated by law.
>
> (GSCC 2008: 4)

What is interesting about this account is how closely the roles and task of social work are linked to government policy requirements. It differs markedly from the plain English 'public description of social work', put forward by the Social Work Task Force (SWTF). This wording was specifically chosen in order to promote 'greater understanding among the general public' (SWTF 2009b: 6) and emphasizes the *help* that social work can provide:

- *Social work* helps adults and children to be safe so they can cope and take control of their lives again.
- *Social workers* make life better for people in crisis who are struggling to cope, feel alone, and cannot sort out their problems unaided.
- *How social workers do this* depends on the circumstances. Usually they work in partnership with the people they are supporting – check out what they need, find what will help them, build their confidence, and open doors to other services. Sometimes, in extreme situations such as where people are at risk of harm or in danger of hurting others, social workers have to take stronger action – and they have the legal powers and duties to do this (SWTF 2009b: 67).

For some authors, the difficulty in identifying the task and purpose of social work is not so much about role confusion as about disagreement. Should social work be about reform or revolution? Should we be seeking to 'fit' people into the system, or to change the system – or do both? Will social work be overtaken by its control function, at the expense of being able to care for people? Are social workers 'inclined either to *pursue causes* or *carry out functions* ... [and] likely to be radical or conservative in the approach to society and its ills' (Howe 2009: 21). Should social work focus on the *maintenance, therapeutic helping*, and *emancipatory* approaches highlighted in Dominelli's (2009: 51–2) conceptualization, defined by Howe in terms of the tension between three functions: *care, control*, and *cure*, with *cure* being used to describe 'therapeutic helping approaches' (Howe 1994: 518)? If we take the dual functions of *care* and *control*, is the current role of social work primarily focused on the enforcement of rules and regulations ('primarily a rational-technical activity') or one that embraces an emancipatory perspective (primarily a 'practical-moral activity') (Parton 2000: 452)? Parton, among others, argues strongly against the more 'rational-technical' stance, highlighting the inadequate and inappropriate way that managerialism's 'audit, procedures, legalism' operates (Parton 2000: 457).

What is missing so far in this discussion is an explicit mention of social work's role as an agent of control, particularly in relation to the bureaucracies set up within the UK Welfare State, although this has been implied. Parton takes up this issue, exploring the difficult balance that social workers have to demonstrate when their work involves both care and control:

> Part of what social workers have sought to do is strengthen the bonds of inclusive membership by trying to nurture reciprocity, sharing and small scale redistribution between individuals, in households, groups, communities and so on. But part is also concerned with the compulsory enforcement of social obligations, rules, laws and regulations. The two are intertwined and invariably the latter provides the ultimate mandate for the former – it is in this context that social work involves both care and control. While it has always been concerned to liberate and emancipate those with whom it works, it is also concerned with working on behalf of the state and the wider society to maintain social order.
>
> (Parton 2000: 457)

A shift has taken place in recent years away from notions of *care* and *cure* towards that of *control*. An example of this shift can be seen in the way that anti-social behaviour among young people has been reconceptualized – and criminalized – under the heading 'youth offending' (Garrett 2007). Of course, 'control measures' may be necessary to provide 'protection' where risk is involved – a situation that calls for sound assessment and intervention skills. The extent to which individual freedom should be controlled is a complex issue but one that falls outside the remit of this text. However, it is worth noting that control can be exercised in a range of different ways, such as controlling the availability of resources and services, or the activities of social workers through the use of targets and performance indicators.

The tension between the three functions of *care, control*, and *cure* (Howe 1994: 518) also reminds us of the central place that caring holds – or should hold – within social work (Phillips 2007). This perspective maintains that caring for people can help bring about positive change, recovery or reparation – or cure (Winnicott 1986: 116). It states that where people have been cared for too little, particularly in childhood – or where we find that basic human needs have not been met – this can lead to emotional insecurity, dependency needs, and a limited ability to deal with the complexities of everyday living. This can sometimes (but not always) result in a range of distressed and disturbed behaviour. The hope is that, by providing care for people who have 'not had enough', we will be able to compensate for the lack of original care and, ultimately, help people to move on independently, and without the continued involvement of health and welfare services. In my experience, the act of caring for others has to be thought through very carefully. To be effective in bringing about positive change, reparation or recovery, it has to be the right kind of care, delivered in a way – and at a time – that maximizes the benefits of that care (Trevithick 1998). This kind of change and reparation is brought about in situations where, through our knowledge and intervention skills, we support the growth process to start up again and to have its own momentum and motivation (Weick 1983; Winnicott 1986).

Theories relating to direct practice

Figure 2.6   Theories relating to direct practice

The third and final sub-heading of the *theoretical knowledge* domain encompasses theories that relate to direct practice (see Figure 2.6). As stated in Chapter 1, social work's particular contribution has focused on attempting to adapt and link theories that originate in other disciplines to the situations regularly encountered in social work practice. Examples of this more holistic or 'whole person approach' can be found in *strengths-based* perspectives (Saleebey 2009); the focus placed on the *person-in-the situation* (Gitterman and Germaine 2008); the attempt to mobilize people's strengths with a systems approach in *social casework* (Hollis 1964); the importance of systemic and ecological approaches and perspectives within social work (Gill and Jack 2007); and the emphasis placed on the social and relational dimensions that are a feature of *constructive* social work (Parton and O'Byrne 2000). To this list should be added the attempt to focus on the underlying reasons why particular social and personal problems emerge, such as the importance of *structural social work* (Mullaly 2007) or *radical* social work approaches (Ferguson 2008; Ferguson and Woodward 2009). Many of these theories emphasize the importance of the relationships we build in social work (Ruch *et al.* 2010; Trevithick 2003).

Practice terminology: the importance of conceptual rigour

When looking at the literature and the theories that inform direct practice in social work, two problems emerge. The first relates to a point discussed earlier, namely the absence of a framework – or conceptual map – that can help to order the different theories that have been proposed, or are being developed in social work. A second problem relates to the differences that can be found in relation to how practice terms are defined and described. For example, theories that might fall in the category of cognitive behavioural, client/person-centred, psychodynamic theories – to name but a few – can be described in some texts as *methods* (Howarth and Shardlow 2003; Stepney and Ford 2000), as *approaches* (Coulshed and Orme 2006), as *perspectives* (Gray 2010: 96–7) or as *practices* (Milner and O'Bryne 2009). The same lack of consistency can be found in the way that groupwork, family work, and community work are described, which can again be referred to as *methods*, *models*, *approaches*, *perspectives*, *practices* or, more uncommonly, *modes* (Howarth and Shardlow 2003).

The term 'model' is also used in a variety of ways. For example, it is described by Howe (1987: 10) as beginning 'to impose some low level order on what is otherwise a jumble of information'. This viewpoint is supported by Chenoweth and McAuliffe (2008: 114), who see a model as having 'less explanatory power than theories. They *show* the relationship between the elements rather than *explain* it' (original emphasis). However, these accounts sit uneasily with concepts such as the *medical/biomedical model* or the *social model of disability*, terms that adopt a particular interpretation of medicine and human behaviour. These inconsistencies highlight the importance of being conceptually rigorous in our use of practice terms so as to avoid confusion. I am not advocating a rigid approach to the use of language and key terms – language has to be free from this kind of constraint for new meaning and new understandings to be allowed to flourish. However, I am arguing for a more self-conscious, questioning, and reflective use of words, particularly in the area of practice terminology, in order to avoid misuse, misinterpretations, and misunderstandings, as well as the idiosyncratic use of key terms. Recently, a greater emphasis has been placed on this issue, with a number of authors adding a glossary to indicate how key terms are being used in their writing (Chenoweth and McAuliffe 2008; Gray and Webb 2009; Taylor and White 2006; Wilson *et al.* 2008).

A knowledge base or a knowledge pile?

It is interesting to note that in 1957, Germain, writing from the USA, identified only three major practice approaches. Twenty-six years later, he had identified 15 (Germain 1983). Similarly, in a publication edited by Turner (1974), 15 'theoretical approaches' were identified. In the UK, the work of Marsh and Triseliotis remains a seminal research study with regard to the subjects taught on social work training programmes. The participants in this research identified over 80 theorists and theoretical approaches taught on social work courses (Marsh and Triseliotis 1996: 51). Almost all had their roots in psychological theories, as opposed to sociologically based theories. A major problem in this area is the fact that social work skills and interventions have not yet become the focus of research, which means that we know relatively little about whether different practices have different outcomes (Parsloe 2000: 145). Again, this problem is not new, although there is evidence of a growing interest in this field (Fraser *et al.* 2009; Rothman 2003). This neglect means that more research is needed if we are to understand and evaluate the effectiveness of social work interventions, and their value and relevance for different service user groups and the different types of problems that are regularly encountered in social work.

Key practice terms defined

In this text, the theories that are relevant to the situations encountered in direct practice have been categorized under four headings:

(a) Skills and interventions
(b) Fields of practice
(c) Practice approaches
(d) Values-based perspectives

(a) *Skills and interventions*
In the past, there has been little attempt in social work to define what is meant by the term *skill*, including *specialist* and *generalist skills* and *interventions* (Trevithick 2011b). In this chapter, I have defined *skill* as follows:

> A *skill* is an action with a specific *goal* that can be *learnt*, that involves *actions performed in sequence*, that can be organized in ways that involve *economy of effort* and *evaluated* in terms of its relevance and effectiveness. Although these characteristics have been described separately, they interweave and overlap.

If we define *skills* in terms of what we learn, then *interventions* describe how we put that learning into practice, that is, the actions we perform to influence events. In this text, *interventions* are defined as follows:

> *Interventions* constitute knowledge, skills, and values in action and are designed to influence – or to alter – a particular situation, course of events or the thoughts, feelings, and behaviour that are evident.

This definition highlights the importance of actions based on knowledge and values. As practitioners, it is important that we too should be open to being changed when intervening in the lives of other people.

Generalist skills indicate a basic knowledge of a given area, situation or context, and the ability to apply that knowledge in the form of an intervention. Generalist skills, which are the skills covered in this text, have the advantage of being more transferable than many specialist skills, and are often the foundation on which specialist skills are developed. The term generalist is sometimes referred to as *generic*. In this text, the term *generic* is used to describe the eclectic range of theories, skills and values that are taught on social work training courses in order to provide students with a broad knowledge base (Trevithick 2011b).

Specialist skills indicate superior knowledge leading to the ability to use advanced skills and specialist types of intervention when working with specific client groups, problem areas, settings, or contexts. In this definition, these skills are acquired by undertaking additional training in a particular theory or practice approach, such as courses that focus on, say, the impact of trauma for practitioners working in the field of family violence, or training in the specific concepts and skills that are central to cognitive-behavioural practice approaches or family therapy. Such training should be consolidated through further practice experience and good supervision.

Eighty generalist skills and interventions

The 80 generalist skills and interventions included in this book are listed on p. 46, with detailed coverage being provided in later chapters. The perspective adopted in this text emphasizes that all actions are intellectual in character, hence the definition of an *intervention* as *knowledge, skills, and values in action*. These actions may be located in particular *fields of practice*, or involve the implementation of *practice approaches*, values-based *perspectives*, *skills*, and *interventions* – but whatever form they take, an intellectual element is always a feature which makes it important for social work to claim the theoretical and intellectual features that underpin the use of certain skills and interventions.

A lexicon of 80 skills and interventions

1. Interpersonal skills
2. Verbal communication skills
3. Non-verbal communication skills
4. Observation skills
5. Listening skills
6. Assessment skills
7. Engaging with the task
8. Planning and preparing for the interview
9. Creating a rapport
10. Welcoming skills
11. Informal opening conversations ('social chat')
12. Sympathy
13. Empathy
14. Professional use of self
15. Use of intuition
16. Information gathering
17. Open questions
18. Closed questions
19. *What* questions
20. *Why* questions
21. Circular questions
22. Hypothetical questions
23. Paraphrasing
24. Clarifying
25. Summarizing
26. Active listening responses ('minimum encouragers')
27. Giving and receiving feedback
28. Sticking to the point and purpose of the interview
29. Prompting
30. Probing
31. Allowing and using silences
32. Using self-disclosure
33. Ending an interview
34. Closing the case and ending the relationship
35. Providing help
36. Giving advice
37. Providing information
38. Providing explanations
39. Offering encouragement and validation
40. Providing reassurance
41. Using persuasion and being directive
42. Providing practical and material assistance
43. Providing support
44. Providing care
45. Breaking bad news
46. Modelling and social skills training
47. Reframing
48. Offering interpretations
49. Adapting to need
50. Counselling skills
51. Containing anxiety
52. Empowerment and enabling skills
53. Negotiating skills
54. Contracting skills
55. Networking skills
56. Working in partnership
57. Mediation skills
58. Advocacy skills
59. Assertiveness skills
60. Being challenging
61. Being confrontative
62. Dealing with hostility, aggression, and violence
63. Managing professional boundaries
64. Respecting confidentiality
65. Record-keeping skills
66. Form filling
67. Updating case notes
68. Minute-taking skills
69. Report writing skills
70. Using supervision creatively
71. Organizational and administrative skills
72. Letter writing skills
73. Skilled use of emails
74. Telephone contact
75. Using mobile phones and text messaging
76. Presentation skills
77. Chairing meetings
78. Coordinating case conferences and reviews
79. Presenting evidence in court
80. Using humour

(b) *Fields of practice*
There are four main fields of practice that can reflect different theoretical orientations. For example, some groupwork may be undertaken from a cognitive-behavioural practice approach, while another approach may adopt a psychodynamic groupwork perspective, and so forth (Trevithick 2012b). The four fields of practice are:

- work with individuals, which can include counselling
- work with families, including family therapy
- work with groups or groupwork, which can include work in teams
- work with communities, including community development.

(c) *Practice approaches*
Practice approaches draw on a coherent and identifiable body of theory that can be applied and adapted in a systematic way in response to the situation encountered and the context. The practice approaches most often covered in social work publications include:

- person/client-centred
- cognitive-behavioural
- task-centred
- psychodynamic or psychosocial
- strengths-based approaches
- ecological practice approaches (derived from systems theory).

These practice approaches are covered in greater detail in the appendices. For more in-depth coverage, see Howe (2009).

(d) *Values-based perspectives*
Clark (2000d: 361) identifies four essential principles that can often be identified in typical statements relating to social work values:

1 The worth and uniqueness of every person
2 The entitlement to justice
3 The claim to freedom
4 The essentiality of community.

Values-based perspectives are often used to understand a subject in greater depth or, where disadvantage or discrimination is evident, to attempt to mediate the impact of oppression in some way. The perspectives that are most commonly adopted in social work include anti-oppressive, anti-discrimination, and empowerment perspectives; feminist and radical or activist perspectives; and those that focus on promoting or advocating for the rights of disabled people, children and young people, and ethnic or cultural minority groups.

Since it is not possible in a general text of this kind to cover these perspectives in detail, the following list provides a number of references to further reading:

- anti-ageist perspectives (Beech and Ray 2009: 356–67; McDonald 2010; Wilson *et al.* 2008: 166–651)
- anti-discriminatory perspectives (Okitikpi and Aymer 2010)
- anti-oppressive perspectives (Burke and Harrison 2009: 209–19)
- black/anti-racist perspectives (Goldstein 2008: 415–22; Owusu-Bempah 2008: 318–25)
- carers' perspectives (Barton 2008: 409–14)
- children's rights perspective (Jackson 2000: 62)
- countering heterosexism/heteronormalism (Brown 1998)
- disabled people's movement (French and Swain 2008: 402–7; Marks 2008: 41–54)
- empowerment perspectives (Adams 2009: 178–88; Sheppard 2006)
- service users' perspectives (Croft and Beresford 2008: 393–401)
- survivors' perspectives:
  - mental health (Rogers and Pilgrim 2010: 250–60)
  - family/domestic violence (Humphries 2008: 27–33)
- welfare rights perspective (Bateman 2008: 148–57).

This section has provided an overview of the different theories that inform social work practice and supports the view that 'better knowledge and understanding tend to make most of us more articulate and authoritative' (Howe 2009: 205–6). It reminds us that the ability to articulate what we know – and to do so in ways that shed a light on 'what is happening and why' for other people – is a central skill in social work. We now look at how ideology can influence our access to knowledge, and what we are allowed to know.

The role of ideology

Ideology shapes the assumptions that underpin key areas of knowledge – assumptions influence the way we see the world and our part within it – such as the Eurocentric assumptions that dominate Western thinking, described earlier. Fook (2002: 56) highlights this point: 'an understanding of the ideological function of ideas ... allows us to make links between the social structure and individual lives, by explaining how people internalize thinking about the social structure and their place within it'. Giddens (2001: 691) has argued that 'the concept of ideology has a close connection with power, since ideological systems serve to legitimate the differential power held by groups'. It is a legitimation that can take the form of overt uses of power or coercion but in Western cultures, ideology is more often represented in an unquestioning acceptance of 'the way things are'. An example of how certain ideologies can acquire greater influence is evident in the way that the biomedical model has become more dominant in recent years. This development can be seen in the *medicalization* of behaviour considered problematic or undesirable and the growing tendency to describe different aspects of human behaviour in terms of medical labels, a situation promoted by drug companies and sometimes supported by government policy. Critics of the 'medicalization' of behaviour 'argue that doctors have too much political influence in issues where they are not in fact professionally competent to make judgements' (Abercrombie *et al.* 2006: 244).

On the other hand, social work also adopts ideological positions and assumptions that can 'function to maintain (or upset) the social order' (Fook 2002: 57). This is evident in the values and perspectives that social work practitioners use to guide their practice, but one of the difficulties for social work is how to stay true to the 'principles of human rights and social justice' (IFSW/IASSW 2000). Sometimes, the absence of what I describe as *a healthy sense of outrage* can be an indicator that the standards we once may have had – and hoped to maintain – have become slowly eroded. An example would be the sense of outrage that should accompany the tagging of children as young as ten years of age. It is a situation that often presents an ethical and moral dilemma for social workers (Drakeford 2008: 306), especially when we remember that as a profession we have an ethical duty to protect the rights of people who are vulnerable. I recall a situation in the late 1970s when a group of probation officers picketed outside a newly created 'short sharp centre' (similar to a 'boot camp'), with placards objecting to the inhumane treatment of young offenders in these units. I have campaigned on similar issues – and still do. The stance we adopt is important because it impacts on the decisions we make and the actions we take. Also, it is a statement in its own right.

Another example of the impact of ideology is the way that dependency is currently portrayed by government policy documents. In my experience, it is not possible for some people to move forward in situations of adversity unless they are allowed to become dependent on professionals in an organized and planned way – that is, in a way that is informed by theory (Winnicott 1965: 83–92) – thereby avoiding the dangers of creating an unhealthy or growth-inhibiting dependency (Trevithick 1995). I address this subject in Chapter 4 where the work of Winnicott is explored. Service users and carers know a great deal about dependency and many would share my perspective. Important opportunities for moving forward are lost, at huge cost to the welfare budget, because of the ill-conceived way that dependency is viewed. For this reason, we need a fundamental review of the way that dependency is portrayed in health and welfare contexts and to do so from a research-based focus, as opposed to one that promotes a particular ideology. In this task, we need to look closely at the reasons that underpin the anti-dependency culture that has been created (Hoggett 2000: 176).

Yet there is a contradiction here because, as a society, we do allow certain types of dependency. For example, according to statistics available for the UK from the National Institute for Health and Clinical Excellence (NICE) for the year March 2002 to March 2003, there were 26 million NHS antidepressant prescriptions written, costing over £380 million in total. Furthermore, 'the number of children in the UK being prescribed antidepressants, stimulants and other mind-altering drugs is soaring faster than anywhere in the world' (Boseley 2004). The number of prescriptions for all psychotropic drugs issued to children in 2000 rose from around 400,000 to more than 600,000 in 2001 and to more than 700,000 in 2002. It is argued that there is not enough funding to pay for more and better direct services for people in need. However, what these figures indicate is the vast amount of public funding that goes to the pharmaceutical industry – an important issue that warrants greater public debate.

The uneasy marriage between theory and practice

I would argue that there are a number of overlapping reasons why the relationship between theory and practice has remained estranged and troubled. First, we have been hindered by the lack of rigour that is evident in the way that different terms are used within social work. If we cannot name what we do, we cannot link theory to action or integrate our knowledge and skills within a coherent map of practice. This difficulty has been described as the absence of a 'comprehensive model of professional knowledge' (Drury Hudson 1997: 37) – an absence that makes it difficult to articulate and defend the boundaries of our professional task, roles, and responsibilities within social work.

Second, there is no established forum or link where policy-makers, academics, practitioners, service users, and carers can come together to discuss what they consider to be essential components of social work's knowledge base. Much of the discussion on the subject of the knowledge takes place in academic circles and not in practice settings – and then mainly in academic journals where the voices and experiences of social work practitioners are noticeably absent. In this regard, it is clear that some social work academics write for other academics, and not for students or practitioners. This is astonishing when considering the fact that social work is an applied professional discipline. The inaccessibility of articles and texts that are highly abstract and conceptually dense can be addressed if terms are clearly defined. Until this happens, we have some way to go if we are to change an ingrained perception that the world of theory and theorizing 'belongs' to academics and the world of practice 'belongs' to social work practitioners.

The last point overlaps with a third factor that contributes to the separation of theory and practice. This lies in the way that social work is organized, whereby the so-called 'producers of knowledge', who are mainly researchers or academics, are divorced from the 'users of knowledge', who are mainly social work and social care practitioners. In relation to social work, it is a division where 'employment structures have institutionalized the division between research and practice' (Marsh and Fisher 2005: 15–16). This situation is not evident in some other disciplines. For example, most academics in medicine and dentistry are expected to run clinics where they see patients, as well as being involved in writing and research. For Marsh and Fisher (2008: 975), this is a division that calls for a 'radical reform of the way we produce knowledge'. In relation to research, they argue that reform is needed in three areas (Marsh and Fisher 2008: 972–94):

(a) relating research to practice concerns;
(b) involving practitioners in generating knowledge that advances social work practice and knowledge production; and
(c) ensuring that research is focused on developing solutions for practice.

Such division is unlikely to be bridged unless a clinical grade is introduced into social work, similar to those in medicine, where academics are paid at a higher grade for working in practice contexts. In some ways, the voice of service users and carers has found its way into some academic publications, due largely to the efforts of some key individuals and the commitment demonstrated by the SCIE and Social Work and Social Policy Subject Centre (SWAP). Also, it is a requirement for service users and carers to contribute to the recruitment, selection, and assessment of students entering social work training programmes. However, the contribution of service users has too often been limited to providing information, a situation that service users have 'expressed increasing dissatisfaction' with (Croft and Beresford 2008: 396). The extensive knowledge, skills, and experience that service users and carers have amassed throughout their lives, particularly in relation to their in-depth knowledge of the social welfare system, warrant much greater recognition if social work is to be enriched by their contribution (Trevithick 2008). At the same time, it is essential to apply this same commitment to social work practitioners through setting up opportunities that can draw on their knowledge, skills, and practice experiences in ways that can lead to new insights and new theories being developed. It is essential that the voice of social workers is heard in ways that shape the future of social work and this is beginning to happen (Munro 2010a, 2010b, 2011a, 2011b; SWRB 2010; SWTF 2009a, 2009b).

The importance of research

This section focuses the relationship between research and social work. It begins with an account of some of the key research terms used in this field, and how the term 'evidence' has been interpreted, particularly the term *evidence-based practice*. It then identifies some of the barriers that exist to inhibit the use of research in social work. As stated earlier, research is viewed in this text as an activity and method by which knowledge can be acquired, analysed, updated, revised, and refuted (Trevithick 2008), but it is not considered to be a distinct body of knowledge in its own right. It is the findings of research – when taken forward in ways that inform *theoretical*, *factual* or *practice knowledge* – that contribute to our existing knowledge. Some research may not reach publication or if published, may not reach social work practice in ways that can be used. However, the process of undertaking research can in itself lead to additional personal and professional knowledge and in the conceptualization I am putting forward, this learning is a feature of *practice knowledge*.

Types and sources of research

There are many definitions of research but the one put forward in a SCIE Knowledge Review defines research quite broadly:

> Research comprises the results from systematic investigations based on planned strategies. This may be primarily research that involves systematic inquiry based on observation or experiment. It may also be secondary research, research that takes primary research studies as its objects of inquiry.
>
> (Walter *et al.* 2004: xiii)

What differentiates research from other activities is the systematic and investigative focus that it involves. This may be categorized as *qualitative* or *quantitative* methods of investigation. The aim of *qualitative research methods* is 'to understand the dynamics of social phenomena in their natural context, and to generate rich description from diverse perspectives. They produce data in different forms but typically as language' (Walter *et al.* 2004: xi). This may draw on small samples, and is often based on interviews. The aim of *quantitative research methods* is 'to measure or quantitatively assess social phenomena; to describe representative samples in quantitative terms; and to estimate or test quantitative relationships. They produce data in numeric form' (Walter *et al.* 2004: xi). These may include the frequency with which phenomena occur, averages and percentages that are often represented and analysed using statistical methods. Qualitative research methods tend to be more established in social work but a growing emphasis is being placed on the importance of using *multi-method research* (Tashakkori and Teddlie 2003), that is, research that draws on a range of different research methods and sources, including quantitative and qualitative methods. However, this calls for greater sophistication in relation to researchers' 'choice and rationale for multi-method approaches' (Marsh and Fisher 2005: 44).

Research sources can be categorized in terms of the extent to which they draw on primary sources and secondary sources. *Primary sources* refer to the original research data that has been collected to inform key findings. Primary sources are written by the people involved in conducting the research, whereas *secondary sources* constitute an analysis or an evaluation of previously collected research data, some of which is likely to be primary data. An example of a primary source could be statistical data collected by the Office of National Statistics, such as the population statistics that can be found in *Social Trends*, covered in the previous chapter, or an account of a service user's personal experience. An example of secondary research sources can be found in literature searches (identifying appropriate material or data) or literature reviews (critically evaluating material or data). Both involve looking for relevant data drawn from a range of sources, including authored books, journal articles, electronic database sources, organizational research findings (e.g. Joseph Rowntree Trust, Age Concern, MIND), systematic reviews (mentioned later), official government sources, and other sources such as *Community Care* or *The Guardian*. Some data may be classified as *grey literature*, which refers to material that falls outside a more rigorous and conventional method of scrutiny and bibliographic control, such as conference proceedings, internal reports, and some books. Grey literature is growing in volume and significance, but the accuracy of information needs to be checked, particularly where the quality control system is either not known or of a questionable nature (Whittaker 2009: 23). A more reliable source of grey literature can be found via the database SIGLE, or System for Information on Grey Literature in Europe.

Depending on the sources used, the research undertaken may involve:

1 *Review*. A review is 'any attempt to synthesize the results and conclusions of two or more publications on a given topic' (Centre for Reviews and Dissemination website).
2 *Systematic review*. A 'review of a clearly formulated question that uses systematic and explicit methods to identify, select and critically appraise relevant research, and to collect and analyze data from the studies that are included in the review. Statistical methods (meta-analysis) may or may not be used to analyze and summarize the results of the included studies' (Cochrane Collaboration website).
3 *Meta analysis*. This describes the 'use of statistical techniques in a systematic review to integrate the results of included studies. Sometimes used as a synonym for systematic reviews, where the review includes meta-analysis' (Cochrane Collaboration website).
4 *Randomized control trial* (RCT). This describes an 'experiment in which two or more interventions, possibly including a control intervention or no intervention, are compared by being randomly allocated to participants. In most trials one intervention is assigned to each individual but sometimes assignment is to defined groups of individuals' (Cochrane Collaboration

website). For example, RTCs can be used to compare and assess the relative effectiveness of two interventions.

5 *Case study.* This describes a 'study reporting observations on a single individual' (Cochrane Collaboration website).

6 *Single case design or evaluation* (also known as a *single-case evaluation, N of 1 design/N = 1 design* or *single-subject design*). A research procedure that addresses the behaviour of a single subject or system, such as an individual service user or carer (Beresford *et al.* 2008) or a local authority (Evans 2011). The research designs are largely quantitative and may not be systematic in the ways described above. Nevertheless, they can provide valuable insights and may have some features that can be generalized and related to other populations, social groups, or particular concerns.

What constitutes 'evidence' in evidence-based practice?

Macdonald (2008: 435) reminds us that the 'impetus to adopt an evidence-based approach to social work came from outside the profession', namely from medicine in the form of evidence-based medicine. However, even within the medical profession there is considerable debate and disagreement about evidence-based medicine, particularly the use of RCT methodology in relation to complex interventions (Prideaux 2002). Within this medical context, one of the most prestigious and widely quoted definitions of evidence-based practice (EBP) can be found in the work of Sackett and colleagues:

> Evidence-based medicine is the conscientious, explicit, and judicious use of current best evidence in making decisions about the care of individual patients. The practice of evidence-based medicine means integrating individual clinical expertise with the best available external clinical evidence from systematic research. By individual clinical expertise we mean the proficiency and judgement that individual clinicians acquire through clinical experience and clinical practice.
>
> (Sackett *et al.* 1996: 71)

In their account, Sackett *et al.* (1996: 72) also emphasize that: 'Evidence-based medicine is not restricted to randomized control trials or meta-analyses. It involves tracking down the best external evidence with which to answer our clinical questions'. A feature of this 'tracking down' is the importance of practice experience, or *practice knowledge*, as well as 'external clinical evidence from systematic research'. The importance of practice experience can also be found in some definitions of the term *empirical*, which can often be defined in different ways. For example, at one end of the spectrum it can refer to findings based on experiment, observation, and research (Munro 1998b: 5) and, at the other end, it can describe the 'position that all knowledge . . . is in some way "based on" experience' (Gibbs and Gambrill 1996: 94). For Walter *et al.* (2004: ix), it is 'the empirical findings of research' that constitutes *evidence*. This broader view of what constitutes evidence is stressed by Thyer and Myers (2011):

> ... in EBP one decides what services to provide by taking into account not only research evidence but also client preferences and values, situational circumstances, professional ethics, the practitioner's existing skills, and available resources.
>
> (Thyer and Myers 2011: 8)

A different view is held by those who link best evidence to randomized control trials. For example, Sheldon (2000: 67–70) has argued for a 'very definite hierarchy (not just a continuum) of methods' with systematic review of randomized control trials (RCTs) or meta-analysis of controlled trials located at the top of this hierarchy, and single case designs at the bottom. The argument here is that where RCTs are well conducted, they minimize the likelihood of bias and error (Sheldon and Macdonald 2009). From this position, other research methods that are not based on RTCs can be represented in some research circles as inferior and untrustworthy. So, too, are some theories that are not derived from 'systematic' sources. As Sheldon and Macdonald state:

> Theories are not created equal. Some are more systematically arrived at on the basis of more and better empirical evidence; some are frankly fanciful and based on the too little examined influence of authoritative figures and their disciplines. Some grand theories place themselves beyond the influence of attempts at refutation ... If some theories prove more valid and reliable than others that are less testable, then the latter must be relegated.
>
> (Sheldon and Macdonald 2009: 54)

The view that 'best evidence' is achieved using randomized control trials has led to considerable disagreement among social work academics – particularly the position that scientific knowledge, or scientific reasoning, enhances professional decision-making. For example, Webb (2001: 60) has questioned whether 'a formal rationality of practice based on scientific methods can produce a more effective and economically accountable means of social care'. Webb goes on to argue that 'evidence at hand is only one determinant of decision-making on the part of the social worker ... They operate with a limited rationality which is circumscribed by legal and organizational requirements which change over time' (p. 60). Similarly, service users do not make decisions based alone on statistical evidence. Other questions on the appropriateness of RCTs in social work highlight the difficulty of finding two parallel groups and the difficulty controlling other variables that could influence the outcome of a study. Also, 'there are practical problems in getting sample sizes which are large enough to have a reasonable chance of showing an effect' (Wilson *et al.* 2008: 251) and the fact that to intervene may be a statutory requirement. In addition, professional ethics and the issue of power need to be considered, particularly where service user choice and informed decision-making lies within the use of RCTs. The following example illustrates the ethical dilemmas that can be involved:

> There are clearly ethical problems in, for example, randomly allocating those suffering from schizophrenia to drug treatment or family therapy, or removing one group of seriously maltreated children from their birth families while leaving others at home, some with and some without support.
>
> (Wilson *et al.* 2008: 251)

Another ethical concern, mainly found in medicine, has been raised in relation to the use of 'placebos', that is, where one group of patients are given a pretend procedure, often a drug, while another group are given the actual procedure or drug. For these and other reasons, some commentators argue against the promotion of a hierarchy of research methods or evidence. Rather than conceptualizing a hierarchy of evidence, this different perspective argues that the research method chosen should be the one that is best able to answer the research question being posed. Taking this approach, the 'evidence' that constitutes evidence-based practice can also include the use of other study designs, such as surveys and qualitative interview studies. Ideally, knowledge will be built up, like pieces of a jigsaw, and in ways that can embrace the complexities, uncertainties, and risks that are inherent in social work (Wilson *et al.* 2008: 4) and ensure that no one factor is given primacy in the evidence sought and found. For Sheppard *et al.* (2000), unless these complexities are acknowledged, evidence-based practice could unwittingly represent 'the process of knowledge application as unproblematic' and fail to recognize 'the complexities of such application, or the intellectual procedures involved' (p. 467).

In many ways, the argument in favour of RCTs as 'the most sure-footed way of piecing together what works' (Macdonald and Macdonald 1995: 49–50) has not been won in relation to social work. This is evident in the fact that there have been very few large-scale RCTs undertaken in the UK in the field of social welfare or social work. Without this research evidence, there is a tendency to rely on RCT research evidence from outside the United Kingdom, or located in other professions that are based in different contexts and settings. In this regard, Sheldon (2000) notes that much of the RCT research evidence to support the effectiveness of behaviourist and cognitive-behavioural therapy (CBT) approaches tends to be based on the work of psychologists and social workers located in North America and that the claims made tend to be based on 'discrete problems in somewhat protected settings' (p. 70). These 'protected settings' primarily relate to the clinics or treatment centres, which are different sites from the 'frontline', locality-based social work settings that can be found in the United Kingdom. Or again, research studies that are based on 'discrete problems' suggest that the impact of other variables has been excluded from the research remit. It is rarely possible to control these variables in UK social work (Matthews *et al.* 2003). Given these differences, the extent to which research from abroad can be considered relevant and transferable across international boundaries is open to question and a point noted by Sheldon (2000: 70), who states that 'extending the use of CBT to routine settings (where things are a whole lot messier) is undoubtedly the next challenge for this discipline'. Indeed, one of the conclusions drawn from a recent RCT that compared the added value of systemic family therapy over individually focused CBT in relation to the impact of trauma noted that 'the challenges of conducting RCTs in "real world" settings should not be underestimated' (Coulter 2010).

Perhaps in response to the way that evidence-based practice has been promoted within certain quarters, some academics in social work have chosen to use different terminology to link theory and practice – and to stress the important relationship between research and practice effectiveness. These include terms such as *knowledge-based practice* (Fisher 1998), *research-based knowledge* (Gray and Schubert 2010; Marsh and Fisher 2008), and *critical best practice perspective* (Jones *et al.* 2008). A different term, *research-informed practice*, is preferred by some because it recognizes 'the diverse and often subtle ways in which research can impact on practice, and the fact that there are other influences on practice' (Walter *et al.* 2004: xii). In a similar vein, the term *evidence-based policy and practice* (Wilson *et al.* 2008: 251) emphasizes the link between policy and practice.

Barriers that inhibit the uptake of research

The importance of practitioners having the knowledge and skills to draw on research findings to inform their work is a central feature of the changes proposed in relation to UK social work (SWRB 2010). However, a number of barriers hinder practitioners' progress in this area. Berger takes up this point in relation to the ability to adopt an evidence-based practice (EBP) approach:

> ... seldom addressed is the limited availability of evidence-based knowledge relevant for social work practice. Consequently, social workers who try to become EBP-informed practitioners often find themselves in a Catch-22. While they are required and interested to perform professionally in a certain manner, the absence of relevant evidence prevents them from doing so effectively and yet, they are blamed for failing to practice based on evidence. This situation may yield frustration, a feeling of incompetence and burnout ...
>
> (Berger 2010: 176)

Access to evidence within research findings was one of the barriers identified in a large-scale literature review. The review focused on the impact of research use in relation to the education, healthcare, social care, and criminal justice sectors where it was found that 'only a minority of practitioners read or referred to research findings' (Walter *et al.* 2003: 13). The list of barriers that inhibited research take-up in this review included:

- lack of access to research findings, including poor or distant library facilities and limited circulation within organisations
- lack of time to access or read research
- lack of skills to interpret research findings
- sheer volume of research literature
- scope and presentation of findings not being 'user-friendly'.

(Walter *et al.* 2003: 13)

This literature search revealed that practitioners 'wanted findings to be provided in clear, jargon-free language, in summary form, and drawing out the key implications for users' (Walter *et al.* 2003: 13). It also found that the use of research was greater when practitioners were involved in the research and dissemination process, thereby highlighting the importance of closer links being developed between researchers and practitioners. These practical reasons for the limited use of research findings are important but wider issues have also been identified, particularly the fact that for a number of years there existed a 'lack of investment in social care research in general, and in practice-based research in particular' (Marsh and Fisher 2008: 971). However, a 'compelling case for further investment in practice based research' (Marsh and Fisher 2008: 984) was put forward and has led to funding opportunities being made available for social work by the Economic and Social Research Council (ESRC), a prestigious and major research funding council for the social sciences in the UK.

I have covered this subject in some detail because of its significance for the future of social work and also to address the fact that some research terms can feel daunting. Yet it is crucial for social workers to be familiar with this terminology, particularly when working in professional contexts, such as multidisciplinary teams, where it is important to understand how research findings are being used to inform decision-making. However, it can take some time to feel comfortable, confident, knowledgeable, and skilled in the world of research and its specialist language. In this context, a number of organizations have websites that provide information on research findings. For example, the National Institute for Health and Clinical Excellence (NICE) provides national guidance aimed at promoting good health and preventing and treating ill health. Organizational websites that provide research findings in relation to systematic reviews include SCIE, the Campbell Collaboration, the Cochrane Collaboration, and the Centre for Reviews and Dissemination (CRD) at the University of York.

The Campbell Collaboration focuses primarily on systematic reviews in education, crime and justice, and social welfare, whereas the Cochrane Collaboration is focused more on health issues, particularly the effects of healthcare interventions. York CRD also focuses on the use of research evidence in health policy and practice. Two organizations, the Cochrane Collaboration and York CRD, provide a glossary of research terminology on their websites. Links to these organizations and their glossary of terms can be found in the Reference List at the end of this text.

This chapter has ordered social work's rich theoretical knowledge domain into three categories: theories that are drawn, adapted or 'borrowed' from other disciplines; theories analysing the task and purpose of social work; and theories that relate directly to practice. I have described the theories drawn from other disciplines in some detail to stress the richness and diversity of our knowledge base and the difficulties this can create in terms of establishing a coherent framework or map of practice. Knowing more about 'parent' theories can help us to recognize their 'offspring', such as the link between psychoanalysis as a philosophy and psychosocial approaches adopted in social work. Included in this chapter is a brief account to the tensions between theory and practice and the importance of research in social work. The perspective put forward in this text emphasizes the importance of social workers being able to establish an ongoing dialogue with the social sciences in order to develop a more rigorous, intellectual approach to knowledge and to be able to apply this knowledge in practice. We now turn to look at the part played by the *factual knowledge domain* within the *Knowledge and Skills Framework*.

3   FACTUAL KNOWLEDGE

Introduction

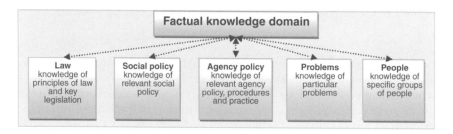

Figure 3.1 The factual knowledge domain

In the *Knowledge and Skills Framework* presented here, the second do-main – *factual knowledge* – includes five sub-headings: knowledge of law/legislation; knowledge of social policy; knowledge of agency policy and procedures; knowledge of particular problems; and knowledge of specific groups of people (Figure 3.1). Figure 3.2 (see p. 62) illustrates how these different domains overlap and interweave in ways that can make any sepa-ration seem arbitrary.

The statistics cited in this chapter relate primarily to England and Wales but for readers in other countries and different contexts, the headings used can provide a basis from which to search for comparable data. Common terms used under the heading *factual knowledge* include research findings, statistics, figures, records, and some types of evidence. These facts can make certain forms of information more accessible and usable but, at the same time, render them open to challenge and, therefore, 'capable of falsifica-tion' (Gambrill 2006: 120). For statistics to be meaningful, they have to be scrutinized and interpreted, particularly in relation to the sources on which they are based, which calls for the application of analytic skills and crit-ical thinking. This highlights the tentative position that knowledge holds, and reminds us that no areas of knowledge should be seen as absolute and

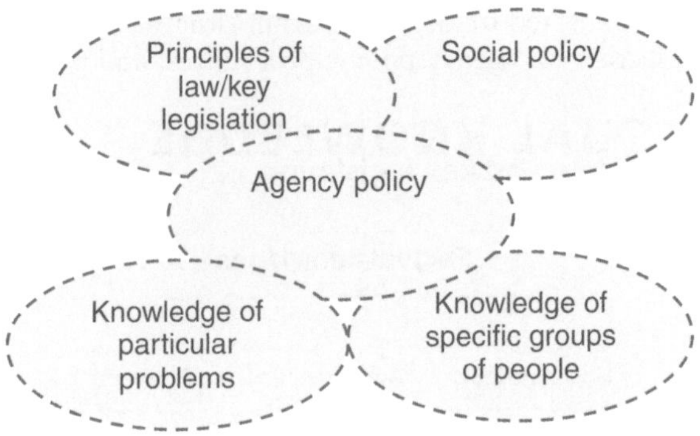

Figure 3.2 The overlapping and interweaving features of factual knowledge

beyond question. Instead, knowledge should be open to scrutiny, review, and revision in ways that invite further exploration and understanding. I would argue that our professional credibility is seriously undermined if we do not have certain facts at our fingertips. Legislation is the most important example of factual knowledge but, as we shall see, this is a vast subject and one that calls for the ability to analyse and to interpret the principles that underpin key areas of knowledge and their relevance within social work.

Knowledge that has a more factual basis can be described in different ways: as *specialist knowledge* (Fook 2002: 37), *technical knowledge* (Eraut 1994), *content knowledge* (Gambrill 1997: 120), *professional knowledge* (Fook 2002: 25) or *formal* or *product knowledge* (Sheppard *et al.* 2000, 2001; Sheppard and Ryan 2003). For the most part, these terms have not found their way into everyday usage by social workers in direct practice. However, they are terms that can be found in academic publications on the subject of knowledge and, for this reason, they warrant some coverage. For example, as stated in Chapter 2, the use of the term *professional knowledge* can, in some contexts, place this form of knowledge in a potentially 'privileged' position in relation to the knowledge that others bring to the situation. Similarly, 'knowledge gained in certain kinds of ways is deemed superior to other forms of knowledge' (Sheppard 2006: 186). This superior status is evident in the status given to randomized control trials (RCTs), again covered in the previous chapter. An important aspect of factual knowledge is 'technical knowledge' because it is 'capable of written codification' (Eraut 1994: 42). This kind of codification means that some types of knowledge are presented as 'given', which Sheppard and his colleagues describe as *formal* or *product knowledge* because 'it refers to existing knowledge, which may be applied' (Sheppard and Ryan 2003: 157). An example of product knowledge can be found in the policy and practice procedures that social work agencies lay down to indicate the kind of rule-based knowledge that practitioners are expected to apply in certain situations – a point we return to later in the section on agency policy, procedures, and practice.

The principles of law and key legislation

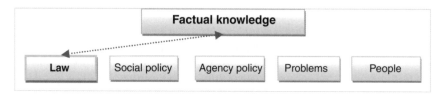

Figure 3.3 Principles of law and key legislation

This first sub-heading of the *factual knowledge* domain highlights the importance that the law holds within social work and the key principles that underpin the English legal system (Figure 3.3). It looks at the stages that Parliamentary Bills pass through before becoming law, including some coverage of the extent to which European legislation can promote human rights. Roberts and Preston-Shoot summarize the legal mandate within which social work operates as follows:

> Social work is empowered, guided and controlled by its legal mandate. This mandate is made up of three elements. The first is organizational, in that most social work in the UK is practised from within the structures of the statutory social services. The second is functional, in that the law determines the powers and duties with which social work is endowed. The third is procedural, in that the law largely determines the nature and extent of social work accountability, both to service users and to the community generally.
>
> (Roberts and Preston-Shoot 2000: 183)

This legal mandate is important from a different standpoint because a familiarity with the law and requirements of government can be an important lever from which to argue for services to be provided (Braye and Preston-Shoot 1995: 66).

Principles underpinning the UK legal system

The English legal system is based on the principle of 'common law', also known as case law, where laws are based on decisions or 'precedents' made by judges, or by the courts. These bind future decisions, until new decisions take precedence. An example of the way that legal precedents work was demonstrated in 1997 when the 'Gloucester Judgement' changed the grounds on which service users and carers could press for services they were assessed as needing under the Community Care (Direct Payments) Act 1996. This judgement stated that local authorities have the right to take resources into account in the provision of services (Horder 2002: 116), thereby making rationing permissible where local authorities have limited funding.

Acts of Parliament

Bills are proposals that start their 'life' in the House of Commons or House of Lords. If amendments are proposed in either House, the Bill moves back and forth between the two until the details have been approved by both Houses when, after receiving Royal Assent, the Bill passes into law (Figure 3.4). (For an informative account of the journey of a Bill into law, see the UK Parliament website listed in the Reference section.) A key point is the consultation stage, which is when the government issues a call for contributions and feedback on the proposals that have been put forward. The British Association of Social Workers (BASW) and other professional associations often respond to these consultation processes but individuals can also respond. This stage provides an important opportunity for social workers to inform the government about issues taking place 'on the front line'.

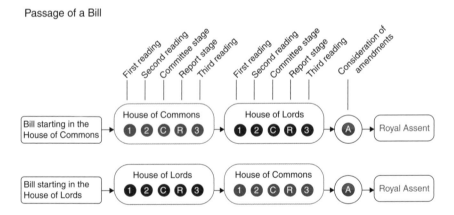

Figure 3.4 Progress of a Bill into an Act of Parliament
Source: UK Parliament (website)

A further opportunity to provide feedback and to engage in the consultation process can be found in several documents that the government publishes, including:

- *Green Papers* – proposals published to encourage public debate.
- *White Papers* – statements of government policy.
- *Command Papers* – papers presented to Parliament by ministers.
- *Guidance documents* – designed to provide guidance to organizations on issues relating to government policies.

For example, *Every Child Matters* (Department for Education and Skills 2003) was published in the form of a consultative Green Paper that later became the foundation of the Children Act 2004. If we are to shape the future of social work, it is important to take up these consultation opportunities, not least because the dilemmas encountered in practice often precede research findings.

Secondary legislation

In addition to Acts of Parliament, delegated powers can be given to government ministers to support primary legislation – powers that are referred to as *secondary legislation* or *delegated legislation*; *statutory instruments* form the majority of secondary legislation (Brayne and Carr 2008: 9). This form of regulation can be introduced without being subjected to Parliamentary scrutiny and the normal legislative processes. The government often uses secondary legislation to indicate what it expects or requires of local authorities. This can take several forms: *codes*, *duties*, *guidance*, or *regulations*, with requirements being more binding for some than others, as indicated below:

- *Codes* – convey to local authorities and other relevant bodies the message '*you ought/should*' (Department of Health 1989: 2).
- *Duties* – 'Where a duty is imposed by law, social services are obliged to carry it out: it is a mandatory obligation to carry out a particular function. The important word is *shall*' (Brammer 2007: 17–18).
- *Guidance* – guidance is issued by the Secretary of State but the role of guidance is not clear-cut. In general, 'guidance must be followed unless there are justifiable reasons for not doing so' (Brayne and Carr 2008: 9).
- *Regulations* – 'regulations in the form of Statutory Instruments, for example, issued under powers granted by Act of Parliament, will be binding in law' (Munby 2008: 463). They convey the message *you must/shall*' (Department of Health 1989: 2).
- *Powers* – convey an 'element of discretion . . . The important word is *may*' (Brayne and Carr 2008: 18).

For example, *guidance* issued under section 7(1) of the Local Authority Social Services Act 1970 means that where local authorities fail to act in accordance with the guidance laid down, a complaint can be made to the Ombudsman (Wilson *et al.* 2008: 207–8). This example shows the overlap and interrelationship that exists between the law, social policy, and agency policy by highlighting the way that both legislation and official guidance render local authorities accountable.

European legislation and international law

In addition to these Acts of Parliament, the UK's membership of the European Union means that social work is subject to EU legislation (Munby 2008: 443). For example, the incorporation of the EU human rights legislation into English law came into force in October 2000 and opened up further protection in terms of the rights of the individual (Williams 2001). Some commentators have argued that the Human Rights Act 'has begun to hold social work decision-making in the UK accountable in a legal sense' (Braye and Preston-Shoot 2006: 21). However, other commentators have remained more cautious: 'Despite the 1998 Human Rights Act, social workers may be denied the legal wherewithal to protect and promote the basic rights to which their clients are entitled' (Williams 2004: 50).

Similarly, the rights of children are embodied in the United Nations Convention on the Rights of the Child (UNCRC) 1998, which the British Government has signed. Criticisms levelled at the British Government by the UNCRC in relation to children's rights led in 2005 to the setting up of Children's Commissioners for England. Other Commissioners have also been appointed for Wales, Northern Ireland, and Scotland. (For a useful summary of the way the law regulates social work practice, including the relevance of European Union legislation, see Munby 2008.)

Social policy

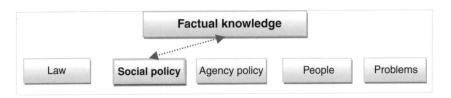

Figure 3.5 Social policy in relation to factual knowledge

This second sub-heading looks at the importance of factual knowledge in the area of social policy (Figure 3.5), beginning with an account of how this subject is defined, and the issues that fall within its realm before providing an account of some of the major changes that have affected social work in recent years. Shardlow (2007: 16) highlights the importance of this subject, stating that social policy decisions can 'enhance or constrain opportunities for the delivery of high quality social work … without an understanding of the social policy … the social work student would not be able to make an informed assessment of need and how need might be met'. Understanding the impact of policy decision is also highly relevant to experienced social work practitioners.

According to Blakemore and Griggs (2007: 1), '*social* policies aim to improve human welfare (though they often fail to do so) and to meet human needs for education, health, housing and social security'. This definition is similar to the 'big five' areas of government policy put forward by Spicker (1995: 3): 'social security, housing, health, social work and education'. A different way to describe social policy is in terms of key themes. For example, Erskine (2003: 12–14) sees this subject as covering three categories: social issues, social problems, and the needs of particular social groups. These three themes echo the coverage I give later in this chapter on *factual knowledge* in relation to particular problems and specific groups of people. The following account summarizes some of the major policy changes introduced by the previous Conservative and Labour governments and the impact of these changes on social work service provision. This coverage is important because it provides a context from which to understand later changes that have been introduced.

Conservative Government (1979–97)

One of the problems confronting the Conservative Government in the 1980s was the escalating costs of welfare provision, particularly residential care for older people (Alcock *et al.* 2008: 272). For example, social security spending on residential care for older people was £10 million in 1981, but by 1991 had risen to £2 billion. In an attempt to address the growing cost of care, and to ensure that professional practice was giving 'value for money' (Harris and White 2009: 12), the Conservatives introduced a policy shift in the form of 'business solutions to social and political problems' (McLaughlin 2007: 5). A central theme of the proposals introduced was the notion of 'value for money', described in terms of the much quoted phrase, *the three 'E's*: economy, efficiency, and effectiveness (Audit Commission 1983: 8).

Health service (NHS) and Community Care Act 1990

The policy changes introduced, which primarily affected adult services, were outlined in the National Health Service (NHS) and Community Care Act 1990. This legislation introduced market forces through the creation of the 'purchaser–provider' split within health and welfare service provision, sometimes referred to as a 'mixed economy of services', 'quasi-market', or 'internal market' (Alcock *et al.* 2008: 245). What this split radically changed was the way that services were to be provided. In the past, it had been the role of social service departments to provide and deliver services based on their assessment of need. The legislative reforms introduced required social service departments to spend at least 85 per cent of their income on services commissioned from the private, voluntary, and independent sector (Alcock *et al.* 2008: 273). To support these changes, a different approach to managing people and services was introduced – New Public Management (NPM), more commonly known as *managerialism*. The 'marketization' of social care

(Dustin 2007) promoted the view that 'market forces' could provide the ideal mechanism to inform and shape welfare policy and practice and that managerialism or NPM would provide the best way to optimize performance and to 'steer human service organizations' (Hughes and Wearing 2007: 21). Running alongside these major policy changes was the deinstitutionalization of care, involving the closure and sale of a number of mental hospitals, local authority children's homes, and other residential establishments, and the introduction of an ideological stance that promoted the importance of greater service user 'choice'.

The NHS and Community Care Act 1990 introduced a second important change that impacted directly on social work because the reorganization of certain services previously provided free as part of NHS 'health care', and funded from general taxation, became redefined under the remit of 'social care'. This meant that key services became the financial responsibility of social services departments, making some services no longer free at the point of delivery. Instead, they became 'means-testable and subject to rationing' (Alcock *et al.* 2008: 274), a change that had a profound impact on the provision of care, particularly for older people. These policies resulted in the privatization and deregulation of services, and gave a boost to private enterprise and the pursuit of the profit motive within social care.

New Labour (1997–2010)

The remit when New Labour came to power, where they were to remain for 13 years, was the reform and modernization of the Welfare State, a task that led to numerous Acts of Parliament and a 'plethora of policy initiatives' (Piachaud and Sutherland 2001). The Labour Party remit also involved taking forward the policy agenda to dismantle the Welfare State, initiated by the Conservative Government, through the privatization of public services. In this account, it is only possible to highlight two major policy changes introduced by Labour: 'personalization agenda' and the dismantling of social services departments.

Personalization agenda

The ambitions relating to adult services were outlined in three important documents. First, *Fair Access to Care Services* (Department of Health 2003: 1) called for local authorities to set eligibility criteria for providing or commissioning services, based on balancing resources against need. Second, *Transforming Social Care* (Department of Health 2008a) described the 'development of a personalized approach to the delivery of adult social care' (p. 1) through the use of *direct payments* and *personal budgets* (p. 5). Finally, *Putting People First* (Department of Health 2008b) located 'personalisation centre stage in social care policy, practice and performance frameworks' (p. 3). These policies were introduced to promote independent living and related mainly to older people, people with chronic conditions, disabled people, and people with mental health problems. The funding for these initiatives has taken two forms:

- *Direct payments* are means-tested cash payments that are given in lieu of community care services. Eligibility for this funding is based on an assessment of need. In this scheme, service users 'take on all the responsibilities of an employer, such as payroll, meeting minimum wage and other legislative requirements and establishing contracts of employment' (Samuel 2009). In March 2008, it was estimated that 55,900 adults in England were receiving a direct payment.

- *Personal budgets* refers to funding that is allocated by the local authority to enable service users to buy services – a system more appropriate for people who do not want to bear employment responsibilities or who want their local council to be responsible for commissioning services on their behalf. Initially it was envisaged that 'social workers will play a key role in delivering personalized services and individual budgets' (Department of Health 2008a: 13).

In 2010, the UK Coalition Government confirmed its commitment to the principles embodied in the 'personalization agenda' and the target is for local councils to offer personal budgets to 1 million social care service users by 2013 as part of its social care provision.

Dismantling of unified social services departments

Following the recommendations of the Seebohm Report (1968), social services departments were created with responsibility for both adult and children's services. In 2005, these departments were dismantled with adult services remaining under the auspices of the Department of Health and children's services relocated with education under the then Department for Education and Skills, and within the remit of the newly formed Children's Workforce Development Council (CWDC). At a local level, new appointments were established for Directors of Adult Social Services (DASS) and Directors of Children's Services (DCS). In children's services, some of the impetus for these changes was fuelled by the concerns that were raised following the public inquiry into the tragic death of Victoria Climbié in 2000. The Laming inquiry, named after its chairman, criticized all agencies involved in Victoria's death – social workers, the police, health visitors, the paediatrician, other doctors and nurses who had examined Victoria – as well as deficiencies in their organizations, described as 'a gross failure of the system' (Laming 2003: 3). The government's reaction to the Laming Report was embodied in *Every Child Matters* (Department for Education and Skills 2003), a document that has been described as the 'biggest shake up of statutory children's services since the Seebohm Report of the 1960s' (Williams 2004: 407). These policy changes were later enshrined in legislation in the Children Act 2004, which laid down the requirement for local authorities to work closely with public, private, and voluntary organizations to improve outcomes for children in five areas: being healthy; staying safe; enjoying and achieving; making a positive contribution; achieving economic well-being (Department for Education and Skills 2003: 7–8). With the creation of the UK Coalition Government, following the general election in 2010, concerns have been raised about the government's commitment to policies enshrined in *Every Child Matters*. Some changes have already been initiated. For example, local councils no longer required to produce an annual children's and young people's plan or to meet the previous legal requirement to set up a children's trust.

The policy changes introduced by the Conservative and Labour governments promoted, in different ways, the privatization and deregulation of services by endorsing private enterprise and the pursuit of the profit motive within social care. These developments raise important questions about how public services should be funded and both governments have been criticized for selling off public-owned services (such as residential or children's homes) to the private sector and creating a situation where service users (and taxpayers indirectly) are required to pay for public services that were once free at the point of delivery when provided by local authorities (Carey 2008: 931). A recommendation by the Royal Commission on Long Term Care (1999) called for a greater use of general taxation to finance care services, as is the case with the NHS and criminal justice system, in order to provide greater funding stability (Brindle 2009). These debates are ongoing and highlight the part played by social policy and legislative developments within social work.

Agency policy, procedures, and practice

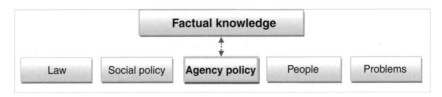

Figure 3.6 Agency policy, procedures, and practice

The third sub-heading of the *factual knowledge* domain focuses on knowledge of relevant agency policy, procedures, and practice (Figure 3.6). It is important to understand the context within which social work is located, and the general principles that shape the organization and delivery of services. This section begins with an account of how different social work and social care agencies are categorized and then looks at key statistics relating to the statutory and voluntary sectors.

Statutory organizations are required by law, such as social work located in the area of child protection, mental health, criminal justice, education, housing, and health provision. *Non-statutory* organizations can be described using a range of terms, including: the private, voluntary, and independent sector (including charities) or PVI; the *third sector*; and voluntary and community organizations (VCOS). Within these different categories, the range of work that different agencies undertake can vary greatly depending on the services on offer. The philosophy of an organization is often summarized in a *mission statement* that describes the vision, aims, and objectives, as well as the roles, responsibilities, and expectations placed on the agency and its staff, including its accountability structure.

Local authority statutory agencies

As indicated earlier, the reforms introduced under the NHS and Community Care Act 1990 gave local authorities two central roles. First, they operate as a major employer and, second, they are the main body responsible for auditing and commissioning (or for joint commissioning) local services. In relation to both roles, local authorities have both mandatory and discretionary powers (Local Government Association 2010). On the one hand, they can exercise some discretion and a degree of autonomy in how they interpret and implement government policy. This offers the opportunity to respond to local needs but can lead to inconsistencies in relation to service provision between local authorities. Jones (2008) has described this situation in terms of councils 'inventing their own policies to determine who gets help'. On the other hand, local councils have mandatory responsibilities – and in some areas their autonomy has become increasingly controlled and restricted by central government's hold on the 'purse strings'. This increased pressure has been made worse by under-funding and the diversion of resources to meet the regulation and inspection requirements laid down by the government. This has created an audit culture and produced a situation 'in which accountability is achieved through constant checking and verification' (Means *et al.* 2008: 81). The development of this 'audit society' or 'audit culture' (Munro 2004) is a feature of a more 'centralist' and 'managerialist' policy framework (Harris 2003), which is the context within which local authorities – and some voluntary agencies – operate. However, the extent to which this approach is considered appropriate for social work has been – and continues to be – seriously challenged not least because it has not been shown to increase efficiency and to raise standards. In fact, the opposite appears to be the case: 'Too often in recent history, the child protection system has, in the pursuit of imposed managerial targets and regulations, forgotten that its raison d'être is the welfare and protection of the child' (Munro 2011a: 8).

Before leaving this coverage of responsibilities that fall within the remit of local authorities, it is important to understand local authority funding, which comes primarily from four sources: central government grants, council taxes, business rates, and miscellaneous charges (e.g. parking fines). For example, the total expenditure for 2007–2008 shows that local authorities in England and Wales spent £22 billion on personal social services, which is broken down as follows:

42 per cent (nearly £9.3 billion) was spent on older people aged 65 and over;

26 per cent (£5.8 billion) on children and families;

29 per cent (£6.5 billion) on adults with learning difficulties, physical disabilities, or mental health needs aged under 65 years.

(Office for National Statistics 2010: 111)

Although the funding for local authorities is considerable, the figures can be deceptive because much of the funding pays for residential care for older people, mainly in private care homes, covered later. For example, the cost of a care home now averages roughly £36,000 a year, but with some homes in the south of England costing as much as £50,000 per year (Simon 2010). Privatization can also mean that services can be withdrawn – sometimes at short notice – if profit margins fall, which for some older people placed in private care homes can mean that they lose their home and risk eviction (Scourfield 2004). A similar situation is evident in relation to children's services. For example, for Buckingham Council the closure of local authority residential homes for children meant that the cost of out-of-county residential care for children spiralled to up to £5400 per week – producing a total cost of £7.4 million for out-of-county placements in 2010, compared with a cost of £3.4 million for in-county placements (Evans 2010). Here it is important to remember that local authorities are expected to spend roughly 85 per cent of their funding on services commissioned from the private and voluntary sectors.

Non-statutory sector (private, voluntary, and independent sector or third sector)

The requirement for local authorities to commission services from other organizations led to a marked increase in the privatization of public services and expansion of the social care workforce, which currently stands at around 38,000 employers, some of whom only employ two or three staff members. The social care workforce in England is estimated to be in the region of 1.5 million workers (Skills for Care 2010). Within this picture, in 2008 there were nearly 5000 home care agencies in England, with 84 per cent located in the private and voluntary sector (Land and Himmelweit 2010: 15). Another change worthy of note has been growth in new charities. For example, in 2006 the then Minister of Communities and Local Government, David Miliband, stated in a speech that over 6000 new charities were being registered each year – giving a figure of 190,000 charities in England and Wales. According to Miliband, the income from these registered charities ran to a total of over £27 billion, which included a paid workforce of 600,000 and a volunteer army of six million people, with more volunteering their time than ever before (Miliband 2006). Within this picture, the government is, indirectly, an important funder of charities through the funding it allocates to commissioning bodies, such as local authorities and primary care trusts. For example, a report based on survey responses from over 3800 charities found that:

- Over 60 per cent of charities with an income above £500,000 currently deliver public services.
- One-third of charities that deliver public services obtain 80 per cent or more of their income from public service delivery sources. This figure rises to almost 67 per cent for charities with an income above £10 million.

(Charity Commission 2007: 3)

The heavy dependence on government contracts is likely to see some charities in a state of crisis if funding is withdrawn. In addition to these difficulties, the Charity Commission also noted the threat that some funders pose to charities' independent decision-making processes. Also, charities can be vulnerable to 'mission drift', that is, where charities lose sight of their original purpose or 'mission' in response to the need to acquire funding or to meet the requirements set by funders (Charity Commission 2007: 23).

In this section, I have highlighted the major changes that have taken place in relation to the provision of services within the statutory and non-statutory sector in social work and social care and the extent to which government policy influences and shapes the type and quality of service provision that can be provided. What is striking in this account, and one this is highly relevant to social work, is the extent to which the reforms introduced in the NHS and Community Care Act 1990 have changed the landscape of care service provision.

The impact of policy changes on agency policies and procedures

The impact of policy changes on agency policy and procedures, particularly in the statutory sector, have changed working practices in social work. Two interrelated changes are particularly noticeable. First, there has been a shift away from the discretionary powers and autonomy once afforded to frontline social workers towards a situation where practitioners are required to enact government requirements that are embedded in agency and practices. As a result, in a number of practice contexts social workers' breadth of knowledge and skills has been replaced by surface considerations in the form of one-size-fits-all, rule-based responses and procedures:

Without knowledge of underlying theory and principles, the practitioner is confined to performing surface responses according to pre-coded procedures. Information checklists, problem categories and recommended responses do not need the knowledge, skills and discretionary powers of the autonomous professional.

(Howe 1996: 92)

The need for more in-depth knowledge, together with the ability to communicate that knowledge in the form of complex and appropriate interventions, is not required where surface responses are paramount.

A second, integral change came with the introduction of new information and computer technology systems, such as the electronic online Common Assessment Framework (CAF). This system was introduced to standardized procedures in relation to assessment, planning, intervention, and review for all professionals working with children and their families or carers. However, the introduction of this and other electronic online computer systems, particularly the Integrated Children's System (ICS), has given rise to serious criticisms. For example, the findings of a research project on the impact of information and communication technologies in children's services found that in some situations the use of electronic online systems have led to a stripping of knowledge. In one research site, practitioners failed to complete certain sections of the form even though these sections related to an area that reflected their personal knowledge and expertise (White *et al.* 2009: 1211). Further concerns relating to the ICS were highlighted in the research findings of Shaw and colleagues, who called into question whether ICS was 'fit for purpose' (Shaw *et al.* 2009: 625) – a point taken up in the Laming Report, where the ICS was described as 'hampering progress' (2009: 33). In the light of these criticisms, some changes have been introduced in local authorities' information and computer technology systems. Nevertheless, one fundamental problem remains, namely the extent to which social workers will be required to spend long periods of time completing computerized forms as opposed to working directly with service users and being allowed to draw on their professional judgement and the 'discretionary powers of the autonomous professional' (Howe 1996: 92).

Knowledge of particular problems

Figure 3.7 Knowledge of particular problems

The fourth sub-heading of the *factual knowledge* domain focuses on the problems regularly encountered in social work (Figure 3.7). In a generalist text of this kind, it is not possible to look in detail at this vast subject but some common concerns can be identified, such as the impact of social inequalities on people's well-being and life chances. In the cross-section of society that we come across, many people experience considerable adversity. Some live in 'disadvantaged' sectors of society where life can be tough, but it is important to note that not all people who experience significant hardship and adversity seek the help of social work or health and welfare agencies. It is clear that some people are sustained and supported by the help and understanding they receive from others – the relationships they have been able to create and to nurture. Yet in this area, I have encountered extraordinary courage and determination and also deeply moving gestures of unselfish generosity and compassion – actions of kindness sometimes from individuals who themselves have very little material comforts but who offer their care and concern for others in a very particular way. When thinking about people's generosity, I am reminded of a survey conducted by the Samaritans, which showed that poor people are more likely to give to charity than rich people. Also, that people from the north of England are likely to be more generous than people from the south and that women are more charitable than men (Samaritans 2005). A similar picture is evident in the USA. This makes it important to avoid seeing people merely in terms of the problems they present. Again, the point made by Maya Angelou is worth repeating – that, as human beings, we are complex and unique individuals and always more than our suffering (Angelou 1994).

However, for another group the difficulties they encounter call for the skilled input of another human being – or several human beings – if they are to be given the help they need to move forward. These problems may be manifest in relation to drug and alcohol addiction (Barber 2002), substance abuse (Goodman 2009), child abuse and neglect (Corby 2006; Doyle 2006), violence (Kemshall and Pritchard 1999), including domestic violence (Hague and Malos 2005), mental illness (Rogers and Pilgrim 2010), crime/offending behaviour (McGuire 1995), physical ill-health (Bywaters *et al.* 2009), poverty (Joseph Rowntree Foundation 2009; Palmer 2010), social isolation (Jack 2000), homelessness/rootlessness (McCluskey 1992; Thornicroft 2006), or manifest in the trauma experienced by people who seek asylum or arrive as refugees (Joseph Rowntree Charitable Trust 2007). Yet it is also clear from the evidence that we have that the problems listed above are rendered more profound and complex where the long-term impact of poverty, adversity, deprivation, and disadvantage is a feature. A strong overlap exists between certain social problems and specific groups of people, a situation that calls for caution if we are to avoid stereotyping certain groups. For example, research indicates that working-class people are more vulnerable than their middle-class counterparts to mental illness (Rogers and Pilgrim 2010: 51). This highlights the fact that some problems stem from the way that society is organized, which calls for interventions to be targeted at those elements that are in part the cause of certain problems that emerge.

To avoid the danger of seeing some human beings as 'problem people' it is important to identify some of the reasons why people encounter problems.

As stated in Chapter 1, in general terms I see the problems regularly encountered in social work as falling into three categories: how people feel about themselves, about others, and their place in society as a whole. This last category includes the status that society gives to certain people, including governments, and links to the way that social inequalities give rise to many of the problems that people present and that we encounter in our work. The following section looks briefly at key issues on this theme, referring to official UK statistics and other scholarly works to support the points put forward.

Poverty

There is considerable disagreement about what is meant by the term *poverty*. The number of people affected can be underplayed, not only by governments but because, for understandable reasons, people may want to hide the fact that they are poor, sometimes believing that poverty is due to personal failure and, therefore, must be their fault. Yet government policy plays a central role in determining the extent to which people fall into or are lifted out of poverty. In the UK and in Europe, governments recognize the notion of relative poverty, whereas in the USA the concept of absolute poverty is more commonly adopted. The following covers how these terms are defined in this text.

Absolute poverty describes the minimum requirement needed to sustain life and a concept that can be applied to all countries in ways that do not change over time. An example would be the number of people living on less than $10 a day, which is estimated to be 80 per cent of the world's population. Of the 1.5 billion people living on $1 a day or less, the majority are women – a situation termed the *feminization of poverty*. According to the United Nations, absolute poverty is:

> ... a condition characterized by severe deprivation of basic human needs, including food, safe drinking water, sanitation facilities, health, shelter, education and information. It depends not only on income but also on access to services.
>
> (UN 1995, cited by IFSW 2010)

Relative poverty, in contrast, differs between nations and is defined according to the standards needed for an individual to take part in the life and activities of that country:

> Individuals, families and groups in the population can be said to be in poverty when they lack the resources to obtain the types of diet, participate in the activities, and have the living conditions and amenities which are customary, or are at least widely encouraged and approved, in the societies in which they belong. Their resources are so seriously

below those commanded by the average individual or family that they are, in effect, excluded from ordinary living patterns, customs and activities.

(Townsend 1979: 31)

In the above definition, social exclusion is a feature of relative poverty. However, one of the difficulties that the term *social exclusion* presents is that it can imply that people exclude themselves and, therefore, it can fail to emphasize the structural, financial, and cultural barriers to inclusion, particularly the impact of poverty. For this reason, some authors prefer the phrase 'poverty and social inequality' (Palmer 2010), while other definitions highlight the importance of structural factors as a feature of social exclusion:

Social exclusion is a process that deprives individuals and families, groups and neighbourhoods of the resources required for participation in the social, economic and political activity of society as a whole. This process is primarily a consequence of poverty and low income, but other factors such as discrimination, low educational attainment and depleted living environments also underpin it. Through this process people are cut off for a significant period in their lives from institutions and services, social networks and developmental opportunities that the great majority of a society enjoys.

(Pierson 2002: 7)

As stated earlier, I consider social inequalities to be the major problem that we face in the UK today, something that is acknowledged in official circles: 'there are still large variations in income and wealth, as well as in health and educational attainment' (Office for National Statistics 2010: xxvii). The following section provides a brief overview of key terms that are used to calculate the threshold of low income.

The poverty line and low income thresholds

The low income threshold – or *poverty line* – is calculated in terms of the average (median) British household income in a particular year. This figure is then used to determine the extent to which the income of a particular household falls at 60 per cent or below this median figure after income tax, council tax, and housing costs have been deducted and a threshold figure that varies according to the number of adults and children in a particular household. It is important to note that paid work cannot guarantee that people will be free of poverty. For example, statistics for 2008–2009 reveal that 61 per cent of income-poor children were in households where one or more parent was in work, showing that 'low wages, part-time work and not having two adults in work in a couple household all increase the risk of poverty' (Child Poverty Action Group 2010). The following statistics make stark reading:

- In 2009–2010, 13.4 million people in the UK (22 per cent) were income poor. This is around a fifth (22 per cent) of the population – and the highest level since 2000 (Child Povery Action Group 2010).
- In 2010, the minimum wage was £3.64, £4.92, and £5.93 depending on age, which comes out at £145.60, £196.20, and £237.20 respectively for a 40-hour week. These rates were 7 pence, 9 pence, and 13 pence higher respectively compared with 2009.
- 'Up to age 44 women are better qualified than men. However, women's median hourly pay is 21 per cent less than men's' (Hills Report [National Equality Panel] 2010: 3).
- In 2010, the Trades Union Council (TUC) PensionsWatch survey showed that the pensions of 329 directors from 102 of Britain's biggest companies averaged £227,726 per year, 26 times the average occupational pension of £8736.

Other statistical comparisons worth considering include:

- The Chief Executive of Shell is reputed to have the largest pension pot at £21 million.
- It is estimated that payments for leading bankers will total £7 billion in 2010.
- It is estimated that the outgoing chief executive of Lloyds Banking Group is in line for a bonus of about £2 million in 2010.
- One report suggests that the boss of the Royal Bank of Scotland, which is 84 per cent owned by the taxpayer, could receive a £2.5 million bonus in 2011.

These facts indicate that the problem is not a lack of national wealth but an unequal distribution of that wealth. (For a helpful summary of the Hills Report, see Gentleman and Mulholland (2010), and for a summary of pension increases for company directors, see Inman (2010).) Unemployment can also result in people's income being located below the poverty line. According to statistics published by the Joseph Rowntree Foundation Poverty Site, in 2010 there were around 4.7 million people of working-age who wanted to be in paid work but who were not employed (Palmer 2010). Of this group, one in four adults with a work-limiting disability were not in work but wanted to be employed.

People on benefit

Box 3.1 provides an overview of the benefits taken up by different groups. In 2008–2009, total expenditure on benefits in the UK was £152 billion.

Box 3.1 Overview of benefits uptake

- £81.7 billion (60 per cent of the UK total benefit expenditure) was paid in state pensions to older people.

- £34 billion (25 per cent) was taken up by people of working age.

- £2.6 billion was for the benefit of children, paid to adults who were responsible for their well-being. The figure for children includes 'elements of income support, disability allowances, housing benefit and council tax benefit paid because of the presence of children in the family' (Office for National Statistics 2010: 110) but with child benefit payments being paid by Revenue and Customs (HMRC).

- £17.5 billion (13 per cent) was benefits paid to people with disabilities. This is not age related and, therefore, covers people of all ages, including people drawing state pensions, people of working age, and children.

- £152 billion total expenditure in 2008/09.

Unclaimed benefits

A considerable amount of money is spent on welfare benefits, but every year a significant amount of money goes unclaimed. This issue was taken up in February 2010 when 27 leading charities, spearheaded by the Citizens Advice Bureau (CAB), called on the UK Government to improve the take-up of welfare benefits and tax credits. According to statistics cited by the Citizens Advice Bureau, which are based on official figures issued by the Department for Works and Pensions (2009) and Her Majesty's Revenue and Customs (2007), it is estimated that:

- £16 billion in welfare benefits and tax credits went unclaimed, despite efforts by the Department for Works and Pensions to simplify the procedures involved in claiming benefit (Citizens Advice Bureau 2010).
- The complexity of our benefits system is evident in the fact that the Citizens Advice Bureau deals with 8000 new benefit enquiries every working day. The lack of publicity to encourage people to claim their entitlement sits uneasily with the publicity given to benefit fraud.

Other statistics to consider

From a different perspective, it is important to compare the welfare benefit figures against other budgets set by the government. For example:

- The budget for defence for 2010–2011 has been set at £36.9 billion (Ministry of Defence), higher than the £34 billion paid out in benefits to people of working age in 2008–2009.

- On top of this £36.9 billion on defence, the wars in Afghanistan and Iraq have cost an estimated additional £20 billion, less than the cost of disability benefits for 2008–2009 and ten times the amount it would cost to scrap student fees in England.
- The cost of replacing the Trident nuclear missile system was set by the government in 2006 at £15–20 billion, which Greenpeace, an environmental campaigning group, state could rise to £97 billion over the system's 30-year life (Norton-Taylor 2009).
- 'Tax dodgers': it is estimated that if we add together tax evasion, tax avoidance, and late tax payments, the figure comes to more than £120 billion owed to the state – 'enough, at least in principle, to close the whole current government deficit' (Murphy 2010).

However, addressing tax loopholes and the failure to comply with taxpayers' obligations has not been a government priority. The department responsible for taxation is Her Majesty's Revenue and Customs, which, since 2005, has seen 26,000 jobs lost, a point taken up by Murphy:

> Last year 5,000 frontline staff went and more still are to go. This makes no sense: each frontline member of staff brings in on average 30 times in tax what it costs to employ them. The result is that tax that is so badly needed to keep services going is being given away.
>
> (Murphy 2010)

As human beings, and as social workers, we can easily feel overwhelmed by statistics relating to social injustices of this kind. Yet within this bleak picture, it is important to keep hold of a *healthy sense of outrage* and also the sense that change is possible – and vital – but to be successful in our efforts we need to know the scale and nature of the problem. The remedy to feeling immobilized is to take action: at a more immediate level by undertaking welfare work and, in the longer term, by confronting the structural inequalities that give rise to poverty and problems that are poverty related (Dorling 2010; Marmot Review 2010; Wilkinson and Picket 2009). An excellent example of the benefits that can derive from welfare rights work is described in the Marmot Review, which gives an example of a mental health initiative in Salford, run by the Citizens Advice Bureau (CAB). In 2007–2008, this agency saw 696 clients – and had innumerable points of contact with the individuals concerned. This resulted in the agency being able to help to 'write off over £15,000 in debt, secure more than £25,000 in benefit back pay, and increase income through benefits by over £290,000' (Marmot Review 2010: 122).

We can all effect change but we are more likely to be successful in this endeavour if we work with others. In this section, I have focused on the impact of poverty and social inequalities because I consider these to underpin many of the problems we encounter in social work. They call for interventions that are not only directed towards the individual but also targeted at those elements of society that give rise to – and condone – inequalities in wealth and life opportunities. I return to this theme later in this text. (For an informative account of 'welfare rights practice' and the range of interventions this can involve, see Bateman (2008). For a detailed account of how the *poverty line* and low income threshold is calculated, see Office for National Statistics (2010: 68) and the websites for the Child Poverty Action Group (CPAG) and Joseph Rowntree Foundation (JRF).)

Knowledge of specific groups of people

Figure 3.8 Knowledge relating to different groups of people

This fifth and final sub-heading of the *factual knowledge* domain looks at the trends that can be identified in relation to different groups of people within our society (Figure 3.8). Again, it is only possible to cover some key issues that different groups of people present. However, a number of helpful references are included should you wish to follow up some of the points covered. The section begins with a brief overview of the population profile of the United Kingdom, followed by an account of the occupational and social class classifications that are used in official statistics, before looking at the importance of terms such as deprivation, disadvantage, and discrimination in social work.

The groups we encounter in social work include people who are described based on their social class, gender, race/ethnicity, age (children, young people, older people), disability, sexual orientation, and those who are described according to their status, such as asylum seekers and refugees, travellers, and so forth. These groups of people constitute social work's 'disciplinary territory':

> Social work's disciplinary territory is the poor, troubled, abused or discriminated against, neglected, frail and elderly, mentally ill, learning disabled, addicted, delinquent, or otherwise socially marginalized up-against-it citizens in his or her social circumstances. This is a dauntingly broad remit, particularly since some of these circumstances line up together on the fruit machine of life.
>
> (Sheldon and Macdonald 2009: 3)

One reason for working within specific categories is because people identify themselves – and often identified by others – as belonging to certain groups. Also, as we shall see, official statistics are gathered using specific categories. For example, a major source of data in relation to the people living in the United Kingdom can be found in *Social Trends*. This research publication is produced each year by the Office for National Statistics and identifies the developments and shifts taking place with a particular subject area, category, or group of people, some of which are used to guide government decision-making. There are dangers and benefits in all classification systems, which makes it important to look for the assumptions that underpin different classifications and the extent to which they reinforce or challenge dominant ideology. In this regard, as an official document it is likely that the themes covered in *Social Trends* are shaped by government priorities. Box 3.2 provides a population profile of the United Kingdom, based on national population projections by the Office for National Statistics for 2008.

Some groups more than others may look to social work for help and support but what the list in Box. 3.2 indicates is how important it is for social workers to be able to work with different groups of people. In the previous section on *knowledge of particular problems*, I looked at the subject of poverty and social inequalities, and the unequal, unjust, and unfair distribution of wealth and opportunities within this country. It is clear that the people who are consistently disadvantaged in this unfair and unjust system are working-class people, yet this theme has tended to be a neglected subject in social work – although this is changing (Ferguson 2008; Ferguson and Woodward 2009). To understand what we mean by the term *social class* or *socio-economic classification*, it is important to understand the classification systems used in official statistics and surveys because these are used to categorize different groups within society and to assess one classification against another.

Classification systems used in official statistics and surveys

From 1913 to 2001, the main systems adopted in official statistics to identify population trends within the United Kingdom, particularly in health, was the Registrar General's Social Classes (RGSC). This used six social class categories to classify people's occupation and socio-economic group but presented serious limitations in terms of women's employment and those not in employment. Because the Registrar General's classification is often referred to in publications that pre-date 2001, the system is illustrated in Box 3.3 (see p. 84). Also, its explicit reference to social class offers an interesting comparison with the new National Statistics Socio-Economic Classification NS-SEC classification (see Box 3.4 on p. 85).

Box 3.2   Population profile of the United Kingdom, 2008

Overall population profile
- United Kingdom: 61.393 million people
- England (approximate): 51.460 million people
- Wales (approximate): 2.990 million people
- Scotland (approximate): 5.169 million people
- Northern Ireland (approximate): 1.775 million people

Social class. No accurate figures are available and definitions vary a great deal:
- upper class: roughly 1–10+ per cent of the total population
- middle class: roughly 50+ per cent of the total population (made up of lower, middle and upper middle class categories)
- working class: roughly 30–40 per cent of the total population (Scott and Marshall 2009)

Gender. In 2008, the female population outnumbered the male population by one million (31.2 million females compared with 30.2 million males) (Office for National Statistics 2010).

Older people. In mid-2008, the population of people of pensionable age (65 for men and 60 for women) was 11.8 million, or 19 per cent of the total population, including 1.3 million people who were aged 85 and over (2 per cent of the population) (Office for National Statistics 2010).

Children under 16 years. The proportion of the UK population aged under 16 in mid-2008 was 19 per cent (11.5 million children) (Office for National Statistics 2010).

Racial/ethnic composition. In 2008, around 83 per cent of the population came from a 'White British ethnic background'. The remaining 17 per cent that identified as coming from a 'distinct ethnic minority group within the general population' included: 'Other White' (5 per cent), Indian (2 per cent), Pakistani (2 per cent), and people from other ethnic minority groups (8 per cent) (Office for National Statistics 2010).

Disabled people. In 2008–2009 there were just under 2.7 million working age recipients of Invalidity Benefit and other benefits in the UK. About a third of people of pensionable age receive disability-related benefits (Office for National Statistics 2010).

Refugees seeking asylum. There were roughly 25,900 UK applications for asylum (excluding dependants) in 2008, an increase of 11 per cent on the previous year and the first annual increase since 2002 (Office for National Statistics 2010).

Gay, lesbian, bisexual, and transgender people. There are no accurate figures but according to the charity Stonewall, around 3.6 million people are lesbian, gay, or bisexual in Britain. There are also roughly 5000 transgender people in the UK (Gender Identity Research and Education Society 2009).

Other minority groups, such as travellers. There are no accurate overall figures but the Department for Communities and Local Government keep a count of the number of caravan sites. In 2010, it was estimated there were roughly 18,383 gypsy and traveller caravans in England (Department for Communities and Local Government 2011).

Carers. It is estimated that there are 6 million carers in the UK, that is, one carer per eight people. By 2037, it is anticipated that the number of carers will increase to 9 million. According to Carers UK:
- every day another 6000 people take on a caring responsibility – that equals over 2 million people each year
- 58% of carers are women and 42% are men; over 1 million people care for more than one person
- 625,000 people suffer mental and physical ill health as a direct consequence of the stress and physical demands of caring
- 1.25 million people provide over 50 hours of care per week

Box 3.3   Examples of employment or occupational categories based on the Registrar General's Social Classes (RGSC) classification

Social class		Example occupations
Non-manual		
Social class I	Service/professional	Higher grade professional, such as administrators, dentists, doctors, accountants, lawyers
Social class II		Lower grade professionals, such as teachers, managers, farmers, nurses, social workers
Social class III	Intermediate/ routine skilled non-manual	Secretaries, clerical workers, shop assistants
Manual		
Social class IIIM	Skilled manual	Electricians, cooks, carpenters, builders
Social class IV	Semi-skilled or partly skilled manual	Agricultural workers, assembly workers, bus conductors, miners
Social class V	Unskilled manual	Laundry workers, cleaners, labourers

The new National Statistics Socio-Economic Classification (NS-SEC) is a conceptual model that is broken down into eight, five, or three socio-economic categories (Box 3.4). In *Social Trends*, eight classifications are used for most analyses (Office for National Statistics 2010: 215).

A different definition of social class can be found in the work of Karl Marx, who defined the working class in terms of the concept of *surplus value*, that is, the added value or profit that is created by employees over the wages their employees are paid. This concept was developed at a time when there were many more manual workers than at present. For example, if we view working-class people to constitute social classes IV and V in the Registrar General's classification, in 1911 the working class was estimated to be 75 per cent of the employed population, whereas in 1991 the figure had fallen to 42 per cent. Current figures suggest that working-class people constitute roughly one-third of those who are 'economically active' (Scott and Marshall 2009: 811).

A definition of social class, however, involves more than an account of the type of work that people undertake. Other considerations include cultural

Box 3.4 National Statistics Socio-Economic Classification (NS-SEC) (Office for National Statistics 2010)

Eight classes	Five classes	Three classes
1 Higher managerial and professional occupations		
1.1 Large employers and higher managerial occupations	1 Managerial and professional occupations	1 Managerial and professional occupations
1.2 Higher professional occupations		
2 Lower managerial and professional occupations		
3 Intermediate occupations	2 Intermediate occupations	2 Intermediate occupations
4 Small employers and own account workers	3 Small employers and own account workers	
5 Lower supervisory and technical occupations	4 Lower supervisory and technical occupations	3 Routine and manual occupations
6 Semi-routine occupations	5 Semi-routine and routine occupations	Never worked and long-term unemployed
7 Routine occupations	Never worked and long-term unemployed	
8 Never worked and long-term unemployed		

issues, education, income, and lifestyle choice, since these also influence how people classify their social class. For example, I define myself as a member of the educated working class but also as a person who lives a middle-class lifestyle. The different ways that people define their class is a subject of considerable confusion and a highly contested subject and there is no universal agreement about what these terms mean. This confusion is exemplified by David Cameron, the current Prime Minister of Britain, who describes himself and his wife as 'middle class'. However, Mr. Cameron was educated at Eton (the most exclusive public school in the United Kingdom), is a descendant of King William IV, and his wife is the daughter of a Baronet and the stepdaughter of a Viscount. Together, Mr. Cameron and his wife are reported to have a personal fortune of £3 million (Shackle *et al.* 2009), although others estimate it to be £30 million (Brennan 2007). In 2011, 23 of the 29 UK Coalition Cabinet members were reputed to be millionaires (Owen 2010). It would be interesting to know whether they too would describe themselves as middle class. Classifications of this kind are important because they highlight 'occupational advantage and disadvantage in British society' (Giddens 2001: 288).

The distinct characteristics of working-class people

The term *working class* tends to be used to reflect some of the following characteristics: people who are manual workers, who are paid weekly wages, often in cash, who live in rented accommodation, often in local authority 'council' houses (social housing) or in poor housing conditions, and who have limited savings or disposable income. Abercrombie *et al.* (2006) take up this theme and identify a number of distinct characteristics that many working-class people demonstrate. These characteristics, they argue, have not been 'eroded' but are clearly evident and include:

- lower incomes
- less job security
- more unemployment
- a greater likelihood of poverty
- more boring jobs
- worse conditions of employment
- fewer chances of a structured career
- higher rates of morbidity (illness)
- an earlier age of mortality
- less chance of success within the educational system than the intermediate and upper classes.

(Abercrombie *et al.* 2006: 426)

If, for example, we take the subject of housing, in 2007 it was noted in *Social Trends* that 'there were an estimated 3.2 million households in England living in poor quality environments' (Office for National Statistics 2010: 146). The sorts of problems described included crime, litter and rubbish, vandalism and hooliganism, noise, difficulties with neighbours, racial harassment and other forms of harassment, traffic problems, graffiti, and problems relating to dogs. These types of problems are simple listed in *Social Trends* – with no attempt to identify and to analyse which sections of society are likely to live in these 'poor quality environments' – and why. Without this analysis, there is a tendency to deny the hardships experienced by working class people and why they are forced to live in 'poor quality environments' (Office for National Statistics 2010: 146).

Health inequalities

One of the major ways in which the Registrar General's classification and now the new NS-SEC classification have been used is to measure inequalities, particularly in the area of health and health-related behaviour. There is a growing concern for what has been described as the *social determinants of health*, a term used to reflect 'the conditions in which people are born, grow, live, work and age, including the health system' (World Health Organization website). Several measures are used to indicate the quality of health within and across different populations, including life expectancy, infant mortality, rates of limiting long-term illnesses and disability. Edwin Chadwick first noted the impact of social conditions on life expectancy in 1839, when the average age of death in Bethnal Green for labourers was 16 years compared with 45 years for 'gentlemen'. More recently, a number of health publications have highlighted the importance of social conditions in relation to life expectancy, such as the Black Report (Department of Health and Social Security 1980) and the Acheson Report (1998). The most recent review on this subject, chaired by Professor Sir Michael Marmot, noted that although many people now enjoy good health in the UK, there are cases where dramatic comparisons can be found:

> In England, people living in the poorest neighbourhoods will, on average, die seven years earlier than people living in the richest neighbourhoods ... For example, in the wealthiest part of London, one ward in Kensington and Chelsea, a man now has a life expectancy of 88 years. But the contrast is stark. A few kilometres away in Tottenham Green, one of the capital's poorer wards, male life expectancy is 71.
> (Marmot Review 2010: 37)

In addition to poorer people dying earlier, more will experience disability during their lifetime:

> Even more disturbing, the average difference in disability-free life expectancy is 17 years. So, people in poorer areas not only die sooner, but they will also spend more of their shorter lives with a disability.
> (Marmot Review 2010: 16)

The review states very clearly that 'health inequalities result from social inequalities. Action on health inequalities requires action across all the social determinants of health' (Marmot Review 2010: 15). For example, Marmot highlighted income inequality as one of the underlying social determinants of health and called on the government to increase the minimum wage and introduce a minimum income standard to ensure that everyone has the opportunity to live a healthy life. In particular, the review criticized government policy in relation to income tax, where in overall terms the poorest 20 per cent of the population paid 38 per cent of their income in taxes, 3 per cent more than those earning the most, with 'the top 20 per cent gaining at the expense of the bottom 60 per cent' (Marmot Review 2010: 74). Class-based health inequalities are also reflected in the quality of care provided is described in terms of the *inverse care law* (Hart 2004; Shaw and Dorling 2004). This concept states that those who need health care the most, such as people living in poverty, are least likely to be able to access that care and, conversely, those groups that have less need for health care, such as the wealthier sections of society, are more likely to access health services – and to use these more effectively. Several other terms are used to describe the impact of social inequalities, such as *deprivation* and *disadvantage*. Again, there is no one agreed definition but the following provides a flavour of how these terms are used.

Deprivation

To be *deprived* means to experience *loss*, such as bereavement, something we are all likely to experience at some point in our lives, perhaps due to an accident of birth, bad luck, or personal failings. But it can also mean *having to do without*. Three different types of deprivation are referred to in social work:

- *material deprivation*, which reflects the limited access that some people have to material goods and resources
- *social deprivation* (covered in the previous section)
- *multiple deprivation*, or the extent to which several forms of deprivation are evident at any one time, such as low income, poor health, unemployment, poor housing, debt, and poor education.

Disadvantage

Multiple deprivation is similar to the notion of disadvantage because it describes the systematic barriers to opportunities and life chances experienced by some people. Its impact can mean that people are trapped in a position where they are permanently disadvantaged, sometimes for generations:

> The disadvantaged are those whose access to a range of goods or desirable life chances is restricted because of some characteristic or condition ... Deprivations of all kinds – material, physical, social or emotional – may happen to anyone in any social group. But the disadvantaged are those who are consistently exposed to the highest risks of being deprived. Put crudely, the disadvantaged are those whose deprivations occur not because they are foolish or unlucky but simply because they belong to a particular social group.
>
> (Brown 1983: 4–5)

When people or organizations behave in ways that disadvantage particular individuals or social groups, or that consistently expose them to risk, this could be considered to constitute *discrimination*. From this perspective, 'disadvantage and discrimination tend to go hand in hand' (Sheppard 2002: 782). The coverage of key terms such as deprivation, disadvantage, and discrimination helps to draw attention to the impact that inequalities can have on people's quality of life and to remind us that part of our remit as social workers is the 'pursuit of social justice (which) involves identifying, seeking to alleviate and advocating strategies for overcoming structural disadvantage' (BASW 2002). I have argued that to achieve this end calls for a sound knowledge and skills base, which includes drawing on factual information in ways that can inform and illuminate the context within which our work is located.

A major difficulty encountered when attempting to identify the knowledge base of any profession is how best to order and classify that knowledge. In this second domain within the *Knowledge and Skills Framework* I have highlighted the importance of the factual in terms of five overlapping components: knowledge of the principles of law and key legislation; knowledge of social policy; knowledge of agency policy, procedures, and practices; knowledge of particular problems; and knowledge of specific groups of people. Although the ability to promote a relationship-based or reflective approach is essential in social work, there must be more than this – there must be a theoretical and factual basis to our practice and the ability to articulate what we know. It is our ability to reflect on – and to scrutinize – what we bring to our work that indicates that our practice is theory-based and updated through the inclusion of relevant factual information.

4   PRACTICE KNOWLEDGE

Introduction

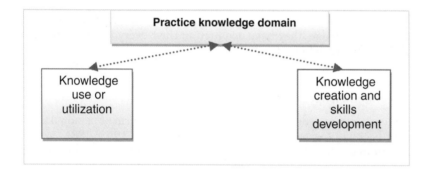

Figure 4.1 The practice knowledge domain

The *practice knowledge* domain is the third and final part of the *Knowledge and Skills Framework* – a domain that overlaps and interweaves with the two knowledge domains already covered (see Figure 4.1). This chapter focuses on how we draw on abstract theories (*theoretical knowledge*) and the facts at our disposal (*factual knowledge*) to guide and inform practice. It concerns the way in which *knowing that* can be related to *knowing how* (Ryle 1949). The chapter begins with an overview of personal and professional sources knowledge, before describing two facets of this domain, namely *knowledge use* or *utilization* and *knowledge creation and skill development*. However, at the outset it is important to state that 'knowledge *use* and knowledge *creation* cannot be easily separated or distinguished' (Eraut 1994: 54). For example, concepts that are included under the heading *knowledge use*, such as *reflection/reflexivity*, *analysis* and *synthesis*; *forming hypotheses*; *critical thinking*; *problem-solving* and *judicious decision-making* all have features that could be routinely or creatively applied. On the other hand, some features, such as intuition, clearly indicate a more creative form of knowledge.

This differentiation between knowledge *use* and *creation* is likely to be influenced by four factors. The first is the problem presented, which may be relatively simple and straightforward and only require a more standard response, or may be more complex and multifaceted, thereby requiring a more creative approach; second, the orientation of the organization or agency, which may promote standardized responses as opposed to interventions that call for a greater degree of creativity and imagination; third, the orientation of the practitioner, who may not feel they have adequate knowledge, skill, or support to provide a response that is more creative, unusual, or unorthodox; and fourth, the extent to which the service user considers a more routine or creative response to be appropriate under the circumstances. These four points link to the coverage in the Introduction of the different capacities that different parties bring to an encounter or to problem-solving. In relation to service users, it is again important to stress that they have their own body of knowledge that they bring to the encounter, which includes personal and 'practical knowledge' they have acquired in their everyday lives (Beresford *et al.* 2008; McLaughlin 2010).

Personal knowledge

Of course, all knowledge that we acquire becomes a form of personal knowledge or becomes 'personalized knowledge' (Sheppard 1995: 283) – whether gained from teaching and learning opportunities, reading, social interaction, or the personal knowledge acquired through our own 'conduct of practice' (Sheppard 1995: 267). For many people, the personal store of experience that we acquire provides a framework through which new experiences can be interpreted in ways that order and synthesize past experiences and enable predictions to be made in relation to future events. This ordering distinguishes one experience from another. It also allows a differentiation to be made between those experiences that are considered important and meaningful, and those that are not. How we interpret and perceive what is important and/or meaningful can vary widely from person to person, and is often adjusted in the light of new information. In both a personal and professional context, the attempt to order experiences in this way could be seen as a feature of reflection and reflexivity and linked to the notion of *experiential learning* (Kolb 1984). One way that this personal form of knowledge is described is in terms of working from 'common sense' – a subject that some authors link to *practice wisdom*, covered later.

The role of common sense

Considerable disagreements exist about whether the use of common sense constitutes a distinct form of knowledge and also whether social workers should rely on knowledge that falls within this category. So much depends on how common sense is perceived or defined. For example, it has been described as 'practical, experimental and critical, but also fragmentary and incoherent' (Abercrombie *et al.* 2006: 69); as 'an anecdotal ragbag of folk remedies' (Pinker 1990: 64); as knowledge that 'is not learnt in the formal sense but is a product of socially acceptable order and reason' (Drury Hudson 1999: 41); and as 'genius dressed in its working clothes' by the American poet, Ralph Waldo Emerson. Emerson's comment is worth noting because for people who have not had access to higher education or access to reliable sources of knowledge, the ability to 'use common sense' can be an important attribute. On the one hand, the use of common sense can indicate a desire and an ability to order ideas and experiences in an intelligent and reasoned way. This kind of 'thinking things through' can involve a more practical, methodical, and logical problem-solving approach to certain tasks, particularly when faced with new situations. On the other hand, common sense notions can be used to describe beliefs that are misinformed – or even prejudiced. To challenge these beliefs, particularly those that are firmly held or put forward as 'universal truths', can produce strong reactions. Some sociologists, such as Durkheim, viewed sociology as a discipline whose task was to break free from common sense notions in order to produce scientific knowledge about the social world that we inhabit. In a different interpretation, Karl Marx linked common sense notions to ideology – as a way that the dominant class or ruling elite imposes its views on the 'masses'. We may not agree with these views but in relation to social work practice, to work solely from unsubstantiated or unconfirmed viewpoints, impressions, assumptions, or ideas – whether based on intuition, tacit knowledge, or common sense notions – is not sufficient.

Heuristics

Heuristics, a term that is sometimes used in social work publications, refers to a more experientially based approach to problem-solving, perhaps involving common-sense or 'rule-of-thumb' approaches. The *Oxford English Dictionary* (OED) defines heuristics as 'enabling a person to discover or learn something for themselves' (Soanes and Stevenson 2003: 815), often where the rules are loosely defined. A different definition describes heuristics as 'pertaining to an experimental, trial-and-error kind of procedure' and 'the art of discovery' (Mautner 2000: 249). For Fiske and Taylor (1991: 381), it constitutes a 'rapid form of reasoning', where judgements are made 'under conditions that may not be best suited to accuracy or thoroughness'. For example, there are situations where a seemingly unlimited amount of information could be brought to bear on a decision, 'but much of it would be of uncertain value' (Fiske and Taylor 1991: 381) and, therefore, shortcuts may be helpful to make problem-solving more manageable.

Professional knowledge

In professional circles, for knowledge to be capable of being used, it must have 'practice validity' (Sheppard 1998: 763) or be 'fit for use', that is, it has to be relevant and presented in a form that is accessible:

> Knowledge should be appropriate to the decision setting in which it is intended to be used, and to the information need expressed by the seeker after knowledge. For knowledge to meet this standard, it should be 'fit for use', providing answers that are as closely matched as possible to the question.
>
> (Long *et al.* 2006: 4)

An important source of knowledge is practice experience, that is, knowledge that 'is expressed only in practice and learned only through experience with practice' (Eraut 1994: 42). The emphasis placed on learning through experience is important but, at the same time, it is not easy to identify the extent to which learning is taking place. One influential factor is the degree to which social work agencies actively promote the importance of learning, and knowledge and practice development. Other factors that impact on learning include practitioners' attitude to learning and the variable nature of the problems encountered. One of the most influential texts on the importance of learning by experience, or *experiential learning*, is that of Kolb (1984).

Kolb's reflective learning cycle

Roughly at the same time that Schön (1983) was writing about reflection and professional practice, Kolb (1984) was writing about *experiential learning* and the *reflective learning cycle*, ideas that were influenced by the work of Rogers and Piaget, described in Chapter 5. Kolb stressed the importance of 'active engagement' or experimentation as the basis from which new learning and new knowledge can be acquired. In this conceptualization, 'learning is the process whereby knowledge is created through the transformation of experience' (Kolb 1984: 38) – that is, learning involves being changed by the experience. This emphasis is important because it moves away from the notion of passive or rote modes of learning to a more process-oriented focus where the engagement and experience of learning is central to the task of learning. Kolb's cyclical nature of learning is represented in Figure 4.2.

This conceptualization embodies four components:

- *Concrete experience (CE)* – or feeling/doing
- *Reflective observation (RO)* – or observing
- *Abstract conceptualization (AC)* – or thinking
- *Active experimentation (AE)* – or trying out new ideas

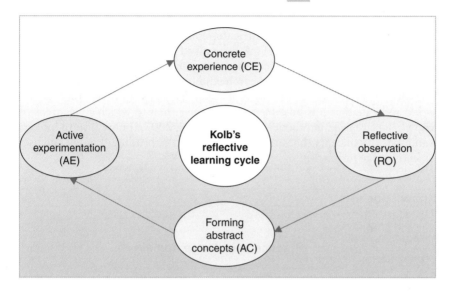

Figure 4.2   Kolb's (1984) experiential learning cycle

Taken together, these four features highlight the interrelationship between experience, perception, cognition, and behaviour. Kolb's work has been highly influential in social work because of its accessibility and visual appeal and also because it can be easily related to different aspects of social work education, particularly the learning that is acquired on practice placements and in supervision.

The extent to which social workers draw on theory to inform decision-making and to underpin action is a subject of constant debate. Some academics writing on this subject support the view put forward by Schön that theory *is* being synthesized by practitioners but not in ways that are clearly evident in terms of producing 'a good verbal description' (Schön 1983: 31) of what they do. One of the difficulties encountered is that practice terminology tends to be implicit, rather than explicit. For example, the findings of an empirical study on knowledge utilization suggest that knowledge may be communicated in diverse ways that may not be easily recognizable because it is not 'always formal and labelled' (Osmond and O'Connor 2004: 677). This point is supported by Eraut, who states:

> ... the intellectual problems of attempting to describe, share and develop practical knowledge so that it becomes more widely available are formidable indeed ... Practical knowledge is never tidy, an appropriate language for handling much of it has yet to be developed.
>
> (Eraut 1994: 56)

Similarly, Bogo (2006: 15) writes in terms of practitioners' knowledge being 'incorporated to create an intricate, complex, multilayered knowledge framework and practice model'. A difficulty I have with this perspective is that it tends to mystify practice, suggesting that what happens in practice can never be understood. Yet research studies that attempt to test the use of knowledge in terms of certain concepts, such as the use of reflection in social work, indicate that it is possible to assess the extent to which some areas of knowledge are used in practice contexts (Tsang 2007). I now turn to look at a number of concepts that are included under the heading 'knowledge use' or knowledge utilization.

Knowledge use

Figure 4.3 Knowledge use

This first sub-heading of the *practice knowledge* domain introduces a range of terms that are central features of social work practice, including: *analysis* and *synthesis; forming hypotheses; critical thinking; problem-solving* and *judicious decision-making*. Because of the importance afforded to *reflection* in social work, and its link to Kolb's *reflective learning cycle* outlined above, this account begins with coverage of this concept beginning with a brief account of the work of Schön. I then look at how the terms that are central to reflection have been conceptualized in social work.

Schön

When Schön introduced the notion of *reflection* about 30 years ago, it marked an important and innovative development in professional practice. Schön trained as a philosopher. In his writing, his primary aim was to demonstrate the extent to which a *technical-rational* model, or *technical rationality*, which has its roots in the positivist tradition, fails to explain how practical competence operates in 'divergent' situations. His work marked an important and innovative development in professional practice, and focused on a search that involved identifying 'the artistic, intuitive processes which some practitioners ... bring to situations of uncertainty, instability, uniqueness, and value conflict' (Schön 1983: 49). In this task, Schön proposed three key concepts. First, *reflective conversation with the situation* describes a way of building on our knowledge base so that we can observe and attend to the uniqueness of every situation, and human experience, in order to link 'understanding, action and effect' (England 1986: 154). It involves reflecting on 'the construction of the problem' and 'the strategies of action' (Schön 1983) that are implicit in helping to formulate a more rigorous approach to the judgements and decisions made in practice situations. Second, *reflection-in-action* is sometimes described as 'thinking on our feet'. It involves thinking about our practice in the here-and-now, while a problem is being addressed – that is, the action and thinking about the action take place simultaneously. Eraut (2008: 6) describes this self-awareness in terms of *meta-cognition*. A third concept, *reflection-on-action*, describes the reflection process that is undertaken later, after the encounter or event. This may occur when reviewing and discussing the practice experience with a colleague or supervisor or when documenting or recording events. It involves exploring what was happening, and why certain actions were taken, thereby raising a number of questions or hypotheses about a practitioner's professional practice.

In a well-known metaphor, Schön differentiates between a small minority of practitioners who choose the 'high, hard ground' of precise and narrowly defined technical practice (Schön 1983: 42) and those practitioners who:

> ... choose the swampy lowlands. They deliberately involve themselves in messy but crucially important problems and, when asked to describe their methods of inquiry, they speak of experience, trial and error, intuition, and muddling through.
>
> (Schön 1983: 43)

Schön's work has been criticized on the grounds that some of the terms he developed lack intellectual coherence and consistency. However, for Eraut (1994) it was Schön's determination to develop an 'epistemology of professional creativity' and to 'refute the technical-rational model' (p. 143) that marks his important contribution but one that tends to be overlooked in his work. Schön's comments on the impact of technical rationality in the area of research, education, and practice are highly relevant for social work, where we have seen the professional autonomy and creativity of social workers being compromised by the introduction of a managerialist culture in the form of 'targets, performance indicators and procedures detailing how tasks should be carried out' (Munro 2010a: 1144).

The following account looks at the family of terms used to describe some form of reflective process: *reflection, reflective practice, critical reflection,* and *reflexivity*. Some difficulties are identified in relation to these concepts and I explain how these terms are used in this text.

Reflection/reflexivity. For Schön reflection involves practitioners discovering and restructuring the 'interpersonal theories of action which they bring to their professional lives' (Schön 1983: 353). It describes a commitment to examine and to think critically about the approaches we adopt in practice with a view to improving how we work.

Reflective practice. A different emphasis is evident in the work of Ruch who, echoing the stance adopted by Schön and others on the limitations of a technical-rationalist approach, locates the concept of reflective practice as standing in contrast to the culture imposed by managerialism:

> The essence of reflective practice involves acknowledging precisely that which the competency culture avoids – the uniqueness of each situation encounter, the extraordinary complexity of human functioning whether in relation to individual personalities, family dynamics or inter-professional relations and, perhaps most pertinently, the anxiety invoked in practitioners by the work they do.
>
> (Ruch 2004: 202)

Ruch's account combines an intellectual and emotional awareness in ways that enrich our understanding of service users and ourselves, thereby allowing for complicated emotions to be acknowledged and worked with as an essential feature of reflection.

Critical reflection. The term critical reflection is similar in many ways to the term reflection:

> A reflective stance points up the many and diverse perspectives which can be taken on knowledge itself, and the shaping of that knowledge. The important difference is that critical reflection places emphasis and importance on an understanding of how a reflective stance uncovers power relations, and how structures of domination are created and maintained.
>
> (Fook 2002: 41)

As such, it is a concept that has been linked to other theories and theorists, such as critical postmodernism, the work of Lukes (1974) and Foucault (1984) on power, and Habermas (1968) on the form and content of emancipatory knowledge or ways of knowing (Hayes and Houston 2007; Lovat and Gray 2008).

Reflexivity. Reflexivity, like critical reflection, involves putting ourselves in the picture and within this process, identifying how our presence might be influential:

> The notion of reflexivity emphasizes the social worker (i) as an active thinker, able to assess, respond and initiate action and (ii) as a social actor, one who actually participates in the situation with which they

are concerned in the conduct of their practice. Thus the reflexive practitioner, in practical terms, is one who is aware of the socially situated relationship with their client(s).

(Sheppard 1998: 767)

Sheppard's account is similar to Eraut's definition of *meta-cognition*, which describes 'a person's ability to be aware of what they are doing or have just done' (Eraut 2008: 6). Fook uses the terms reflective and reflexive interchangeably, stating that: 'In a developed critical practice, practitioners will be both reflective and reflexive, able to use a variety of methods to confront the ways in which their own backgrounds, embodiment, personalities and perspectives intermingle' (Fook 2002: 43–4). Like Fook, in this text I use the terms reflective and reflexive interchangeably.

While the family of terms outlined above carry important currency in social work, their value and relevance has been questioned. For example, the interchangeable way that these terms are sometimes used, often without being defined, can lead to confusion (Ixer 1999) and misrepresent their essential features and purpose. As a result, reflection can be interpreted differently and to mean anything or everything, which calls for a 'more rigorous examination of the conceptual issues related to reflective practice in social work' (Tsang 2007: 684). In this task, I would emphasize the importance of identifying what areas of knowledge are informing the use of reflection in practice. Other criticisms relate to the relationship between 'action and reflection', which is not always evident (Parsloe 2000: 10), particularly the question of how to balance self-awareness in ways that avoid becoming introspective and neglectful of service users' needs. Finally, from a practice perspective, adopting a stance that is more reflective and questioning may not be possible in working environments that are hostile to this approach (Trevithick 2012a). Where this is the situation, collective support is needed but difficult to achieve because of the way that social work has become fragmented and fractured by the role adopted by successive governments. With important exceptions, in recent years we have not demonstrated a strong history or tradition of coming together in ways that are evident in other professions through their involvement in interest groups, membership of professional associations and trade unions. It is my hope that this situation will change and that together we can reclaim the professional autonomy that enables social workers to be reflective in their approach.

Analysis and synthesis

An *analysis* describes the process of examining or unpicking the components of a particular encounter, event, situation, or structure in ways that lead to understanding. A *synthesis* is the opposite procedure but has similar aims because it combines the different components into a connected whole in an attempt to provide a coherent understanding of the situation under consideration. Both terms originate from classical Greek and mean literally 'to unloosen' and 'to put together' respectively. A central activity outlined in the Benchmark Statement for Social Work is the ability to 'analyze and synthesize knowledge gathered for problem-solving purposes' (QAA 2008: 11). This includes the ability to 'analyze information gathered, weighing competing evidence and modifying their viewpoint in light of new information, then relate this information to a particular task, situation or problem' and to 'synthesize knowledge and sustain reasoned argument' (QAA 2008: 11).

Part of this analysis and synthesis involves providing a 'social analysis', that is, an analysis that involves not only the personal characteristics of the individuals involved, but wider social or ecological factors such as the family situation, relevant issues that are located in the neighbourhood or community context, societal attitudes, and policy issues. For example, an analysis of a particular intervention could focus on: the quality of information provided in the original referral, both with regard to individual circumstances and the context within which the work is located; assumptions that are evident; the purpose of the work and the desired outcome being sought; whether the actions taken achieved the desired outcomes and the purpose for which they were intended; how practice effectiveness might be measured; where the voice of service users is located within the analysis and decision-making process, and so forth. This analysis can lead to findings that clarify and confirm – or challenge and question – the value and effectiveness of decisions made and actions taken.

Similarly, an analysis of existing approaches or practices could lead to new insights, perspectives, and theories. For example, the development in the early 1990s of a strengths perspective stimulated 'a significant paradigm shift in social work practice as a whole' (Sullivan 2012). In doing so, it posed a challenge to academics and practitioners working from a 'deficit' model, that is, an approach where the focus is placed on people's limitations – as opposed to working with the strengths and attributes that they and others bring to an encounter or work at hand. The ongoing changes taking place in social work's 'increasingly diverse knowledge base' (Reid 2002: 10) mean that gathering the literature available into a *conceptual syntheses* is growing in importance as a way to bring together and to integrate different theories to guide practice priorities and effectiveness. An example of a conceptual synthesis is my *Knowledge and Skills Framework*, which integrates a range of theories and perspectives to provide a coherent map of social work practice.

Formulating hypotheses

Once a referral has been received – or a new problem or situation has emerged – an important feature of the analysis and synthesis undertaken in the assessment process involves formulating hypotheses, sometimes described as 'hypothesis generation' (Sheppard 1995: 275). It is a term that has been defined in a number of ways. For example, Giddens (2001: 691) defines a hypothesis as 'an idea, or an educated guess, about a given state of affairs, put forward as a basis for empirical testing', whereas the Cochrane Collaboration predictably defines hypotheses in research terms as 'unproved theories that can be tested through research'. Thus, hypotheses could be seen in terms of 'informal' theory-making in an attempt to define, explain, and predict certain events to increase our understanding and to act as a basis for action. As such, they are generally formulated at an early point in the intervention process and, for this reason, tend to be based on limited available data or information. For example, in a referral concerning non-attendance at school, we might formulate a variety of hypotheses: that the child is absent from school because he or she is looking after a parent or younger sibling; his or her parents do not have the money to buy essential clothing; he or she may be being bullied; he or she finds the teacher frightening; he or she finds the culture of school bewildering; or that he or she is unwell.

Initial propositions may be described in terms of *working hypotheses*. As further information unfolds, these too are tested in ways that either 'confirm or refute' any testable proposition put forward (Schön 1983: 146). This testing is only possible if hypotheses are clearly specified and articulated. Sheppard summarizes the tasks involved in 'hypothesis generation' as follows: 'Three themes are evident for practice: clear hypotheses, the search for disconfirming data and reformulation of hypothesis or redefinition of problem in the face of disconfirming evidence' (Sheppard 1995: 275). Testing hypotheses in this way is an important feature of Schön's notion of reflection-in-action. The proposition that 'most successfully resists refutation' is the one to be accepted, but tentatively. Other factors, not yet recognized, may come to light that 'resist refutation more successfully still' (Schön 1983: 143). The emphasis placed on verification is consistent with an evidence-based approach, where a focus is placed on identifying the extent to which there is a 'fit' between the hypotheses put forward and the evidence available.

It is important to remember that hypotheses are not error free but tentative proposals that call for sound cognitive and reasoning skills. These skills are needed, for example, to ensure that certain factors are not over- or underestimated and also to avoid giving equal weight to 'all confirming and disconfirming issues, when some may be much more reliable and significant than others' (Eraut 1994: 139). Taylor and White (2006) highlight other concerns. First, there can be a strong commitment to the first hypothesis formulated, or initial 'anchor' hypothesis, which can make it more difficult for practitioners to revise their proposition later. Second, there can be a 'related tendency to seek out evidence that confirms a hypothesis, rather than searching for "disconfirming' evidence"' (Taylor and White 2006: 939). The tendency to fit the facts to the existing hypothesis is known as 'confirmation bias'. For Taylor and White (2006: 939), this problem is 'magnified in relation to social work where there are no reliable diagnostic tests to confirm or disconfirm anchor hypotheses'. It is important to note that hypothesis testing differs from the term *hypothetical questions*, which is an intervention that can be used to encourage an individual to consider new possibilities (see Chapter 6).

Critical thinking

Critical thinking is often linked with the notions of *reflection, critical reflection*, and *reflexivity*, terms that are again described separately in this section to highlight their main features. At the outset, it is important to note that the word 'critical' is not used to suggest criticism or fault-finding but instead to encourage a questioning, challenging, and investigative stance. *Critical thinking* can cover a range of different terms, such as the attributes that are central to the 'critical intellectual' (Gray and Webb 2009: 76) or an 'active thinker' (Sheppard 1998: 767). One of the most important proponents of critical thinking is the American scholar, Eileen Gambrill, who defines it as follows:

> Critical thinking is a unique kind of purposeful thinking in which we use standards such as clarity. Critical thinking involves the careful examination and evaluation of beliefs and actions in order to arrive at well reasoned ones ... Critical thinking involves clearly describing and taking responsibility for our claims and arguments, critically evaluating our views no matter how cherished, and considering alternative views ... This involves paying attention to the process of reasoning (how we think), not just the product.
>
> (Gambrill 1997: 125–6)

To apply critical thinking in this way, we must have acquired sound background knowledge in key areas (Gibbs and Gambrill 1996: 5) so as to be able to recognize and analyse the thoughts, feelings, behaviour, and actions that we encounter and to link these features with other elements within the wider system or environment. Critical thinking involves reviewing the assumptions we may have made prior to becoming involved in a particular event or incident, thinking carefully about the different elements we are able to recognize, and what evidence we have to confirm and disconfirm the tentative explanation or hypothesis we have formulated. It then involves considering carefully the possible consequences of any action taken.

For some authors, critical thinking stands in contrast to the more positivist, 'technical-rational mode of knowledge use' (Taylor and White 2006: 944) because it involves the ability to reason and to think through what decisions and actions to take, as opposed to complying unquestioningly when presented with rule-based, prescriptive procedures that dominate certain areas of social work. As such, it introduces an ideological and political dimension (Fook 2002; Gray and Webb 2009). Gambrill approaches this subject from a different perspective, seeing critical thinking as a way to avoid the 'effects of propaganda' and 'indoctrination', including the indoctrination that can be 'presented as education' (Gambrill 2010: 314). However, the ability to apply this more challenging and questioning stance is not solely dependent on the individual: it requires an environment that is committed to promoting these attributes. Supervision can be an important resource in this area because it offers the opportunity to link critical thinking with practice effectiveness and continuous professional development (Lishman 2009a: 65–7). But even with good supervision and a supportive environment, for some individuals this more questioning and challenging perspective requires a kind of confidence that can be difficult to achieve.

Problem-solving

The extent to which social workers should engage in direct problem-solving, rather than helping individuals to develop their problem-solving abilities, is a complex issue and highly dependent on the context. Similarly, the extent to which our efforts should focus on the wider social issues is another difficult area. Some social failures give rise to certain problems that lie beyond an individual's immediate control and, increasingly, problems and problem-solving in social work are being individualized. This is evident in the tendency for governments to present social problems, such as unemployment or poverty, as 'private troubles' rather than as 'public issues' (Mills 1959) – over which governments have considerable control. To counter this tendency, it is helpful to develop problem-sharing strategies and alliances that unite people who share a common concern.

Our involvement in problem-solving is often more straightforward when problems are well-defined and when agreed solutions can be enacted relatively easily. However, in social work some problems presented tend to be ill-defined. There may be no obvious solution, or require more time, resources, and/or funding that cannot be found. This can lead us to turn 'to tried and tested treatments without attempting to engage in more appropriate problem-solving strategies' (Eraut 1985: 47–8), which, if unsuccessful, can mean that relatively uncomplicated *difficulties* can deteriorate to a point where they become complex or intractable *problems*. Watzlawick and colleagues identify three unhelpful problem-solving actions that are likely to produce negative results:

- 'action is necessary, but is not taken', that is, 'a solution is attempted by denying that a problem is a problem';
- action is taken when it should not be taken, that is, 'change is attempted regarding a difficulty which for all practical purposes is unchangeable ... or nonexistent';

- action is 'taken at the wrong level', that is, action is taken which does not address the problem at the correct level (Watzlawick *et al*. 1974: 39). This may occur if we ask service users to attempt to resolve a problem for which they are ill-prepared, perhaps because they lack appropriate skills or confidence or because they are frightened.

Watzlawick *et al*. distinguish between two types of change: 'one that occurs within a given system which itself remains unchanged, and one whose occurrence changes the system itself' (1974: 10). Too often we opt for changing the person and not the system – a point looked at later in the coverage of organizational learning loops.

Persistent, unhelpful problem-solving actions can leave people feeling demoralized and defeated and can result in states of learned helplessness (Seligman 1975). One way to avert this kind of deterioration involves understanding the relationship between what is expected in terms of skills and ability to perform a particular task and a person's emotional and practical capacity to achieve this. This calls for empathy – the ability to understand the problem being faced from another person's point of view. We cannot know everything, and events can change quickly, but from this standpoint it should become possible to identify whether the individual in question has the capacity to problem-solve independently or with the help of others and, if not, for decisions to be made about how best to approach the problem(s) presented. One of the difficulties here is that time constraints can sometimes make it easier to undertake the problem-solving ourselves, thereby running the risk of creating an unhealthy dependency. Taking action on the behalf of others can also lead to us denying the opportunity for people to learn about themselves and the world around them through their problem-solving efforts. Of course, these points are not relevant where individuals are struggling with some form of difficulty or impairment that hinders their capacity to act on their own behalf, and it is crucial that the position taken up is not so 'hands-off' that people feel abandoned. These decisions are complex and call for sound and sensitive appraisal and analysis of the different factors involved, both personal and political.

An important starting point when helping people to problem-solve is to gather adequate information on the nature of the problem and to review what solutions have already been tried and with what success. This can identify the depth of the problem and the extent to which personal, social, and political barriers inhibit the chance of resolution. This exploration also offers the opportunity to 'get alongside' the individual and the problem being faced and may involve teaching new skills. A different approach involves dividing the problem into manageable 'bits'. Here it is important that the different 'bits' or manageable parts are achievable or solvable and that the person in question is actively involved in breaking the problem down and deciding how each 'bit' should be ordered and addressed. This approach is particularly important where an individual is clearly emotionally overwhelmed and demoralized by the weight and sheer number of problems that have to be 'sorted out' or 'dealt with'. When people become 'problem-saturated' in this way it is important to recognize this fact, which Saleebey notes as follows:

> First, it is incumbent on the practitioner to provide the words and images of strength, wholeness, and capacity where they may be lacking. Second, it is important for the practitioner to be an affirmative mirror, beaming back to the client a reflection of that person's positive attributes, accomplishments, skills, and talents. Last, it is wise to carefully lay out with an individual what may be possible in his or her life – big or small things, it doesn't matter. And all of this must ring true to the person and be grounded in the dailiness of life.
>
> (Saleebey 2006: 89)

This compassionate and humane comment from Saleebey serves to remind us of the emotional burden that some people face in relation to the problems they encounter. Our role can be crucial in supporting people and teaching new skills.

Judicious decision-making skills

A central feature when formulating hypotheses, unpicking (analysing) and bringing together (synthesizing) different features or evidence is the ability to make professional judgements and to arrive at well thought through decisions. For Eraut, a *professional judgement* is defined in terms of 'practical wisdom, a sense of purpose, appropriateness and feasibility' (1994: 49). It involves the balanced interpretation of different features in ways that enable a position to be reached. In a similar vein, *decision-making* is defined as the conclusion reached, or the opinion, judgement, or position adopted, after careful and reasoned consideration of the different factors involved. In recent years, considerable criticism has been levelled at the quality and effectiveness of social workers' judgements and decision-making skills. In this regard, critical thinking, critical reflection/reflexivity provide an important opportunity to review our judgements and decision-making processes, and to learn from our experiences – both positive and negative. A feature of this reflective process involves finding ways to overcome barriers that block judicious decision-making, such as time constraints or limited resources. In most of the situations we encounter, we are required to make decisions on the best available evidence at that time (Nevo and Slonim-Nevo 2011), which, by necessity, is most often based on 'imperfect knowledge' (Munro 1996: 793–4).

It is generally agreed that the implementation of a decision is likely to be much more successful where the recipient of that decision has been directly involved in its formulation and action strategy. Beresford and Croft take up this point in relation to service users:

User participation implies active involvement in the social sphere and refers to a range of involvements which individuals and groups may have in organizations, institutions and decisions affecting them and others. These extend from having control to being a source of information or legitimation. Participation is crucially judged by the extent to which people can exert influence and bring about change.

(Beresford and Croft 2000: 355)

As well as having practical benefits, participatory approaches in decision-making embody a higher moral and ethical commitment to the principle of social justice and human rights, often described in terms of social work values or 'emancipatory practices'. These acknowledge the inequalities that exist in terms of status and power and the importance of challenging those factors that impact on people's sense of worth and well-being. In the next section, the vulnerability to error in social work is examined in two key areas: individual error and organizational error in decision-making.

Vulnerability to error

Individual errors and omissions

Reason (1997, cited in Munro 2010a: 1141) distinguishes between 'active' errors, that is, actions taken or avoided by practitioners that contribute to adverse outcomes, and 'latent' conditions, which describe structural and organizational features that impact on decision-making, such as policy priorities, resources, etc., which 'create conditions in which error is more or less likely' (Munro 2010a: 1141). Irrespective of our experience and status, Gambrill (2010: 29) reminds us that 'we are vulnerable to a variety of cognitive biases that may lead us astray'. For example, Munro cites a research project that looked at decision-making in child protection in relation to 45 inquiry reports into the deaths of children known to social services. Munro (1996: 793) found 'one persistent error: social workers are slow to revise their judgements'. This could indicate a lack of intellectual rigour and critical thinking and reflection or, as stated earlier, a failure to question the initial position adopted or 'anchor' hypothesis (Taylor and White 2006: 939). A linked failing is the desire to make 'certainty out of uncertainty', which refers to a tendency for some social workers to make 'early and certain judgements' (Taylor and White 2006: 937) when a position of 'respectful uncertainty' (Laming 2003: 2005) might be more appropriate. The kind of errors that I have tended to make as a social worker include giving too much weight to the views of people of a higher professional status, such as doctors and also senior managers, and being caught up in *groupthink* (Janis 1982), that is, the desire to avoid conflict and to comply – or to 'go with the tide' – in ways that fail to question the assumptions or the quality of the decisions being made. Also, in situations where my knowledge of a particular subject is limited, I am more likely to be thrown off guard and to fail to question the views of someone who appears to be knowledgeable or who asserts their views forcefully. I am seriously at a loss when research findings are cited in support of a position, particularly if the findings are complex and difficult to understand.

Organizational errors

It is essential to recognize how the culture and priorities of an organization can hinder judicious decision-making. Decisions in the real world – and also in the world of practice – are made in a context where complexity, uncertainty, and risk abound. In an attempt to control or to manage these insecurities, a range of measures have been introduced, such as checklist and other rule-based procedures, based on the untested assumption that these measures will improve – or at least regulate and standardize – the quality of service provision. In some situations, the measures have been appropriate and helpful, particularly for problems that are quite simple and correctable. However, a standardized, one-size-fits-all approach to service provision can never meet the different needs and concerns that are presented in social work. This approach has created a situation where meeting performance targets has been prioritized over meeting the problems that service users present, and has been shown to limit the range of options and choices open to practitioners in terms of what it is possible to achieve. The most obvious and recent example of what I have termed organizational errors is evident in the criticisms that have been raised in relation to the Integrated Children's System, mentioned in Chapter 3, a criticism summarized in the following quotation from the Laming Report:

> Professional practice and judgement, as said by many who contributed evidence to this report, are being compromised by an over-complicated, lengthy and tick-box assessment and recording system. The direct interaction and engagement with children and their families, which is at the core of social work, is said to be at risk as the needs of a work management tool overtake those of evidence-based assessment, sound analysis and professional judgement about risk of harm.
>
> (Laming 2009: 33)

What was evident in the Laming Report was an organizational inability, within the organizations concerned, to identify and correct the administrative and technological errors, such as the limitations evident in the operation of the Integrated Children's System. For Munro (2010a: 1141), this indicated the absence of good feedback loops and 'a bias towards single, not double-loop learning'. That is, when problems emerge, the initial action adopted in organizations is to look for an alternative strategy that will work and to ignore the underlying cause of the problem. This is termed *single-loop learning*. *Double-loop learning* takes place when errors are detected and corrected in ways that lead to changes in the organizational structure, policies, objectives, and assumptions. The failure of organizations to address the cause of an error, and the context in which it occurs, can reinforce 'the tendency to consider the error was avoidable and to blame the individual' (Munro 2010a: 1146).

This point about the extent to which child deaths can be avoided is important because the findings of public inquiries and serious case reviews suggest that some tragedies are predictable and, therefore, preventable – but for others, this is often not the case (Devaney *et al.* 2011; Sidebotham *et al.* 2008). For example, in an analysis of 161 serious case reviews, dated from 2003 to 2005, it was concluded that the majority of cases studied were 'essentially unpredictable' (Brandon *et al.* 2008: 7). However, in most reviews there were numerous childhood adversities and difficulties that were not known to practitioners – issues that could have 'aided professionals' understanding of the children's circumstances' (Brandon *et al.* 2008: 7). It is also important to note before leaving this subject that not all decisions involve decision-making errors. For example, in 42 per cent of 45 inquiry reports mentioned earlier, social workers were not criticized (Munro 1996: 793). Nevertheless, for many practitioners the changes introduced in social work in recent years have not laid the foundations for decision-making to be based on 'wise judgement under conditions of considerable uncertainty' (Eraut 1994: 17).

Knowledge creation

This second sub-heading of the *practice knowledge* domain explores several terms that describe the more creative forms of knowledge used in everyday social work practice. These concepts, which include the *professional use of self*, *intuition*, *tacit knowledge*, *transferability*, and *practice wisdom*, describe a type of knowledge that is less formal, abstract, and rule based than the 'technical-rational decision pathways' (Schön 1983: 338). Essentially, these terms describes those occasions when it is necessary to leave the territory of what we think we know, in order to enter the territory of the unknown. While it remains true that knowledge *use* and knowledge *creation* overlap and interweave and cannot be easily separated out, it is also clear

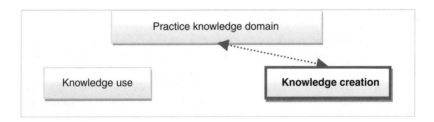

Figure 4.4 Knowledge creation

that in some areas the creative features of social work are more evident and, to emphasize this difference, the terms listed above are allocated under this 'creative' heading.

Creativity

This section highlights the creative and imaginative ways in which social workers have approached their work. A starting point is to state that 'the interpretive use of a new idea in a new context' constitutes an example of an action that is creative; that is, practice knowledge is *created* when 'knowledge is developed by practitioners "solving" individual cases and problems' (Eraut 1994: 54). The unpredictable nature of the work is evident when we knock on a service user's door. From the moment the door is opened, we have to make on-the-spot, speedy judgements about what to do – what response to make and what actions to take – and these decisions are determined by what we encounter. It is a situation that calls for a repertoire of skills and interventions that can be adjusted, often intuitively, to respond appropriately 'to a more or less infinite range of circumstances' (Lymbery 2003: 105). It indicates the uniqueness of every encounter. We may have a tentative frame of reference to work from but this cannot be imposed on the situation without producing a routinized or mechanical response. Such an imposition could easily jeopardize the two-way nature of every communication, and the meaning that is embedded in the encounter. It is the subtle, unfamiliar, and complex nature of this interaction that lies at the heart of the creative practice – a creativity, artistry, or 'art', where the 'art is in the practice skill' (England 1986: 89). Clark eloquently takes up this point, linking 'the rules of basic knowledge and the creative arts of practice':

> . . . it is the qualities of creativity and imagination which enable solutions to be sought for unfamiliar, complex and subtle problems. But this creativity and imagination must be formed by a deep understanding of a logic and method of enquiry, and must be disciplined by the internalized understanding of the procedures for making investigations and checking conclusions. It is accurate to call this a discipline, both in the purely academic context and in wider sense of self-chosen adherence to a philosophy for pursuing understanding.
>
> (Clark 1995: 578)

There are numerous other examples of the creative way that practitioners approach their work. For example, as fieldworkers in a run-down neighbourhood, my colleagues and I had regular meetings with local councillors, largely initiated by the local MP (Labour Party), who insisted on regular briefings about what was happening 'on the ground'. On these occasions we mainly discussed how local officials, in particular benefit and housing personnel, were treating service users. Occasionally, the councillors raised issues with the appropriate department. One locality team where I worked had set up a charity some years earlier. Its purpose was to pay for one-off expenditure for service users and carers, such as travel costs, children's shoes and clothing that could not be met by our agency or the charities that we regularly approached. As a staff group, we all contributed to this charity by setting up and attending discos, sponsored walks, etc., and made decisions collectively in response to applications for funding. Similarly, I once worked in a very poor area where problems associated with poverty were an ongoing concern but largely not discussed openly, mainly because of the feelings of shame and sense of personal blame that often runs with 'being poor'. Our response as a team was to set up a group called *Money Matters*. Its purpose was to attempt to find new and different ways to help people to make ends meet, and also to provide an opportunity for people to come together and to share their feelings about poverty and its impact. Two initiatives that emerged involved a group of boys setting up a car washing service and a group of women running a small household cleaning service, both of which were offered in middle-class areas of the city. Crucially, the emotional benefits of attending this group were enormous.

Professional use of self

The *professional use of self* is a term that describes the use of self-knowledge or self-awareness in professional practice to aid understanding and action. It is a term that has been described in a number of ways: as the 'positive use of self', 'self-understanding' (Coulshed and Orme 2006: 108), 'intuitive use of self' (England 1986), or simply as the 'use of self' (Howe 2009: 159). How we are constructed by our social environment – and construct ourselves – is shaped by our earlier experiences, particularly the extent to which our unique 'selfhood' has been allowed to flourish (Frost 2008), a perspective that links to Maslow's (1954) concept of *self-actualization* or Carl Rogers' (1961) *actualizing tendency*. Shulman emphasizes the importance of self-knowledge in relation to our capacity to understand others:

> The capacity to be in touch with the service user's feelings is related to the worker's ability to acknowledge his or her own. Before a worker can understand the power of emotions in the life of the client, it is necessary to discover its importance in the worker's own experience.
> (Shulman 1999: 156)

On the one hand, the term *self-knowledge* describes the extent to which we understand ourselves – how we behave and come across to other people. It includes what we know to be our strengths and limitations. On the other hand, *self-awareness* describes how we use this self-knowledge in the service of others, particularly in relation to our ability 'to engage effectively with others who are different', which is a central feature of anti-oppressive practice (Dominelli 2009: 49–64). In the emphasis I propose, the professional use of self is underpinned by our ability to be open and available in how we relate to other people. It describes the capacity to become involved but not merged with service users and to be sensitive, reflective, and intuitive about the verbal and non-verbal communication taking place. It is about allowing ourselves to be affected by the experiences and hardships that people face in ways that move us. In the case of injustice, it can encourage an appropriate *healthy sense of outrage*, which can propel us in our efforts to help bring about change. In emotionally fraught situations, our self-awareness can guide us to take up an appropriate position of separateness, while also maintaining a clear connection to service users, so that we are not too distant or inflexible on the one hand, nor too merged or inappropriately accommodating on the other. It can act as a litmus test that helps to ensure that we do not slip into a need to 'rescue' people (Karpman 1968), perhaps by taking on too much responsibility or promising more than we can deliver.

As stated earlier, every encounter with another human being offers the opportunity for us to be changed by the experience but often there can be a tendency to hold back from really engaging in this way and, as a result, we limit the possibilities that the encounter can offer. It is a point of contact that has both conscious and unconscious dimensions – features that cannot be measured in terms of targets. In one way or another, we are always communicating who we are – our 'moral identity' and the personal qualities that we bring to the situation. For McBeath and Webb (2002: 1030), this links to the notion of 'virtues', where 'virtues connect the inner self to action; they set the baseline as to what we should not do'. This moral perspective is taken up by Kelly and Horder:

> In a world of continuing poverty, oppression and abuse, our society needs to hold onto the possibility that individuals and families can receive personal services characterized by knowledge and skills but also by integrity and creativity. Future social work education needs to be designed with this in mind.
>
> (Kelly and Horder 2001: 698)

It is a subject that links directly to the importance of critical reflection/reflexivity, covered earlier in this section, and also to our capacity for empathy, mutuality, and reciprocity. Self-knowledge is not always easy to acquire because it involves that capacity to tell ourselves the truth. We may only begin to know the limits of our self-awareness when presented with problems that trigger reactions inappropriate to the situation. For example, we may feel we have come to terms with childhood experiences of rejection until we encounter a service user who is deeply rejecting of us, and we find ourselves shaken unexpectedly by our reactions. Once we realize our vulnerability, we have a professional responsibility to attend to these unresolved emotions so that we can continue with the work at hand. Our personal commitment to *sort out* and *work through* these personal dilemmas can lead to new insights that can be used later to help others. Unless we do this, we are for ever vulnerable to falling into pockets of distress 'that lead to inattention, poor listening and inappropriate responses and actions' (Lishman: 2009a: 93). Two important examples of the professional use of self can be found in our capacity to create and maintain *professional boundaries* and the *judicious use of self-disclosure* – two skills covered in Part 2 of this text.

Intuition

Like other themes covered in this chapter, intuition has been described in a number of different ways: as a 'persistent mystery' and a 'puzzle' (England 1986), as 'gut feelings' or 'hunches', and as 'semi-conscious' (Broudy *et al.* 1964). The following account looks at its main features and the difficulties that the use of an intuitive approach embodies. Intuition is used in this text to describe the emotional exchange that occurs between people where explicit conscious reasoning is not evident. It is mainly used to describe the ability to pick up or sense the unspoken thoughts and feelings of others in ways that aid understanding. Munro unpicks the mysterious quality of intuition:

> It is only mysterious in the sense that it is generally an unconscious process that occurs automatically in response to perceptions, integrating a wide range of data to produce a judgement in a relatively effortless way. It is very rapid and relatively independent of language, oriented towards identifying patterns. It need not remain unconscious but can be articulated and this ability can be improved with practice. Supervision of casework typically involves helping practitioners draw out their reasoning so that it can be reviewed.
>
> (Munro 2008: 10)

In addition to the understanding gathered through self-awareness, the ability to be intuitive is linked to the importance of empathy and emotional intelligence (Goleman 1996: 2009), and is also linked to the concepts of *transference* and *counter-transference* (Koprowska 2010; Lishman 2009a; Wilson *et al.* 2008) – all of which are covered later. Like the human qualities of empathy, warmth, care, and concern, I do not believe it is possible to teach people how to be intuitive. However, being able to identify our intuitive abilities is important – as England notes, 'there will always be people who have an unusually developed yet untrained ability to understand others and to act upon that understanding. Social work can only be distinct because of the *reliability* with which its workers master such an unusually developed understanding' (England 1986: 32–4).

Like other attributes, there are occasions when the capacity to be intuitive is less pronounced, such as when practitioners are stressed, exhausted, feel 'put down', or preoccupied with other concerns. In other words, environmental factors can inhibit or enhance the capacity for practitioners to be intuitive. This calls for an employment culture that recognizes the contribution that such an emotionally based form of reasoning can make. Yet it is important to note that the emotions involved can be elusive and difficult to identify, a situation that is most evident when social workers have been traumatized by events. Painful and confusing feelings of this kind make it essential for emotions to be unravelled by creating a culture that encourages practitioners to talk openly with colleagues and supervisors about their own and others' emotional state and the 'baggage' they are carrying. Without opportunities of this kind, it is possible for practitioners' capacity to reason to be adversely affected and vital clues to be missed, or for practitioners to operate from an unquestioning confidence about their intuitive 'hunches' without these impressions being supported by 'hard facts' or different types of evidence. Until our intuition can be clarified in this way, our thoughts, hunches, instinctive reactions, impressions, associations, insights, impulses, or sheer guesswork must be considered as hypotheses (tentative propositions) or as possible indicators (a sign, warning, or a pointer to a particular direction, event, or outcome). It is a process that integrates different forms of knowledge, including intuitive and 'practical reasoning, emotion and, most of all, an intelligence that is disciplined and creative' (Taylor and White 2006: 950).

Case example: Bea

The following example is drawn from my experience as a social worker. It describes a group that I once set up for 8- to 10-year-old girls who were encountering serious difficulties at home and vulnerable to being brought into care. One member of the group, Bea, displayed particularly disturbing behaviour. She seemed oblivious to the social conventions and uninhibited in relation to when and where to physically touch other girls, and she was bewildered yet seemingly unaffected by the hostility that her behaviour provoked in the other girls. This situation was made more complex because Bea had been assessed as having mild learning difficulties and it was not always clear whether she fully understood what was being communicated.

One night, after the group, I was asked to drop Bea home because her social worker was unwell. As we drove nearer to her house, Bea started to become more agitated and quite bizarre in her behaviour. Her father was waiting at the door, frowning with arms crossed. We arrived late and as I moved to get out of the car to offer my apologies, Bea began to panic. She hurriedly gathered her belongings together, and insisted that I drove off immediately. I did as asked but on my way home I felt deeply confused and concerned about Bea's reaction. I felt frightened and felt that I had picked up this fear from Bea. The following day I mentioned this to her social worker who reassured me that Bea was 'always like that' and that the behaviour I had witnessed was quite 'normal for Bea'. Apparently, her father had a profound mistrust and dislike of social workers and the agreement was that Bea could attend the group on the proviso that this did not involve having any contact with social services or the group leaders.

Bea never found her way to the group again. Over the weeks and months that followed, I continued to feel concerned and encountered the same reassurance from her social worker that she was fine. Several months passed until it came to light that Bea's 16-year-old sister was expecting a baby by her father. A careful police investigation led to questions being raised about Bea's relationship with her father. In time, it came to light that both Bea and her sister had been physically and sexually abused for some time, not only by their father but by other men he invited into the home. Bea and her sister were both received into care and the father sent to prison.

I learned a great deal from my contact with Bea in the girl's group but I learned almost as much from my brief but fraught encounter with her father when I dropped her off home. For example, I learned the importance of trusting my intuition but also how difficult this can be when such concerns are not shared by others and when concrete evidence is not forthcoming. I also learned that attempting to differentiate between learning difficulties and the effect of sexual and physical abuse on children can be a complex and difficult undertaking, and a situation in which the clues that children may send out can easily be ignored if their disturbed or distressed behaviour is interpreted solely in terms of their learning difficulties. Children who live in fear can develop extraordinary strategies to survive. Bea's worrying compliance and desire to please adults should have alerted me to the fact that she felt unsafe. This was constantly evident when asked a question or to do something, when she would respond as if trying to read my mind – as if somewhere at the back of my head was the answer to what she should do – and she needed to find what the answer was before she felt confident to act or to offer a response. Howe takes up this point in relation to disabled children, but the following quotation also describes a behaviour that I have encountered in non-disabled children and young people:

> With carers who are unavailable and frightening, children begin to take control of their own safety and needs. This results in various *controlling* strategies, including compulsive compliance, compulsive care-giving and compulsive self-reliance (Crittenden, 1997). These are very partial, incomplete and brittle strategies which quickly break down under stress, leaving the child once more frightened, angry, sad . . .
> (Howe 2006: 746)

I have focused in some detail on the coverage of intuition because it is an attribute that has tended to become lost, for as Munro (2011a: 35) notes, 'previous reforms have concentrated too much on the explicit, logical aspects of reasoning and this has contributed to a skewed management framework that undervalues intuitive reasoning and emotions and thus fails to give appropriate support to those aspects'. It is an attribute that is often linked with the concept of tacit knowledge, which I now explore.

Tacit knowledge

If intuition is considered somewhat mysterious, so too is the concept of *tacit knowledge*, a term coined by Polanyi (1967) to describe the fact that it is possible for people to know – or to infer – more than they can sometimes say or identify. Schön takes up this point:

> In my analysis of these cases, I begin with the assumption that competent practitioners usually know more than they can say. They exhibit a kind of knowing in practice, most of which is tacit.
>
> (Schön 1983: viii)

The theoretical or factual knowledge described in this text would be classified as explicit types of knowledge, whereas tacit knowledge refers to implicit forms of knowledge, that is, 'knowledge gained from watching what colleagues do, trial and error, reflective practice, peer approval, client satisfaction and so on' (Pawson *et al.* 2003: 11). Eraut also suggests that at least some of the components of tacit knowledge can be acquired through experience and through watching the work of others:

> *Working alongside others* allows people to observe and listen to others at work and to participate in activities; and hence to learn some new practices and new perspectives, to become aware of different kinds of knowledge and expertise, and to gain some sense of other people's tacit knowledge. This mode of learning, which includes a lot of observation as well as discussion, is extremely important for learning the tacit knowledge that underpins routines and intuitive decisions and is difficult to explain.
>
> (Eraut 2008: 19)

A different conceptualization describes tacit knowledge in terms of 'unconscious knowing', that is, 'the key educational message is that practice can be informed by both explicit (consciously aware) and tacit (implied, unconscious) knowledge' (Osmond 2005: 884). The example given is the awareness we have of non-verbal behaviour. However, I consider it unhelpful and inaccurate to consider the non-verbal behaviour that we pick up as being an aspect of *unconscious knowing*. A psychodynamic definition of the unconscious refers to an aspect of the mind that is not directly accessible and not part of our awareness. For tacit knowledge to be viewed as unconscious locates what is happening outside of our capacity to know and to recall events and their features (John and Trevithick 2012). If a psychodynamic concept has to be deployed – and I would argue that tacit knowledge need not be conceptualized in this way – then this form of remembering lies in the realm of the *pre-conscious*, which is where memories are located and thus what is happening can be recalled, though often only with help.

Clearly, we cannot put into words all the thoughts, feelings, and sensations that we accumulate in our work and, when communicating with others, there will always be certain aspects that are elusive. However, where these elusive features inform our decision-making, it is important to try to identify what might be obscured by the phrase 'we know more than we can say'. Some intangible and obscure issues that we pick up should be 'amenable to investigation and explanation through various methods' (Gould 2006: 119), particularly through being reflective and through discussion with colleagues and supervisors (Munro 2011a: 53). In the meantime, we may need to live with the conundrum that tacit knowledge 'has not been, and may never be, clearly articulated' (Eraut 1994: 18).

Transferability of knowledge, skills, and values

The importance given to the transferability of knowledge and skills can be seen in the fact that it is mentioned in the three guidance documents governing UK social work education and training (GSCC 2002; QAA 2008; TOPSS 2002). Transferability involves 'applying knowledge from past situations, in order to practise effectively in new situations' (Fook 2002: 145). In the United States, the subject of transferability is sometimes called 'translation skills' and can involve having to 'borrow' or 'to translate concepts from one discipline to another' (Gambrill 1997: 173).

In my earlier writing on this subject, I stated that for 'knowledge and skills to be transferable, they have to be related to a sound knowledge base and an understanding of human beings in their particular social contexts' (Trevithick 2008: 1231). It is a process that involves pattern recognition, that is, analysing and identifying those features that are unique to a particular situation and those features that can be generalized, and relating these to theory. When similar features are identified in a new situation, these generalized theories can then be related and tested for their accuracy and relevance. It is an analysis that calls for a sound understanding of – and ability to draw on – theoretical and factual knowledge, including an understanding of the immediate and wider systems that impact people's everyday lives.

This transition can be seen in three ways. First, it describes what we 'borrow' from other disciplines – a borrowing that I have described in detail in Chapter 2. Second, it describes the way that different subjects that have been taught on social work training courses are related to the situations that are commonly encountered in practice. A third feature of transferability describes the ability to relate the learning that has been acquired in one context or situation to a new and different situation that we encounter in our work. The task of analysing what is unique and general in each situation is a life-long learning process but I have argued in earlier chapters that the failure to integrate knowledge, skills, and values into a coherent practice framework or map of practice has hindered theory development in relation to the transferability of expertise. The following account looks at how the concept of transferability is evident in the areas of knowledge, skills, and values.

Transferability of knowledge

The transferability of knowledge identifies how different theories can be related to different fields of exploration. For example, if we explore the particular features of lifespan theory, it is possible to see how this theory can be applied to the continuities and discontinuities that exist within the growth process for children, young people, middle-aged people, and so forth. However, other theories tend to be less straightforward. For example, some years ago I was involved in transferring and adapting the writing of Winnicott to my work with women suffering from depression. I was guided in this task by my supervisor at that time, Barbara Dockar-Drysdale, but even with a sound theory base and good supervision, it took some time – and considerable trial and error – before my colleagues and I were able to transfer knowledge in ways that enabled the development of a practice approach that was appropriate for the women who sought our help (Trevithick 1993, 1995, 1998). From this example, it is clear that the transfer of knowledge from one situation to another is not always as straightforward as is sometimes implied (Matthews *et al.* 2003). This is particularly true in relation to professional services that are located in different disciplines and in different work contexts. For example, professional services that are located in clinical settings, perhaps where only one problem is the focus, differ markedly from the contexts found in social work. An example is the use of cognitive-behavioural approaches for depression where, for the most part, those aspects of the problem that relate to wider social issues, sometimes involving variables that cannot always be controlled, do not form part of the 'treatment' or approach on offer.

Transferability of skills

It is often social work skills that are referred to in much of the coverage on transferability. Here again, for skills to be reliable and enduring across different – and sometimes difficult – situations, and to be used with a degree of accuracy and efficiency, they have to be related to a sound theory base. In this task, the actions taken have to be related to individual clients and not just routine behaviour (Parsloe 1988: 8). The point to be stressed is that the transferability of skills is an intellectual activity, as well as a practical one. For example, skills and interventions cannot be transferred if they have not yet been named, which is an intellectual activity. Or again, when confronted with complex human behaviour, such as an encounter with someone who is being aggressive, it is important to have a body of knowledge and repertoire of skills and interventions to draw on to help us to understand and to respond appropriately. Linking our knowledge to practice in this way means that both are constantly in dialogue, each informing the other in ways that 'invigorate, fascinate and professionally uplift' (Howe 2002: 87). A further account of the transferability of skills is given in Chapter 7.

Transferability of social work values

What is often missing in the coverage of transferability is the extent to which it includes social work values – again, a phrase that resists 'satisfactory definition' (Clark 2000a: 26). Values are most commonly described in terms of the attitudes – the personal qualities and 'moral character' that practitioners adopt in their everyday contact with people: 'it is worth reasserting that good professional practice is not sufficiently described either by technical competence or by grand ethical principle; it also subsists essentially in the moral character of the practitioner' (Clark 2006a: 88).

The general and transferable features of this commitment indicate an adherence to 'the broad general principles of liberal rights' and also include the 'moral standards and cultural values' that are communicated in work with service users and others (Clark 2006a: 85). Thus, a values perspective embodies a professional commitment to provide services that promote the equal treatment of all people, based on a recognition of 'the impact of injustice, social inequalities and oppressive social relations' (QAA 2008: 7). When working with people who experience discrimination, the capacity to communicate 'a respect for the equality, worth, and dignity of all people' (IFSW/IASSW 2000) constitutes a particularly important attribute. Social work values tend to embody a range of beliefs about the kind of practice we consider appropriate and the attitudes that we wish to promote in society as a whole, including 'general beliefs about the nature of a good society, general principles about how to achieve this through actions and the desirable qualities and character traits of professional practitioners' (Banks 2006: 7).

Practice wisdom

Practice wisdom is an elusive term and one that has been described in a number of ways. For example, O'Sullivan notes how practice wisdom is presented in terms of two contrasting images, that is, 'as unreliable, personal, idiosyncratic knowledge built up through practice experience and ... as the ability to make sound judgements in difficult, complex and uncertain situations' (2005: 222). Where most practitioners would locate themselves along this spectrum of contrasting images is largely not known, but the picture is likely to be uneven, partly due to practitioners' individual practice orientation and also because of the culture of the organization or agency. O'Sullivan comes down on the side of practice wisdom as 'the capacity for reflective judgement, and the associated flexible and creative use of knowledge' but, importantly, goes on to state that 'practice experience alone is unlikely to be enough to gain practice wisdom' (O'Sullivan 2005: 239). From a different perspective, the conceptualization of practice wisdom put forward by Klein and Bloom (1995) attempts to merge 'phenomenological experience' with 'scientific information' (p. 799) and also to incorporate a strong values component, which serves 'as rules to translate empirical knowledge, prior experience, and other forms of knowing into present professional actions' (p. 801). In my experience, it is the absence of 'rules' that makes practice wisdom an attractive concept among practitioners. Sheppard offers a less prescriptive and wider view of the different sources of knowledge that make up practice wisdom:

> Practice wisdom may be defined, for our purposes, as the accumulated knowledge practitioners are able to bring to the consideration of individual cases and their practice in general. This would appear to have three main and distinct potential sources: knowledge gained from 'everyday life', derived from the process of living in society and interaction with others; knowledge gained from social science, specifically research and ideas; and knowledge gained from the conduct of social work practice.
>
> (Sheppard 1995: 279)

The three features of practice wisdom indicated by Sheppard are covered in this chapter under the earlier headings of *personal knowledge* and *professional knowledge*. Coverage of 'knowledge gained from social science' is a theme covered in detail in Chapter 2 on Theoretical Knowledge.

Pattern recognition

Many of the terms described in this chapter rely on *pattern recognition*, described by Eraut as *semi-conscious patterning* or *generalizing*. This describes the way we remember, recognize, and draw on previous personal and practice experience to guide decision-making and action:

> The effectiveness of most professionals is largely dependent on the knowledge and know-how they bring to each individual case, problem or brief. Much of this knowledge comes from experience with previous cases, so its use involves a process of generalization. Some idea, procedure or action that was used in a previous situation is considered to be applicable to the new one. While most of the previous cases scanned for this purpose are likely to be from the professional's own experience, some may be known only through the reporting of other people's experiences (formally in the literature or on courses, or informally via colleagues or social networks) . . . Semi-conscious patterning of previous experience may also occur, making it difficult for the professional to trace the source of, or even to clearly articulate, the generalization he is using.
>
> (Eraut 1994: 44)

The extent to which experiences can be generalized varies greatly, but the concept of *pattern recognition* can often help to illuminate the thoughts, feelings, impressions, or sensations that guide particular actions. Citing the work of Benner (1984) and Dreyfus and Dreyfus (1986), Gould and Kendall (2007: 487) suggest that *pattern recognition* or 'scenario recognition' are likely to become an integrated feature of practice when social workers become more expert and begin to move away from a reliance on explicit, evidence-based rules in favour of a more intuitive form of practice. The notion of pattern recognition links to my earlier definition of *transferability* where I add the importance of relating general features to theory in order to identify and analyse their relevance in other contexts.

This chapter has explored a number of different practice terms: analysis and synthesis; forming hypotheses; critical thinking; problem-solving and judicious decision-making; professional use of self, intuition, tacit knowledge, transferability, and practice wisdom. What is clearly evident is the difficulty encountered when trying to separate out knowledge use from knowledge creation and, for this reason, it could be argued that no distinction should be made. The rationale for attempting to do so is to highlight the fact that social work practice can be undertaken at many different levels depending on the context, the orientation of the social worker, the service user, and the problem or difficulty presented. The tendency to constrain social work practice within routines and targets fails to address the fact that a great number of the situations that regularly occur cannot be predicted – nor can many of the variables that impact on the effectiveness of our work be controlled, such as the impact of poverty, homelessness, alcohol, or drug misuse. Therefore, the opportunity to employ a more flexible, adaptive, imaginative, and creative practice approach is essential, not least because it is an approach that ensures practice effectiveness by locating the needs and best interests of service users and carers at the centre of social work practice (Trevithick 2012a).

From my coverage of knowledge *use* and *creation* in this chapter, I consider the argument that practitioners do not use theory to be less and less convincing – and particularly so if we take the definition of theory as being an attempt to 'explain a particular phenomenon' (Barker 2003: 434), as indicated in Chapter 2. The following quotation from Clark on the use of theory in relation to the knowledge that practitioners apply in practice provides a helpful summary of this topic:

> Despite the importance attached, at least by educators, to the learning of theory, most of the previous research appeared to suggest that if social workers do use theory, they are seldom aware of it and hardly ever able to cite it explicitly. However, given the subtlety and complexity of many tasks in social welfare practice, it seemed quite unsatisfactory to conclude that practitioners do not theorise.
>
> (Clark 1995: 570)

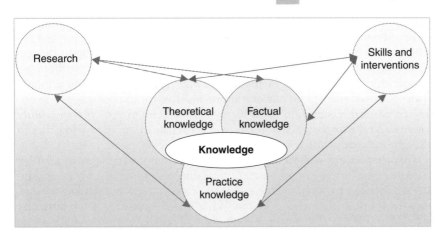

Figure 4.5   Three overlapping domains of knowledge

In this third and final section of my *Knowledge and Skills Framework*, it seems fitting to end this chapter on the *Practice Knowledge* domain with Figure 4.5, where the interrelated features of this triangular relationship are highlighted. All areas of knowledge are represented as influencing – and being influenced by – research. Similarly, interventions – as knowledge, skills, and values in action – are represented as being shaped and informed by knowledge and, in turn, influence all areas of practice.

5 UNDERSTANDING HUMAN BEINGS

Introduction

This chapter provides a brief overview of some of the main theories that are relevant and useful in contemporary social work. It is not my purpose to sketch a comprehensive review of different psychological theories but to provide a foundation from which to begin to raise key questions that are important to social work. Why, for example, do people behave in certain ways, sometimes becoming 'stuck' or locked into 'self-destructive scripts' (England 1986: 16)? What enables people to keep going, sometimes in the face of extreme adversity or demoralizing experiences (Howe *et al.* 1999: 30)? How do these experiences differ, if at all, for people who carry additional oppressions because of their gender, race, class, age, disability, sexual preference, culture, religion, and/or health. Above all, how can we effectively help people to address the concerns they present so that they can begin to move forward?

Many of the concepts described in this chapter are based on the belief that emotional development is a continuous process, and that the capacity to develop – to learn, grow, and change – is present in human beings throughout their lives (unless there are biological and neurological conditions to impede this process). The theories outlined here also seek to address a complex issue, that is, to identify the factors – environmental and internal to the individual – that influence the possibilities for growth and development. The study of the 'life-long process of change' (Reber *et al.* 2009: 212) is usually undertaken within the discipline of developmental psychology. However, this term is often taken to refer to child psychology, rather than an investigation of human development throughout the whole of life from the cradle to the grave. Within this discipline, two major fields of investigation have emerged: stage theory and lifespan developmental psychology.

- *Stage theory*. Some examples include: Freud's stages of psychosexual development; Maslow's hierarchy of needs; Erikson's eight stages of man (Erikson's work is also described as belonging to lifespan developmental psychology); Piaget's stages of cognitive development; and Kohlberg's stages of moral development. Some theories assume that each stage must

be completed more or less successfully before the next stage can be negotiated but others do not and, as 'grand' theories (i.e. as theories that seek
to explain certain features of human behaviour), they have serious shortcomings in terms of whether they can provide a 'complete explanation of
developmental processes' (Rutter and Rutter 1993: 3). Nevertheless, their
contribution is important because of the questions raised in relation to
the different processes and influences involved in development.

- *Lifespan developmental psychology.* Developmental psychology argues
  that *continuities* and *discontinuities* exist within the growth process, and
  that psychological functioning and development change throughout the
  course of our lives. 'We are social beings and our psychological functioning is influenced by the interactions and transactions we have within our
  social environment' (Rutter and Rutter 1993: 6). It looks at how people's behaviour is shaped by past experiences, their attachment history,
  and other social factors and how, for example, risk and protective factors
  operate in terms of the developmental process. It also touches on social
  learning theory: how people, particularly children, develop through observing and imitating the behaviour of others. (For further reading on
  lifespan theory, see Daniel and Bowes 2010.)

The following is a brief summary of some of the main psychological
theories that are important in social work. It looks at theories in relation
to: need, human motivation and self-actualization (Maslow); the search to
reach our 'true' potential (Rogers); the learning we can gain from observing
human behaviour (Skinner); the relationship between conscious and
unconscious thoughts, feelings, and actions (Freud); the impact of life stages
on human beings (Erikson); attachment theory (Bowlby); and the struggle
of human beings to achieve independence (Winnicott). It then looks at other
important developments that include the notion of *resilience*, the challenge
posed by feminists in relation to women's emotional development and
oppression, and the limitations that exist when we base our understanding
on normative and Eurocentric assumptions.

Psychology's three forces: psychoanalysis, behaviourism, and humanism

Psychology is sometimes described as having three 'forces': psychoanalysis,
behaviourism, and a 'third force' – humanistic psychology. Psychoanalysis
is based on the belief that, as human beings, we are born with the capacity
for good and evil and that much of our life is determined by the tension
and conflict between these two elements. Behaviourism, on the other hand,
is based on a belief that feelings of distress or neurosis come about through
faulty conditioning and that what needs to be changed is maladaptive behaviour. It stresses the importance of observable, testable, measurable, reproducible, and objective behaviours: we are as we behave. As such, unlike

psychoanalysis and humanism, behaviourism is not primarily concerned with the meaning and understanding that human beings ascribe to their thoughts and feelings. Finally, humanistic psychology emphasizes a belief in the essential goodness, wholeness, and potential of human beings (Feltham and Dryden 2004: 104). This school of psychology, sometimes described as the 'human potential movement', stresses the importance of individuals exercising freedom of choice in relation to their lives.

Psychoanalysis, behaviourism, and humanistic psychology have all had an impact on social work but, as we shall see, in different ways. For example, psychoanalysis has influenced the development of other theories, such as the work of Bowlby and Erikson. More recently, behaviourist theories, particularly cognitive-behavioural approaches, have become important. Yet in relation to the choices made by social workers, many gravitate towards humanistic approaches, primarily because of their theoretical accessibility, their 'holistic' approach, their adaptability, and the sense of hope they engender. The practice approaches covered in the Appendices of this text highlight how these three main theories – psychoanalysis, behaviourism, and humanistic psychology – have been developed in ways that can be applied in practice (Trevithick 2012a).

Humanism

Maslow's (1954) hierarchy of needs

Abraham Maslow (1908–1970), an American academic, is often described as the founder of humanistic psychology. His quest to understand human behaviour and motivation led him away from psychoanalysis, which he found too absorbed with neurosis and disturbed behaviour, and away from behaviourism, which he found too mechanistic, remarking after the birth of his first child that anyone who had seen a baby born could not be a behaviourist. Instead, he put forward the concept of a *hierarchy of needs* where the need for *self-actualization*, that is, the need that human beings have to realize their full potential, which can only be fulfilled once other needs have been met. Self-actualization describes an inborn tendency for human beings to grow and to maximize innate talents and potentialities.

According to Maslow, the first level includes basic physiological needs for food, shelter, clothing, and so on. Once these needs have been met, the actualization process creates a momentum for the next level of needs to be realized, namely, for security and safety and to feel free from danger. Again, once these have been met, there is an innate motivation to move on to the next stage, and so forth (see Figure 5.1).

In his conceptualization of a hierarchy of needs, Maslow was one of the first people to attempt to analyse human needs and to relate the meeting of needs to a notion of human growth and development, motivation, and the maximization of human potential. As such, 'Maslow's model' is most

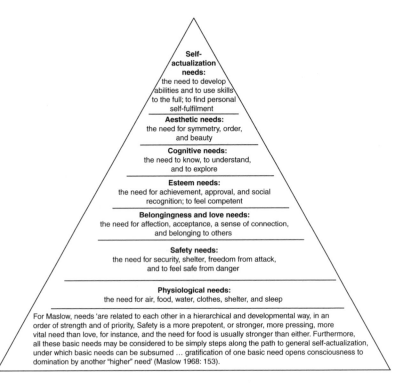

Figure 5.1 Maslow's hierarchy of needs. Fundamental or basic needs must be met or satisfied, at least partially, before other 'higher' needs can be met

often used to provide a rough working generalization about most people in most situations, but as an explanation of human motivation, his theory has serious limitations. Some people do not address their needs in ways that fall within Maslow's conceptual framework. Creative people have been known to sacrifice basic physiological needs for, say, food and rest, in pursuit of their creativity. Similarly, some people who appear to have satisfied their basic needs somehow fail to move on to address higher needs. For reasons that this theory cannot explain, some people can become stuck and, seemingly, unable to move forward.

We have, all of us, an impulse to improve ourselves, an impulse toward actualizing more of our potentialities, toward self-actualization, or full humanness or human fulfillment or whatever term you like. Granted this, then what holds us up? What blocks us?

(Maslow 1973)

For Maslow, an 'unhealthiness' blocks human potential but this suggests that responsibility for 'self-actualization' lies solely with the individual. However, it is clear that other factors, such as 'social interaction and culture' are also important, but these aspects are seriously downgraded in Marlow's conceptualization (Webb 2010: 2368).

In social work we encounter situations where some people find it extremely difficult to move beyond the first two levels. For some, the energy spent on trying to survive in the face of adversity necessarily means that emotional resources – or energy – are not free to be used on other courses of action, such as sorting out family problems, finding a job or meeting other needs. This has important implications for our work because it could mean that providing the right kind of practical or material assistance, and appropriate emotional support for service users, could release the momentum and motivation towards self-sufficiency and independence (self-actualization). Without this understanding, we run the risk of providing help and support where fundamental change cannot – and does not – happen. The difficulties inherent in working alongside service users to bring about change are well documented in the work of Saleebey (2009) and Miller and Rollnick (2002) (see Appendix 6 on Motivational Interviewing and Appendix 10 on Strengths Perspectives).

Rogers' client-centred approach

Carl Rogers (1902–1987), an American psychologist and founder of client-centred therapy (also called person-centred counselling), shared Maslow's view that human beings have an innate drive or motivation to develop and to maximize their inherited potential. Rogers described this as an *actualizing tendency*, a term similar to Maslow's terminology. However, unlike Maslow, whose theory is descriptive and speculative and located at the level of ideas, Rogers formulated not only a complex theory of human growth and development, but a practice approach: client-centred therapy (Rogers 1951: 61). Its aim was to help create the conditions for individuals to overcome the constraints placed on them from the impact and internalization of negative and invalidating experiences and criticisms.

Rogers stressed the need for positive self-regard and noted in detail the impact of adverse conditions on the capacity of individuals to be self-directing, to trust their innate abilities and resourcefulness, and to be in touch with their own 'locus of evaluation', that is, their ability to trust their thoughts and feelings in relation to decision-making and to choose particular courses of action. For Rogers, the *actualizing tendency* (Rogers 1961: 351) is motivated by the drive for emotional and intellectual growth but this growth is only normally possible when the individual is released or freed from the fear of punishment, coercion, inhibiting social pressures, and other negative or constraining experiences. Central to Rogers' theory is the belief that individuals know more about themselves and their lives than anyone else and, because of this, are in the best position to deal with personal problems that emerge (Rogers 1961: 76). The role of the therapist or practitioner is to create the conditions necessary for people to find their way to a new self-concept and self-regard:

> ... the client should experience or perceive something of the therapist's congruence, acceptance and empathy. It is not enough that these conditions exist in the therapist. They must, to some degree, have been successfully communicated to the client.
>
> (Rogers 1961: 284)

From this new position, it is hoped that people can develop the capacity to solve their own problems and to function in ways that feel satisfying, so that any opportunities for growth and development that emerge can be explored and maximized.

From this theory of human growth and development, Rogers went on to develop a practice approach to help individuals to overcome these constraints. This involves a therapist or practitioner creating a particular kind of relationship using *congruence, unconditional positive regard*, and *empathic understanding* (Rogers 1961: 282–4) to understand an individual's subjective experience. The therapist's or practitioner's aim is to get alongside the client in ways that show a willingness to enter the world of another human being and to provide an experience and presence that is validating, releasing, and restorative.

Through this process, individuals are presented with a different way of perceiving and experiencing themselves, so that a new self-concept can emerge and, with this, the capacity to solve their own problems. This is not easy to achieve because it requires great commitment, skill, and discipline on the part of the counsellor. It also requires the individual to recognize and work with the qualities that the counsellor brings to the relationship, so that trust, a particular kind of intimacy, and a degree of mutuality can be reached (Thorne 2002: 178). Although not without its critics or shortcomings, Rogers' theory stands out for its profound optimism and belief in the capacity of human beings to embrace difficult experiences, to take hold of their lives and to move forward, and for the important role that others can play, including social workers, within this process. (For a more detailed account of Rogers' work, see Thorne 2002.)

Behaviourism

The behaviourist school of psychology is based on the theories of Pavlov (1927), Watson (1970), Skinner (1974), and others. It attempts to explain behaviour in terms of observable and measurable responses and starts from the position that behaviours are learned, which means, therefore, that behaviours can be unlearned. Thus, neurosis is considered to be the result of faulty conditioning, which means that when people feel distressed, what needs to be changed is the maladaptive behaviour. This places the focus on the behaviour itself, as opposed to analysing the underlying conflicts or causes. For example, Watson considered introspection to be unscientific – a view still held by some behaviourists. As a therapy, it is considered to be particularly effective in relation to fears and phobias and also for obsessional states, such as compulsive hand-washing.

Most behavioural perspectives share the following characteristics:

- Reliance on empirical findings rather than speculation to inform assessment and intervention
- Identification of personal and environmental resources that can be drawn on to attain desired outcomes
- Description of baseline levels of relevant outcomes and skills
- Clear description of assessment and intervention procedures
- Close relationship between assessment and intervention
- Clear description of desired outcomes
- Concern with evaluation.

(Gambrill 1985: 184)

Behaviourist approaches include four major techniques: systematic desensitization, aversion therapy, operant conditioning, and modelling, although therapists may use these interventions differently. *Desensitization* is often used as an effective means of alleviating fear and anxiety by attempting to weaken the anxiety response to a given stimulus by exposing the individual to a series of similar anxiety-provoking situations until a more relaxed response is reached. *Aversion therapy* is, in some ways, the opposite of desensitization because it consists of administering unpleasant, painful, or punishing stimuli to individuals whose 'unacceptable' behaviour is in some ways felt to be gratifying, with the intention of altering this reaction and behaviour pattern. The use of this technique on certain groups of people, such as 'sex offenders' and alcoholics, has been criticized and has also proved less successful than anticipated (Miller and Rollnick 2002). As a result, aversion therapy tends to be less popular – and used less – than other behavioural techniques. *Operant conditioning* is a technique where 'the environment has been specifically programmed to support certain behaviours and discourage others' (Sheldon 1995: 62) by altering the consequences that follow. The reinforcement may take the form of a reward, such as those found in token-economy schemes. Finally, Bandura (1969) emphasizes the importance of *modelling* as an effective way to bring about behaviour change. This involves encouraging an individual to acquire behaviour by imitating the actions or behaviour of others. According to Gambrill:

Several characteristics distinguish the behavioural approach from other social work frameworks. A behavioural approach constrains social workers to draw on empirical research in selecting assessment and intervention procedures. For example, if research demonstrates that the observation of behaviour in the natural environment offers valuable information that can complement and correct impressions given by self-reports concerning the interaction between clients and significant others, then this kind of information would be used if feasible and ethical. If the literature shows that one kind of intervention is more effective than another, then within ethical and practice limits, social workers would use this approach regardless of personal theoretical preferences.

(Gambrill 1985: 185)

It is probably true to say that behaviourism itself has had little impact on social work. However, the use of behaviourist theories and concept has grown in influence since the 'marriage' that led to the development of cognitive-behavioural approaches (Cigno 2009). According to Sheldon (1995: xii), combining behaviour therapy and applied behavioural psychology has led to a 'cognitive revolution' in recent years. As the term implies, cognitive-behavioural approaches attempt to link behaviour with how human beings organize, think, and feel about their world – and how these beliefs become known, perceived, and understood. Two important concepts that link behaviour and thoughts in this way are *learned helplessness* and *locus of control*.

Learned helplessness

A particularly valuable concept, based on social learning theory, is learned helplessness (Seligman 1975). This describes the generalized view that helplessness is a learned state, brought about when individuals are exposed to unpleasant, harmful, or corrupting situations where there is no avoidance or escape. Such individuals learn through experience that there is nothing they can do to bring about change or to modify their situation, that is, they become powerless. Seligman's view, and that of cognitive-behaviourists, is that if behaviour can be learned, it can also be unlearned 'in a sympathetic, step-by-step way, by teaching the skills necessary for the reassertion of some control over their unpredictable environments' (Sheldon 1995: 61). Working alongside service users in this way can help to enable them to overcome the doubts and fears that they harbour. This concept is particularly useful and adaptable within a social work context because it helps to understand why some people fail to take action or fall victim to events.

Locus of control

A different way to conceptualize the degree to which an individual has internalized a sense of helplessness and powerlessness would be to explore the extent to which they believe they can control their destiny and behaviour. This helps to understand where the individual is located in relation to the process of change. The locus of control (Lefcourt 1976) is measured along a scale from a high internal to high external locus. Individuals with a high internal locus of control tend to accept responsibility for their actions and to believe that it is possible to influence or to control ('master') their circumstances and lives. At the other end of the spectrum, individuals with a high external locus of control believe that control is located elsewhere and that 'things happen to them' – both positive and negative – over which they have little or no control. The usefulness of this concept is that it helps to identify whether, when presented with a new situation or dilemma, individuals will consistently and spontaneously perceive a situation as something over which they can or cannot exercise a degree of control. This has important implications when, as practitioners, we are attempting to assess the degree of responsibility that service users can take on and what role we should play.

For further accounts of the use of behaviourism within social work, see Hudson and Macdonald (1986), Sheldon (1982), and Appendix 1. In relation to cognitive approaches, see Appendix 2 and for cognitive-behavioural approaches, see Cigno (2009) and Sheldon and Macdonald (2009).

Psychoanalysis

Like many writers, Freud (1856–1939) described people's tendency for growth and emotional development as innate: as an 'instinctual propelling force' (Freud 1919/1924: 396). Some people have sufficient inner, emotional resources to set in motion this opportunity for growth and development but for others, the impact of depleting experiences in childhood and/or ongoing and snowballing adversity in adulthood means that any movement forward will depend on the quality and nature of help given. Some psychoanalytic concepts are not easily applicable to social work but others are highly relevant. For example, concepts such as those relating to *conscious*, *preconscious*, and *unconscious* states and human *defences* are enormously helpful in our efforts to understand others (see Appendix 8). From 1920 onwards, Freud introduced different topographical distinctions linking the *unconscious* to the *id* and the *conscious* to the *ego*, *with the superego* having both *conscious* and *unconscious* elements. The following account describes these concepts in greater detail:

- *Ego*. The *ego*, which comes from the Latin for 'I' or the 'self', is characterized as the conscious and reasoning part of the mind. It mediates between the conscious and the unconscious, although it too is partly unconscious. Its primary function is to deal with external reality (sometimes called *reality testing*) and to make decisions. Enhancing the capacity of the *ego* to deal with stress and conflicts is what is often being referred to in the phrase 'helping people to cope'. Working alongside people to enhance their coping strategies is an essential feature of social work and a strategy that is central to ego psychology, popular in the USA (Goldstein 1995; Parad 1958).
- *Id*. For Freud, the *id* represents primitive instincts and impulses. It is governed by the pleasure principle and, as a result, demands immediate gratification. Like the *superego*, the *id* is largely unconscious and describes actions that are propelled or triggered by an impulse of which the

individual is not aware of at the time. Therefore, *id*-driven behaviours are difficult to predict or to control, but they can often be identified by the irrational nature of the behaviour and also because they have a timeless feature. Here I am reminded of a young 'joy rider' I was asked to visit, whose only explanation for stealing the bike was that he 'felt like it'. When asked to describe the details surrounding the theft, this young man had no memory of what time he stole the bike, where he was, and had no thought for the consequences or repercussions. Of course, not all impulsive behaviour could be said to be *id* driven – but some certainly fall within this category.

- *Superego*. The *superego* is conceptualized as being responsible for self-imposed standards of behaviour. It is the 'conscience' of the mind, the place where rules, moral codes, taboos, and censorship are harboured to control behaviours. To violate or transgress these rules often gives rise to feelings of guilt. Individuals who have an over-developed *superego* can find themselves racked with guilt or with intense feelings of responsibility and blame that are inappropriate to the situation. If the *id* is concerned with pleasure, and the *ego* with responsibility and reality, the *superego* is concerned with idealism, often based on an internalization of parental attitudes. It is important to stress that the *superego*, *ego*, and *id* are hypothetical constructs, metaphors to help us to understand human behaviour.

Box 5.1 shows the differences between the *id* and *ego*.

Box 5.1 The differences between the *id* and *ego*

Id	Ego
the *id* is primitive/impulsive	the *ego* is civilized/reflective
the *id* is unorganized	the *ego* is organized and perceptual
the *id* observes the pleasure-principle, that is, the *id* is irrational and foolhardy	the *ego* adheres to the reality-principle, that is, the *ego* is rational
the *id* ignores the demands and restrictions of time and space	the *ego* conforms to demands and requirements of time and space

Defence mechanism

To protect the ego – or the self – from thoughts, feelings, or actions that are felt to be threatening, defensive strategies are employed, often unconsciously (Jacobs 2010: 110; Trevithick 2011a). All human beings have defences, some of which are unconscious, that is, they are reactions that for the most part lie beyond our immediate awareness and control. For example, events may be forgotten or *repressed* to protect us from memories that would produce anxiety or guilt if they became conscious (Reber *et al.* 2009: 679). Or defences can distort what is remembered, which means it can be difficult to gain an accurate picture of experiences and events. It is worth remembering that the greater the wounding that an individual has experienced, the greater the level of defensiveness that is likely to be evident. Thus, it is the most defensive people who greatly need our help, but any offer of help runs the risk of being rejected because the same defences that are designed to protect the individual can also block the opportunity for helpful contact to be made. Given the understanding and sensitivity that is required, it is often unhelpful to confront defences head on. A feature of a psychodynamic approach could involve the use of interpretations to help individuals gain an understanding or insight into their behaviour, thereby opening up the possibility of change. However, the effective use of this skill requires additional training because if badly timed or premature, interventions can increase defensiveness and inhibit progress (Feltham and Dryden 2004: 120). A different approach involves helping to contain the anxiety that underpins the defensive reaction. This is a much more grounded intervention and one that can introduce a sense of safety and reassurance into an otherwise emotionally charged situation. Both skills are covered in greater detail later in this text.

The following are two common defensive reactions that we regularly encounter in social work: denial and avoidance. They can be conscious or unconscious in character – and it is often not clear which is being deployed. They are included in this text because in social work, there can be an understandable reluctance to acknowledge that some service users present challenging and deliberately deceptive behaviour – but such behaviour exists and needs to be acknowledged. For example, in Haringey's closing submissions to the Laming Inquiry into the death of Victoria Climbié, it was stated that social workers 'are not used to dealing with wholesale deception' (Laming 2003: 260). Regrettably, that is not my experience and given this fact, we need to acquire the knowledge and skills that are appropriate when we encounter deception, misinformation, and other dishonest forms of communication.

Denial is most often evident when people refuse to accept any responsibility for their behaviour, sometimes blaming events or their behaviour on other people. Information that is considered threatening, frightening, or anxiety provoking is rejected or blocked from awareness – and people can communicate this denial with great intensity. There may be no deliberate intention to deceive – instead denial can be a form of protection from an assumed or real threat. For example, a person may say 'I am not angry' when their body language indicates that they are indeed angry.

Avoidance describes the different ways that people dodge or evade information or events that give rise to worrying thoughts, feelings, sensations, etc. This may be communicated, for example, by diverting the communication away from certain issues, or by being late for appointments, arriving unprepared, leaving early, and so forth.

The other main defences that we regularly encounter in social work include projection, regression, repression, introjection, and splitting (for a fuller account, see Brearley 2007; Jacobs 2010; Trevithick 2011a).

The importance of the relationship between practitioner and service user lies at the heart of psychoanalytic approaches, not only as a basis for helping people to move forward but as a way of understanding inner conflicts that are unconscious. These are communicated through transference and counter-transference reactions, in other words, in the ways we are experienced by service users and what we represent: *who we have become for service users* or *what part we are expected to play*. For example, a mother whose child is refusing to attend school may experience our communication as critical (negative transference), where in fact our reaction may be the opposite – sympathetic and uncritical. Or again, we may end an interview feeling unexpectedly immobilized and dismayed, perhaps having picked up feelings of hopelessness and despair communicated unconsciously by the service user (Stevenson 1998: 18). Picking up negative or troubling feelings in this way is inevitable: these are the reactions on which 'hunches' or intuitive reasoning are built (Munro 2011a: 35). Supervision can help to understand these experiences. However, being able to work directly with transference and counter-transference reactions, rather than just understanding these terms as concepts, requires additional training but even with training, we must always check that we are not bringing our own unresolved feelings into the encounter or into the relationship. (For articles on the application of psychoanalytic concepts in social work, see the *Journal of Social Work Practice*.)

Erikson's (1965) life cycle approach to development

Erik Erikson (1902–1994), a German immigrant to the USA in the 1930s, built on Freud's theory of psychosexual development (oral, anal, phallic, latency, and genital phases), and the impact of biological and social and cultural influences on human development. His theory was one of the first to emerge as part of the discipline of 'lifespan psychology' – a framework that attempts to categorize human experience from the cradle to the grave and to understand how human beings operate, find an identity, and meet the demands placed upon them within a changing social and cultural context.

Erikson's proposition was that the ego – the self – of the infant is not fixed at birth, or during childhood, but that the infant has all the elements necessary for development to take place at different stages. From this basic premise Erikson saw development being moulded throughout life, as part of a lifelong response to the demands and challenges placed on individuals. These demands provoke 'crises', where difficult challenges or problems have to be confronted and successfully resolved, from which 'vital strength' is gained. Although it is not essential for each stage to be fully resolved, failure to meet these challenges can be damaging to development and self-esteem, and can result in developmental stagnation or 'stuckness'. This can, however, be overcome with help. Erikson's eight stages of psychosocial development are shown in Box 5.2.

Box 5.2   Erikson's eight stages of psychosocial development (eight stages of man)

Approximate age* (chronological ages are not always clear)	Stage	Psychosocial crisis	Favourable outcome (potential 'new virtue')
Stage 1: Birth to 18 months	Infancy	Trust vs. mistrust	Trust, optimism, hope
Stage 2: 18 months to 6 years	Early childhood	Autonomy vs. shame and doubt	Sense of control, adequacy, self-confidence
Stage 3: 6– 8 years	Play age	Initiative vs. guilt	Direction and purpose
Stage 4: 10– 14 years	School age	Industry vs. inferiority	Competence in social, intellectual, and physical skills
Stage 5: 14– 20 years	Adolescence	Identity vs. role confusion	Fidelity; an integrated sense of being a unique individual
Stage 6: 20– 35 years	Young adulthood	Intimacy vs. isolation	Love; ability to form close relationships and to make commitments
Stage 7: 35– 65 years	Mature adulthood/ maturity	Generativity vs. stagnation	Care and concern for family, society, and future generations
Stage 8: 65+ years	Late adult- hood/old age	Integrity vs. despair and disgust	Wisdom; a sense of fulfilment and satisfaction with life and a willingness to face death

*A person's actual chronological age in years can differ from their emotional age. Also, different authors present slightly different ages in relation to the different stages, which makes it important to see the ages cited as generalizations. Erikson summarized the eight stages as follows: 'I . . . speak of *Hope*, *Will*, *Purpose*, and *Competence* as the rudiments of virtue developed in childhood; of *Fidelity* as the adolescent virtue; of *Love*, *Care*, and *Wisdom* as the central virtues of adulthood. In all their seeming discontinuity, these qualities depend on each other' (Erikson 1965: 115).

Erikson's work continues to be influential, particularly in relation to adolescent psychosocial development and the ageing process. In relation to old age, Erikson (1965: 261) noted: 'healthy children will not fear life if their parents have integrity enough not to fear death'. Like Freud and Maslow, Erikson's theory of psychosocial development lacks a sound research and evidence base but at the level of ideas, his theory identifies the kinds of concerns that human beings encounter at different points in their lives. (For a more detailed description and critique of Erikson's different stages, see Gibson 2007.)

Bowlby's attachment theory

John Bowlby (1907–1990), a British psychiatrist and psychoanalyst, was commissioned after the Second World War to investigate children orphaned or separated from their parents as a result of the war. In 1951, Bowlby published a report for the World Health Organization entitled *Maternal Care and Mental Health*, which concluded that human beings have an innate and fundamental need to form meaningful attachments with others, particularly in childhood but also throughout life, and that within this process the mother–child relationship or 'bond' is of central importance. Bowlby later revised his views on the prominence given to mothers to include other significant adults (Bowlby 1988: 27). Bowlby defined attachment theory as follows:

> ... a way of conceptualizing the propensity of human beings to make strong affectional bonds to particular others and of explaining the many forms of emotional distress and personality disturbance, including anxiety, anger, depression, and emotional detachment, to which unwilling separation and loss give rise.
>
> (Bowlby 1979: 103)

According to Bowlby, the *affectional bonds* created between the mother and baby help to establish a secure base, particularly in the first year of life, where positive and trusted attachment figures foster feelings of confidence and self-worth and act as a source of emotional stability and security (Bowlby 1979: 130). From this secure base, children develop self-confidence, self-reliance, trust, and cooperation with others (Bowlby 1979: 117). On the other hand, negative attachment figures who are inaccessible, unreliable, unhelpful, or hostile, can result in children feeling anxious, insecure, rootless, mistrustful, and lacking in self-confidence. Within this process, Bowlby emphasized the importance of children being able to recognize and to collaborate with attachment figures in ways that feel reciprocal and rewarding (Bowlby 1979: 104), stressing that a healthy personality involves both self-reliance and reliance on others:

Paradoxically, the healthy personality when viewed in this light proves by no means as independent as cultural stereotypes suppose. Essential ingredients are a capacity to rely trustingly on others when occasion demands and to know on whom it is appropriate to rely. A healthily functioning person is thus capable of exchanging roles when the situation changes.

(Bowlby 1979: 105)

He also stressed that the pattern of relationships that are established first will tend to persist throughout life, although a significant relationship with another human being can change a person's circumstances (Howe 2011: 226). These models are internalized, to become *working models* of the self, from which children hold an inner picture of themselves: their self-image, self-esteem, and sense of worth. These may be positive or negative, depending on the nature and quality of a child's past and present internal and external experience (Bowlby 1979: 118). They lead to a range of expectations being established and a particular outlook on life and the future.

Bowlby (1980) revealed that infants formed different kinds of attachments, influenced by the behaviour of their parents/carers, as well as the situation and social context. He identified three stages of reaction to separation from an attachment figure, namely:

- *Protest.* At this stage, children demonstrate clear signs of being tearful, upset, and agitated, sometimes calling for the attachment figure or searching for them.
- *Despair.* When the protest fails to bring the attachment figure back, children enter a period of despair, characterized by withdrawn behaviour, tearfulness, refusing to eat, bed-wetting and soiling.
- *Detachment.* At this stage children become detached, appearing to have adapted to the situation and to be disinterested in the attachment figure. They have learnt to fend for themselves and may use thumb-sucking, rocking or masturbation in an effort to comfort themselves.

Alongside Bowlby, others studied infant–parent relationships, including James Robertson and Mary Ainsworth, and developed new theories based on their observations and classifications. For example, the research of Ainsworth *et al.* (1978), particularly the 'strange situation' test (Howe 1995: 79), led to the development of a different attachment classification system: *secure attachment*; *insecure attachment: avoidant*; and *insecure attachment: ambivalent*. These attachment strategies are also referred to in terms of A (avoidant), B (secure), and C (ambivalent). A fourth category, *insecure: disorganized attachment* (disorganized D) was added to the original group by Main (1995) (see Box 5.3).

Box 5.3   Different types of attachment

Securely attached (Type B)

'In secure parent–child relationships, care is loving, emotionally attuned, respon-sive, predictable and consistent. There is a sensitivity to children's needs, thoughts and feelings. Parents tend to have children who are secure in their attachments, if they:

• are good at reading their children's minds and meeting their emotional needs
• treat their children as burgeoning psychological beings in their own right
• are good at making their children feel emotionally safe and contained
• are skilled at finding effective ways to comfort their children' (Howe 2009:141).

Insecure attached: avoidant patterns of attachment (Type A)

This form of attachment is also described as *insecure resistant*. It can indicate a deceptive degree of self-reliance and independence, largely due to the failure of parents to provide comfort and attention when the child is in distress. As a result, any attempt at reassurance or comfort is likely to be rebuffed to protect the child from further pain and rejection.

'Children who develop avoidant patterns of attachment have parents who are either indifferent, rigid or rejecting . . . When separated from their parents, these children show few signs of distress' (Howe 2009: 142).

Insecure attached: ambivalent patterns of attachment (Type C)

Children who fall within this category often lack a sense of confidence in relation to the world around them, and because of their insecurities, can come across as needy, demanding, and fretful. There is the sense of 'non-enough' love and care, largely because parents tend to be engrossed in their own emotional needs.

'When parental care is inconsistent and unpredictable, children begin to experi-ence increasing levels of anxiety. The problem is one of neglect and insensitivity rather than hostility. Parents often fail to empathize with their children's moods, needs and feelings' (Howe 2009: 142).

Insecure: disorganized (Type D)

'This type of attachment is observed most often where children suffer abuse, neglect, and trauma in relationship with their attachment figures. It must be noted that even in these cases of hostile (abusive) and helpless (neglectful) parenting, the primary carer is still the child's attachment figure' (Howe 2009: 143).
Some parents not only neglect and frighten their children but also fail to recognize their children's distress. As a result, children have to take charge of their needs and safety – a situation marked by children's need to adopt controlling strategies, which links to Winnicott's concept of *premature self sufficiency.*

Over the years, the work of Bowlby and others has been important within social work in making links between children's emotional development and behaviour and the quality of their relationships with their parent(s), and other attachment figures. As a result, attachment theory has been used extensively, in day care settings, in residential establishments and fostering, and is a central feature in the *Assessment Framework* used in relation to children (Department of Health 2000). It continues to be particularly useful in mapping continuities and discontinuities in care, and the degree to which a lack of permanence or consistency can have an impact on children's emotional development and on their capacity to relate to themselves, to others, and to their wider environment. I have focused on attachment theory because of its significance in social work and multidisciplinary context. On a final note, it is important to recognize that despite the adversity that children experience, change is always possible:

> The more significant the relationship with a key other – whether parent, partner, lover, therapist – the more radical the shift in the life circumstances, the more likely it is that an individual's attachment organization will change. Children placed with warm, loving, insightful foster carers gradually develop secure attachment. Insecure people with secure partners might begin to feel loved and valued, and with those feelings their attachment grows more secure . . .
>
> (Howe 2011: 226)

Winnicott's writing on dependence and points of failure

Donald Winnicott (1896–1971) was a paediatrician and psychoanalyst whose work had a significant influence on social work and teaching, as well as medicine, in the 1950s and 1960s. His influence on social work was due, in part, to the fact that his wife, Clare Britton Winnicott, was a trained social worker and writer, whose contribution in the area of children's emotional development was substantial but largely overshadowed by the work of her husband (Kanter 2004). Donald Winnicott wrote extensively on many subjects but here I focus on his writings on the journey we must all make from dependence to independence, and finally towards interdependence. I also present a brief account of Winnicott's writings on the points of failure.

The journey towards interdependence

The journey towards interdependence begins with the *almost absolute dependence* of the newborn baby, whose needs must be responded to and adapted to almost totally to enable physical and emotional growth to take place. This leads to the possibility of moving towards a state of relative dependence, where the mother or carer introduces less adaptation to ensure that the child can begin to look outward to have their needs met, to look to themselves and their wider social environment. This time of great exploration is marked by infants and toddlers being able to leave the security of their parents/carers and to venture further afield in search of new experiences. If all goes well at this stage, a movement towards *independence* begins to develop, marked by a desire on the part of the child to find ways to do without actual care and to undertake more things for themselves (Winnicott 1965: 84). This stage should not be confused with *premature self-sufficiency*, which occurs when individuals are failed and forced into a false independence before they have the emotional resources or maturity to manage properly for themselves (Winnicott 1986: 21). This kind of failure can result in the development of a *false self*, designed to protect the individual's *true self* from the impact of further failures, trauma or 'impingement' (Winnicott 1958: 291–2).

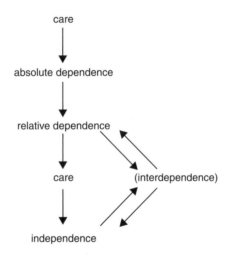

care

↓

absolute dependence

↓

relative dependence

↓

care   (interdependence)

↓

independence

Figure 5.2 Winnicott's stages of dependence

In relation to the movement in and out of dependent states, the concept of *interdependence* is important because it describes the capacity of the individual to give and to receive from others without undue anxiety. This can lead to the individual being able to engage in more reciprocal relationships with others, and to be able to relate with a degree of confidence to their wider environment and to society. This conceptualization stresses the fact that, as human beings, we need one another. For this reason, Winnicott regarded independence more as an illusory ideal than a realizable or even desirable goal:

Independence is never absolute. The healthy individual does not become isolated, but becomes related to the environment in such a way that the individual and the environment can be said to be interdependent.

(Winnicott 1965: 84)

This involves being able to seek help and the company of others without feeling compromised or depleted by the experience and can help to explain why some service users do not take up services that are offered. This journey is illustrated in Figure 5.2.

Points of failure/failure situations

Neglect in infancy can result in 'delays and distortions' in development. One way to attempt to understand when and where the developmental process has become delayed or stuck could be to look at how past failures are continuing to have an impact. 'Failure situations' or 'points of failure' (Winnicott 1958: 281) describe experiences of being disappointed, 'let down', or failed by others in crucial ways. These unthinkable memories and failures remain 'frozen' but they are waiting for a safe and reliable situation where they can be 'unfrozen'. The most severe and enduring failures often occur in childhood and the involuntary revival of these memories can catapult service users into a different, often earlier time zone and 'space'. From this place it can be difficult to distinguish between past and present, primarily because unresolved and painful feelings of the past are experienced in the present, often becoming merged with present-day events. For example, the ending of a significant relationship can revive unresolved feelings of grief from the past about the death of a loved one or the loss of an earlier relationship, no matter how long ago this occurred. Whatever triggers a return to these points of failure, and this may never be fully known, the fact that they have come back into prominence – into our memory or half-awareness – is significant on two accounts:

- these feelings take up emotional energy and reserves in ways that exhaust service users and threaten their capacity to cope; and
- they provide an opportunity to recover from earlier failures and for the developmental process to start up again where this has become stuck.

This perspective sees all behaviour as providing important clues. For example, repeating harmful or self-destructive behaviour can be seen quite simply as a manifestation of distress, which it clearly is. However, it can also be seen as a return to previous traumas or points of failure in a service user's attempts to become free of their constraining impact. The energy that is taken up trying not to feel the pain of these earlier experiences – to forget, to control or to repress difficult feelings or failures – can be freed up and used creatively in other areas of our lives.

Too often, these points of failure are left unhealed or unresolved, which means that the developmental process can become locked or 'frozen' at these points. As a result, certain aspects of an individual's emotional development can become stuck. An example of this uneven development can be seen when an individual communicates a balanced perspective until we touch upon a painful, unresolved issue when suddenly the dialogue takes a different, less rational tone. Sometimes it can feel as if the individual has gone back to a younger age. For those areas where growth has become stuck, it can be difficult for people to work through these painful experiences without help because they may be unaware of them, that is, they are unconscious (John and Trevithick 2012).

Alongside these aspects of developmental delay or 'stuckness' exist pain-free areas, that is, areas where an individual has not been hurt or where there has been the opportunity to resolve painful issues that they may have experienced. In these areas of resilience and strength there remains the possibility to grow, to change, and to embrace the challenges that life brings. Experiences of success and achievement can expand an individual's emotional reserves. These resilient aspects of the personality can help compensate for those areas where a person feels hurt and vulnerable, perhaps by guarding or steering the individual away from the experiences, thoughts, and feelings that are likely to trigger difficult emotions. But sometimes this vigilance is not possible, because the ongoing experiences of adversity are too severe and also because it takes energy to continuously protect those parts of the personality that are vulnerable. Life has its own way of intruding into the best-laid plans and deepest defences. Again, the death of a loved one is an example of an experience that is likely to 'throw' most people, but particularly those who already carry a great deal of unresolved grief and loss. (For an account of Winnicott's relevance to social work, see Applegate and Bonovitz 1995 and Lesser 2007.)

In their different ways, the theories outlined above provide a generalized account of human growth and development – how we come to be who we are. A central theme is an attempt to identify those factors that lead to the development of a healthy individual and what barriers exist to hinder this process. One way to assess this balance between growth-enhancing and growth-limiting experiences can be found in the following *resilience–vulnerability framework*.

Resilience

Resilience was first coined by Fonagy and colleagues (1994: 233) to describe 'normal development under difficult conditions', a phrase that is often used in social work when attempting to assess why some children cope better with adversity than others. Howe defines 'psychological resilience' as follows:

When the individual's self-system is under stress, resilient people are able to maintain psychological integrity; they remain able to draw on a range of personal strengths to cope with adversity and life's ups and downs. They continue to be purposeful and focused problem-solvers. Other people continue to be seen as a resource and not necessarily part of the problem. Resiliences include self-esteem, self-efficacy, self-reflexivity, social empathy and autonomy.

(Howe *et al.* 1999: 30)

The matrix shown in Figure 5.3 illustrates how different dimensions interact to impact on a child's capacity to cope with adversity. Vulnerability is defined as 'those innate characteristics of the child, or those imposed by the family circle and wider community which might threaten or challenge

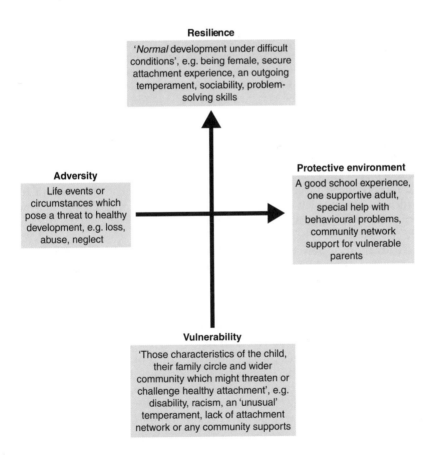

Figure 5.3 Resilience–vulnerability matrix
Source: Daniel *et al.* (1999: 61)

healthy development' (Daniel *et al.* 1999: 73). What is important about this matrix is the link that is made between emotional and social factors. There are many factors associated with resilience, but Gilligan distils from the literature three fundamental 'building blocks of resilience':

1 A secure base whereby the child feels a sense of belonging and security.
2 Good self esteem, that is, an internal sense of worth and competence.
3 A sense of self efficacy, that is, a sense of mastery and control, along with an accurate understanding of personal strengths and limitations.

(Gilligan 1997: 15)

Although resilience can seem a relatively straightforward concept, Howe reminds us that:

Resilience is a complex phenomenon. It is not a unitary concept. No-one possesses across the board resilience. Each of us may show varying degrees of resilience in different situations.

(Howe 2008b: 106)

For example, some children may appear to manage difficult situations very well yet may be quite distressed. This can be difficult to detect, particularly if children or adults present a *false self* to protect themselves. Here I am reminded of a case I was allocated where the little girl in question, Dora, had recently been placed in a residential home. When I visited Dora, the residential workers felt that she had settled well and that she did not miss her mother. The opposite was true but it took many weeks before Dora felt safe enough to show her true feelings.

If this more secretive and withdrawn reaction is persistent, this would suggest that a child has been traumatized and when this is the case, more in-depth therapeutic help needs to be provided. The term *trauma* tends to be used in a range of different ways in social work. My preference in this text is to use a definition proposed by Freud: trauma is a memory that 'acts like a foreign body which long after its entry must continue to be regarded as an agent that is still at work' (Breuer and Freud 1893/1955: 56–7). It is a memory that can be triggered by a range of different associations – some of which will be unconscious – but once triggered, an agitated state can often be identified. However, different types of trauma can be noted. For example, Kris (1956) differentiates between 'shock trauma' and 'strain trauma'. Shock trauma describes a totally unexpected experience that is difficult to assimilate, such as a road accident, whereas strain trauma describes a situation where a feeling of fear, anxiety, or stress is ongoing. Women who live with violent partners often suffer from strain trauma, and their children can also experience the trauma, whether they witness the violence or not. We now turn to look briefly at other theories that are important to social work.

Other developments within psychology

Feminism and patriarchal assumptions of women's psychology

One of the most important developments in relation to psychology, particularly psychoanalysis, can be found in feminist writings on these themes, both in the USA and in the UK. The focus of feminist writings has been twofold: first, to challenge male-dominated and sexist assumptions about women's lives and emotional development; and second, to create a new and different women-centred theory and practice, loosely labelled 'feminist therapy'. The challenge posed by feminists, particularly in the 1970s and 1980s, to psychology, psychoanalysis, and the mental health system was formidable.

In relation to psychoanalysis, for example, feminist attack was focused on Freud's concept of penis envy and his abandonment and revision of women's accounts of sexual abuse. In the field of psychology, assumptions held by professionals who effectively saw women as being less well adjusted than men were challenged. Similar analyses were made in relation to psychological theories and research, particularly the assumption that girls' experience could be understood in terms of boys' experience. For example, Carol Gilligan identified a clear gender bias prevalent within certain developmental theories. A former student of Kohlberg, Gilligan challenged the work of Kohlberg (1969) and Piaget (1932) in particular because girls were not included in their research: 'the child' is male and 'females simply do not exist' (Gilligan 1993: 18). Gilligan notes that Kohlberg's 'six stages that describe the development of moral judgement from childhood to adulthood are based empirically on a study of eighty-four boys whose development Kohlberg followed for over twenty years' (Gilligan 1993: 18). The absence of girls from the study meant that 'prominent among those who thus appear to be deficient in moral development when measured by Kohlberg's scale are women' (Gilligan 1993: 18).

The attempt to create an alternative field of feminist theory and practice in relation to women has led to many interesting developments. In relation to Gilligan's work, it led her to explore the ways in which women and men deal with experiences differently, with men seeking to 'protect separateness' and women to 'sustain connections' (Gilligan 1993: 44–5). She explains that 'the failure to see the different reality of women's lives – and to hear the differences in their voices – stems in part from the assumption that there is a single mode of social experience and interpretation' (Gilligan 1993: 173).

Gilligan's concepts form part of the theoretical framework for the Stone Center, a feminist organization based in Boston, Massachusetts (Jordan 1997, 2007, 2009; Jordan *et al.* 1991; Miller 2003). The work of this centre exemplifies the quest among feminists to develop a theory and practice based on women's experiences of oppression and social inequality. The work of Jean Baker Miller, author of the seminal text *Towards a New Psychology of Women* (1986b), has been a central influence on the theoretical and practice perspective developed at the Centre, which stresses the importance of the *interconnectedness* between people. This has led to a radical reappraisal of the concept of dependency as a necessary and important element in relating. It has also led to a critique of concepts such as *mutuality* and the central place that empathy plays in terms of establishing a sense of *relatedness* and *connection*. These concepts have led to an important reappraisal of the therapist–client relationship, suggesting that the distance that is commonly promoted in therapeutic circles in the therapist–client relationship may not be appropriate or empowering within a feminist context.

Much of the development of 'feminist therapy' within the UK in the 1980s focused initially on the work of Luise Eichenbaum and Susie Orbach (1982, 1984) and other feminists involved in the London Women's Therapy Centre (Ernst and Maguire 1987; Krzowski and Land 1988). This centre drew on psychoanalysis, particularly object relations theorists such as Fairbairn (1952), Guntrip (1977), and Winnicott (1958, 1965), as well as feminist writers and theorists from the United States (Chesler 1974; Chodorow 1978; Dinnerstein 1978; Flax 1981; Mitchell 1974, 1984). This work also drew on a broader framework and a range of different therapeutic and practice approaches, such as gestalt, bioenergetics, psychodrama, assertiveness training, etc. Over time, a number of other therapy centres were set up in UK cities. The work of these centres tended to be focused on addressing issues that had been largely ignored in the past, such as group and individual therapy for women who were struggling with the impact of sexual abuse, rape, anorexia, bulimia, infertility, terminations, and so forth. The experiences of women from minority groups were also explored and workshops were run for black women (Hibbert and van Heeswyk 1988), lesbians (Ryan and Trevithick 1988), and working-class women (Trevithick 1988). Although feminist therapy is now less prominent, the learning acquired during this period was profound and had an impact at many different levels: the personal, professional, and political. And in some contexts, the impact of feminism is still evident. As an example of its professional impact, I was involved with other women in organizing three national women and social work conferences. (For further reading, see Benjamin 1998; Jordan 2009; Miller 2003; Seu and Heenan 1998.)

Normative theories and Eurocentric assumptions

It is important for us to engage in a dialogue in social work about whether 'normative' theories relating to human behaviour illuminate our understanding, given the fact that generalizations of this kind can be dangerous, particularly in relation to minority groups. An aspect of social psychology – and one where social workers, carers, and service users have much to contribute – concerns the impact of poverty, social inequalities, and discrimination on the quality of people's lives and what we can do, if anything, to strengthen people living in situations of adversity (Sheppard 2002). But to do this well involves being clear about the dangers of 'normative' theories. Daniel takes up this point:

> Because psychology is based heavily upon the construction of norms, there is a danger that people who deviate from the norm are considered to be 'abnormal', even though a norm is only an average of the spread of possibilities. When the norm becomes that which is desired and normative there is a danger of labeling people as deviant, even when they represent a part of the natural diversity of human beings.
>
> (Daniel 2008: 351)

Robinson takes this point further in relation to the normative assumptions made about black people:

> A main feature of Eurocentric psychology is the assumption among psychologists that people are alike in all important respects. In order to explain 'universal human phenomena', white psychologists established a normative standard of behaviour against which all other cultural groups were to be measured. What appeared as normal or abnormal was always in comparison to how closely a specific thought or behaviour corresponded to that of white people. Hence, normality is established on a model of the middle-class, Caucasian male of European descent. The more one approximates this model in appearance, values and behaviour, the more 'normal' one is considered to be.
>
> (Robinson 1995: 12)

In the case of women and black people, and in relation to all minority groups, the problem in establishing norms based on the values and assumptions of a dominant group is that they reinforce *their* reality *as reality*, with those at odds with this reality being seen – or seeing themselves – as deviant or deficient, or their experiences irrelevant in some way. Robinson highlights three models that have been used to describe human development:

- *The inferiority model*, which maintains that black people are 'intellectually, physically and mentally inferior to whites – due to genetic heredity' (Robinson 1995: 13).
- *The deficient (deprivations) model*, which states that black people are deficient in terms of intelligence, cognition and family structure, 'due to lack of proper environmental stimulation, racism, and oppressive conditions' (Robinson 1995: 13).
- *The multicultural model*, which differentiates between the difference and deficiency by acknowledging the strengths and limitations that all cultural

groups possess. Like Gilligan's work, it emphasizes the importance of minority groups defining themselves.

The conclusion that Robinson (1995) draws is that 'social work policies and practices are fundamentally Eurocentric' (p. 3), based on middle-class values and made up of 'mostly white middle-class people who are very much removed from the black population' (p. 4). In this context, cultural differences describe the beliefs, attitudes, values, and sanctioned behaviour that are shared by a group of people and community over time, or from one generation to another. Eurocentric is defined as:

> Understanding the ideas or practices of another culture in terms of those of one's own culture. Ethnocentric judgements fail to recognize the true qualities of other cultures. An ethnocentric individual is some-one who is unable, or unwilling, to look at other cultures in their own terms.
>
> (Giddens 2001: 688)

Robinson (1995: 5) further states that 'traditional principles and theories in psychology have not had sufficient explanatory power to account for the behaviour of black people in Britain'. Research in this area is limited – a point taken up by Ungar in relation to our understanding of how resilience is manifest in different cultures: 'We do not yet know what resilience means to non-western populations and marginalized groups such as Aboriginal people who live side-by-side with their "mainstream" neighbours in western settings' (Ungar 2004: 219). This criticism is important and one that could be extended to include other minority groups because none of the theories described in this chapter explore their relevance in relation to differences of class, race, gender, age, disability, sexual orientation, culture, and creed. The limitations of psychological theories in relation to black people calls for a revision of the existing theories to ensure that they are culturally sensitive and indicate a deeper understanding of the lives and culture of black people and the psychological characteristics that they tend to share.

In writing this chapter, my intention has been to keep alive the oppor-tunity to explore and debate whether different theories illuminate our un-derstanding of human beings and our current, day-to-day experiences as social work practitioners. They may not, but it seems important to arrive at this viewpoint from examining their strengths and limitations before casting them to sea. The perspective I have taken is that no one theory can speak to all aspects of the human condition or the different situations that we face. Also, theories have to be located in their own history and the cultural influences and limitations prevalent at particular times. We may believe our current awareness to be superior, but future generations may not be so kind. Most of the theories covered have been criticized for the fact that they do not have a research or an evidence base. However, the absence of evidence should not be taken to imply the absence of benefit – or the absence of relevance. If these theories illuminate our understanding of people and their social situation, then they have some relevance, despite their limitations. Uncertainty is a feature of social work and it is unlikely that we will ever be able to differentiate with confidence those areas of human behaviour that are knowable and those that are not. It is for these reasons that it is important to commit ourselves to exploring a range of explanations, positions, and theoretical underpinnings in the hope that this may provide greater understanding.

PART 2

SKILLS AND INTERVENTIONS

6 COMMUNICATION, OBSERVATION, LISTENING, AND ASSESSMENT SKILLS

Introduction

This chapter describes how *theoretical, factual,* and *practice knowledge,* covered in the previous chapters, can be applied in practice. Again, it is important to stress that the points covered do not relate solely to work with service users and carers. A great deal of our contact in social work is with other professionals, and with other people who play a significant role in relation to decisions that need to be made. Therefore, the application of all areas of knowledge needs to encompass every situation where, as practitioners, we are interacting with others in some way. The perspective emphasized in this section, and in other parts of this text, is that practice is an intellectual activity, as well as a practical endeavour. *Interventions,* therefore, constitute knowledge, skills, and values in action. As stated earlier, there is a tendency for social work educators, practitioners, students, and others to use practice terms differently, thereby making it difficult to give a coherent and 'intellectual account' of ourselves (England 1986: 56). It can also mean that the effectiveness of our interventions may be lost if we fail to used key terms in a rigorous way – in ways that have no agreed and precise meaning. And if we are confused, then it is likely that service users, carers, and others can be confused, which places our commitment to promoting partnership, empowerment, and service user/carer involvement on shaky foundations.

This chapter looks at a range of practice terms and how these have been defined, beginning with the importance of communication skills, and what is meant by the terms *skill* and *intervention,* before moving on to look at the following core skills that are covered in this chapter. These include:

1 Interpersonal skills
2 Verbal communication skills

3 Non-verbal communication skills
4 Observation skills
5 Listening skills
6 Assessment skill.

Interviewing skills belong to this 'family' of core skills but are covered separately in Chapter 7. Coverage of competences or a competency-based approach can be found in Chapter 10.

Communication skills

To understand another person, and their world of meaning, we need to start by acknowledging our ignorance of that person and their social world. This involves learning to ask good questions, in ways likely to provide information that is both relevant and sufficiently detailed, and to watch for clues. It also involves the importance of being 'culturally sensitive' (Robinson 2007: 160), that is, to combine being both sensitive and purposeful with being able to acknowledge the uncertainty that is inherent in looking across into another person's world.

Communication involves the exchange of information in verbal and non-verbal forms. As human beings, we are always communicating something, although this may not be in words. This can be evident in other areas of activity, such as what is communicated in writing and also in the actions we undertake. The knowledge, skills and values that we bring to our work are conveyed through our capacity to communicate with others.

Learning to understand what people are communicating – the meaning that is being conveyed – and communicating what we have understood in words is a crucial skill within social work. This may involve attempting to understand the young person who is disruptive in school, the person addicted to alcohol or drugs, the mother too depressed to get out of bed, the person whose strategy for getting what he or she wants is to steal, to lie, or to cheat, and the old person too fiercely independent to seek help when needed – they are all communicating something about how they feel about themselves, their lives, and the hardships and adversity they have experienced, and may still be experiencing.

These skills involve being able to communicate across a wide spectrum, from those located at the 'higher end' of the professional ladder, such as magistrates, doctors, consultants, solicitors, chief officers, or directors, to people who are struggling to survive at a different, often 'lower end' of the social ladder. In my experience, most social workers feel more comfortable talking to service users than people in senior positions. Our own reactions when we feel nervous or intimidated can be a valuable reminder of how intimidated some service users or carers may feel in relation to us. However, it is important that our own lack of confidence is not allowed to disadvantage the people we work with, remembering that we are less effective as social workers if we cannot communicate precisely and persuasively.

Skill

A central feature of competence is the term *skill*. However, it is a word that is rarely defined in social work texts and often used interchangeably with a range of different concepts such as *competence, intervention, aptitude, expertise,* and *technique.* For Shulman (1999: 4), the term skill refers to 'a specific behaviour that the worker uses in the helping process'. Many of the key skills of social work involve interpersonal skills that Dickson and Bamford (1995: 85) describe in terms of enabling the 'worker to engage meaningfully with the client'. Barker defines the term skill as follows:

> Proficiency in the use of one's hands, knowledge, talents, personality, or resources. A social worker's skills include being proficient in communication, assessing problems and client workability, matching needs with resources, developing resources, and changing social structures.
>
> (Barker 2003: 399)

This and other definitions tend to highlight the use of skills to achieve a particular purpose or outcome but fail to identify its specific features or how a particular skill might be acquired. As such, there is a tendency to see the term *skill* as being synonymous with the term *intervention* – which I define as two separate categories, with interventions being covered in the following section. Earlier, in this text I described the specific features of a skill as embodying five interweaving and overlapping characteristics:

> A *skill* is an action with a specific *goal* that can be *learnt*, that involves *actions performed in sequence*, that can be organized in ways that involve *economy of effort* and *evaluated* in terms of its relevance and effectiveness. Although these characteristics have been described separately, they interweave and overlap.

Although skills have distinct features, in relation to their use it is important to note that 'within any skilled performance these characteristics are closely bound together, and in order to gain an adequate view of the nature of skill all must be considered' (Welford 1958: 18). For example, the skill of driving a car involves a pre-set collection of actions that need to be carried out in sequence or in chronological order; that is, we generally put the gear stick into neutral, switch on the ignition, press the accelerator, press the clutch, and so on. In time, these tasks can be performed without conscious thought, although at the outset considerable mental concentration is required before we can drive in a way that is reliable and safe. The interrelated nature of different actions supports the argument against a competency-based approach, which separates out different actions or activities into their component parts. Driving would involve no movement if we only focused on one aspect of the task, such as switching on the ignition and turning on the engine. However, because skills cannot be divorced from the context within which they are used, the scene has to be taken into account – and this is constantly changing. For example, other drivers need to be considered, pedestrians, road conditions, rule-based requirements, such as traffic lights, and so forth (Koprowska 2010: 2). Thus, skills are inherently interactive in character and their use involves highly tuned intellectual skills.

It is essential to remember that ability can be taught but the perfecting of ability is dependent on deliberate and focused practice, not just doing the same actions over again. Here I am reminded of the well-known phrase *practice makes perfect* but it would be more accurate to state that *practice with honest and accurate feedback makes perfect*, since it is the opportunity to learn from our strengths and weaknesses that sound learning is acquired. Without feedback on how well we are performing, it is not possible to know how we can improve. The skills involved in giving and receiving feedback are covered later in this text. This learning is best acquired where time is set aside to prepare for the performance of a particular skill – and where guidance is also provided beforehand as well as afterwards. In addition, the capacity for self-reflection and self-criticism is important when working to consolidate existing skills and develop new ones.

As human beings, there are huge individual variations in relation to the skills we do – and do not – learn and how easy we find this learning. In general terms, one factor that enables a skill to be learned is a degree of innate or developed aptitude that an individual possesses. In this context, aptitude is defined as a natural or innate ability to do something. It is a relatively stable ability but one that can be modifiable by practice and that can enable the development of other abilities, including the development of new skills. For example, the ability to speak one foreign language often signals the ability to learn other languages, just as acquiring basic skills can lead to the development of more advanced skills. Yet the highest level of achievement in any area is largely acquired through practice.

If we define skills in terms of what we learn, then interventions describe how we put that learning into practice, that is, the actions we perform to influence events. For example, we do not know how well a skill has been learned until we try to put that skill into practice – as an intervention. For this reason, it is not always easy to separate the two concepts because they overlap and, for this reason, at times I have grouped skills and interventions together in this text. The next section covers how the different levels of skill can be categorized.

Categorizing different levels of skill

In Chapter 2, I gave an account of how generalist and specialist skills are defined in this text. The following coverage looks at the work of Dreyfus and Dreyfus (1986), who categorized skills in terms of five stages: *novice, advanced beginner, competent, proficient,* and *expert* levels of 'human skill acquisition'. Their five-stage typology of 'human skill acquisition' is shown in Box 6.1.

The typology proposed by Dreyfus and Dreyfus was used in a longitudinal study by Fook *et al.* (2000) to follow the progression of Australian students through a degree programme, and by Benner (1984) in relation to nursing. My interest in this typography has focused on attempting to identify the factors that enable students to progress in terms of their communication skills. For example, a student at the level of *novice* is likely to communicate in ways that indicate a greater concern with their own performance than a concern to communicate effectively, with the primary task being to 'get the demonstration over with'. Questions are likely to be basic and formulaic in character, with little emotional affect and clues not followed up. The body posture and facial expression are likely to come across as self-conscious or somewhat nervous, worried, or aloof. At the other end of the spectrum, at the level of *expert* a student is likely to demonstrate the ability to follow cues and to ask good questions in ways that communicate a clear engagement with the task. Questions emerge spontaneously and the direction of the interview tends to be determined by the service user but with some attempt to adhere to the purpose of the interview. This approach is an adaptation from the one proposed by Dreyfus and Dreyfus, who were interested to note the changes that could be identified in relation to the 'detached, rule-following beginner', who shows little capacity to engage and to be spontaneous and intuitive, compared with the 'involved, intuitive expert', who demonstrates a thoughtful and reflective engagement with the task (Dreyfus and Dreyfus 1986: 50).

Interventions

The word *intervention* is used a great deal, but rarely defined. It comes from the Latin *inter* (between) and *venire* (to come) and means *coming between.* As such, interventions lie at the heart of everyday social interactions and 'inevitably make up a substantial majority of human behaviour' (Kennard *et al.* 1993: 3) through our desire to shape events and to influence other

Box 6.1   The five stages of 'human skill acquisition' – Dreyfus and Dreyfus (1986)

Skill level	Description
Level 1 *Novice*	'... the novice learns to recognize various objective facts and features relevant to the skill and acquires rules for demonstrating actions based on those facts ... rules are to be applied to these facts regardless of what else is happening' (Dreyfus and Dreyfus 1986: 21).
Level 2 *Beginner*	'Performance moves to a marginally acceptable level only after the novice has considerable experience in coping with real situations ... Through practical experience in concrete situations with meaningful elements ... the advance beginner starts to recognize those elements when they are present' (Dreyfus and Dreyfus 1986: 22).
Level 3 *Competent*	'In general, a competent performer with a goal in mind sees a situation as a set of facts. The importance of the facts may depend on the presence of other facts ... [and] requires choosing an organizing plan. The competent performer ... feels responsible for, and thus emotionally involved in, the product of his choice ... and intensely involved in what occurs thereafter' (Dreyfus and Dreyfus 1986: 24–6).
Level 4 *Proficent*	'Usually the *proficient* performer will be deeply involved in his task and will be experiencing it from some specific perspective because of recent events ... As events modify the salient features, plans, expectations, and even the relevant salience of the features will gradually change.' An intuitive feature is evident: 'When we speak of intuition or know-how, we are referring to the understanding that effortlessly occurs upon seeing similarities with previous experiences' (Dreyfus and Dreyfus 1986: 27–9).
Level 5 *Expert*	'An expert generally knows what to do based on mature and practised understanding ... We usually don't make conscious deliberative decisions when we walk, talk, drive, or carry on most social situations. An expert's skill has become so much a part of him that he need be no more aware of it than he is of his own body ... experts do what normally works ... this deliberation does not require calculative problem solving, but rather involves critical reflecting on one's intuitions' (Dreyfus and Dreyfus 1986: 30–2).

human beings. Thus, interventions are not confined to professionals. In any given encounter, different people are intervening on their own behalf, or on the behalf of others, in an attempt to influence the course of events in some way. The social work interventions described in this text refer to:

The purposeful actions we undertake as professionals in a given situation, based on the knowledge and understanding we have acquired, the skills we have learned, and the values we adopt.

Interventions, therefore, constitute knowledge, skills, understanding, and values in action – a term that is 'analogous to the physician's term *treatment*' (Barker 2003: 226).

The context for an intervention in social work may focus on individuals, families, communities, groups, or organizations – actions that may be categorized in terms of *micro*, *mezzo*, and *macro* skills and interventions. These terms are featured in the Benchmark Statement for social work, which requires social workers to 'employ a critical understanding of human agency at the macro (societal), mezzo (organizational and community) and micro (inter and intrapersonal) levels' (QAA 2008: 11).

- *Micro* skills and interventions primarily focus on helping individual service users to address or solve the problems they encounter. This often involves looking at relationship difficulties in relation to partners, family members, friends, and neighbours.
- *Mezzo* skills and interventions 'refers to the nature of the neighbourhood and community, the expectations and atmosphere in the work setting, and the programmes and services available through relevant social and health delivery services' (Bogo 2006: 160). Interventions at this level are often focused on bringing people together, perhaps using negotiating and mediating skills.
- *Macro* skills and interventions emphasize the 'sociopolitical, historical, economic, and environmental forces that influence the overall human condition, cause problems for individuals, or provide opportunities for their fulfillment and equality' (Barker 2003: 257). Interventions at this level tend to be focused on organizational or agency policy and procedures, and the resource opportunities or access barriers that these bodies present. They are often focused on trying to alter the balance of forces or events in ways that favour service users' best interest and well-being.

Terms such as micro and macro link closely to the ecological model proposed by Bronfenbenner (1979) (see Appendix 4). In relation to UK social work training, there is a tendency to focus solely on teaching micro skills and interventions and for *macro* skills to be neglected (the term *mezzo* tends to be used less). A different way that interventions are categorized is in terms of the extent to which they focus on being directive and non-directive:

Directive interventions attempt to purposefully change the course of events and are often driven by an external imperative, such as agency policy and procedures, or the rules that govern a particular encounter. For example, they can involve providing information and prescriptive suggestions about what to do, or how to behave in certain circumstances, such as guiding a young person who has been involved in an incident and has been called to the head teacher. This range of interventions can be important, and a professional requirement, where immediate danger or risk is involved. However, caution is required particularly where differences in status are involved because directive interventions can fail to ensure that service users' wishes remain central to the decision-making process (Coulshed and Orme 2006: 268).

In *non-directive interventions*, the practitioner does not attempt to guide the decision-making process or to persuade an individual towards a particular choice or outcome. Instead, the task is to work with service users, carers, and others in ways that enable individuals to decide for themselves. This may involve helping people to problem-solve, or helping people to talk about their thoughts and feelings, and the different courses of action open to them (Lishman 2009a: 165). Counselling skills and strengths-based perspectives can be important in this regard.

Often our work involves both directive and non-directive elements and, once again, it is important to see both types of intervention as having something to offer in particular situations, since both have advantages and disadvantages. Some interventions may be better suited to certain problems, or the characteristics of a particular individual. The same is true of different practice approaches. For example, cognitive-behavioural approaches are generally considered to be more directive, but subject to some differences in emphasis depending on the disposition of the practitioner and the perspective adopted. On the other hand, community work and strengths-based perspectives almost always fall within this more non-directive category.

The focus of interventions

Some social work academics have expressed concern about the potentially 'invasive' nature of interventions and the different ways they can be used to control others (Dalrymple and Burke 2006). Certainly, an intervention in 'wrong hands' can be unhelpful and disempowering if delivered in ways that have no clear purpose or in-depth understanding of key issues and concerns. However, depending on the nature of the problem for which our help is being sought, some service users look for – and find – interventions that are supportive and helpful. Research indicates that service users value interventions where social workers demonstrate 'relevant experience and show appropriate knowledge' (Lishman 2009a: 12–13). Also valued are interventions where social workers communicate their commitment, concern, and respect for other people (Wilson 2000: 349).

A different concern, and one on which there is considerable disagreement, is focused on whether interventions should be targeted on personal change (micro intervention) or wider societal, environmental or political change (macro interventions). Here it is suggested that a micro practice orientation has tended to dominate macro perspectives, the latter often being linked to the importance of social justice and changing social structures (Hugman 2009). Once again, so much depends on the kind of help that is being sought. Some people may want help accessing a particular service, or other forms of help, and may not welcome interventions that are designed to steer them in a particular direction – such as behaviour change or social action. On the other hand, some problems are likely to persist or recur – or become intractable – if collective action is not taken. For example, I once worked on a council estate where the electricity tariff was set at an unacceptably high level by the electricity board for that region and, as a result, tenants were experiencing considerable financial hardship. The interventions that my colleagues and I adopted involved helping the tenants in question to set up a Tenants Association. The collective action that they initiated resulted in the tariff being significantly lowered. Similarly, proposed changes to the welfare benefit system, or the cost of social housing, are likely to impact negatively on the quality of life of a considerable number of people, unless these policies are challenged and modified by people coming together to take collective action.

We do not yet live in a fair and just society and it is our professional and moral duty to draw attention to the 'social ills' that disadvantage certain sectors of the population, namely people who are poor, sick, frail, or disadvantaged and discriminated against in some way. Advocacy skills are important in this context. Also important is the voice of 'users'. Lishman takes up this point:

> We need to acknowledge with users of services the social, political, economic and structural pressures which disadvantage them. When faced with structural problems for users of services, we need to work in ways which are empowering and do not individualize structural problems.
>
> (Lishman 2009a: 163)

Within this picture, the danger of individualizing problems is profound – and a danger that is difficult to avoid within a context where working with groups and communities is not considered to be a legitimate and essential social work activity. However, a major advantage of generalist skills is their transferability, which means that most of the skills and interventions covered in this text can be adapted in ways that enable practitioners to work with different groups of people but within a framework where people's right to privacy and the rules of confidentiality are acknowledged.

When and how to intervene

What is evident in the findings of the public inquiries into the deaths of children known to social services is the tragic consequences that can occur if we intervene in ways that are inappropriate and ineffective, that is, if we act in ways that fail to draw on a sound knowledge base and a clear understanding of the actions that need to be taken. Similarly, deciding not to intervene can lead to serious consequences. This kind of indecision may be based on the incorrect belief that by doing nothing, we will not be held responsible for later developments. It is not my intention to be alarmist but as professionals working with complex situations we are all likely to intervene in ways that are poorly thought through, ill-timed, badly expressed, or lacking a clear purpose or direction. Good supervision can help to avoid these shortcomings, as does eliciting feedback and support from our colleagues.

If we decide that we must act, it is important to ensure that our involvement is justified and falls within our professional and legal mandate (Roberts and Preston-Shoot 2000: 183). Establishing a mandate for our involvement is important in all situations, but particularly where we have a statutory responsibility to intervene, which may be the case when children or adults are at risk. In addition to our legal mandate, other decisions may influence our involvement, such as the urgency of the problem and the possible consequences that could ensue if we fail to act.

Writing in a groupwork context, Kennard *et al.* (1993: 6) provide a guide to the kind of questions that we might ask ourselves before making an intervention. I have adapted and extended this guide in ways that allow the questions posed to be relevant for use in different social work contexts, such as work with individuals, families, groups, communities, or organizations.

What is the situation that I am observing or have encountered?
↓
What data/evidence is there to confirm/refute my hypothesis?
↓
What factors or processes are contributing to this situation?
↓
Do I judge the situation/interaction to be constructive, destructive, or neutral?
↓
Would it be advantageous to change this situation/interaction?
↓

Is it possible to change it?

↓

What intervention(s) might influence this situation/interaction?

↓

Is the necessary intervention within my repertoire?

↓

Is the time/opportunity ripe for an intervention?

↓

What measures can I use to assess the effectiveness of my intervention?

↓

What measures can I use to assess the effectiveness of my work overall?

Clearly, it would not be possible to ask ourselves this range of questions in all situations, particularly those that call for immediate action, but questions of this kind can be useful when preparing for an interview, when reviewing what happened after the event, and when attempting to explore the impact and effectiveness of our interventions. The ability to deliver immediate, on-the-spot interventions is an important skill and one that becomes less daunting with practice and experience. Nevertheless, on-the-spot interventions can still be stressful, particularly when we feel nervous, pressured, tired, or when confronted with complex problems or confusing situations.

The first section of this chapter has looked at what is meant by the terms communication, skills, and interventions. We now turn to cover six specific skills mentioned at the beginning of this chapter.

Specific skills

1. Interpersonal skills

A different way that communication skills can sometimes be described is in terms of *interpersonal skills*, which is mainly used to describe what happens between people who are in direct contact. Koprowska emphasizes the interactive nature of interpersonal skills and the fact that the interaction, and our own reactions, can be far less predictable than we might imagine:

> We therefore bring consciousness and deliberation to interpersonal skills, and we constantly reassess what is happening, from moment to moment. This happens between people all the time, not just in social work encounters.
>
> (Koprowska 2010: 3)

Some individuals use the term 'people skills' (Thompson 2009) to describe the quality of contact, rapport, and relationship that has been established, although Dickson and Bamford note that 'relatively little has been published by way of a systematic exploration of current social work education/training provision in promoting skilled professional interaction' (1995: 85). This exploration has been a focus in counselling where the term interpersonal skills is commonly used. For example, McLeod describes interpersonal skills as a feature of competence in counselling:

> Competent counsellors are able to demonstrate appropriate listening, communicating, empathy, presence, awareness of non-verbal communication, sensitivity to voice quality, responsiveness to expressions of emotion, turn-taking, structuring time, use of language.
>
> (McLeod 2009: 613)

Most of the skills and interventions described in this text could be described as interpersonal skills. However, it is important to note that communication skills extend beyond the direct contact with other people to include activities, such as numeracy skills or information technology/computer skills.

2. Verbal communication skills

We use language to inform and shape the way we think, how we experience life, and to relate to other people. As professional social workers, it can be our choice of words, and the gestures, meaning, and understanding that accompany the words we use, that enable relationships to be formed and work to be done. This fact is evident when we consider the ongoing struggle within social work about which words to use, or what language to adopt, to describe certain situations or categories of people. The hope is that by changing the words we use, such as replacing the word 'client' with that of 'service user', there will be some fundamental shift in how people are viewed – and, of course, this can happen. A new word can give us hope, and help us to identify one another, but this cannot guarantee equality or justice. This can only be achieved through our commitment to strive for social justice and by being honest with ourselves, and others, about the real differences that exist – and the difficulties we encounter when trying to establish more equitable relationships. In relation to our own language, and the language that others adopt, this calls for a 'linguistic sensitivity' (Pugh and Williams 2006: 1229), so that we are aware of our language and can explain to other people, in a kindly and respectful way, what we might find problematic or discriminatory about their choice of words.

An example of the confusion caused through differences in language is demonstrated very clearly in *Getting the Message Across* (Social Services Inspectorate 1991), where one member of the project group circulated a questionnaire to 100 service users listing a range of words frequently used within social work. Others from the project consulted service users with a variety of special needs. The following shows how this group of service users understood certain terms. Their responses are shown in italics:

- voluntary agencies – *people with no experience, volunteers*
- maintain – *mixed up with maintenance – money paid for children in divorce settlements*
- sensitive – *tender and sore*
- encompass – *a way of finding direction*
- agencies – *second-hand clothes shops*
- common – *cheap and nasty (it is not advisable to talk about 'common' values)*
- eligibility – *a good marriage catch*
- allocation process – *being offered re-housing*
- function – *wedding (party), funeral*
- format – *what you wipe your feet on at the front door*
- gender – most did not know this word
- criteria – most did not know this word
- equitable manner – most did not know this term
- networks – no-one knew this word
- advocacy – some users thought this word meant that if they did not agree with the assessment they would have to go to court. They wondered who would pay the bill.

(Social Services Inspectorate 1991: 20)

In the light of these findings, the Social Services Inspectorate recommended that agencies should consider developing a local glossary of terms likely to be misunderstood and to involve service users in this task. For example, the term 'common purpose' used within this book – as well as other terms – may need to be clarified in this way. On the other hand, it is important for all people to be in a position to extend their vocabulary. As professionals, developing our 'linguistic aptitude' is important because, according to Hargie and Dickson (2004: 181), 'those with a wider vocabulary are better listeners, since they can more readily understand and assimilate a greater range of concepts'. At this point I am reminded of a service user I once worked with who began to cry when I said I was leaving my job. When I asked her to put into words what her tears meant, to my absolute surprise she replied, 'I feel sad because now I won't be able to learn new words'.

For the most part, the coverage of this theme has been based on the assumption that people have the ability to communicate with others and to use language without difficulty. However, some people have specific communication needs. For example, people who have a hearing impairment may need the support of a trained competent British Sign Language (BSL) interpreter. Loop systems are important for some people with hearing difficulties and good lighting for people who are sight impaired. Information for people with hearing and visual impairments needs to be provided in an appropriate and accessible format (Beresford *et al.* 2005). Some individuals who have communication problems, perhaps due to a disability, may require specialist support to aid communication, such as Makaton, a system of signing sometimes used with people with learning disabilities. The use of Braille for people who are visually impaired tends to be less popular than other low-vision aids.

3. Non-verbal communication skills

The importance of non-verbal forms of communication, sometimes described in terms of body language, should not be underestimated. For example, in the classic study by Birdwhistell (1970), an early authority in this field, it was 'claimed that the average person actually speaks for a total of only ten to eleven minutes daily, the standard spoken sentence taking only about 2.5 seconds' (Hargie and Dickson 2004: 46). Birdwhistell's research used slow-motion film footage of people talking and an interesting conclusion drawn from this research suggests that no gestures convey the same meaning universally. For example, all human beings smile but the significance and meaning that can be attributed to smiling can vary in different cultures. The following quotation highlights the ambiguity of our non-verbal communication in relation to interviewing:

> Detailed studies have identified many items in the nonverbal vocabulary, including five thousand distinctly different hand gestures and one thousand different steady body postures. Precise observation of nonverbal behaviour is important, but it is only a first step. The interviewer still has to infer some valid meaning from the data. Accurate observation is a necessary but insufficient requisite for understanding the psychological relevance of the gesture.
>
> (Kadushin and Kadushin 1997: 315)

Another influential author in this field, Mehrabian (1972), estimated that in a typical encounter involving two people, 'the overall communication is made up of body language (55 per cent), paralanguage (the non-verbal aspects of speech) 38 per cent and the verbal 7 per cent' (Hargie and Dickson 2004: 45–7). These findings are sometimes referred to as the '3 Vs' – verbal, vocal, and visual or as the '7%–38%–55% rule'. In addition, it is estimated that more weight is given to non-verbal forms of communication, particularly when there is a conflict between verbal and non-verbal forms, because the assumed meaning, once picked up, cannot easily be accessed or refuted (Hargie and Dickson 2004: 45).

The analysis of what is being communicated non-verbally is a complex undertaking and one prone to 'common-sense' interpretations that may not be accurate. For example, I once worked in a residential setting where the self-injuring behaviour of a young woman, Anna, was described by a staff member as 'attention-seeking'. Another understood the same behaviour to be an indicator that Anna was feeling 'safe'. One had a negative understanding, the other a positive one, but others felt both to be inaccurate or incomplete understanding. Anna's own understanding, which had not been sought, was that she had 'had enough', having been let down by her parents and foster-carers. She had every reason to be distressed but this information was not sought and, as a result, her behaviour was not understood. This example illustrates a tendency within social work to attribute the behaviour of service users to personality characteristics rather than outside forces, while service users are more likely to cite external causes and situational variables as responsible for many of their problems and choices. In all communication, but particularly the non-verbal forms, there can be a miscommunication between the message sent and the message received. This is more likely to happen when we are operating from a set of assumptions. We see and hear through our histories and this can have advantages and disadvantages. Our best safeguard is to check our perceptions directly with the person in question but this too may fail if the person is not able, for whatever reason, to reveal his or her true thoughts and feelings.

Lishman (2009a: 34–9) divides non-verbal communication into two broad areas: proxemics (distance and physical closeness) and kinesics (movements, gestures, expressions). Lishman also includes the importance of 'symbolic communication', where 'punctuality, reliability and attention to detail are symbolic of the worker's care, concern and competence' (2009a: 30). In texts from the United States, these may adopt a more specialist range of terms. For example, Kadushin and Kadushin (1997: 287–320) included the following terms as specific features of non-verbal communication. The italics indicate my explanation of what these terms cover:

- chronomics (*time keeping, such as the likelihood of people being too early or too late; preparedness*)
- artificial communication (*the language of the physical setting, such as how the home is arranged and personal presentation, such as personal dress, choice of clothes*)
- smell (*emotional states communicated through subtle changes in body odour*)
- touch (*handshaking, hugs, which tend to be defined according to the situation and cultural norms*)
- paralinguistics (*cues that depend on hearing and how words are said in terms of their tone, pitch, volume, speed, emphasis, intonation, articulation, and intensity*)
- proxemics (*communication through space and distance; the distance people need to feel comfortable*)
- body language kinesics (*visual communication through the face, eyes, hands and arms, feet and legs*)

For example, I would describe returning a telephone call to service users, carers, and other professionals as a 'symbolic communication' because it communicates to other people that their communications are important. It can also communicate the sense that we are disciplined and rigorous in our professional approach. Similarly, how we dress can be significant: 'The way we dress communicates symbolically something of ourselves, and will have symbolic meaning for users of services and colleagues depending on age, culture, class and context' (Lishman 2009a: 29). I recall a social worker being bewildered by a service user who complained when the social worker arrived to introduce himself wearing dirty jeans and a combat jacket. Or again, I recall my own shortcomings when I have let children and young people down by cancelling appointments or failing to turn up on time. My explanations felt insignificant compared with the distress I caused. Our mistakes can sometimes be worthwhile if we allow ourselves to be changed by our errors.

Given the central importance of communication skills in social work, it is surprising to realize the limited research that has been undertaken in this field. For example, in a study that looked at the communication skills employed by child care practitioners, an extensive literature search by the authors could only locate 'three studies published since 1985 that directly collected information on interviews with parents where there were child welfare concerns' (Forrester *et al.* 2007: 42). This research analysed 24 taped interviews involving social workers, where an actor played the part of a parent, as a 'simulated client'. The findings indicate:

> ... that often social workers are *not* communicating well with parents. The implications for training, professional supervision and research are profound ... this is perhaps just one manifestation of a general lack of attention to directly observing and improving the skills we use in practice. As a profession we need to focus far more on what social work communication skills are, what impact they have on the process of interviews and outcomes for clients, and how we can help individuals develop and maintain them.
>
> (Forrester *et al.* 2007: 50)

Our failure to focus on the importance of communication skills in social work is also evident in the fact that, to date, no adequate test of student or practitioner performance has been developed and accepted within the social work community in relation to communication skills (Clark 1995), although some progress has been made in this area in other countries, such as Canada (Bogo 2006; Bogo *et al.* 2004). It is an area, as Forrester and colleagues note, where the 'systemic lack of support for the development of communication skills within the profession' needs to be addressed (Forrester *et al.* 2008: 1317).

4. Observation skills

Our understanding of non-verbal forms of communication is usually gathered through our observations. These help us to understand and to formulate hypotheses about what is actually happening and why, and to check out the reliability of our perceptions against those of other people and other information available. We can learn a great deal through observing other people, such as what is being transmitted through their tone of voice, the speed with which they communicate, their volume and intonation, posture and gestures. However, what we see has to be interpreted, and our assumptions noted, because without some form of interpretation, hypothesis, or analysis, our understanding can only be descriptive. Gambrill stresses the importance of observation skills in social work:

> Observation in real-life settings may be required to clarify problems and identify related circumstances. Without a fine-grained (detailed) description of problem-related contingencies based on careful observation, you may make inaccurate assumptions about maintaining conditions. You may overlook problem-related behaviours and misapplied and unapplied contingencies. Observation systems are available for observing and recording collective action ... Each individual and each environment is unique. Only through careful observation may interaction patterns between clients and significant others be understood.
>
> (Gambrill 2006: 487)

Observation skills can be used quite generally or as a specific intervention. Inviting another colleague to sit in on a particular meeting or interview to gain a different perspective would be an example of using observation as an intervention. Whether used as a general or specific tool to understand both the content and process of a particular interaction, observations can be important when attempting to understand the nature of the interaction between individuals. In addition, our capacity for self-observation, although always somewhat limited, provides us with an opportunity to analyse our own role and impact (Sheldon 1995: 132–3). Le Riche and Tanner outline the advantages that 'intentional observation' can offer:

> Observation can best be understood as a complex concept which not only includes sensory processes such as seeing, but also incorporates purpose and action. An observation continuum locates informal, everyday 'tacit' processes at one end and more purposeful 'intentional' observation leading to action at the other. Social workers are involved in observation at all points in this continuum, but, in their professional roles, intentional observation can contribute to the development of good practice in a range of activities such as assessment, planning, supervision and service delivery. Observation also plays a significant part in social work education.
>
> (Le Riche and Tanner 2000: 233)

Common errors when observing others include:

- Failing to see the significance of what we are observing. This may be due to relying too heavily on our own experiences, the views of others or common-sense notions.

- Failing to link our observations to what is known about the behaviour, situation, or individual in question, that is, the theoretical, factual, and experiential knowledge available.
- Being unaware of our assumptions and preconceptions in ways that interfere with our capacity to observe behaviour and events from a more impartial and open-minded perspective, such as labelling or stereotyping people, including other professionals.
- Failing to give adequate importance to factors that may give rise to certain behaviour, reactions, or events such as the context or setting, the triggers (antecedents) and impact (consequences), and how these different factors impact on people.
- Being imprecise and woolly in our account of the behaviour or events we observe.
- Generalizing behaviour in ways that may not be accurate. For example, what occurs in one situation (school) may not occur in other situations (youth club).
- Being too hasty in our need to draw conclusions from our observations. Our inferences need to be tentative hypotheses – unless there is ample evidence on which to base our conclusions.
- Assuming that the agreement of others implies accuracy and valid inferences have been formulated. This links to the concept of *groupthink* (Janis 1982) – where groups arrive at faulty decisions based on the belief that the greater the number of people that agree, the greater the truth or accuracy of the conclusions drawn.

If an observer is to be invited to 'sit-in', it is important to explain the purpose of the observation and to seek the permission of the service user before the session, so that they have the chance to refuse without feeling 'put on the spot'. This is important for the person being observed, because it can be quite unnerving to be watched by another human being, particularly when the observation is in silence and undertaken by a professional. As human beings, we all have parts of our personality that we do not want to be seen by others. Also, being observed can give rise to a range of worries and fantasies about the observer, particularly what the observer is thinking: some people interpret silence as someone being critical. Again, these concerns need to be addressed. Where part of the process involves giving feedback, unless the purpose is to be more confrontational, it can help to be more descriptive than interpretative in the observations offered, thereby allowing the individual to form their own conclusions and inferences. Finally, it is worth remembering that if invited to observe a session in silence, particularly when it involves the disclosure of abuse or other traumatic experiences, the observer can sometimes leave the session feeling distressed from being exposed to feelings in an unguarded way. In this situation, I have found it helpful for the observer to be able to take notes or to sit in a place where some distance can be established. These difficulties need to be explored beforehand

and discussed in supervision so that the benefits of direct observation are not lost.

5. Listening skills

Barker defines listening skills as follows:

> The ability to acquire and process the verbal and other cues of another and generally comprehend the meaning of the communication. When such skills are effective, they include looking at and acknowledging the communicator; hearing and noting the other's words and accompanying gestures; and providing feedback, questions, and expressions of understanding when appropriate.
>
> (Barker 2003: 279)

Listening skills are essential in a whole range of different situations – when listening to colleagues, attending meetings, engaging in inter-agency collaboration – in fact, in all situations where communication is a central theme. A characteristic of a 'good listener' is that they are 'oriented to other people rather than to themselves. They are good observers of other people. They accurately note what others say and how they say it, as well as nonverbal cues' (Gambrill 2006: 306).

It is estimated that something like 45 per cent or more of our waking lives is spent listening. However, where listening performs part of our professional role this figure is higher. As people and as professionals, there are several reasons why we listen to others. The following list indicates some of the main benefits involved in listening, such as the opportunity to:

- gather information and to begin to understand the hopes, fears, and expectations, and ongoing concerns that a person is harbouring
- gain an impression of a person's strengths and areas of vulnerability and fragility
- understand the meaning attached to certain experiences and events, and their ongoing impact
- identify what is not being said, and to hypothesize why this might be the case.

Providing an unhurried and safe opportunity for people to express their thoughts, feelings, and reactions is particularly important for people who have been silenced or have lost confidence in their ability to express themselves. Being sensitive in this way is essential when listening to children and young people (Lefevre 2010). A range of adjectives are used to describe listening skills so as to stress the different aspects involved within this process, such as *attentive* listening, *intuitive* listening, *empathic* listening, *active* listening, *credulous* listening, *non-selective* or *non-directive* listening, *interpretive* listening, *reflective* listening, and so forth. In their different ways, they all emphasize the importance of understanding another human being and being able to express that understanding in words and gestures. The following examples provide a flavour of the different emphasis that might be deployed.

- *Active listening* (Moss 2008: 14–22). Active listening describes a special and demanding alertness on the part of the listener, where the aim is to listen closely to the details of what is being conveyed and to ensure that the person is aware that this is happening.
- *Credulous listening* (Feltham and Dryden 2004: 129). Credulous listening is believing what is being communicated. This description aptly fits much of social work where, in the face of evidence to the contrary, we might doubt the evidence before we doubt the individual. While this might be the correct initial approach to follow, we must always be open to reviewing our judgements in the light of new information.
- *Non-selective listening* (Lishman 2009a: 98). This is sometimes called *non-directive listening* or *evenly suspended attention*. This is where listening occurs at several levels, such as: what people say, how they say it, at what point they say certain things, whether certain themes recur, and also what people do not say. This is sometimes described as 'listening with the third ear'. This form of listening allows us to be sensitive to the wider social and cultural context from which an individual speaks. The intention is to minimize our own personal bias and stereotypical assumptions and to follow the speaker's lead.

The skills involved in listening
The importance of creating a safe environment, free from distractions, when listening to others has to be stressed. Listening provides a creative opportunity to demonstrate our commitment and care: it is an essentially respectful undertaking, particularly if done with generosity. When listening in silence, this commitment, warmth, and concern must be conveyed through our body language, which, if done well, may speak so clearly that the individual never realizes that we have said nothing in words. The following is a list of the 20 basic skills involved in listening:

- being as open, intuitive, empathetic, and self-aware as possible
- maintaining good eye contact
- having an open and attentive body orientation and posture
- paying attention to non-verbal forms of communication and their meaning
- allowing for and using silence as a form of communication
- taking up an appropriate physical distance
- picking up and following cues
- being aware of our own distracting mannerisms and behaviour
- avoiding making vague, unclear, and ambiguous comments
- being aware of the importance of people finding their own words in their own time

- remembering the importance of the setting and the general physical environment
- minimizing the possibility of interruptions and distractions
- being sensitive to the overall mood of the interview, including what is not being communicated
- listening for the emotional content of the interview and adapting questions as appropriate
- checking out and seeking feedback wherever possible and appropriate
- being aware of the importance of timing, particularly where strong feelings are involved
- remembering the importance of tone, particularly in relation to sensitive or painful issues
- avoiding the dangers of preconceptions, stereotyping or labelling, or making premature judgements or evaluations
- remembering to refer to theories that are illuminating and helpful and also, where appropriate, take the opportunity to explain, in an accessible language, theories that may aid understanding
- being as natural, spontaneous, and relaxed as possible.

Most people think that listening is an easy activity. As a result, for many it is considered an innate skill that comes naturally and, therefore, needs no training – but this is not the case. The essence of good listening is learning about how to reach the emotions and thoughts of others – this is not a skill that can easily be taught. The misconception that listening is easy can be based on a failure to differentiate between listening and hearing. We may hear what is being said, but this may be a passive activity, whereas listening requires a more active involvement. Kadushin and Kadushin (1997: 50) differentiate between the two by describing hearing as a physiological act, the appreciation of sound, whereas listening is seen as a cerebral act – that of understanding.

Inadequate listening

Egan (2002: 75–6) uses a range of terms to describe inactive or inadequate listening, including *non-listening, partial listening, tape-recorder listening* (merely repeating the client's words), and *rehearsing* (where the interviewer stops listening to rehearse a response). Smith divides poor listeners into three categories:

- *Pretend listeners* – are 'not actually listening at all but only pretending to'. They have learnt to respond in appropriate places, thereby giving the impression of listening.
- *Limiting listeners* – practise 'a type of partial listening where the listener consciously determines that he [*sic*] will attend only certain portions of the speaker's remarks', often those aspects considered more interesting.
- *Self-centred listeners* – 'are concerned only with themselves and pay little or no attention to others'.

(Smith 1986: 261–2)

There are times, particularly when we are tired or preoccupied, when we are all prone to being poor or inadequate listeners. However, to become locked into the habit of not listening is serious because these patterns can be difficult to shift. For example, in a study that evaluated the level of skills achieved on a two-day workshop on motivational interviewing for experienced social workers, it was found that 'practitioners did not . . . demonstrate high-quality listening skills post-training' (Forrester *et al.* 2008: 1308). Instead, practitioners tended to be more confrontational in their approach to the role-play scenario chosen. However, this approach was amenable to change because the findings of this study suggest that the experience of attending the workshops led most workers to increase their listening skills and to be less confrontational in their approach (Forrester *et al.* 2008: 1314).

6. Assessment skills

An assessment involves an attempt to understand the nature of a problem, its cause, and what needs to be done to resolve or to minimize its impact. It is a term that could be considered to embody both task and process elements. For example, an initial assessment could be a one-off task where the case is closed at an early point. Or an assessment that requires our continuous involvement could be considered in terms of an ongoing process:

> Assessment is not a single event, it is an ongoing process, in which the client or service user participates, the purpose of which is to assist the social worker to understand people in relation to their environment. Assessment is also a basis for planning what needs to be done to maintain, improve or bring about change in the person, the environment or both.
>
> (Coulshed and Orme 2006: 24)

The ongoing involvement that is described above can be portrayed differently – in terms of monitoring, reviewing, or evaluating progress, but whatever term is used, almost all assessments stress the importance of collaborating with others, particularly service users and carers, but also other professionals and involved individuals. Also central to the task and process of assessment is the emphasis placed on social and environmental factors. This emphasis means that the focus of the assessment will differ depending on the context and the particular problems and specific characteristics of the people involved – a point I return to.

Three points are worth noting. First, that undertaking an assessment can involve almost all the repertoire of interventions described in this book. The skill is in *knowing how* to use certain interventions – and decisions of this kind cannot be based on a formula because they are dependent on the unique features of the situation or context. Second, 'traditionally in social work, assessment has been about identifying deficits or difficulties rather than strengths, with an emphasis on matching needs with eligibility for services' (Crisp *et al.* 2003: 2). The problematic features of this deficit model are covered in Chapter 4. Third, it is interesting to note that a SCIE Knowledge Review on assessment found 'no singular theory or understanding as to what the purpose of assessment is and what the process should entail' (Crisp *et al.* 2003: v). This may in part be due to the fact that assessments take a different form depending on the problem presented and the area of practice, such as children's services, adult care, mental health, criminal justice, and carer services. In addition, complex legislative requirements often also shape the assessment process.

'Difficulties' and 'problems'

When attempting to conceptualize what constitutes a problem and how they arise, it is worth noting that we know more about *what* happens than *why* certain events or incidents occur. In relation to serious social problems, such as child abuse, substance misuse, suicide, and crime, there 'are the many uncertainties and controversies about the nature, immediate causes or explanations of these problems' (Parton and Kirk 2010: 29). Situations that are defined as 'problems' tend to be influenced by ideology and what people are prepared to tolerate. For example, taking illicit drugs has been outlawed much more than alcohol, despite the fact that the health and social problems that arise from alcohol consumption outweigh those associated with the use of drugs. Alcohol consumption is a source of revenue for the UK Government.

In most social work texts, the words 'problem' and 'difficulty' tend to be used interchangeably. However, Watzlawick *et al.* (1974) use 'difficulties' to refer to everyday, undesirable or unbidden events that can be resolved through relatively straightforward solutions. They can describe dilemmas that have 'no known solution and which – at least for the time being – must simply be lived with' or accommodated in some way (Watzlawick *et al.* 1974: 39). The idiosyncratic and irritating behaviour of some family members is an example of a difficulty that must be endured and tolerated. 'Problems', on the other hand, are situations, thoughts, feelings, or experiences that are too troublesome, perplexing, distressing, or complex for people to deal with, solve, or overcome without help and support. Often several difficulties occur together, and where people are not helped, this can result in a transition from difficulties to problems. This highlights the importance of preventative measures and early intervention.

Common problems

In a previous paper (Trevithick 2003), I cited Reid's influential categorization of nine 'unsatisfied wants' (Reid 1978: 25–30). Here, I wish to reorder and simplify this list and to categorize these 'unsatisfied wants' in terms of problems relating to *self*, *others*, and to *society* at large (SOS). Eight of Reid's 'unsatisfied wants' could be categorized as follows:

- Problems that predominantly focus on how people relate to themselves, i.e. *difficulties in role performance, reactive emotional distress, decision problems, and psychological or behavioural problems not elsewhere classified* (S).
- Problems relating to other people, i.e. *interpersonal conflict* and *dissatisfaction in social relations* (O).
- Problems relating to how people fit into society or relate to large institutions, i.e. *problems with formal organizations* and *inadequate resources* (S).

The last category identified by Reid covered *other and unclassifiable* areas (Reid 1978: 314), which could be said to include all – or a combination of – his previous categories. All these problems interlink and overlap but the reason for trying to simplify different 'wants' is to identify what problem, if any, tends to dominate and how does this problem impact on others and society at large. For example, depression is a distress that is felt personally (S) but one that is likely to impact on other family member (O) and one that has consequences for society at large as a measure of people's well-being and in terms of the financial cost involved in health care provision (S).

Six main tasks involved in an assessment

1 *Interpret and analyse information received.* This may begin with an analysis of the initial referral or in relation to ongoing work, may focus on new information or data that has emerged. This is likely to involve further information gathering and searching for confirming and disconfirming information/data.

2 *Clarify the problem.* This may involve forming hypotheses on what is happening and why, and possible solutions to be sought. It may include a systemic or ecological approach to the problems initially identified, thereby ensuring that environmental factors are not overlooked. Of particular importance will be the urgency of the situation, degree of risk, and any safety issues that may be involved.

3 *Identify the collaborative framework to be adopted.* This includes identifying the role that service users and carers will play in the assessment process, plus the input that other professional organizations, agencies, or individuals might perform.

4 *Identify an agreed set of goals and an action plan.* This action plan needs to include, whenever possible, baseline data that indicates the frequency, intensity, or severity of problems identified so that this information can be compared at a later point. Where appropriate, it can be important to engage service users in data collection. At an early point, it can also be helpful to identify possible barriers to progress and how these might be addressed or overcome.

5 *Implementation strategy.* This involves identifying the decision-making process, particularly the actions or interventions that different individuals or organizations have agreed to undertake and also what monitoring, review, or ongoing system will be put in place to provide an update on any changes or developments that have occurred.

6 *Evaluation of effectiveness.* This involves thinking about what format or system will be adopted to evaluate the effectiveness of the interventions adopted and the extent to which agreed outcomes have been achieved. For example, it could involve reviewing any changes that have taken place against the initial baseline data collected and any follow-up work that may be undertaken to identify what progress, if any, has been maintained over time.

The course of action outlined above might appear relatively straightforward and this may be the case if the problem presented is not complex and clearly defined. However, in social work this is often not possible. Instead, we are often trying 'to achieve a satisfactory balance between diverse needs, recognized risks and restricted resource provision' (Milner and O'Byrne 2009: 18). Other difficulties include time restraints and also the fact that many of the situations encountered are fraught with uncertainty.

In relation to the meaning of events, and what may be the underlying cause of a particular problem, there can be a tendency to want to 'search for long-lost causes' – to become a Miss Marple or Sherlock Holmes – which Sheldon regards with suspicion, except in the case of major trauma, for the following reasons:

(a) there is no guarantee that they will ever be found;
(b) because the exercise is costly in time and resources;
(c) when views as to the original causes of problems *can* be elicited they are not always agreed upon by the protagonists, nor are they necessarily valid;
(d) dwelling on the history of problems can sometimes serve to intensify bad feelings and can distract from the necessity of doing something positive in the here and now.

(Sheldon 1995: 112–13)

This last point is important. Sometimes we may focus on the past because we do not know how to address the problem that has been presented. On the other hand, it is sometimes clear that service users want to explore past events, and it can be unhelpful and over-prescriptive to steer them away from their natural inclination. Narrative approaches, and some psychosocial and strengths-based approaches, use self-selected 'story-telling' as a specific intervention and assessment approach. Recounting their lives in this way can lead some people to change their perceptions and outlook on life.

Practice emphasis in assessment

Within some practice approaches, the assessment task is likely to have a different focus, with greater weight being given to certain factors or problems over others, and different solutions being proposed. For example, in a cognitive-behavioural approach to assessment considerable focus is placed on the here-and-now picture, and the causes (antecedents) and effects (consequences) that influence problems. (For further coverage on the emphasis that tends to be adopted in different practice approaches, see Milner and O'Byrne 2009.) All practice approaches and perspectives emphasize the importance of practitioners being empathic, respectful, and caring and also warm and genuine or 'congruent' (Gambrill 2006: 51) in their contact with service users and others.

The *Knowledge and Skills Framework* used within this text provides a rigorous and systematic approach to the task of assessment (Box 6.2 on pp. 180–1). Its advantage is that it identifies different aspects of the assessment process that tend to be taken for granted or forgotten, such as the part played by legislation or agency policy and practice in relation to service delivery. In Box 6.2, the six main tasks involved in an assessment are indicated in bold italics, and are described in greater detail elsewhere in this chapter.

The following example gives an account of an incomplete assessment and the kind of issues that can be overlooked within this process:

- Problem-related behaviours are not clearly described
- The functions (meaning) of behaviours of concern are unknown
- Cultural factors are overlooked
- Clients' assets (strengths) are overlooked
- Positive alternative behaviours to undesired behaviours are not identified
- Baseline data are not available (i.e. descriptions of the frequency/duration of behaviours, thoughts, or feelings before intervention)
- The cause of behaviour (e.g. aggression) is assumed to be another behaviour (e.g. low self-esteem)
- Higher level contingencies are overlooked (e.g. loss of welfare payments).
  (Gambrill 2006: 526)

Different ways of doing an assessment

Different organizations and agencies adopt different ways of undertaking an assessment. These can include:

- *Practitioners working alone*, which is the most common format.
- *Joint assessment*, which mainly refers to two practitioners working together. This is particularly valuable where the situation is fraught or the problems are complex.

- *Group* or *team assessment*, where everyone who has had contact with the family or group contributes what they have experienced or perceived.
- *Multidisciplinary assessment*, which involves professionals from different disciplines working together, sharing their knowledge and expertise in ways that effectively meet the different needs of service users.

The opportunity to work with other colleagues is important. In the section on interviewing skills in Chapter 8, there is coverage of the different settings that may be the context for an assessment to be undertaken.

Needs-led versus resource-led assessments

A *needs-led* assessment is based on the needs of an individual and is often contrasted with *service-led* assessments where access to services is determined largely by the availability of local authority funding rather than by individual need.

> In a needs–led model, social workers are required to undertake an assessment to identify a person's needs, such as 'needs help to wash and dress', and to gain an understanding of a person's circumstances to enable them to establish the provision that will best meet identified needs.
>
> (Leece and Leece 2011: 209)

Identifying the needs of service users and carers is included in the legislation that regulates certain areas of social work practice, such as the needs-led policies defined under the National Health Service and Community Care Act 1990, The Carers (Recognition and Services) Act 1995, and Chronically Sick and Disabled Persons Act 1971 (Munby 2008: 458–68). An example of the shift in thinking in relation to meeting the needs of service users can be seen in the enactment of the Community Care (Direct Payments) Act 1996, where local authorities were given powers to make cash payments to enable service users to purchase their own assistance.

However, a tension exists between needs-led and service-led assessments – a tension is likely to persist where demand for resources exceeds supply. Who gains access to resources and what happens to those who fail to qualify is a crucially important issue and an ongoing concern for practitioners and policy-makers committed to creating a more equitable system for the allocation of resources. It is a situation that can often lead to public complaints and media criticism.

Risk assessments

Increasingly assessments are being focused on the extent to which a particular individual or problem poses a risk to themselves, to others or to society

Box 6.2   Assessments based on *the Knowledge and Skills Framework*

Theoretical knowledge	What theories would illuminate our understanding of the nature of the problem and what needs to be done? What theories would enable me to: 1. *Interpret and analyse information received?* 2. *Clarify the problem?*	
Adapted theories	What theories would help to illuminate what is happening and why?	*Psychology* • humanist? • behaviourist? • psychodynamic? *Sociology* • class and stratification? • gender relations? • racism and equality?, etc.
Role and task	What role I am expected to adopt or what role do I consider most appropriate?	• care or control? • pursue causes (radical) or carry out functions (conservative)? • a 'rational-technical' activity or 'practical-moral' activity?, etc.
Theories that inform direct practice	What generalist and specialist skills would be appropriate?	*Generalist skills and interventions* (see the lexicon of 80 skills on p. 46): information gathering, analysing and synthesizing the data, decision-making, taking action, etc.
	Where should our primary and secondary focus lie?	*Fields of practice:* work with individuals, families, groups, communities?
	Which practice approach – or combination of approaches – would be better?	*Practice approaches:* cognitive-behaviourist, ecological, person-centred psychosocial, task-centred?, etc.
	Would a particular perspective provide a clearer picture of the nature of the problem and what is to be done?	*Values based perspectives:* anti-oppressive practice, feminist, child-centred, radical, strengths-based?, etc.
Factual knowledge	What factual information or data would ensure that the approach adopted is knowledge and research-based? 3. *What is my agency's policy in relation to the collaborative framework to be adopted?* 4. *What factual knowledge do I need in order to draft an agreed set of goals and action plan?*	
Law	What legislation is mandatory in this assessment?	• Carers (Recognition and Services) Act 1995? • Criminal Justice Act 2003? • Children's Act 2004? • Mental Capacity Act 2005? • Mental Health Act 2007?

Social policy	What social policy is relevant?	• *Every Child Matters* (Department for Education and Skills 2003)? • *National Framework for Older People* (Department of Health 2001)? • *Our Health. Our Care, Our Say* (Department of Health 2006)? • *Transforming Social Care* (Department of Health 2008a)? • *Putting People First* (Department of Health 2008b)?
Agency policy	What is my agency policy and practice in relation to this case?	• CAF (ICS) assessment? • rule-based and procedure-driven interventions? • recording system? • what is the agency's approach to partnership collaborative links? • what influence can service users and carers have on agency policy and practice? • inter-agency collaboration? • multidisciplinary approach?
Knowledge of problems	What knowledge do I need to have about the nature of the problems already identified?	• emotional, physical, sexual abuse; neglect; mental health/capacity; bereavement and loss; adoption/fostering; domestic violence/abuse; family disruption/breakdown; health/ill-health; homelessness; aggressive or violent behaviour?, etc.
Knowledge of people	What knowledge do I need to have about the specific group of people involved?	• social class; gender; race/ethnicity; infants; children; young people; older people; physical disability; learning disability; asylum seekers; gay/lesbian/bisexual/trans-gender people; other minority/indigenous groups (e.g. travellers)?, etc.
Practice knowledge	**How can I use the theoretical and factual knowledge I have acquired in ways that ensure that agreed outcomes can be achieved?** 5. *How can I use the knowledge and skills that I and others bring to the encounter to draft an appropriate implementation strategy?* 6. *Evaluation of effectiveness – what system should I set in place?*	
Knowledge use	What knowledge, skills, and interventions can I use to help bring about the changes that have been agreed or that are being sought?	• reflection/reflexivity? • analysis and synthesis? • forming hypotheses? • critical thinking? • problem-solving? • judicious decision-making?
Knowledge creation	How can I use what I know to be more imaginative and creative in my approach?	• professional use of self? • intuition? • tacit knowledge? • transferability? • practice wisdom?

at large. The following quotation highlights the rationale for focusing on risk:

> There is a balance to be struck between enabling people to have control over their lives and ensuring that they are free from harm, exploitation and mistreatment, particularly if they have the capacity to make informed choices.
>
> (Department of Health 2005: 28)

However, the changes introduced in the NHS and Community Care Act 1990 have led to a situation where 'a preoccupation with risk and its management has engulfed public sector services' (MacDonald and MacDonald 2010), a situation that has had particular implications for social workers in child protection. Munro takes up this point:

> Many of the imbalances in the current system arise from efforts to deal with that uncertainty by assessing and managing risk. Risk management cannot eradicate risk; it can only try to reduce the probability of harm. The big problem for society (and consequently for professionals) is working out a realistic expectation of professionals' ability to predict the future and manage risk of harm to children and young people.
>
> (Munro 2011b: 38)

Munro (2011b: 43) reminds us that making 'decisions in conditions of uncertainty (i.e. risk taking) is a core professional requirement for all those working in child protection', something that applies to other areas of social work practice. What is questionable is whether it is possible to predict the likelihood of risk within an assessment process where both uncertainty and risk are key features. The link between these two concepts is evident in the definition of risk that can be found in HM Treasury publication, *The Orange Book: Management of Risk – Principles and Concepts*, where risk is defined in terms of uncertainty:

> **Risk:** uncertainty of outcome, whether positive opportunity or negative threat, of actions and events. It is the combination of likelihood and impact, including perceived importance:
>
> (HM Treasury 2004: 49).

However, MacDonald and MacDonald (2010) argue that it is important to differentiate between risk and uncertainty. For example, we can predict that where an individual is known to have been persistently violent there is a high probability of further violence. Situations of uncertainty are far less predictable and produce 'uncertainty about the meaning of events, the reasons for referrals, the accuracy of assessment, and the consequences of taking one course of action compared with another' (MacDonald and MacDonald 2010). Yet where problems are well-defined, where information is accurate and up-to-date, and where practitioners work from a sound knowledge and skills base, the likelihood of either underestimating (false negative) or overestimating (false positive) the risks involved is likely to be reduced.

Nevertheless, even with judicious decision-making, it is only possible to reduce the level of risk, not to eliminate it completely. For Munro, a way forward involves realizing that it is not possible to be *risk adverse* but it is possible to be 'risk sensible', that is, to formulate risk decisions and assessments that are judged in terms of 'the quality of the decision making, not by the outcome' (Munro 2011b: 43), or in terms of retrospective judgement based on hindsight (MacDonald and MacDonald 2010). But decision-making in relation to risk assessments can also be skewed because of scarce resources and rationing of services and can lead to a situation where practitioners may sometimes use the term 'risk' to argue 'for and against a particular decision' (Webb 2006: 154).

At this point in time, 'practitioners are obliged to comply with risk re-duction technologies' (Broadhurst *et al.* 2010: 1046), that is, to work within systems and procedures that they know fail to meet the needs of service users and the problems they present. Yet at the same time, there are examples of practitioners being able to work in ways that are more creative and that stress the 'importance of continuity in human relationships' (Munro 2011b: 20). I have argued elsewhere that since social workers are not watched on a minute-by-minute basis, there will always be the opportunity to work creatively – the skill lies in finding these opportunities.

This chapter has looked at a range of skills and interventions and set the scene for further coverage of key skills. On a final note, it is important to remember that it is not always easy for people who seek our help to communicate their needs or put words to their thoughts and feelings, partic-ularly when these are tangled amid feelings of confusion, fear, humiliation, anger, and despair. At these times, it can be hard for people to remember the courage and determination that has enabled them to get this far. Within this tangled mass of jumbled experiences, misunderstandings between people and agencies can occur, sometimes with tragic consequences (Gough 1993; Laming 2003; Munro 1996). As practitioners we still have more to learn about how to work with people in ways that communicate the purpose of our work, clearly and sensitively, and in ways that shine a torch on what is happening and why, and possible ways forward. We may not always be able to provide evidence of effectiveness but, as I stated earlier, the absence of evidence does not necessarily mean the absence of benefit.

This learning is an ongoing process and never complete. Indeed, one way to view every interaction is as a learning experience for both parties. Some service users may add to our learning by testing our resilience, particularly those who have a different value base, or who 'have no interest in being helped' and are not motivated to change (Trotter 2006: 1). Others may teach us how to pose questions in ways that lead to greatest openness and honesty, and the chance to take things forward. Or we may learn how to listen to what is *not* being said, rather than what is actually said, and to be able to hypothesize from this experience. At the same time, through the process of actually putting thoughts, feelings, and experiences into words, service users and carers may be able to order events and emotions in ways that are helpful. And, in this process, they may learn more about their strengths and limitations – their capacity to cope or the limits of their coping ability – when faced with too many demands or too much stress. As stated earlier, what we gain from this involvement is that we too can grow and be changed by the encounter – it is this, and the benefits that others reap from our best efforts, that is our ultimate reward.

7 INTERVIEWING SKILLS

Introduction

This chapter looks in some detail at interviewing skills and describes how our knowledge can be put into words to aid effective communication. This includes being able to communicate our understanding, and the meaning given to experiences, and being able to respond in ways that foster action and the opportunity for people to move forward. In addition, we need to be able to communicate effectively with other professionals, family members, neighbours, and the general public. Within social work, interviewing plays a vitally important role:

> Although social work involves a great deal more than interviewing, social workers spend more time in interviewing than in any other single activity. It is the most important, most frequently employed, social work skill.
>
> (Kadushin and Kadushin 1997: 3)

An interview constitutes a conversation with a purpose that is designed to meet a 'specific and usually predetermined purpose' (Barker 2003: 227). For this reason, good planning and preparation are the hallmarks of a successful interview: 'failing to plan is planning to fail'. The purpose of many interviews is laid down by the type of task being undertaken. For example, the primary purpose of some interviews may be roughly divided into more formal interviews, such as child protection 'investigations', mental health or community care assessments, and those less formal interviews more common to everyday problems presented. Skills have to be developed in both areas because the two can overlap and the balance can shift between one and the other. An interview may be the medium through which important connections and relationships are developed, and where important concepts such as partnership and empowerment are taken forward. Although our purposeful conversation may be focused on one individual, the impact of a good interview can impact on the lives of a wide cross-section of people – service users, carers, their families, friends, and neighbours. Therefore, interviews need to be planned and followed up thoughtfully.

Specific skills

Interviewing skills
FOUNDATION SKILLS

  7 Engaging with the task
  8 Planning and preparing for the interview
  9 Creating a rapport
10 Welcoming skills
11 Informal opening conversations ('social chat')
12 Sympathy
13 Empathy
14 The professional use of self
15 The use of intuition

QUESTIONING

16 Information gathering
17 Open questions
18 Closed questions
19 '*What*' questions
20 '*Why*' questions
21 Circular questions
22 Hypothetical questions

CONFIRMING WHAT HAS BEEN SAID AND HEARD

23 Paraphrasing
24 Clarifying
25 Summarizing
26 Active listening responses ('minimum encouragers')
27 Giving and receiving feedback

PROBING DEEPER

28 Sticking to the point and purpose of the interview
29 Prompting
30 Probing
31 Allowing and using silences
32 Using self-disclosure

DRAWING THE CONTACT TO A CLOSE

33 Ending an interview
34 Closing the case and ending the relationship

Foundation skills

This first heading in relation to interviewing skills looks at the personal attributes and key issues that ensure that the interview is a thought–through undertaking.

7. *Engaging with the task*

Purposefully engaging with an individual or group requires that a number of points be considered:

> In thinking about engagement, we need to be conscious of *who* we are connecting with, *what* we are connecting with them about, *where* we are making the contact, *when* this contact takes place, why we are making the contact and *how* the contact is initiated.
>
> (Chenoweth and McAuliffe 2008: 202)

As indicated in the above quotation, engaging skills entail being explicit about what we are doing and why (Munro 1998a: 89). They indicate our willingness, as practitioners, to engage with the concerns that people are experiencing and, in this process, can be an important way that we communicate our commitment, care, and concern. Our success in this communication can be seen when individuals leave the interview with an increased sense of self-confidence, self-respect, and energy because they feel that the encounter has been worthwhile – that they have been heard, and their difficulties have been understood and shared. People who feel positive about themselves tend to have a greater capacity to influence others, and are more likely to be successful in changing their lives. McLeod describes this connection as:

> ... a consistent willingness to engage empathically with the reality or 'world' of the person seeking help. In practice, empathic engagement is expressed through statements that a counsellor makes in summarizing what they have understood from what the client has been saying.
>
> (McLeod 2007: 145)

It involves 'tuning in' and being alongside the person seeking help. However, this approach is more one to adopt in social work, as opposed to counselling, and I do not want to imply that our efforts to engage with people will always be successful or lead to a positive outcome. For example, it is important to remember that the extent to which we can engage with others depends, in part, on their capacity and willingness to engage with us. This kind of connection can be extremely difficult for people who have been traumatized or seriously let down by other people, including professionals. Similarly, it is worth remembering that some service users approach their contact with professionals harbouring a range of fears that include worries that they may be blamed, criticized, or turned away. For these reasons, it is important to be aware of these concerns and to consider how they can be addressed (Lishman 2009a: 28). I return to this subject later, when looking at working with challenging situations.

8. Planning and preparing for the interview

Before beginning an interview, it is important to think carefully about its purpose and what you hope to achieve in the time allotted. Good planning and preparation are essential. Also, it is helpful to think about the interview in its widest context, which involves taking into account the particular needs and/or expectations of:

- the individual or group of people seeking our help
- other people involved with this individual or group of people (e.g. family members, neighbours, and other involved individuals)
- ourselves as practitioners, in terms of our personal and professional expectations
- agency policy, procedures, practice, resources and requirements of us, as employees or representatives of the agency
- other professionals connected to this individual or group of individuals.

There are essentially two ways of preparing ourselves for this task. Both cover many of the same issues but in different ways. One could be called a *reflective* approach, where information is gathered in ways that are less systematic but more empathic and intuitive. This is my preferred approach, and involves using our empathic skills to 'enter imaginatively into the inner life of someone else' (Kadushin and Kadushin 1997: 108). This involves considering the thoughts and feelings, fears, expectations, and fantasies of the interviewee, and what we know about their situation in terms of their personal characteristics, home life, financial situation, and so on. If, for example, we imagine that the service user might feel nervous, what evidence would we look for to confirm or deny this hypothesis or our intuitive reasoning (Munro 2011b: 90)? If confirmed, what can we put in place to help this individual to feel at ease? A different way to prepare for an interview involves the use of a *checklist*, which records a list of the tasks or issues that need to be considered (for an example of an interview checklist, see Trevithick 2000).

Both the reflective and checklist approach require that we familiarize ourselves with the case notes, if any, and update our knowledge of recent events, particularly in relation to others involved in the case. This is an important point and one where social workers are not always rigorous. For example, of the 45 public inquiries into child abuse cases between 1973 and 1994, 'eight reports noted that social workers failed to read their own files and so overlooked important facts such as previous child abuse' (Munro 1998a: 91). To have overlooked a family's past history in this way is a serious omission. Finally, it is essential for us to make a note of our own thoughts and feelings, particularly the extent to which we may be harbouring negative stereotypical attitudes or beliefs about the individual in question. For any interview or interaction to be successful, service users and others involved in the work need to feel that, as professionals and as people, we are competent and caring human beings, capable of understanding their concerns and worries, both from a general and specific standpoint.

These considerations help to give the interview some structure and establish a clear role in terms of the boundaries of the task, time, and territory. Once having scanned these factors, it is then important to concentrate on being as open, relaxed, and natural as possible to ensure that a rapport can be created and a relationship established with the person seeking our help. Every individual is unique and every interaction different and this needs to be remembered in our planning and preparation. Otherwise, the interview runs the risk of being perceived as a cold, uncaring, impersonal experience, which hinders the possibility or quality of future contact. Being able to respond with flexibility and adaptability to an individual's needs is also a sign of a successful interview.

However, agency policies and the constraints placed upon resources may limit the options available to us, particularly in relation to the availability of services. For example, in relation to the list of services to support families cited in the Children Act 1989, some surveys indicate 'considerable discrepancy in the way in which these provisions are implemented. Some authorities have adopted a minimalist approach, whilst others provide a much wider range of services' (Thoburn 2008: 212). Similar inconsistencies have been highlighted in relation to other service user groups. These points stress that interview planning and preparation needs to include information that is drawn from a wide range of sources, and using our knowledge of relevant legislation and policy guidance to push for more and better services.

Interviews in different settings

Our work can involve conducting interviews in other settings, sometimes called 'secondary settings' (Lishman 2009a: 205). These include:

- a workplace or agency setting
- the home (including foster homes/adoption placements)
- schools
- hospitals (psychiatric and general hospitals)
- day centres
- community centres
- residential settings
- prisons
- informal settings, such as holding a conversation in a café or during a journey by car.

These settings provide different restraints and opportunities – and characteristics and idiosyncrasies. For example, interviews that take place in a hospital setting can be difficult because busy wards are often noisy and confidentiality can be difficult to maintain if it is not possible to access a location that offers more privacy. Similarly, the use of informal settings, such as car journeys, might be subject to distractions from other motorists, but this context can provide an ideal opportunity if the interviewee is less comfortable in more formal surroundings or perceive eye contact as something to be avoided or as a threat (Kadushin and Kadushin 1997: 306).

Home visits are particularly important (Ferguson 2008). They provide an opportunity to observe people in a setting where their behaviour is likely to be more natural and spontaneous. What we observe in terms of the interactions taking place and how the home is organized can provide important information. The smell of poverty is unique and deeply memorable but caution is needed to ensure that our assumptions and intuitions can be justified. Kadushin and Kadushin give an interesting account of interviews that take place in the home, where service users can defend themselves through the intelligent use of 'arranged distractions':

> The interviewee can exercise a measure of self-protection by using 'arranged distractions' – letting a radio or TV blare at full volume, giving a warm welcome to neighbours who drop in, or vigorously rattling pots and dishes while washing them during the interview. Because the setting is the interviewee's home, the interviewee has to take the initiative to turn down the radio or TV, although the interviewer can request this. Of course interviewers can, somewhat more subtly, gradually lower their voices until the interviewee is prompted to turn down the radio in order to hear.
>
> (Kadushin and Kadushin 1997: 83)

Whatever the context that is used, it is important that clear professional boundaries are maintained but this can be difficult in more natural settings where it is possible to be easily taken off-guard. This danger is well known among residential workers who have to be their 'best selves' for longer periods.

9. Creating a rapport

For any interview to be successful, a rapport must be established. It involves some features that are similar to the notion of a relationship but with some differences (see Chapter 1 for a detailed account of the important place that relationships hold within social work). Rapport is often defined in one of two ways. First, it describes a meaningful first point of contact and an initial step towards building a relationship. A second and more common meaning describes rapport in terms of a 'chemistry' that gives a particular kind of important connection. For Kadushin and Kadushin (1997: 101), a 'rapport suggests that the participants are in tune with one another, on the same wavelength, in sync with each other'. Barker (2003: 359) takes up this theme and describes rapport as 'the state of harmony, compatibility and empathy that permits mutual understanding and a working relationship between the client and the social worker'.

As such, it is possible to establish a good rapport quite quickly with a complete stranger, as if by chance – but 'hitting it off' with someone in this way can be facilitated if we are in a position to think carefully about the interviewee before the meeting and to use our ability to empathize as a basis for a meaningful connection. The advantage of being able to establish a rapport in this way is that it is possible to create a climate that facilitates the opportunity for people to discuss their situation in an unguarded way.

10. Welcoming skills

One way to establish a rapport is to ensure that the welcome people receive is warm and respectful (Lishman 2009a: 28). This helps to allay some of the fears and uncertainties that may exist. For some service users and carers, these anxieties may be due to the difficulties inherent in asking for help: some may have never asked for help before. For others, it may be their first experience of social services, the probation service, or a voluntary agency. As a result, they may have little idea of what to expect or what help can be offered, and this kind of uncertainty can be worrying. A different group of people may be wary because they have had contact with social services or similar agencies in the past and these experiences have left them feeling negative and perhaps defensive about the prospect of future contact. Whatever the concerns, to provide a warm welcome on all occasions is central to creating a good rapport and sound 'working alliance'.

Shaking hands

Although shaking hands has become less popular, in the UK it is still used as a formal gesture in some circles. This is particularly the case in professional settings, where the event may begin with people shaking hands as they are introduced. For this reason, it is important that we know how to shake hands not least because it indicates that we are not reluctant to make contact in this more formal way when the situation requires it.

In relation to service users and carers, the picture is more complex and subject to wide variations according to individual preference and cultural influences. For example, women tend to shake hands less than men and children almost never offer their hand unless they do so for fun. Generally, men tend to be more at ease and practised in this type of physical contact but even among men there are wide variations according to class, race, and age.

Deciding whether to shake hands can be a test of our intuitive skills. Clearly, no-one should ever be coerced into shaking hands. However, if a service user or carer comes across as relatively relaxed and able to manage this more formal contact, my preference is to shake hands because it marks a clear beginning and end to an encounter. I also find it helpful to have the opportunity to 'touch' a person physically and to gain some impression, however tentative, about where they are coming from, although I would exercise great caution before drawing any firm conclusions from a handshake. Shaking hands also creates an opportunity to say a few warm words of welcome or farewell (Kadushin and Kadushin 1997: 90). This too can be quite revealing. Whatever our personal preference in relation to handshaking, the point to stress is that it is important to think about how to welcome or bid farewell to people we encounter.

Other forms of physical contact

A question that constantly arises is whether or not it is appropriate for service users, or others being interviewed, to be touched during the course of an interview. As a general rule, this is not wise, although there are some exceptions to this rule. For example, if someone is crying it might be considered inhuman and unprofessional not to offer some physical contact – perhaps a touch of the shoulder or hand or the offer of a cup of tea. However, a word of caution is needed because what we consider comforting is not the same for all people. Some people who have been abused find any kind of physical contact difficult, and can experience any form of touching or accidental physical contact, including being hugged, as a violation. For some, it can lead to an awakening of memories of abuse. Similarly, to touch someone when they are crying might make them feel guilty or inhibited about expressing emotions in this way, and may have the effect of closing them down. They may worry that they have upset us: here it is important to offer reassurance that this is not the case.

These complexities are difficult to unravel and call for us to be intuitive. They highlight the importance of self-knowledge and the distinction that needs to be drawn between our personal reactions and our professional responses as a person-in-role. One of the most useful things we can do is to try to 'be with' the feelings being expressed and to provide comfort in ways that feel appropriate. Another is to encourage the expression of emotion by talking to the individual who is upset. A soft, gentle voice offering realistic reassurance can feel like a blanket, wrapping itself around someone to keep them safe. However, the ability to soothe another human being in this way cannot be learned because it must come from a different, more sensitive, and intuitive part of our personality – and is all the more important for this reason.

11. Informal opening conversations ('social chat')

Another way of providing a relaxed welcome might involve starting up an informal conversation. This frequently involves talking about uncontroversial subjects, such as the weather or the journey. Again, our intuitive skills are needed to gauge how long a discussion of this kind should last. Being too brief can leave people feeling hurried and rail-roaded. However, it can create unnecessary anxiety or mistrust if these informal conversations are dragged out longer than necessary. This kind of conversation, sometimes called a 'social chat' or a 'chit-chat', should not be trivialized because it allows people to gain an impression of the kind of person we are before the interview begins. As practitioners, it gives us the opportunity to create a climate that makes it possible for people to ask for help or to discuss difficult subjects. Initial impressions are important and are formed within the first few moments of contact, hence the phrase 'you only get one chance to make a good first impression'. What is inappropriate is to use this more informal point of contact as an information-gathering experience – as an opportunity to take people off guard so that information can be obtained in ways that are not honest and transparent. It is important that we work within agreed professional boundaries, which means that it is inappropriate to engage in general 'chat' sessions that lack 'a clear set of objectives to work towards' (Moss 2008: 102).

Receptionists

Receptionists can do a great deal to create a caring environment. Over the years, however, I have seen some shameful behaviour on the part of receptionists and, whenever possible, I have communicated my concern. But more frequently, particularly in recent times, I have seen some very sensitive and kind interactions between receptionists and visitors to an agency. I can think of a locality team that I visit regularly where the receptionist goes out of her way to ensure that she is warm and caring in the welcome she provides. I am sure that this person's skills makes it easier for people to visit this agency and to keep in touch with the practitioners who work there. Too often these gestures of kindness and concern go unnoticed, particularly in relation to so-called 'junior' or 'support' staff.

Another way to think about the reception a service user and carer might receive relates to the decor of the reception area in relation to whether:

- it is too formal or informal
- it is comfortable, tidy, and well decorated
- it has an appropriate range of seating (comfortable seats, including seating appropriate for older people, chairs and a desk if needed)
- it is private and confidential, and located in an area where interruptions and disruptions can be avoided
- it reflects the multi-racial, multi-cultural, age and gender composition of people seeking a social work/probation service
- it is wheelchair accessible and can accommodate children's buggies and prams
- it provides enough sufficiently current and interesting magazines to help pass the time away if service users and carers have to wait to be seen.

As practitioners, it is part of our professional responsibility to ensure that the reception and welcome that service users and carers receive when they first visit our agency is, as far as possible, a warm and welcoming experience (Lishman 2009a: 28).

12. Sympathy

Sympathy and empathy are discussed separately because they involve different skills. Sympathy describes the sense of being moved by the situation that another human being is experiencing, or has experienced: 'Sympathy can be a genuine expression of concern for another; a polite but not deeply felt expression of condolence for another who has suffered a particular personal loss' (Feltham and Dryden 2004: 230). It is sometimes described as feeling *for* another person (passive) as opposed to empathy, which is described as feeling *with* another person (active) (Shulman 1999: 156). In some texts, this emotion is described quite critically and as inferior to empathy. For example, Egan (2007: 186) sees sympathy as a 'form of collusion', whereas Feltham and Dryden (2004: 230) describe certain expressions of sympathy as an unhelpful attempt to reassure by identifying with another person (as in the phrase 'I know exactly how you feel').

However, sympathy can be, and often is, a genuine, human response to another person's experience of hardship or suffering. We cannot be empathic all the time. That would be exhausting and fail to do justice to the unique features that are central to being empathetic. But we can allow ourselves to feel sympathy with the plight of others and, from this perspective, it is an important skill when we meet someone for the first time, where the need to convey a sense of concern, commiseration, and compassion is paramount.

Example: Sympathetic response

Service user: My husband died last year.
Practitioner: I am very sorry to hear that. How are you managing?
Service user: I had to take to the streets when I left care because I had nowhere else to go.
Practitioner: That must have been a difficult experience. Where did you sleep?

13. Empathy

Creating good working relationships involves being able to empathize with others. It describes an attempt to put ourselves in another person's place, in the hope that we can feel and understand another person's emotions, thoughts, actions, and motives. Empathy involves trying to understand, as carefully and as sensitively as possible, the nature of another person's experience, their own unique point of view, and what meaning this carries for that individual. It goes beyond sympathy (passive understanding) and conveys a willingness to 'enter imaginatively into the inner life of someone else' (Kadushin and Kadushin 1997: 108). Shulman divides the skills involved in empathy into three:

- *reaching for feelings*, which involves 'stepping into the client's shoes', thereby coming as close as is humanly possible to another person's experience;
- *displaying understanding of client's feelings*, which entails suspending disbelief or similar reactions and instead 'indicating through words, gestures, expression, physical posture, or touch the worker's comprehension of the expressed affect'; and
- *putting the client's feelings into words*, which is particularly important when clients are unable to articulate certain feelings, because they do not fully understand the emotion or because 'the client might not be sure it is all right to have such a feeling or to share it with the worker'.

(Shulman 1999: 158–60)

Being empathic involves conveying 'interest, warmth, trust, respect' (Kadushin and Kadushin 1997: 124) and, for this reason, at times it can be difficult to differentiate empathy from those attributes that are about being concerned professionals. However, I consider empathy to embrace an intuitive quality because it is our intuitive reasoning that is the antenna that enables us to interpret people's reactions in ways that reflect or mirror the mood of another person. This mood is often communicated in non-verbal ways but people's verbal communication can also be crucial, especially what is *not* said. However, Rogers (1957: 4) reminds us that it is important to be cautious about the extent to which we intrude into another person's world and that we need to take our lead from service users.

There is some debate about whether empathy is a skill that can be taught or whether it should be considered a personal attribute or quality. My view is that the natural ability to empathize is based on the extent to which people have experienced empathy growing up and as a feature of their attachment to others. Where the experience of empathy is limited, I think that students and practitioners can be made aware of the features that are an aspect of empathy but that this teaching is more likely to be successful if it draws on – and is embedded in – students' and practitioners' actual experiences with service users. Some important work in this field has been undertaken in medicine (Mercer and Reynolds 2002), where a Consultation and Relational Empathy (CARE) measure has been developed (Mercer *et al.* 2004). Another development in this field can be found in the area of social cognitive neuroscience, where it is stated that in relation to empathy four 'physically observable neural networks' can be identified that include: affective sharing; self-awareness; mental flexibility and perspective taking; and emotion regulation (for an interesting article on this subject, see Gerdes *et al.* 2010: 6–7).

The ability to be empathic is one of the most important skills in social work. When attempting to put into words a sensitive and accurate understanding of another's experience, our own subjective experience is a useful starting point but in some ways our attempts to understand the meaning others give to their experiences will always be elusive. The difficulties we encounter can sometimes be forgiven because it is our willingness to try that is important – but being able to establish an accurate 'reading' of the meaning that underpins people's thoughts and feelings can have a profound impact and one that may be remembered for a lifetime. As stated earlier, being understood by another human being is enormously important. It can lead to self-understanding, an awareness that can last and much longer than our professional involvement, which may be fleeting, yet our role in this process of self-discovery may be deeply significant.

The words used to convey empathy need to be easily understood and consistent with the mode of communication with which the individual is familiar. For this reason, it is important to avoid seeing empathy as an opportunity to indulge in philosophical ramblings or personal statements about the meaning of life or how much we admire the individual in question. Empathy is based on self-knowledge and self-reflection and an ability to reach into and to communicate that knowledge, in words and/or body language. One way to see this two-way communication is as a conversation using two mirrors, where the reflection of another person is always seen alongside our own reflection. Sympathy, on the other hand, is more about looking solely at the mirrored reflection of another person.

Example: Empathic response
Service user: My husband died last year. It's been hard without him.
Practitioner: You seem very sad. How have things been since he died?

To ask a general question, such as 'how have things been?', is sometimes preferable to asking a more specific question, such as 'are you still finding it difficult to adjust to life without your husband?' General questions allow the individual to self-select the issues and concerns they choose to include in the word 'things'. However, closed questions are often more appropriate if a person is distressed or withdrawn in some way.

Example: Empathic response
Service user: I had to take to the streets when I left care because I had nowhere else to go.
Practitioner: That's a very difficult experience to have to bear – to feel that you had nowhere to go, no home, no-one that you felt you could turn to ... how did you manage to keep going?

14. The professional use of self

The professional use of self is based on the use of self-awareness in professional practice and a subject that is covered in detail in Chapter 4, *Practice Knowledge*. This section looks at how we use self-knowledge when communicating with others, a subject that overlaps with the earlier coverage on empathy and the following section on intuition. It is through our self-knowledge that we become aware of our strengths and limitations. As professionals, our task is to use this knowledge in ways that enable us to communicate clearly and effectively with other people. This means that once we are aware that we find certain subjects troubling – or there are areas where we are unable to act from our *best selves* – as professionals our next step should be to work out what action to take to overcome this difficulty. For example, at one time I found doing an initial home visit and knocking on someone's door a hugely anxiety-provoking experience. The thought that flooded my mind – and that blocked my concentration – was that I would encounter unmanageable hostility. I first realized the extent of my anxiety when I talked with a colleague about a home visit that had gone disastrously wrong. What became clear during this conversation was the extent to which my anxieties were impacting on my work and she suggested that I learn to use a cognitive-behavioural technique – *thought-stopping* – as a way to keep my feelings manageable. This I did, which worked well. This example highlights the importance of talking about our experiences with other people because it is conversations of this kind that can enable us to learn more about ourselves. It demonstrates that our self-awareness is always limited and that we need other people to help us to realize why we might come across in a certain way. We have to be open to that learning but the more open we can be, the more we are free of our own preoccupations and able to fully engage with other people.

15. The use of intuition

The important place of intuition in social work is also covered in detail in Chapter 4, *Practice Knowledge*. Here I wish to highlight the importance of testing our intuition and the kind of phrases that might be helpful. For example, because we can never be sure of the accuracy of our intuition and the feelings or mood that we have picked up, it is important to think carefully about whether sharing our intuitive impressions would be a helpful intervention. Some people feel that interventions of this kind are intrusive – we may be indicating more than they wish to reveal. On the other hand, some people may find it helpful for us to put into words what may be present in the encounter but has not yet been expressed in words – a decision has to be based on the best interest of the service user. Appropriate interventions need to be tentative and speculative and could begin with the following, spoken slowly:

I may be wrong, and please correct me if I am, but I seem to be picking up a sense that you're afraid of your husband. Could that be right, or am I well off beam?

I wonder if I can take this interview to a different level ... [*pause*] ... could you manage that? ... [*wait for a response and if it is positive*]

... What I'm picking up is a feeling of despair, that you feel that the situation is hopeless and that I can't help you. Is that's what's happening?

An important point to remember is that interventions of this kind need sufficient time to be set aside so that the issues raised can be explored in detail.

Questioning

This second heading looks at the importance of information gathering and questioning skills in social work.

16. Information gathering

Chapter 4 provides detailed coverage of the importance of information gathering skills in social work. Here, the focus is on the initiative, determination, and courage that it can take for us to gather the range of information that is needed to inform and guide the assessment process, judicial decision-making, and action. The extent to which we are prepared to be thorough can make the difference between a well-informed decision and one that is not. It can involve intruding into territories that others do not want us to explore. We are sometimes working with people who do not want us to know what they know. I include in this category some professionals and it can take courage and a particular kind of determination to be able to bypass the barriers that are created. Being inquisitive and naturally questioning is an indispensable asset. As we shall see, asking good questions is an essential feature of good information gathering skills but so too is the ability to plan how best to approach this task. We also need to bear in mind what is at stake: that service users can benefit from our actions, or they can be let down. The other point to remember is to cast our net as widely as possible, as the following example illustrates.

Case example: Alice

I once worked with a 6-year-old girl, Alice, who was allocated to me at the point where she needed to be found a new placement while the adoption process was in motion. Alice had been made the subject of a care order due to her father's cruelty. Tragically, this had resulted in her being brain-damaged but, because of her trauma, it was not clear to what extent. Almost by accident I found an old reference to her paternal grandparents in her case file, dating back several years. We had no address but the case notes stated that Alice's grandfather worked for the local gas board. With this information, through a range of informal networks, I was eventually able to track down the grandparents' whereabouts. They had lost contact with their son because of his threatening behaviour towards them and, as a result, had also lost contact with Alice (in fact, their son was by then in prison). They did not know of her abuse or that she was now in care but they were pleased to hear of Alice and delighted at the prospect of seeing her again. To cut a very long story short, Alice's grandparents eventually adopted her. She now attends a special school and, as sometimes happens, she appears to be less permanently disabled than originally thought (Howe 2006). Her grandparents love her enormously and I believe that for the first time in her life she knows what it means to live in a peaceful, secure, and permanent environment. Not all children are so fortunate and it may be quite rare for us to bring about this kind of change because too much is working against us. Nevertheless, most social workers can describe situations where they felt truly helpful and, amid the doom and gloom of everyday practice, it is important to remember that positive outcomes are sometimes possible, but may call for us to be imaginative and determined and to cast our nets wide.

Asking good questions

Asking a range of different questions is central to interviewing. Different authors highlight the qualities that practitioners need to demonstrate to frame questions in ways that are helpful and illuminating (Lishman 2009a: 40–1; Seden 2005: 28). Most stress that *before asking a question, we must be interested in the answer*. Also, it can be very easy to think that as practitioners we know how to ask questions, but most of us come to the task of interviewing with fixed patterns of behaviour of which we are largely unaware. Some of these behaviours may be facilitating, but others may be off-putting or unhelpful, such as 'putting words into other people's mouths' (Seden 2005: 29) – hence the value of watching ourselves on videotape. For example, many practitioners think they can manage silences relatively easily until presented with a situation in which they are required to remain silent, or to work with someone who is silent. Here the compulsion to speak is almost unbearable and can lead to all kinds of strange questions being asked to break the intense discomfort that silence can engender.

Seven common errors when questioning

Gambrill (2006: 143) describes seven common errors and unhelpful questions:

- Asking leading questions
- Asking questions at the wrong time (they serve as distractions or interruptions)
- Asking closed-ended questions calling for a *yes* or a *no* answer when more information is desired

- Asking irrelevant questions (knowing that the answer will not be helpful)
- Asking more than one question at a time
- Asking complicated questions
- Asking a person why something occurs with the assumption that she knows the answer.

17. Open questions

The advantage of open-ended questions is that they are designed to give freedom of choice, enabling service users to express their thoughts and feelings in their own words and in their own time – and to choose to ignore certain issues. As stated earlier, most people know whether they are being listened to, and whether their thoughts and feelings are being given the importance they deserve. This form of questioning sometimes stimulates self-awareness and self-reflection. It can act as a catalyst that returns people to their own thoughts and their own knowledge base, which is the place where the kernel of self-determination and empowerment is located. However, for people to benefit from this exploration, sufficient time needs to be set aside.

Unless there are reasons to do otherwise, open-ended questions should form a major part of an initial interview or first encounter. However, this approach can appear threatening or overwhelming for service users who find it difficult to formulate their thoughts and feelings. Some individuals may deal with the confusion and anxiety that is provoked by trying to guess the response we are looking for. This kind of mind-reading can seriously detract from the purpose of the interview unless it is addressed. Other people find difficulty answering open questions because they do not yet have words with which to explain what has happened to them.

Some fear is due to worry about coming across as 'stupid', or of being judged or criticized. It may be possible to overcome these concerns by addressing them directly, or by stating the purpose of the question, what we are hoping to achieve, and the benefit that this entails in terms of ensuring that we understand that person's situation before making a decision. It may help to ask a range of open and closed questions. These different approaches require that we are flexible and able to change the form or content of the interview in ways that enable people to tell their stories and to gather their thoughts and feelings with greater freedom. When people remain agitated and defensive, the only option may be to stop the interview or to spend time explaining in greater detail why it is important for us to ask these questions. At this point, and at other points in this and other interviews, it is important to inform people of their rights and of agency policy in relation to information that is recorded about them or other members of their family. For example, 'I've got some information about an offence [shows a copy of the charge sheet] but I want you to tell me what happened – in your own words'.

Example: Life-story work

Practitioner: One way for me to get to know you would be for you to say something about yourself. How does that sound? ... [*nod*] ... Where would you like to begin?

18. Closed questions

Closed questions can often be answered with a simple 'yes' or 'no', or with other responses that only require a few words, such as when asking a person's name, address, age, and so on. This form of questioning is useful when trying to elicit factual or detailed information, particularly when time is limited. It can also be used to keep the interview focused, to open up new areas, to change the direction of the interview, to draw the interview away from or towards sensitive or emotional topics, to slow an interview down, and to allow missing details to be covered. However, this does place more responsibility on the interviewer, who must both choose and formulate relevant questions and listen carefully to the answers so that questions follow on naturally. This can require a great deal of concentration and is one reason why interviewing can be so tiring. On the other hand, closed questions can foreclose exploration. For example, doctors seeking to diagnose a patient quickly are more likely to ask closed questions.

Closed questions can be particularly valuable when working with people who do not have a great deal of confidence, perhaps because they feel reticent or mistrustful or find it difficult to formulate their thoughts and feelings. People involved in accidents or who have been traumatized in other ways may find themselves uncharacteristically unable to answer open questions but able to manage closed questions relatively well. People are different, so it is important that we are able to adapt.

The main disadvantage when using closed questions is that they may steer the interview in the wrong direction by being too focused. This can lead to a sense of frustration on the part of the interviewee, who can easily feel that their experiences are being disregarded or categorized and squeezed into little boxes. Here, it can be helpful to spend time before and after the interview talking about the difficulties involved in having to answer questions in this way and reaffirming why it was important. It is sometimes assumed that open questions are more in keeping with anti-discriminatory/anti-oppressive practice than closed questions. This implies that all people are the same and that all interviews can be conducted in the same way. This is clearly not the case.

Combined questions

In most circumstances it is unhelpful to ask combined questions, but where a great deal of factual information is being sought, combined questions may be necessary to avoid the interview feeling like an interrogation. For example, rather than ask 'Are you on medication?', which may require a follow-up question ('What are you taking?'), it may be better to ask a combined question: 'If you're on medication, can you tell me what you're taking?'

Example: Gathering basic information

Choice of words, tone, and timing are important when trying to gather information of this kind. It is also important to say why the information is needed and who will have access to it.

Practitioner:	I'm afraid I have a number of rather boring questions that I have to ask. What I'd like to do is to get them over with quickly so that we can talk about things that you want to look at. Is that okay? Right, can I have your name and address, please?
Service user:	Okay. Michael Smith, 37 Baron Street, Newtown.
Practitioner:	Thanks. What's your date of birth, Michael?
Service user:	Fourth of September 1983.
Practitioner:	So you're sixteen?
Service user:	Yes.

Example: Clarifying the reason for the referral

Practitioner:	I see from the letter from your doctor that she thinks you need a social worker to help you to sort out some problems you're having at home. Is that how you see the situation?
Service user:	No. I didn't know that my doctor had written. I came because I got a letter from you asking to see me.
Practitioner:	Okay. I think it would help to take a step back and start at the beginning so that I can understand why your doctor has referred you to us. Is that okay?
Service user:	Yes.
Practitioner:	When did you last see your doctor?
Service user:	Last week.
Practitioner:	What was that for, Mrs Day? ['What' question]

19. 'What' questions

This form of questioning is particularly popular in family therapy and in certain types of brief therapy. Its main advantage is that it is quite unspecific in terms of what constitutes the 'what' implied in the question, thereby leaving the interviewee free to define for themselves the issues or concerns that they wish to focus on. Another advantage is that its emphasis is on the present rather than the past, but with an opportunity for additional questions to be asked relating to the past, if that is considered necessary (Lishman 2009a: 117).

Sometimes there is insufficient time, and it is not always useful, to explore the past or the cause of a problem, because this may not help us to formulate what the current impact of the problem is and how it might be rectified or solved (Watzlawick *et al.* 1974: 84). Indeed, an exploration of the past can be a way of avoiding what is happening in the present. Some 'what' questions can be interpreted as accusatory or blaming, although this can be overcome by using a sensitive and caring tone of voice.

'What' questions are immensely adaptable, particularly when attempting to explore wider issues and the part that other individuals or factors play in the perpetuation of the problem encountered. This emphasis is consistent with a systemic perspective that stresses that no one person is solely responsible for a problem or a difficulty that exists, although as human beings we are all responsible for our actions. For example, 'what' questions can be asked in most situations: 'what is going on?', 'what plays a part in perpetuating this problem?', 'what part does this problem, individual or family play in relation to the whole (system, family, community, etc.)?', 'what needs to happen to bring about change or a solution to this problem?', 'what is needed to keep the momentum for change alive?', and 'what would tell us that the intervention, approach or work has been effective?'

Examples: Initial interview

Practitioner: What's happening – as you see it – Mr Black?
Practitioner: What do you think will happen if we leave things as they are?
Practitioner: What can I say, or do, to make a difference?

As stated earlier asking a purposely vague question, such as 'what is happening?', allows the individual to decide what they see to be 'happening'. This can include anything and take us to some unexpected places. This in turn can enable us to judge whether different parties see the situation in the same way and, if not, to explore what these differences are and, if important to the task, how they can be bridged and a common purpose agreed.

20. 'Why' questions

A major difficulty with *why* questions is that they can often be experienced as accusatory or authoritarian (Seden 2005: 29). It suggests that people have to account for their behaviour, which they may not be able or want to do, thus introducing a more confrontational tone without this being intended. Thoughtful wording, accompanied by the skilful use of tone and timing, can help to avoid this danger. A different approach involves adopting an inquisitive tone, perhaps extending the word *why – w h y?* However, in general I consider this kind of wording can easily lead to people being defensive and where possible should be avoided. Lishman draws our attention to an interesting point in relation to *why* questions:

> I was struck when someone pointed out that we only use 'why' questions with children in a negative way: 'Why did you do/steal/lose that?' We do not ask: 'Why did you do so well?'
>
> (Lishman 2009a: 117)

21. Circular questions

A further style of asking good questions is what is known as 'circular questioning'. Developed within the family therapy field, circular questioning assesses family functioning and interaction by asking one member of the family to comment on the relationship or behaviour of two other members. Thus, 'When your wife tells Peter that he is grounded and not allowed out for a week, what does Mary (sister) do?' 'Mary, when your mother tells Peter that he is grounded, what does your father do?' Because the communication can be witnessed by all family members, circular questioning allows new connections to be made. In my experience, it takes some practice to use circular questioning well. The following are its advantages:

Using circular questions
• Broaden the frame from the individual to inter-action
• Shift from linear cause–effect to inter-action
• Demonstrate the importance of relationship
• Bring forth unheard voices
• Make connections between the meaning of important events
• Make links between the present, future hopes, and past stories
• Keep therapist's curiosity alive
• Help the client become more curious about their own life
• Enable both parties to test out and refute hypotheses
• Introduce news of difference
• Open space for new connections
• Enable therapists to respect the client as the expert in their life
• Change the stories
                                   (Hedges 2005, cited in Wilson *et al.* 2008: 290)

22. Hypothetical questions

Hypothetical questions can easily be confused with testing a hypothesis but this communication skill is designed to encourage an individual to consider new possibilities by presenting a hypothetical situation (Kadushin and Kadushin 1997: 263).

Examples: Hypothetical questioning
Practitioner: If you were asked to deal with the situation, what do you think you would do?
Practitioner: If you were to think about where you'd like to be in two years time, what would your life be like? What do you think you would ideally like to be doing?
Practitioner: I wonder if you can think what life might be like if you weren't being abused in this way? Can you imagine how you might think and feel?

An advantage of this approach is that it enables us to understand the extent to which it is possible for someone to imagine a different life – what life might be like in a different situation. If a person is unable to imagine anything different, this may indicate the extent to which they feel bogged down or trapped within their present situation, which could open up the chance to explore these feelings. If a person is able to imagine something different, this could provide a catalyst for other options to be explored and pursued. However, the hypothetical situation needs to be carefully chosen and relatively realistic if the question is not to be viewed as irrelevant and frustrating.

Confirming what has been said and heard

This third heading in relation to interviewing skills focuses on interventions designed to ensure that we have understood the content and meaning of what has been communicated so far. This is sometimes referred to as *tracking*, that is, the 'skill of listening intently and empathetically to the moment-to-moment explorations of the client, with an ability to reflect back and/or to summarize what is said' (Feltham and Dryden 2004: 239). It combines creative listening with responding to and reflecting back what is being communicated (Seden 2005: 27).

The skills include paraphrasing, clarifying, summarizing, and giving and receiving feedback. Each offers a different way to ensure that we have understood what is being communicated and provides an opportunity to demonstrate that understanding in words. This allows for misinformation to be corrected and for knowledge and expertise to be returned to the individual concerned. Putting our observations and perceptions into words also allows the individual to hear their own comments and statements but in a different way. This can be both illuminating and thought provoking, sometimes enabling new and different options to be explored. When feeding back in this way, it can be easy to slip into jargon: 'what I hear is' or 'I want to share with you what I hear'. Some people find this kind of language off-putting, which makes it important to choose words that are in everyday use and easy to understand (Social Services Inspectorate 1991: 20).

23. Paraphrasing

In paraphrasing, the essence of the person's statement is restated, although not exactly as an echo. It is a selective restatement of the main ideas with words resembling those used by the individual, but which are not the same: 'para' means 'alongside'. Its main purpose is to ensure that we have grasped the sense and meaning of what is being communicated. Sometimes the only way to know this is for us to put into words our own thoughts and impressions. In doing so, practitioners:

... demonstrate they have heard the client, they offer their understanding of what they have heard (to be confirmed or otherwise), and their use of paraphrase casts a slightly different light on the original statements, allowing the client to hear their own statements in a way which itself can powerfully move her (or him) into new personal perspectives.

(Feltham and Dryden 2004: 158)

Paraphrasing is not the same as imitation, repetition, or mimicking, which can be experienced as humiliating and should be avoided. We seldom have permission to be familiar in this way, although sometimes this permission is assumed if the service user is young or 'unequal' in other ways: this is inappropriate. Paraphrasing carries other dangers. Restating points already covered can make some people feel that their own words are not adequate or clear. This can elicit the response, 'What was wrong with the way I said it?' Some people have a history of being taunted for their style of speaking or choice of words. This is particularly true of members of ethnic minority groups and young people, who may find paraphrasing offensive or undermining. Where this is the case, paraphrasing should not be used unless it is to enable service users to recover from the inhibitions they feel about their capacity to communicate (Seden 2005: 88). Another danger with paraphrasing is that it can be used to change the meaning of what was said. This kind of trickery can be deeply alarming because it 'sets people up' by making it seem as if they said something that they did not. Nevertheless, despite these dangers, the ability to relate accurately or restate another person's words is an important skill and the basis of good report writing.

Example: Putting what has been said into your own words

Practitioner: Let me put what you have said into my own words so that it is clear that I've understood you properly. Please interrupt me if I get anything wrong. You want John to live at home but only if he behaves himself properly. You are prepared to put up with his laziness, late nights, and loud music but you draw the line when he smokes or truants from school ...

Service user: [*Interrupting*] I don't like the fact that he smokes but I can't stop him. What I won't have is John smoking in the house in front of the other kids. That's different.

Practitioner: Right. So the line you draw is that for John to live at home he has to agree not to smoke in the house and he has to go to school. Is that right?

Service user: That's right.

24. Clarifying

Clarifying is primarily used to sort out confusions and to ensure the listener has an accurate grasp of what is being conveyed. It is also used to put words to thoughts and feelings in a language that can be easily and clearly understood, but without falsifying and changing the original meaning. More generally, clarifying can help the individual to identify, confirm, and rank the problems that are currently most troubling. This is particularly useful when individuals have many problems and need to focus on those that might have the greatest impact on them. Clarifying can also be used to extend an individual's knowledge base or deepen their understanding of themselves and others they are close to. It differs from paraphrasing because, when clarifying, we frequently choose the same words used by the individual, whereas, when paraphrasing, the emphasis is on putting some of the points covered into our own words. Another role that clarifying can play is in relation to checking out assumptions and expectations that may be present – on the part of either the interviewee or interviewer. This allows for differences to be addressed and, it is hoped, worked through.

Like many of the skills described in this chapter, clarifying can have advantages beyond the technique itself. It can reveal that we are listening carefully and giving importance to what is being said. This can be a particularly important and validating experience for people who have rarely had their thoughts and feelings confirmed in this way. However, clarifying what has been said can interrupt the flow of the interview and, like paraphrasing, can make some people feel ill at ease because it can feel like a veiled criticism or imply that they are communicating poorly. If these concerns emerge, they need to be addressed before the interview can proceed further.

Example: Identifying and confirming events

Practitioner: Let me see if I have this right. Tell me if anything's wrong. You went into the Women's Refuge with your children in May 1998, where you stayed for six months? When your husband tracked you down there, you then went to your sister's in Nottingham where you were for three months until your husband followed you there. Then you returned to the refuge, where the workers there have helped you to take out an injunction. But in this process, you have run up a lot of debts. Is that right?

Service user: Yes.

25. Summarizing

Summarizing can be useful in a number of ways. First, we can begin a new session by drawing together and summarizing points covered in earlier sessions. Second, it can provide an accurate and succinct partial or detailed breakdown of what has been covered so far. This allows us to gather together the disparate strands and central themes of what has been covered and to check out that the understanding we have is the same as that of the individual being interviewed. Again, this can help service users to clarify their own thoughts and perceptions, and sometimes lead them to look at the issue from a slightly different angle (Egan 2007: 203). Third, a well-timed, brief, and accurate summary can be particularly useful when the discussion has started to drift or the session to lose direction. It can be used to draw one line of enquiry to a close so that a new one can be opened. Finally, summarizing is used to draw the session to a satisfactory end. Within this process, summarizing what has been covered can highlight issues that have not been explored and provide a useful opportunity to plan future sessions.

Example: Summarizing issues still to be covered

Practitioner: Let's look at what we've discussed so far. You've talked about your experiences of being in care, your foster parents, how you got on at school. Is there anything I've left out? [Service user shakes head] ... What we still need to look at with the time we've got left is where you plan to live when you leave care. Is that okay? [Service user nods] ... Where would you like to start – what ideas have you already had?

Example: Final summary of the points covered in an initial interview

Practitioner: I think that's all we can cover today. What we have looked at is your childhood, your history of going in and out of hospital, your current living situation and how you are coping right now. We can talk more when we meet again next week. Does that sound all right?

Service user: Yes, that's fine.

26. Active listening responses ('minimum encouragers')

Different responses can encourage people to continue what they are saying. They often take the form of responses such as 'uh-huh', 'right', 'mmmm', 'I see', 'really?', 'wow', 'ok', which may or may not be accompanied with physical gestures, such as nodding the head. This skill might seem trivial but some people need ongoing encouragement of this form and for some, failing to offer encouraging indicators, particularly at the beginning of an interview, can suggest to them that we do not agree with what is being communicated or that we are disinterested. The use of a facilitative tone is essential when using minimum encouragers – all of the responses indicated above could seriously backfire if they are not communicated thoughtfully. Also, where they fall in the overall communication is important because too many encouraging sounds can be interpreted as wanting to hurry the communication or that we are impatient. For example, the comment 'I see', if communicated quickly, could suggest that we want the communication to come to an end. The other advantage that encouraging comments and gestures can have is that they can be communicated while the person is actually speaking. Kadushin and Kadushin emphasize the importance of this form of communication:

> Although the word *minimal* refers to the activity of the interviewer, the effect on the interview is more than minimal. Such utterances have a potent effect in reinforcing the interviewee's behaviour. Because they are meaningless interventions without content, they are unintrusive. They do not impede the interviewee's flow, and they do not cause the interviewee to shift the nature of the material being shared.
>
> (Kadushin and Kadushin 1997: 139)

27. Giving and receiving feedback

Giving and receiving feedback, both negative and positive, has advantages for both practitioners and service users. First, clear and honest feedback can provide a way of ensuring that a particular course of action is 'on course' in terms of achieving agreed objectives. Second, feedback can be used as a way of noting the emotional content of the communication: 'reflecting feelings entails responding to clients' music and not just to their words' (Nelson-Jones 2000: 130). This can help service users to learn more about themselves – how they come across – which can be important in ensuring the success of a particular endeavour. For example, where someone is approaching a particular task with a sense of defeat or pessimism, feeding back these impressions may be essential to avoid the task being sabotaged and effort being in vain.

In practice, giving and receiving feedback is a difficult undertaking because it requires the ability to deal with the feelings that arise. Some service users find any form of feedback, whether positive or negative, difficult and upsetting. People who have been hurt in the past by negative feedback can easily worry that they are going to be 'got at' again. To allay these concerns, at the outset it can help to carefully and caringly stress the value of feedback in terms of meeting agreed objectives. Egan highlights the benefits of what he describes as 'confirmatory' and 'corrective' feedback:

- *Confirmatory feedback*. 'Through confirmatory feedback, significant others such as helpers, relatives, friends and colleagues let clients know that they are on course – that is, moving successfully through the steps of their action programs toward their goals'.
- *Corrective feedback*. 'Through corrective feedback significant others let clients know that they have wandered off course and what they need to do to get back on'.

(Egan 2002: 361)

Positive feedback can also create problems, particularly where people have been tantalized and lured into painful or humiliating experiences through the use of kindness and flattery. For example, I once worked with a young woman who associated any compliments or words of appreciation as an attack or a cause for concern. Her response to kindness was to ask, quite spontaneously, 'What do you want?', that is, 'What's the payback?' Therefore, before giving feedback it is vital to think carefully about how people might react and adjust your comments accordingly. It can help to remember that some things can be left for another time. Furthermore, feedback is more likely to be taken on board if it is brief and to the point, and if it focuses on actual behaviour in ways that are descriptive as opposed to interpretive. It also helps to give sufficient time for service users to comment and to remind them that our views can be wrong and are not 'gospel'. It may be helpful to include an opportunity for service users to comment on how well we performed when giving them feedback.

Probing deeper

This fourth heading looks at the skills that can be valuable when we need to remain focused and to probe deeper in order to gain a clearer understanding.

28. Sticking to the point and purpose of the interview

The ability to ask questions that change the pace or direction of an interview, or that probe deeper, is an important skill, particularly when interviewing people who aimlessly ramble on about topics that are not relevant, or if they are reticent, confused, anxious, or unable to give a clear picture of what they want and why. Some responses may stem from a deliberate desire to mislead. However, most occur because, as human beings, it is natural for us to be guarded to some extent about what we are prepared to reveal about ourselves, particularly to strangers. For example, it can be difficult for some people to broach certain issues, and we need to be able to offer reassurance that these subjects can be discussed, and discussed in ways that are not without clear boundaries. However, this reassurance can come across as half-hearted if a practitioner feels uncomfortable when called upon to address difficult issues. Avoidance can be as much a defence for practitioners as it can be for service users. This avoidance may be evident when practitioners adopt 'a non-questioning, non-directive style' that leaves service users having to 'identify and to address their problems themselves' (Munro 1998a: 99).

Our attempts to stick to the point or purpose of an interview can be experienced as either helpful or coercive, depending on the individual and our skills in drawing people away from issues that are less relevant. The skill here is to be able to return to the purpose without disturbing the rapport and trust that has been established. There are several reasons why we might want to intervene in this way:

- the discussion has become overly focused on one issue at the expense of others

- the content has been exhausted and the communication is becoming repetitive
- the discussion has moved on to peripheral issues or irrelevancies
- the discussion has moved away from difficult issues and needs to be brought back
- the discussion has become emotionally charged and a sense of calm and balance needs to be introduced.

Example: Sticking to the point by focusing on issues not fully covered

Practitioner: I now have a good picture of your mother's health problems so I wonder if we could leave this issue here, so that you can say some more about the housing problems you mentioned?

Practitioner: If I can return to something you mentioned in passing, can you say more about your children's contact with their father? How often do they see him?

Example: Steering the interview away from an upsetting issue

Practitioner: I can see how upset you are about being separated from your daughter – let's hope that this need not be for long ... Since this is a difficult situation for you, perhaps we should leave this discussion about her foster home for now, so that you have the chance to take it all in and to feel less upset. What do you normally do to help to calm yourself when you feel upset in this way?

Service user: I usually have a cup of tea and a cigarette – that's what helps.

Practitioner: Well, I can offer you a cup of tea – and am happy to go and make this for you – but I'm afraid I can't offer you a cigarette in here but you can go outside and I can bring your tea out to you. What do you want to do? Do you want to go outside and have a cigarette and cup of tea? Can we talk again when you've had a break?

It is helpful to speak slowly and distinctly when addressing someone who is visibly upset because the capacity to assimilate information when we are emotionally distressed is often severely limited. In my experience, people tend to remember the tone we use more than anything else. However, when speaking slowly in this way, it can be easy to come across as patronizing. This is evident when a person is being spoken to in ways that are condescending – as if an inferior human being or someone whose faculties are less than our own. This may be evident in our choice of words 'come on dear' or if we speak to someone very slowly or loudly, or using exaggerated intonation (Hargie and Dickson 2004: 29).

29. *Prompting*

This intervention differs from the previous coverage on 'minimum encouragers' and describes the use of prompting where there is some reluctance or difficulty on the part of the interviewee to continue to speak or to explore certain issues. It can take many forms, such as inviting further comment through direct suggestion, by providing a link between one statement and another in order to encourage further dialogue or by helping the individual to return to unfinished sentences or comments. The need to prompt can sometimes be reduced by our making it clear why we need certain information. If a person's reticence is due to anxiety about what the information will be used for, it helps to address this concern by stating openly where information is recorded, who has access to it, where it will be kept, and how service users can access their records (see pp. 293–5 on record-keeping skills).

When prompting, there is a temptation to finish off another person's sentence. This should be avoided at all cost because it is important that people find their own words to describe their thoughts and feelings. Like paraphrasing and other skills described earlier, prompting someone to continue speaking can be experienced as encouraging or coercing. Timing, sensitivity, a kind tone and caring approach are crucial in helping people to differentiate between the two.

Example: Inviting further comment
Practitioner: Earlier, you said that prison 'was hell' but then moved on to talk about problems finding work. How do you know what prison is like?

Example: Unfinished comment
Practitioner: That's twice you've started to say something about having no money but stopped. It's always hard to talk about money issues – particularly when there isn't enough to go round – but what do you mean when you say you have no money?

Example: Linking
Practitioner: If I can go back to something you mentioned earlier, you said that Peter doesn't get on with your new partner. Later, you also said that Peter now wants to live with his father. Is there a link between these two comments?

Service user: [Silence] I don't know what you mean – what you're getting at?

Practitioner: I am trying to find out whether Peter wants to leave because he is unhappy about your new partner – perhaps he feels put out. You lived alone together for a long time, didn't you?

Service user: He probably is – but so what. What can I do about that?

Practitioner: Well, it depends on whether you feel you can do something about it – and what Peter really wants . . .

30. Probing

Probing is used to elicit more detailed or specific information and can be a useful intervention when trying to gather information from individuals who are prone to adopt more misleading patterns of communication. It is a skill central to risk assessments. Probing can take the form of questions, statements, or requests (Egan 2002: 120), and can be an invaluable skill in providing information that helps to make sense of people's experience or to provide a clearer picture of the whole situation. However, probing must be undertaken skilfully so that the person in question does not become more defensive and guarded. To avoid meandering into areas that are private and personal, it helps for probing questions to be linked to a hypothesis or line of enquiry and, if possible, to explain why certain questions are being asked.

Example: Asking more in-depth questions

Practitioner: You seem to know your way round this office. Have you been here before?

Service user: What makes you say that?

Practitioner: You seemed to know where the interview room was without my having to lead you. Have you been here before?

Service user: Yes.

Practitioner: When?

Service user: About three years ago.

Practitioner: What brought you here then?

Service user: Just a little misunderstanding. [Changing the subject] . . . Are you going to help me with my benefit problem or not?

Practitioner: Yes, in a minute. What was that misunderstanding?

Service user: My daughter hurt herself.

Practitioner: Hurt herself in what way?

Service user: She slipped and fell down the stairs.

Practitioner: Why did that involve this office?

Service user: I can't remember – it was so long ago and all a misunderstanding. Can we talk about my benefit?

Practitioner: Let's start at the beginning, Mrs Wood. Tell me what happened from the beginning so that we can move on to look at your benefit problem. Where do you want to start?

Example: Making a statement to encourage a response

Practitioner: You appear to be troubled about the contract we have just agreed.

Service user: Yes, I never realized that I would be expected to do so much myself. I thought you'd do it all for me and I don't know whether I am up to it.

Practitioner: Okay. Maybe I'm expecting too much of you but I'm trying to find the right balance. It's important that you play your part because otherwise, you won't feel that any headway we make was because of you. Let's take a step back, shall we? What is it that bothers you the most about the things you have to do?

Example: Making a request

Service user: When I left your office last week I felt a bit upset about what we had talked about.
Practitioner: A bit upset?
Service user: Well, very upset really.
Practitioner: What upset you? Can you remember?
Service user: I hate it when you're late. When you leave me sitting in that horrible waiting room with those useless old magazines. I hate it.
Practitioner: I'm sorry. That's my mistake and something that should not have happened. I'll do all I can to make sure it doesn't happen again and I'm sorry it upset you. [Pause] . . . It's good you're able to tell me – is there anything else that I do, or don't do, that bothers you?

31. Allowing and using silences

Silence can generate difficult feelings both for service users and practitioners, so much so that it is not always easy to know who is feeling the most uncomfortable. This section explores some of the assumptions that are made about silence and how we can best work with this 'period filled with lack of speech, in which both interviewer and interviewee participate' (Kadushin and Kadushin 1997: 214).

The assumption is that talking is better than not talking, and that nothing is being communicated when silence prevails. That is not the case. Words can be used to create or kill real dialogue, to conceal rather than reveal what is happening. Other assumptions include the views that:

• silences should always be broken
• that the interview is not successful if there is too much silence
• that it is mainly inexperienced practitioners who feel uncomfortable with silences
• that silences indicate poor communication skills on the part of the interviewee
• that silences indicate a failure on the part of the practitioner to engage with the interview or the interviewee.

In addition, silence within English culture can easily be confused with a lack of politeness, incivility, or poor social skills. Silence can also be used as a sign of rejection or disapproval. Although there will be times when these assumptions ring true, they may also be far from accurate. For these reasons it is important to attempt to identify what is being communicated through silences – how silence is being used. This in turn helps us to understand how long we should allow the silence to run for.

Creative and troubled silences

What might be called 'creative silences' describe a period of non-speech that is communicating something meaningful and important about the individual and his or her situation. Creative silences indicate that the individual is happily preoccupied with his or her own thoughts and feelings. This stands in contrast to a more 'troubled' form of silence that indicates a feeling of anxiety, embarrassment, or confusion on the part of the interviewee, or a withholding or punishing withdrawal. Troubled silences can also reveal that the individual is too upset or too fearful to speak, perhaps because they feel overwhelmed or feel that they need to protect themselves or others.

Several points need to be emphasized. First, it takes two to create a silence in an interview: the service user and the interviewer. If a service user is silent, we need not be – unless we decide to be so. Second, we often do not know for certain what is being communicated through the use of silence – and this includes our own silence – and whether it is a 'productive silence' or not. One way to overcome this difficulty would be to ask the person in question what their being silent means but, of course, we may not get a response! In relation to our own silence, it can help to think about what we are communicating in our silence and what our silence means to us. Third, it is crucial to remember that the briefest silence can appear to last a long time. This very quickly comes to light if we have the opportunity to do a time-check. One 'trick' I use cautiously – and always as a 'last straw' when working with an adolescent who is determined to remain silent – involves planting a deliberate error in my soliloquy. The one most likely to produce a response is when I purposely describe the young person in question to be younger than they actually are (see example below). Once a silence has been broken, it is generally considered unwise to try to analyse immediately what the silence meant. For some service users, this can feel like they have lost control or they are being manipulated. This is particularly important to remember when working with children and adolescents.

The ability to be calm, silent, and still in an interview is an important skill and one that every competent interviewer needs to acquire. One way to see a pause is as a brief silence – a resting place – that allows time to gather thoughts and feelings. However, like silences, long pauses can be difficult to bear. When a person is known to show a pattern of being silent, it can help to sit facing a clock, so that we can check the time without interfering with the flow of the interview. This allows for silence to be measured against reality, rather than our own internal clock, which tends to tick very slowly in an interview where silence is present (see Kadushin and Kadushin 1997: 213–18).

Example: Speaking into the silence of a young person determined not to speak

Practitioner:	Well, you're a very silent 12-year-old ...
Service user:	I'm not 12, I am 13! So there!
Practitioner:	Sorry – my mistake. So you're 13 – not 12?
Service user:	Yeah. Do I look like a 12-year-old? [said with contempt]
Practitioner:	No, you don't. When's your birthday, Jake? ...

Example: Speaking into the silence

Practitioner: You have been silent for some time now Jenny. I wonder why you don't want to talk today?

Service user: [Silence]

Practitioner: [Pause] ... I wonder if you are afraid that I might be angry because you didn't manage to turn up last week?

Service user: [Silence]

Practitioner: [Pause] ... I'm sure that you came all this way for a reason ... but at this point in time, it's not easy for me to see what help I can be ... why you feel you cannot speak. Has something happened?

Service user: [Silence]

Practitioner: [Pause] ... Are you angry with me?

Service user: [Silence]

Practitioner: [Pause] ... Maybe it's best if I don't ask you any more questions. Maybe I should fill this silence with my words and tell you what I think has been happening – and you can tell me if I'm right or wrong. [speaking slowly] ... My guess is that last week, you couldn't come to see me because you were grounded again. I think you had another row with your mother. Maybe you both said some tough things – and she said you had to stay in your room until you apologized. I think you find apologies difficult and this meant you missed seeing me. I'll bet that since the row, you've felt very confused and hurt. Maybe you've said to yourself that it's better not to talk at all since talking gets you into trouble. Instead, you're left talking to yourself but the problem is that it's very hard for any of us to sort things out without talking. I think you have found talking helpful in the past and it can help you now. I am here to help you.

Service user: [Silence]

Practitioner: My guess is that you are talking but you are not talking out loud. I think that you are talking to yourself. Am I right? I wonder if you can bring yourself to tell me what is going on in your head – what you are saying to yourself ... It can help you to feel less alone with these feelings ... what do you think?

Service user: [Silence]

32. Using self-disclosure

Self-disclosure highlights the importance of our being able to draw on our own personal knowledge and history to gauge what course of action is appropriate and necessary to be effective in a particular situation or encounter (Lishman 2009a: 78). However, this self-knowledge and 'professional use of self' is taken one step further because self-disclosure relates to revealing present or past personal information about ourselves. These self-statements can be invaluable for people who feel isolated and alone in their suffering, or who worry about revealing themselves in any way. For us to reveal that it is all right to be *known* in certain ways can help to break down feelings of shame, guilt, or self-blame – the feelings that say 'I'm not like other people', when in fact many reactions that people may experience as 'odd' or 'strange' are common to much of the human race. This can bring an enormous sense of relief. For example, if we have been bereaved it can help to disclose how we overcame our feelings of devastation and grief at losing someone we loved. Sharing thoughts and feelings through self-disclosure can help service users to see us as 'ordinary human beings' as well as professional workers. Similarly, it can help us to feel more empathic and in touch with what is being said and felt.

However, *the general rule is that self-disclosure should not occur unless it is in the interest of the individual seeking help*, and even then it must be handled sensitively. For example, I recall an incident when a social worker shared his history of sexual abuse with a service user. He did so for many reasons but none related to the best interest of the service user, who was left feeling bewildered, confused, and distressed. This is an extreme but true example and one that highlights how inappropriate it can be for us to share our personal or professional problems and history in this way. Or again, it is important to avoid using certain phrases that are not accurate, such as 'I know what it's like' or 'I know what you're going through'. We can have some idea of what it is like, but all human beings are unique, which means we cannot know from our own experience what another person's experience is actually like. For this reason, it is often better to be quite vague and to keep our comments to a minimum, unless there are good reasons to do otherwise.

Example: Self-disclosing past experiences (truanting)

Practitioner: I never used to like going to school so I know a bit about what it's like to have to go somewhere that you don't enjoy. In my case, I managed to keep going because I found a teacher who I could really talk to. Is there any teacher, or pupil (student) that you like or get on with quite well?

Service user: There's a few people I like the look of but I don't come across them.

Practitioner: Well, maybe it's our task to ensure that you do come across them. How does that sound?

Service user: Rubbish ...

Example: Self-disclosing past experiences (depression)

Practitioner: I have had bouts of depression in the past and so I have some idea about how you're feeling but people experience depression in very different ways. Can you describe what this depression is like for you and when it started?

Service user: Do you still suffer from depression?

Practitioner: No, I'm fine now. It is important to say that depression can and does lift. What we have to look at is what will help you to overcome this depression.

Some practitioners would not feel comfortable disclosing personal information of this kind and that is a valid position. There are no hard-and-fast rules but whatever the situation, it is important to use self-disclosure thoughtfully. If there is any indication that it may not be received well, I would avoid it.

Drawing the contact to a close

In this final section, the importance of providing a good ending is explored.

According to Kadushin and Kadushin (1997: 271), 'preparation for termination [of the interview] begins at the start of the interview'. This perspective encourages us to think of our contact with people as complete experiences: as encounters that have a beginning, middle, and end, all of which should be considered at the planning and preparation stage of the work we are about to undertake. An intervention plan that has a focus and purpose should mean that we are able to identify how long the work will run and what outcome we are seeking when we reach the end. However, the impact of unexpected variables can lay to waste best laid plans.

One reason why significance is given to endings is because they provide an opportunity to do a great deal of important work. For service users who have experienced painful, abrupt, and sometimes traumatizing endings in the past, experiencing a good ending can provide the chance to begin to sort out and work through any issues that inhibit them from moving forward. Some of these painful experiences may be due to unresolved grief at the premature death of someone close to them. Other experiences may be due to social workers and other significant figures leaving them without saying a proper goodbye. Children 'looked after' describe poignant experiences of feeling abandoned and their trust betrayed by social workers who only came once or who never came to say goodbye, thereby giving them no time to prepare for the fact that they may never see this individual again.

Case example: Diane

For example, I once worked with Diane, who felt she had a special relationship with a particular health visitor: she felt understood and accepted by this individual in ways that were important. However, one day the health visitor did not turn up as agreed. In fact, she never turned up again. The reasons for her departure were never revealed to Diane but this experience continued to haunt her. It acted as a barrier when Diane encountered other professionals, despite the years that had elapsed. So much so that at the beginning of my work with her, the focus had to change (but not the overall purpose) in order to address the grief and anger that she felt about being abandoned in this way. Perhaps something untoward happened to this health visitor. We will never know. What we do know is that it is likely that Diane could have adjusted to her health visitor's untimely departure had she been offered some kind of explanation – something that said to Diane that she was important. This example shows how crucial it is that we do not forget or underestimate our importance to the service users we come into contact with.

To provide a good ending allows the opportunity for individuals to work through what it feels like to be left or to be left behind. It also provides an opportunity for people to experience what a good, well thought-out ending should involve. For example, a good ending can allow the understanding, knowledge, or wisdom gained to be reviewed and consolidated in ways that can be built on and used in the future. However, some individuals find endings very hard, perhaps because they have a history of being 'let down' and failed. As a result, changes of any kind, but particularly endings, can feel very final and devastating. For this reason, it is essential to remember that endings can give rise to a whole range of unexpected emotions. These include feelings of bewilderment, helplessness, fear, and a terrifying sense of aloneness, abandonment, and rejection. These reactions can happen, perhaps less intensely, when we go away on holiday or are absent for other reasons, but may remain hidden because it can be difficult for service users to reveal how much we mean to them. It is therefore important that we do not underestimate our significance, or the impact that an ending can bring about.

33. Ending an interview

Interviews are enormously varied, as are their endings. Where a clear time boundary has been stated at the beginning with regular but unobtrusive time-checks and reminders, one can assume that most people will feel ready to end the interview. However, despite these boundaries and safeguards, it can be hard for some service users to 'let go' and to move on. Some desperately try to get all they can out of the interview – right up to the end. As a result, the interview can end up being drawn to a close in a way that feels rushed, with insufficient time to review what has been covered or to work through any feelings triggered by our departure.

'Doorknob revelations'

One way that people reveal a difficulty working within boundaries can be encountered in the form of 'doorknob revelations'. These occur where significant or painful information is revealed at the end of the interview when we are about to leave. As a practitioner, these revelations put us in a difficult 'no-win' situation. To extend the time boundary could mean we have lost control of it, and could also make us late for other appointments, but to be too rigid could involve missing an opportunity to understand the service user better. Also, on occasion it can be very important to show that we are willing to change the time boundary – to be flexible and to adapt – to meet the needs being expressed. Whether we decide to respond or not, the request and our response should be reviewed and considered in terms of the overall purpose that has already been agreed. There are no easy solutions to these difficulties except to provide an opportunity early in the interview for service users to talk about what it feels like when the end of an interview is in sight.

Example: An uncomplicated ending to an interview

Practitioner: Okay. We've got ten minutes left and I wonder how you would like to use the rest of the time we have?

Service user: Can we talk about what will happen when my husband comes out of prison?

Example: A 'doorknob revelation' at the end of an interview

Practitioner: It's 10.20, which means we have ten minutes left. I wonder if we could use the time remaining to look at what we've talked about and then to decide what we plan to cover when we meet again next week. How does that sound to you?

Service user: Okay but there's something I want to tell you before you go. You know I said my mother died of cancer when I was seven. Well that wasn't right. My aunt told me last year that she killed herself. That's why I went to live with my aunt – there was no-one else to take care of me. [She begins to cry]

Practitioner: I'm sorry. [Pause] . . . I did not realize that your mother died in that way. That's very upsetting for you to hear. You said your aunt told you this last year. What prompted her to tell you then, Sarah? [This ill-timed question is ignored]

Service user: [Sarah begins to sob]

Practitioner: It's okay . . . it must have been a real shock to hear this.

Service user: [Still sobbing deeply]

Practitioner: [Pause] . . . I can see how upset you are . . . and I feel for you. [Pause] . . . But I'm afraid I have to go in a minute because I have to be elsewhere.

Service user: [No reply]

Practitioner: Sarah, is there anyone you would like me to contact who could come over now to be with you?

Service user: [No reply]

Practitioner: [Pause] . . . Would it help if I asked your aunt to come across? How does that sound?

Service user: No. I don't want my aunt. I'm dead angry . . . she should have told me sooner.

Practitioner:	Okay ... I understand. But who else can I ask? Who would be better?
Service user:	[No reply]
Practitioner:	I'm really sorry to have to leave you when you feel so upset. If you like, you can stay here for a while ... till you feel a bit better. If you need any help to get home, there's a duty officer downstairs – Peter – who'll be able to help ... and I'll give you a ring you later ...
Service user:	Don't bother.
Practitioner:	I'll ring you later ... bye Sarah.

It is important to note that the sense of time we feel when someone is crying is very similar to the time we feel when people are silent. It can seem that the individual has been silent or tearful for longer than they actually have. Unless deeply distressed, most people tend not to cry for long periods, but this does not make the experience of crying any easier to bear for everyone concerned. It is important to check how people are feeling after a prolonged tearful experience. Some may feel physically sick or develop a headache. Others may appear bewildered, as if in an altered state. Where this is the case, it is important to ensure the individual arrives home safely.

34. Closing the case and ending the relationship

Closing a case appropriately when ending the prospect of future contact can be one of the most difficult yet important skills to acquire (Kadushin and Kadushin 1997: 271–84). It is made more difficult to achieve when other forms of help are not forthcoming. This is particularly troubling when working with people who do not have the emotional, practical, or material resources needed to manage without support of a particular kind. These concerns are very real. Sometimes this can lead to a situation where we continue to work with service users longer than is appropriate. We may be justifying this change of plan in sophisticated ways but, nevertheless, extending our involvement longer than is appropriate can create a situation where our work becomes purposeless and devoid of direction. It can also result in an unhealthy dependency being created, based as much on our own concerns as those of the service user. This is not the hallmark of a competent practitioner. Focused, thoughtful, and sensitive supervision can be enormously helpful in addressing these difficulties.

In ideal circumstances, cases should be terminated at a point that has been mutually agreed: when goals have been reached or the time allocated for the work has come to an end and the service user feels ready to end the contact. Well-planned endings often involve a tapering down of services, for example extending the length of time between appointments. This then also allows for the progress to be properly evaluated against agreed goals, aims, and objectives. This may include identifying how to build on what has already been learned and achieved, perhaps by referring the individual to other appropriate agencies, as well as providing the opportunity to work through difficulties, such as those triggered by separation and loss. It also allows the service user the chance to look ahead and to propose appropriate courses of action, including where to find additional help if this is needed.

One of the most valuable skills in relation to endings involves encouraging people to bring other people into their lives to replace us, by helping them to turn to others who can provide the care, concern, guidance, and support that they need. However, for a range of different and complex reasons, in practice many endings are not mutually agreed or carefully planned and prepared. As a result, they do not leave either party with a sense that there has been a satisfactory completion of an important and valuable piece of work. Closing cases in less than ideal circumstances, or at an inappropriate point, does little to enhance the reputation of social work but in a climate of limited resources, there may be no option. This highlights the complexities involved in social work and the difficult decisions we have to make. It can leave us in a 'no-win' situation and vulnerable to criticism, which can sometimes affect our judgement about whether to close a case.

Example: Preparing for the contact and relationship to end
This example involves Greg, aged 11, who has very poor social skills and who is ostracized and bullied at school.

Practitioner: Greg, You may recall that our agreement was to work together for six months. You may also remember that three months into our work, when we'd reached the half-way point, we agreed to look over our progress – what we'd achieved. We now have eight weeks remaining, which means that we will meet eight more times before we stop meeting. Endings can be difficult but they can be made easier by talking things through and by looking at what it will be like when we stop seeing one another. What comes to your mind when I say that our work will be ending in eight weeks' time?

Service user: I don't think I'd realized that we only have eight weeks left. I have been thinking in terms of months and two months seems a long way off. But eight weeks, or eight more meetings, seems like no time at all. I am already feeling that I would find it difficult to be okay without your help.

Practitioner: It's good that you're in touch with how you're feeling. Let's look at this a little more. What do you think you will miss most about not seeing me?

Service user: Having someone to talk to. You let me say whatever comes into my head and you never tell me off or say that I am wrong or stupid.

Practitioner: That's right ... Okay ... what we now need to think about is who else – other than me – doesn't tell you off or put you down? Who would be the best person for you to turn to when our work comes to an end?

Service user: No-one.

Practitioner: Let's try that question again. Of all the people you know, who is the easiest person for you to talk to?

Service user: No-one.

Practitioner: You have to help me Greg. You do know other people. Who is the easiest person for you to talk to? Who do you like being with?

Service user: John.

Practitioner: Right. What is it about John that you like?

Service user: He never puts me down.

Practitioner: So, what John and I have in common is that we don't criticize you or put you down?

Service user: Yes.

Practitioner: What else do you like about John?

Service user: He's a laugh.

Practitioner: How does he make you laugh?

Service user: He fools around a lot. And does crazy things ... and likes to have fun.

Practitioner: Okay. Who else do you know who makes you laugh – who fools around a lot and likes to have fun?

Service user: No-one.

Practitioner: Keep trying Greg. Who else do you know who likes to have fun?

Service user: Alan.

Practitioner: Okay. Now you've named two people that you like and who are important to you. Over the next eight weeks, I want to suggest we need to spend some time talking about your friends and how you can keep in touch with John and Alan – and any other friends that come to mind – so that when the time comes for us to end our work together, you have some friends to talk to.

Conclusion: interviews as 'positive experiences'

This chapter has looked at 28 interviewing skills and interventions. The task of interviewing is a central and essential skill because of the opportunity it provides to gain a greater understanding of people and their situation. This understanding, when shared, can in itself help bring about change. For these reasons, interviewing skills are as important to experienced practitioners as newly qualified staff because they help to ensure that our work has a structure and purpose, with clear objectives located within a meaningful value base. They are also crucial when we encounter difficult or chaotic situations or complex and intractable problems. For example, as an experienced practitioner I still find myself needing to draw on interviewing techniques when I encounter situations that I find overwhelming or frightening, or when I am tired and find it hard to concentrate at the end of a difficult day. They act as a safeguard – as a compass when I find myself lost in the wilderness of my own preoccupations and fears. The two chapters that follow continue this theme and explore interventions that can be used to help people to move their lives forward and to bring about change.

8 PROVIDING HELP, DIRECTION, AND GUIDANCE

Introduction

Unlike in Chapter 5, the interventions covered in the first part of this chapter describe reactions that are not solely the domain of professionals: family, friends, neighbours, concerned individuals or strangers can be skilled in helping a human being who needs help. As practitioners, our role and responsibilities result in different expectations. Accountability is different. The second part of the chapter covers skills that are more advanced.

Specific skills

Skills: Providing help, direction, and guidance
35 Providing help
36 Giving advice
37 Providing information
38 Providing explanations
39 Offering encouragement and validation
40 Providing reassurance
41 Using persuasion and being directive
42 Providing practical and material assistance
43 Providing support
44 Providing care
45 Breaking 'bad news'
46 Modelling and social skills training
47 Reframing
48 Offering interpretations
49 Adapting to need
50 Counselling skills
51 Containing anxiety

35. Providing help

It takes skill to decide what kind of help may be needed and how to offer this in ways that are personally and culturally acceptable to the individual. These skills are at the heart of social work but difficult to acquire. Nevertheless, according to England (1986: 4, original emphasis), 'good social workers *know*, through their experience, the value of their helping work with clients. That value cannot be abandoned'. It is the uncertain nature of the value of helping – what it means to give and to receive help – that must be unravelled, clarified, and articulated so that the essential part that help plays in sustaining and creating positive change can be identified and utilized to the fullest. To fail to enter into this dialogue about the value of helping leaves us trapped between those who desire to care for vulnerable people within a 'caring society', and those who despise and attack vulnerability and who demean those who care for vulnerable people. Without this clarification, we are open to being stereotyped as ineffective 'do-gooders', where our work and the help we offer is characterized as ineffective, coercive and controlling, and beyond scrutiny and evaluation (England 1986: 5).

To begin to unravel what is included in the term 'help' is difficult because there is no uniformity across social work and, as a result, being helpful can involve a range of different interventions. In an attempt to clarify the use of these terms, *practical* and *material assistance, support* and *care* are differentiated in this book and used to describe different activities and different skills. However, none of these interventions is mutually exclusive. For example, most problems have an emotional element. Some service users may feel ashamed or embarrassed about asking for practical assistance. To ensure that they can take up and utilize whatever practical help is needed, emotional support may be required (Lishman 2009a: 10–11). The converse is not necessarily the case. Emotional support itself may be all that is required. For example, practitioners using counselling skills when working with someone who has been bereaved may only focus on the feelings of bereavement and loss, if practical support is being provided elsewhere.

Much of our willingness to help may be conveyed quite subtly through our behaviour. Yet, despite our best efforts, some service users may still dislike having to seek or ask for help. These negative feelings may include a concern about how they might be seen by others, or have their roots in a fierce sense of independence. The possible responses are endless and dependent on what it was like for the individual to have to rely on others in the past. Memories of earlier failures, disappointments, or humiliating experiences can result in people becoming guarded. Some professionals respond inappropriately, by treating service users like children or as if they are stupid. Others demand compliance, insisting that service users should be grateful, cooperative, and deferential. Too often, this can result in people feeling robbed of their self-respect and sense of personal autonomy. It can be difficult for any individual to accept and to benefit from services when these are offered in a demeaning way. Older people are particularly susceptible to this kind of patronizing behaviour. So too are children and young people and others, such as people from minority groups, whose right to be respected does not always come automatically.

All professions are prone to treat people badly, sometimes in ways that are less obvious, such as making people wait for long periods. Citizen and patient charters are designed to address these difficulties and inequalities but have limitations because they neither guarantee people's entitlement to certain services nor the right to be treated fairly.

According to Howe (1987: 113), 'helping is a test of the helper as a person'. This statement emphasizes that much of our ability to provide appropriate help relates to our own personal history of being helped and our ongoing capacity to receive help from others in our everyday lives. It reinforces the importance of self-knowledge and of our being in touch with what we feel when we are at the receiving end of help and the anxieties felt from being beholden to or having to depend on others. Howe's statement also emphasizes the importance of creating and sustaining a more equal, mutual, and reciprocal relationship when working alongside or in partnership with service users. For example, I once worked with a social worker who had a remarkable capacity for being able to empathize accurately with service users and to translate that understanding into appropriate and creative forms of help. However, his ability to communicate that understanding was on the whole quite poor. After some time, and some serious misunderstandings, it came to light that the reason for this difficulty lay in the fact that this worker was brought up in a mixed race, immigrant family where the language used took the form of commands: 'do this/do that'. Questions or requests were not the kind of phrases commonly used. Although his language had changed over the years, the legacy of this early form of communication remained, particularly when he felt under attack or nervous. This example highlights how our early experiences can affect our capacity to provide help, both negatively and positively.

Providing help also offers an opportunity to give more than practical services. It allows us to stretch the experience across other needs. For example, in setting up a nursery place for a child, we could highlight the possibilities this opens up for the mother or father, as well as for the child. We could use it as an opportunity to explore what direction this parent might want for their life and for their child. Clearly, encouraging someone to pursue their hopes and desires in this way has to be tempered by the reality of the situation. However, too much realism can be a reflection of our own depressed outlook, and dampen enthusiasm and the opportunity to herald something new and exciting.

Taking hold of opportunities and stretching them in this way can demand a great deal from and, inevitably, we cannot always put forward our *best self* because there will be times when we do not feel able to respond in this way – when we find ourselves guarding resources as if they are our personal possessions or when we feel too put-upon, depleted, and empty to be able to give at all, let alone to give generously. Service users may pick up on this fact, and in such a situation it may be wise for us to acknowledge our weariness and temporarily bow out as gracefully as possible, in the hope that we can return soon with renewed energy. This may be preferable to our struggling to give from a depleted part of ourselves. If persistent, difficulties of this kind can mark the beginning of burn-out, that is, a situation where we feel disillusioned, undervalued, and exhausted by expectations and demands that feel overwhelming and impossible to process (Feltham and Dryden 2004: 29; Munro 2011b: 91).

36. Giving advice

Advice and guidance are sometimes used interchangeably because both involve recommending something or directing an individual towards one or several courses of action. In a professional context, both can carry the expectation that our views are backed by knowledge and/or experience. However, guidance tends to sound less prescriptive (vocational or career guidance agencies) whereas the word advice tends to have a more definite meaning.

Advice is often sought either to help identify the problem clearly or to help identify possible solutions, but should be offered with the greatest care because we can be inaccurate or simply wrong in the advice we offer. Offering advice inappropriately can also reinforce a sense of personal inadequacy or be experienced as intrusive. For these reasons, it is important to be judicious and thoughtful about the kind of advice we give, perhaps only offering advice when asked and with the proviso that we may be wrong. These safeguards help to ensure that any advice given is sensitive to an individual's personal situation and expectations, including their cultural and social context.

In recent years, some social workers have felt reluctant to provide advice. It can be seen as 'imposing our values or morals' on our clients (Lishman 2009a: 128); as contradicting the principle of client self-determination (Biestek 1961); as failing to acknowledge the importance of service users taking on the role of 'experts' in relation to their own lives; as patronizing and disempowering; or as discouraging self-sufficiency and personal autonomy by creating an unhealthy dependency. As a result, offering advice can generate anxiety among practitioners, in case we give the 'wrong' advice and are held accountable. One way to manage these anxieties is to be honest and open about what we do and do not know, and to avoid bluffing or hedging our responses. However, certain areas of knowledge are required of us and are essential to the social work task, which means that in certain situations we have a responsibility to offer advice that should include, as a minimum, 'detailed, accurate and up-to-date knowledge about the law, welfare rights and local community facilities' (Davies 1981: 52). This links to the point made earlier about the importance of social workers developing a sound knowledge base.

It is interesting to note that service users do not always share our reservations about being given advice (Lishman 2009a: 12). As with the offer of explanations, advice can be particularly important for people who feel bewildered and confused or who need to base their decision on our opinions. For example, offering advice to people who have been recently traumatized can help to structure what they have to do and in what order. For this reason it is important for service users to decide for themselves whether they want to hear advice that is on offer, rather than us deciding for them. Most service users weigh up the advice they are given quite carefully and will tend to ignore advice that seems inappropriate. However, the timing of advice giving is crucial. As a general rule, it should only be offered when other possibilities have been exhausted and the decision-making and problem-solving processes have broken down. It is important that advice is not 'thrown in' at the end of the session, as a parting shot, because this does not give the individual the opportunity to take new information on board and to work through whatever thoughts and feelings have emerged.

37. Providing information

Recent years have seen the development of specialized information services and centres, such as those in relation to housing, welfare rights, legal rights, and those providing information on local resources, such as self-help groups and social networks (Lishman 2009a: 118). This development has left some social workers unsure about whether it is appropriate to offer certain kinds of practical help, such as welfare rights checks, where specialist expertise may be more accurate and up-to-date. Nevertheless, even if we do not undertake welfare rights checks ourselves, it is essential that we know where these more specialist advice centres are and the nature of their referral criteria.

In more general terms, providing information can be central to problem-solving and the decision-making process. For this reason, it is important that any information offered is accurate. Updating the information we have on local resources can be a time-consuming task, particularly without proper organizational structures to feed in new information and developments. However, for service users to act on information later found to be wrong can result in a serious loss of trust and confidence in the competence of social work as a profession.

Where the task involves referring people on to other agencies or organizations, it helps to check the accuracy of the information to hand, perhaps by telephoning the agency before referring people on, having ensured first that we have the service user's permission to do so. It is alarming how many service users are given incorrect information at this stage: for some, it must feel like being sent on a wild goose chase, where only the most charmed or most determined get through. Checking disabled access is particularly important.

The following points need to be stressed. Anxiety and fear can interfere with an individual's capacity to listen and to digest information, because emotional energy is being taken up attending to these anxieties. This may manifest as the individual appearing to be confused or preoccupied. When this is the case, it can be helpful to repeat information, using language that is simple, steady, and accessible. This is particularly true when communicating bad news, such as details of an accident or incident. If this does not work and the individual still seems confused and lost, we need to consider ending the session.

Again, it is vital not to give important information right at the end of a session when concentration may have lapsed: sometimes it is essential to be present to see how well information has been processed. Where we suspect that a person might forget the details covered, a follow-up letter may prove helpful but only where we know the service user has adequate literacy skills and where receiving a letter would not be experienced as daunting.

Leaflets and other written information

The importance of providing written information in the form of leaflets and handouts is likely to depend on the situation and what knowledge the individual already has and needs. This may vary over time. For instance, an asylum seeker who has recently arrived in this country is likely to need a great deal of information, which may have to be translated. This may entail explaining basic information, such as how different services and government departments operate and how to access these. For example, it can save a great deal of time and anguish if we explain the difference between social security and social services. Leaflets must be adapted where service users' capacity to understand and to take in information is limited. Special care needs to be taken in relation to differences of age, physical disability, hearing or sight impairments, emotional state, literacy and comprehension skills, and so on. There are many imaginative ways to overcome such difficulties, such as using drawings, pictures, figurines, and videos.

It is easy for people to be 'fobbed off' with information, as if by handing out a leaflet we are always providing something that is useful, helpful, and appropriate. Sadly, that may not be the case and, instead, we could be handing out worry or confusion, particularly if the leaflet is not written in a way that meets the needs of the person seeking this information. The test lies in whether they were able to use this information, and the best and easiest way to find this out is to ask for feedback. Another way would be to read the information or leaflet as if we were unfamiliar with the issue being communicated to determine whether it is informative. We may find that too much knowledge is assumed, which can raise more questions than answers.

Information giving, whether given verbally or in written form, can be seen as an opportunity to provide new meaning and understanding. As a symbolic communication, providing advice, guidance, or explanations can have far-reaching consequences (Lishman 2009a: 26–32). Information that is passed over well not only helps people to make an informed choice but can also instil confidence in a way that encourages individuals to act independently and effectively on their own behalf in the future (Millar *et al.* 1992: 108). Therefore, how we communicate information can be as important as the information itself. Leaflets handed out with an attitude of indifference, or as an afterthought, are likely to be viewed by service users in the same way. For this reason, it can be helpful to bring the leaflet/information 'alive' by reading it beforehand, marking those areas considered relevant and important, and by making it personal by adding the individual's name to it. These gestures are important because they reveal a commitment and thoughtfulness: they can also save valuable time.

Finally, it is important to note that under the Disabled Persons Act 1986, social work departments and voluntary agencies have a duty to provide leaflets and information in an appropriate and accessible format for people with a disability, such as providing information in Braille, or as tape recordings. Equally, it is required that information is provided in the language of the people who use the service. This expectation also extends to information on health and welfare issues. For example, the current Attendance Allowance leaflet (DS 702) is available in several languages other than English: Bengali, Chinese, Greek, Gujarati, Hindi, Punjabi, Turkish, Urdu, Vietnamese, and Welsh.

38. *Providing explanations*

Explaining is a core skill in social work, and important in other health and welfare settings, but it has received limited attention in social work texts and in communication studies research. Brown and Atkins proposes three reasons for this neglect:

- explaining is a taken-for-granted activity; a great deal of time is spent explaining in everyday life and in various professional contexts, so it is assumed that everyone knows how to explain
- for some professional groups such as counsellors, therapists and social workers, explaining has associations with authority-centred approaches, with telling, instructing and didactics; hence the study of explaining is shunned
- explaining, like so many taken-for-granted activities, is a deep concept. Explaining has interconnections with understanding, with language, with logic, with rhetoric, and with critical theory and with culture.

(Brown and Atkins 1997: 183)

Explanations differ from advice and guidance because their purpose is not to offer direction but to illuminate, clarify, reconcile, or interpret events with a view to providing greater understanding. They attempt to throw light on the cause, nature, and interrelationship of different thoughts, feelings, and events. Explanations can be divided into three types: illustrations, demonstrations, and verbal explanations. Of these, the focus of this section is on verbal explanations, which can be seen in terms of three main categories, each addressing a different type of question (Brown and Atkins 1997: 184–5):

- interpretative explanations – what?
- descriptive explanations – how?
- reason-giving explanations – why?

Some explanations may involve all three categories in an attempt to describe the problem or situation in words that can be understood and absorbed, so that a new understanding can be reached. This endeavour is more likely to succeed if it is (1) sensitive to the service user's thoughts and feelings, (2) delivered in a way that is interesting, involved, clear, and well structured, and (3) where the communication has been planned in a way that maximizes learning and understanding – 'a little remembered is better than a lot forgotten'.

Responsibility for an unsuccessful communication should lie with us and not be blamed, implicitly, on service users. One way to check whether a new understanding has been reached is to ask service users to recall what they have heard or to ask them to apply this understanding to specific and relevant situations in their lives. This needs to be undertaken sensitively, drawing on points made earlier in the text on the 'nature of helping', and the importance of understanding the meaning given to experiences.

Explanations as a way of addressing emotional needs

In relation to emotional needs, explanations can be profoundly important for people who easily become confused or who have little confidence or trust in their own thinking and how to understand and link different experiences. Such confusion may be short term in nature and lift relatively easily. However, for some people this state of confusion is severe and enduring, and in some cases may be the result of discontinuities and disruptions in childhood.

Case example: Jo

I once worked with a young woman, Jo, whose family was always moving house, possibly to avoid debts, although this was never known for sure. Her parents never appeared to offer any explanation about events, which meant that there was never any transition or bridge between one experience and another. This situation reflected a serious lack of consistency and predictability in Jo's life. This difficulty was compounded by the fact that she was not a 'wanted child'. She felt this acutely. Her mother later admitted that she had tried to have an abortion when she knew she was pregnant with Jo. The result of these experiences meant that Jo lived with the dread, throughout her childhood, that one day she would come home and find her family gone and her house empty; she would be left behind, with nowhere to go and no means of knowing where to find her family. Jo found it virtually impossible to link events or to bring cause and effect together. She thought 'things just happened' for no reason, or no reason she could work out. The absence of words and explanations from her parents meant that Jo found it hard to sort out one feeling from another or to know which feelings belonged to her and which belonged to others (Howe *et al.* 1999: 145). This profound sense of confusion and bewilderment haunted Jo's struggle in the world and, when she left care, she eventually became rootless, living in doorways, with no sense of belonging anywhere, as if searching for something. One of her greatest joys was to have things explained to her, which she once described as 'a word lullaby', because it attempted to provide some order, certainty, and predictability in a world that otherwise felt frightening and beyond comprehension.

The importance of explaining the world and what is happening for service users who have not had this experience in childhood, needs to be emphasized. It is for this reason that story-telling (Jewett 1997: 119–23) or narrative accounts are important. We can recognize these gaps and confusions when, as with Jo, we encounter service users who regularly manifest a profound bewilderment, asking what appear to be naive questions but with little capacity to remember the answer. Such bewilderment can be painful and terrifying. For this reason, the ability to explain situations to service users – to help them to understand past and present events and future possibilities – in a language and tone that is accessible and kind is one of the most important communication skills that we can develop as practitioners.

39. Offering encouragement and validation

Offering *positive encouragement* can be an important intervention within social work. However, according to Lishman, research suggests that these interventions may not be widely used by practitioners:

> There seems general hesitancy or ambivalence in social work about the value of explicitly conveying approval or positive encouragement. This may reflect in part a cultural bias against giving or accepting positive feedback or an anxiety that giving approval can be patronizing. It may also reflect underlying traditional values in social work, for example, acceptance and taking a non-judgemental approach ...
>
> (Lishman 2009a: 82)

An exception is where encouragement forms part of a particular practice approach as, for example, in Rogers' (1957) concept of *unconditional positive regard* or where, as with praise, encouragement is used as a 'support intervention' (Kadushin and Kadushin 1997: 205) intended to ensure that certain options are explored or undertakings completed. In relation to cognitive-behavioural approaches, encouragement and validation are described in terms of *positive reinforcement* (Cigno 2009; Sheldon 1995: 63).

Encouragement can be seen in two ways: to help service users *towards* or *away from* a particular course of action, experience, thought, or feeling. Both can be particularly helpful when individuals have poor self-esteem (Mruk 1999: 153), little self-confidence or limited experience, or when they feel overwhelmed and afraid of what they may encounter. Encouragement can help to smooth the journey towards these experiences or can be a low-key means of drawing service users away from certain actions or activities that may be dangerous or damaging, and/or pose a threat to themselves or to others.

Some practitioners are reluctant to attempt to steer another person's behaviour in this way. The concern is that it could be used unethically, perhaps as a means of controlling or manipulating individuals in a particular direction: these dangers have to be guarded against. Nevertheless, some people need encouragement to keep them going and give them confidence and, although it may not always be appropriate to respond to these needs, they should not be ignored. A further difficulty is that it can be hard to know how to express our encouragement in ways that do not sound soppy or 'over-the-top'. This skill comes with practice and experience.

Validation

Whereas encouragement is oriented to inspire or motivate people to think or act differently *before* an event or experience, *validation* tends to provide a positive appraisal *after* the event. In this sense, validation is a form of feedback but often has a more personal orientation because it provides an opportunity to applaud the commitment and effort put into a particular situation and to celebrate any achievement or personal learning that has been gained. Validation of this kind is important when working with people who lack confidence in themselves, perhaps in relation to their appearance or in their ability to make sound decisions and to act independently. However, care must be taken that the validations we give are honest and truthful and not exaggerated or given merely to make someone 'feel better'. Validations sound hollow or patronizing if they are not based on actual abilities or real achievements.

40. Providing reassurance

Offering reassurance can be an important way to ease anxiety and uncertainty – to smooth troubled waters – and to provide comfort. This is particularly important at times when an individual has lost touch with a more balanced view of what is happening in their lives and, as a result, needs someone to reassure them that, despite their worries, everything is basically in order. However, reassurance should not be offered where we are not confident that our words will come true. To be over-optimistic or over-reassuring when the outcome cannot be clearly predicted or controlled is to run the risk of letting people down and putting our relationship and credibility in danger. If our reassurances are later proved wrong or unfounded, this could seriously – perhaps even irreparably – undermine confidence in our judgement. It is worth remembering that people can feel reassured indirectly by the way we conduct ourselves, including the way we dress (Kadushin and Kadushin 1997: 291–4; Lishman 2009a: 29–30), and by our ensuring that they are treated with respect (Clark 2000a: 50).

Some people repeatedly seek reassurance yet somehow they remain agitated, as if the words of reassurance have not been meaningful – have not touched them or 'got through'. Where this is the case, repeating reassurances is unlikely to reduce the anxieties being experienced and, in fact, can be counterproductive because 'the repeated seeking of reassurance undermines the person's confidence to deal with the problem himself [sic]' (Trower et al. 1988: 110). Instead, it may help to draw attention to the fact that our words are not reassuring and to ask the individual to explore what is happening to them at this moment, in this 'here-and-now' conversation. The person needing reassurance may not be able to explain or to understand their behaviour but this line of questioning can help to break into the repetitive nature of the communication and mark the beginning of a real engagement.

In these and similar situations, it can be helpful to ask ourselves 'What is this individual trying to communicate about themselves?' or 'What or who have I become for this person?' and to feed back our thoughts and feelings. For example, it can help to ask 'What do you think I could give you that would be useful or helpful to you right now?' This helps to break into the repetitious nature of the communication and to establish a more direct rapport.

41. Using persuasion and being directive

Persuading service users to behave differently or to see themselves in a different light can be very difficult. People can become very fixed in their ways, and although this intervention attempts to create some possibility for change, it also runs the risk of our being too coercive and influential, sometimes to the point where we persuade service users to do something they are not yet ready to do. This can foreclose exploration and restrict the opportunity for people to find their own way in relation to decisions that affect their lives. Too often the result is failure, which can have a negative impact on a person's confidence and their hopes for the future.

In any attempt to influence others, power differentials have to be taken into account. Being persuaded by someone in authority can feel like an instruction or a command – as a 'should' and an 'ought' – where the only option possible is to comply. Failing to acknowledge inequalities of this kind can mean that we create or reinforce feelings of poor self-esteem or personal inadequacy. It is important that these feelings, and the reality of power differentials, are addressed (Clark 2000a: 200; O'Sullivan 1999: 118).

In some professional circles, such as medicine and dentistry, persuasion is more highly valued than it is in social work, where it tends to be viewed with reserve and suspicion because it involves attempting to influence people. However, this can be a denial of the sometimes uncomfortable fact that, as human beings, we all try to influence one another to lesser and greater degrees, whether in blatant or subtle ways.

Although non-directive approaches seem to be preferred by social work practitioners, particularly those embracing a more client-centred/person-centred approach, there will always be situations that warrant our being directive. For example, there can be risks involved if we do not attempt to persuade someone away from danger, or when we do not use our knowledge and experience to direct someone towards a course of action that could be of benefit. The key is to use persuasion – as with all other directive interventions – judiciously, basing our decision-making on the interest of the service user and on the best information we have about the potential advantages of a particular course of action. There are times when we need to 'respond to the need for a user of services for some structure and direction' (Lishman 2009a: 172) by being more directive, but this should be undertaken as a short-term intervention. Being directive and persuasive is more likely to be successful where we have a good relationship with the individual in question, where the person is open and responsive to our viewpoint, and where we feel we have sufficient knowledge and experience to steer the person in the ways suggested. (Some cognitive-behavioural approaches provide good examples of the use of more directive interventions, such as those found under the heading *positive* and *negative reinforcement*; see Sheldon 1995: 63–4.)

42. Providing practical and material assistance

One of the ways that we communicate our care, concern, and commitment to others is through offering practical and material assistance. Research findings indicate that service users place great value on being given practical help, particularly when it addresses problems they are struggling to deal with themselves, such as writing letters, transportation, or acting as an advocate (Fisher 1983; Lishman 2009a: 12–16; Mayer and Timms 1970). Equally, being given access to resources that would otherwise be difficult to access – such as day-care provision, after-school activities, respite accommodation or laundry facilities – can greatly ease the pressures and stresses that service users experience, often on a daily basis (Dartington Social Research Unit 1995; Thoburn 2008: 212; Thoburn *et al.* 1995). In this respect, the limited financial assistance available to service users remains a serious problem, given the fact that, for many, poverty is their major problem (Bateman

2008; Clarke 1993; Walker and Walker 2009). Sainsbury *et al.* summarize the situation as follows:

> Social workers (compared with their clients) overestimated the relative helpfulness of insight work, the use of authority and giving advice, but underestimated the helpfulness experienced by clients as a result of material and financial help and negotiations with other agencies on their behalf.
>
> (Sainsbury *et al.* 1982: 19–20)

Two problems exist in relation to providing practical and material assistance. First, it is sometimes undertaken without a clear sense of purpose or strategy in terms of a particular outcome or goal: rushing to act before thinking carefully about the meaning of someone else's experience and what it means symbolically to act. Such activity is devoid of purpose and, therefore, prone to having little real impact. For England (1986: 14), providing more 'active' forms of material and practical assistance should be offered to improve a service user's 'coping capacity', that is, they should form part of an identified strategy and always be related to the service user's 'objective resources'.

The second problem relates to the fact that the request for practical assistance may not meet a response at all. Instead, emotional support or counselling may be offered, perhaps because this accords with the orientation of the practitioner or because practical or material problems, such as those relating to social security benefits, debts, poverty, homelessness, unemployment, ill health, and so on, are not given the priority they deserve by the practitioner or the employing agency. Much of the time this shift towards counselling and away from providing practical support goes unnoticed, but can become evident when the service user's perceptions of their problems and their preferred solutions are compared with those of practitioners.

43. Providing support

'Support' is one of the most imprecise words used within social work. It can mean almost anything – offering assistance, backing, sustenance, reassurance, guidance, encouragement, validation, care, concern, and love (Feltham and Dryden 2004: 228). For this reason it is important that we are clear what we mean when we use the term. In this book, 'support' is used to describe *emotional support*; that is, responding to the need that we all have to be able to turn to a person, perhaps located in an agency, who can give us appropriate back-up during periods of strain, stress, or crisis, so that we can continue to cope and to keep going. Talking through problems with a sympathetic listener is a common source of emotional support. This may sometimes be described as social support (Sheppard 1994), which may be preferable because the word 'emotional' may be exposing or off-putting.

Ideally, such support will be met by partners, family, friends, and neighbours (Thoburn 2008: 211). However, where this is not the case, individuals may need help to locate appropriate sources of support, such as a support group for parents or mental health 'survivors'. There is much evidence from mental health and child-care research that the availability of support is associated with less stress and can result in, for example, more competent parenting (Thoburn 2008: 211), and in fewer admissions to psychiatric hospitals (Sheppard 1997: 321). For some people, however, this support may not exist, or may be too difficult to access. For others, the support may be offered too late, or be inappropriate or inadequate, perhaps because their own personal resources and support systems have become seriously depleted. In such cases, service users may look to practitioners for this kind of emotional or social support. This may be difficult to provide on an ongoing basis without adequate back-up in the form of sound, structured supervision, and peer and agency support.

The point to be stressed is that where we encounter a serious breakdown in a service user's capacity to cope with everyday tensions, our responses in terms of alternative sources of support have to be both robust and reliable, if we are to avoid a further deterioration in the quality of life for that individual. This involves our being clear about what support is needed, and is being offered, for how long, by whom, and for what purpose. It also involves checking that the support is being received in the way intended and that it is helpful. When carers are asked to provide this support, they too can show signs of being unable to cope with the demands placed upon them (Phillipson 2008: 50–1). The consequences of this kind of breakdown in support networks are profound. It can lead to greater marginalization, isolation, and loneliness, and further demands being made of social services to provide alternative back-up. As practitioners, this calls for us to use our skills effectively to create or to re-establish support networks and, in the meantime, to find ways to sustain the demands placed upon us by service users who have no alternative source of support.

44. Providing care

In relation to social work, notions of *care* and *caring* have many meanings, including: care orders, care and control, in care, care in the community, care assistant, carers, care packages, care planning and care management, and many more. Implicit in these different terms is an orientation to provide for the well-being of others. To *care* could be seen as allowing ourselves to be affected emotionally by another human being, whereas to be *caring* might involve demonstrating warmth, gentleness, kindness, and concern for others (caring *about*) or providing physical help or comfort (caring *for*).

One way to view the relationship between helping and caring is to see helping as relating to the *task*, and caring to the *process* of providing for others. Cheetham, developing a point suggested by Sainsbury (1987), sees *helping* as tangible and *caring* as intangible:

> Some social work is about *helping*, while some may emphasize *caring*. Helping clients seems to imply some observable difference made to their lives; and there are indeed some quite clear-cut, tangible social work tasks, for example providing information or arranging a specific service, the presence of which can be noted as one outcome of intervention. Caring, on the other hand, may involve the intangibles of a personal relationship without necessarily making an outwardly observable difference.
>
> (Cheetham *et al.* 1992: 12, original emphasis)

The rewards in providing help, whether as a carer or as a professional, can be many. For example, it can be deeply satisfying to know that, through our efforts, we played some part in enabling an individual to keep going, to gain more from life or to move on to new experiences. It is this mutuality and reciprocity that motivates us to want to do our best and to care for others. This mutuality is defined as 'the recognition of mutual obligations towards others, stemming from the acceptance of a common kinship, expressed in joint action, towards a more equitable sharing of resources and responsibilities' (Holman 1993: 56).

The fact that it is predominantly women who care for others, often in difficult and pressured circumstances, has been described as 'enforced altruism' (Davis and Ellis 1995: 146). The lack of understanding in relation to the emotional, physical, and social cost of caring for others was starkly demonstrated by the Audit Commission report that described 'the care provided by relatives and friends as "free"' (Audit Commission 1992: 3). An important role we could play as practitioners would be to highlight these gender inequalities and to agitate for better care, practical assistance and support for those who give and for those who receive this care.

The pitfalls in caring

It is not always clear how to pitch our care and support and there are many pitfalls. For example, our attempts to be helpful can sometimes be experienced as patronizing or condescending. Much depends on our intention, choice of words, timing, and tone. It also depends on the way in which we ourselves have been cared for in our lives and how comfortable we feel in the role of helper. Where practitioners and service users alike have been hurt in terms of their capacity to give and to receive, the 'give and take' that is central to creating a rapport and being empathic can be difficult to achieve without understanding and patience. When these different factors fail to fit together well, we can indeed easily fall into the trap of being patronizing or condescending, and find ourselves speaking down to the person in question. When this happens, it is important that we do not become defensive or apologetic to the point where service users feel they must neglect their own issues to care for us. Instead, it is better to try to understand how our words and gestures have been experienced and learn from our errors.

People's rights to help and the way that help is offered are important. People who have for years prided themselves on their ability to be self-sufficient can find the offer of help offensive or intrusive. To touch on delicate subjects is a skilful endeavour. For example, I recall once suggesting to an elderly couple living in a second floor flat that they might find a second handrail helpful. Both had fallen down the stairs on a number of occasions, but not seriously. My suggestion was poorly received: in fact, it was received as an insult. It took several weeks of gentle persuasion and another fall before they felt able to consider a second rail and then with the proviso that it would be removed if they 'didn't take to it'. Luckily, the handrail was installed by two very thoughtful council workers who played a part in helping this couple to adjust to the change: the couple would not now be without their rail. This example shows that unless we attend to emotional issues – in this example, the importance and meaning that this couple gave to their capacity to be independent – our efforts can be sabotaged.

In relation to the wider picture within social work, a further pitfall in relation to caring for others is that in some professional and personal contexts, caring can be used as a means of control – as a way to engender guilt, obligation and compliance, and to take away an individual's right to self-determination and autonomy. In its blatant form, this kind of 'social control' can be challenged but it can be quite subtle and, therefore, difficult to detect and to confront, particularly in relation to vulnerable groups, such as people with learning disabilities (Clark 2000a: 21–2). The development of 'service user movements', such as those in relation to people with disability and people in receipt of psychiatric services, challenges the way that services are controlled and highlights instead the importance of 'user-led' policies and provision (Croft and Beresford 2008: 397–8).

In relation to social work skills, we need to take account of the wider context within which our work is located because the realities of practice may require great flexibility. We may walk in the door offering one skill and leave having offered another. Once I found myself being asked to 'sort out' the 'problem behaviour' at a particular school, only to find myself acting in the role of advocate for young people's rights. My experience is not unique.

45. Breaking 'bad news'

The ability to break 'bad news' sensitively is an important skill. The following points warrant consideration:

1. Think about how you might feel if you were to be told this bad news. What might you need?

2. Based on the information you have on the service user, how might he or she react?
3. Think about how best to break the bad news in terms of:
   - the setting and where best to communicate the bad news
   - who else ought to be present to provide comfort and support
   - which words to use and how your tone and timing, and other non-verbal forms of communication can be helpful
   - how to avoid being interrupted
   - the role of other staff members, for example informing the receptionist of the bad news you are about to communicate and the fact that the service user is likely to be upset.
4. What additional or follow-up work may be needed to ensure that the service user is able to cope and to manage the feelings and reactions that they are experiencing?
5. What support you might need. How are you likely to react or be left feeling? Who could provide you with that support?
6. Think about how to tie up any loose ends, including any practical arrangements that need to be dealt with.

46. Modelling and social skills training

Modelling is often associated with cognitive-behavioural approaches and is designed to promote and reinforce particular behaviours that are considered desirable or appropriate for the individual concerned (Ronen 2008). These behaviours or new responses can be acquired through various processes, including 'observational learning, vicarious learning, modelling, or imitation' (Sheldon 1995: 81), and can be broadly divided into two categories: inadvertent and deliberate modelling.

Inadvertent modelling refers to behaviour that the service user has learned through watching others. Most behaviour is learned in this way, both good and bad, particularly from parents and, in recent years, through the mass media:

> Modelling accounts for the acquisition of a vast range of very different behaviours: skills simple and complex, from washing dishes to brain surgery, from social good manners to conducting philosophical debate; and also those kinds of behaviours we do not designate as skills, such as reacting with anxiety to thunderstorms or being brave in the face of danger. Numerous experiments have shown that skills, attitudes and emotional responses can all be acquired through modelling.
> (Hudson and Macdonald 1986: 41)

In the social learning approach developed by Bandura (1977), modelling is more likely to be attractive and successful where the model is seen to have some standing and where the respect given to a model is linked to a particular behaviour. Also, it is important for there to be a similarity or shared sense of identity between subject and the model, an opportunity to practise the behaviour soon after it has been modelled, and a climate where the newly acquired behaviour is reinforced by others (Hudson and Macdonald 1986: 45).

Deliberate modelling is generally employed to address behavioural problems, to reduce anxiety, and to help re-establish or reinforce lost or suppressed behaviours (Sheldon 1995: 87). This may involve the live enactment of certain behaviours by the practitioner and, in formal modelling, includes the following steps:

1. Specify the behaviour to be demonstrated and ask the observer to attend to it
2. Arrange demonstration
3. Ask the observer to imitate the behaviour immediately after the demonstration
4. Give feedback to imitate the behaviour immediately after the demonstration
5. Give further practice, and so on.

(Hudson and Macdonald 1986: 141)

Modelling is particularly useful where individuals have encountered worrying situations that they feel ill-equipped to manage. In relation to service users, this intervention can be important in helping to tackle daunting situations such as court appearances, social security tribunals, and school exclusion procedures, with the practitioner running through the various stages likely to be encountered.

Social skills training is based on the same social learning principles used in modelling. It is most often employed in helping service users overcome behaviours that render them vulnerable to being isolated or socially excluded, or to develop and extend certain skills, such as how to respect another person's sense of space and privacy or how to be more assertive. Again, this may involve direct instruction or modelling by a practitioner, video demonstrations, role-plays, and homework. A danger in relation to both modelling and social skills training is that social and cultural influences and differences may be ignored in favour of the norms of the dominant culture.

47. Reframing

This intervention has received little attention in social work texts, yet it is one of the most important skills that a practitioner can have. It is a major technique of neurolinguistic programming (Feltham and Dryden 2004: 193) and family therapy (Watzlawick *et al.* 1974). Reframing also has much in common with cognitive-behavioural approaches where the aim is to change thought processes and behaviour. Its main advantage is that it provides an opportunity to describe a situation or behaviour from a different, more hopeful and optimistic perspective. This allows service users and practitioners to revisit decisions or opinions made previously, often by people in positions of authority, and to pose a different view of 'how situations are to be understood and what knowledge is to count as relevant' (Howe 1994: 526). As a result, factors located within the 'frame' can be viewed differently. For example, people described as having 'no motivation' can, within the same 'frame', be described as not wanting what is on offer, for very good reasons: 'For many stigmatized and oppressed groups "help" has come to equal control because that has been their experience' (Sheldon 1995: 241). To counter the stigmatizing experiences attached to labels such as *alcoholic* or *drug addict*, reframing is used in motivational interviewing to help people to reframe the labels they have been given (Miller and Rollnick 2002: 61–2).

Reframing involves taking the same 'facts' but placing them in a different context or 'frame'. As a result, the 'entire meaning' is changed (Walzlawick *et al.* 1974: 95). Its purpose is to change the meaning that is attached to certain behaviours or ways of relating to make the situation more amenable to change. These redefinitions can help to remove some of the 'sting' – the guilt or shame – and help to bring the behaviour within the grasp of the individual, perhaps through normalizing it. For example, reframing can be used to view a negative behaviour in a positive light or allow a less judgemental and more compassionate understanding of events. This is particularly valuable when working with people who have little confidence or self-esteem or who are racked with self-blame or guilt, such as parents experiencing difficulties with their children. Often the messages that service users give to each other can be deeply critical, harsh, and self-punishing. Reframing offers a way to replace these painful, negative *internal conversations* with words that are more understanding, optimistic, and caring. It is important to stress that for reframing to be successful it must use the same concrete facts, and the alternative 'frame' should be believable and communicated in words that can be easily understood.

Reframing can sometimes be confused with making excuses but it is not the same. Making excuses involves justifying actions, thoughts, and feelings or unacceptable behaviour, sometimes because we cannot deal with the conflict this arouses in us or because we are scared to stand our ground. However, it is important to see the 'gentle art of reframing' (Watzlawick *et al.* 1974: 92–109) in its own right as an intervention that can be enormously valuable in helping people to feel less stuck, and as a way of enabling people to move forward.

Example: Reframing

Service user: I'm too lazy to get out of bed.
Practitioner: Perhaps what you describe as being lazy is a feeling that there is nothing to get up for?

Service user: I think I'm a horrible mother. I'm really tired and bad-tempered and shout at my kids all the time ...

Practitioner: The fact that you felt able to tell me about how you are with your children shows that you want to be different – to have a better relationship with them. It takes courage for a parent to admit that things are going wrong – as you just did. It gives us the chance to build on the fact that you want to do something about these difficulties.

Service user: I decided yesterday not to come to see you today because I felt you would criticize me.

Practitioner: Then you were very brave to come.

48. Offering interpretations

Interpretations offer a new frame of reference, based on information provided by the individual but extended to include inferences derived from that information and from the practitioner's own perceptions and intuition. Three types of interpretation are common. First, in the field of therapy, particularly in psychoanalytic psychotherapy, interpretations are used to bring unconscious conflicts and motives into the conscious to facilitate integration through acquiring insight (Rycroft 1972: 76). This helps 'clients to understand the origins of their problems, and thereby gain more control over them and more freedom to behave differently' (McLeod 2009: 88). This kind of interpretation involves psychotherapeutic training and is, therefore, beyond the practice remit of most social workers. Second, in relation to cognitive approaches, the emphasis is on understanding how service users interpret and misinterpret events, rather than the worker formulating interpretations (Feltham and Dryden 2004: 119). Third, interpretations are used to link and to connect the significance of certain thoughts, feelings, or behaviours to draw the service user's attention to something that they appear to be unaware of (Feltham and Dryden 2004: 119). This is the form of interpretation most used in social work and the one emphasized here.

As social work practitioners, there is an ongoing and understandable tendency to want to 'interpret' a service user's behaviour, that is, to link one event with another. However, this presents problems because the connections we are making may be inaccurate and difficult to evidence (in terms of 'hard facts'). It is always difficult to know with any certainty whether our awareness is accurate unless the situation or relationship is uncomplicated. If it is accurate, however, it can place us in the difficult position of knowing more about an aspect of a service user's behaviour – or life – than they themselves are aware of. It can be difficult to determine how we can use this 'interpretation' in ways that enable service users to gain this awareness for themselves, thereby gaining advantage from this knowledge.

One of the most common examples of this dilemma relates to child sexual abuse, where it is quite common to hear disturbed or distressed behaviour being 'interpreted' as a manifestation of early experiences of abuse, particularly sexual abuse. For some children, this interpretation may be true, but for others it may not. In fact, in my experience it is unlikely that severe disturbed behaviour can be linked to any one cause. This makes it important to analyse and question the assumptions that guide decision-making about when and how to offer an interpretation and to review critically evidence used to support a particular proposition. For example, not all abused children are traumatized by sexual abuse in ways that continue to have an impact on their behaviour or to limit their outlook on life (Corby 2006), but it is also the case that children can be traumatized by the manner in which professionals react and attempt to address their experiences of abuse. To communicate a healthy sense of outrage at the suffering children experience is appropriate and understandable but needs to be kept within professional boundaries through the process of self-reflection, to ensure 'that our responses arise from the client's situation rather than our past or needs' (Lishman 2009b: 376).

Well-timed and carefully worded interpretations have particular value in helping children and adults to understand themselves better but this process can neither be rushed nor imposed from outside. For truth to have meaning in ways that can be integrated, it has to be explored and discovered by the person in question. This can be a difficult undertaking, particularly if the truth is locked within painful memories. For this reason, it is important that careful thought is given to the possible consequences of offering information or interpretations in circumstances where it is unclear whether the service user is ready to 'take in' this information. One way through these dilemmas is to frame our awareness and understanding as tentative hypotheses (Feltham and Dryden 2004: 119) and to present these in a low-key way that leaves service users free to take them up or not, depending on how they are feeling at the time. This emphasis places less importance on the content of the interpretation than on the process of trying to ensure that service users are aware of our commitment and our willingness to get alongside them in ways that facilitate greater understanding and the possibility of moving their lives forward.

49. Adapting to need

Most practitioners have met service users who communicate a need for help but who cannot make use of the services or resources on offer, and frustrate our best efforts to get help to them. Such individuals are sometimes wrongly described as 'unmotivated'. Sheldon (1995: 126) takes issue with this, stating that: 'Psychologically speaking, there is no such thing as an "unmotivated person"'. Instead, he suggests that the poor take up of services may be an indication 'that they have not learned to want what we would like them to want'. This may be true. However, generalizations of this kind can fail to address all that is subtle and complex about human behaviour and motivation (Coulshed and Orme 2006: 109). A different way to understand behaviour that is frustrating or 'unmotivated' would be to emphasize that some service users may want what is on offer but lack what it takes emotionally to allow their needs to be met. This may be because their history of giving and receiving does not allow this freedom (John and Trevithick 2012).

This difficulty in accessing or utilizing services on offer frequently indicates 'failures' experienced in early childhood. Such failures are, I believe, best understood in terms of an individual's attachment history and other 'relationship based theories' (Howe *et al*. 1999: 30), such as those put forward by Bowlby (1979), Winnicott (1958, 1965), and later writers in this field. This difficulty is often manifest in service users being unable to adapt their behaviour or needs in ways that facilitate the helping process. For example, service users may try to control events or the relationship, perhaps by refusing to see us unless we are prepared to visit them at home or unless some other condition is met. In some situations, the need to control what is happening is so powerful that some service users would rather do without than accept services that are not presented on their terms.

Sometimes this need to control is a result of the service user being manipulative or uninterested. In other cases, however, it may be a need to ensure that predictability is preserved and uncertainty kept to a minimum. Another way to analyse this behaviour would be to see it as a manifestation of service users being wounded in the area of give and take or giving and receiving. People who have been given to in ways that were cruel or humiliating, or where the 'pay back' was too great, can find it hard to take from others – it might feel like losing control or exposing themselves to danger and further pain. Giving to others may be an easier undertaking but only if fear of rejection is not paramount.

These difficulties can be compounded in adulthood when service users have been 'abandoned by other sources of potential help' (Sheldon 1995: 118) or 'let down' in their significant attachments in other important ways. Whatever the reason, to be offered something – even something good and desired – can give rise to conflicts that may result in people failing to take up what is on offer, or needing to transform it in such a way that they lose some of the original benefits. For example, they may attempt to control what can or cannot be discussed to a point where the value and benefits inherent in the practitioner–service user relationship are lost.

One way to enable service users to take up the services on offer is through *adaptation to need*, which involves creating a situation in which we attempt to meet the unique needs of each individual. Many social work interventions personalize services in this way but, in the adaptation to need I am describing, this personalization is more detailed, focused, and purposeful. It is based on Winnicott's work, described briefly in Chapter 3, on the importance of adaptation in early childhood development, relating to the journey from almost total dependence to relative dependence, and independence towards interdependence (Winnicott 1965: 83–92). In this theory, healthy emotional development is based on the child being adapted by his or her carers in ways that facilitate growth and the capacity to relate to self, to others, and their social environment. Failures in adaptation can result in infants developing a sense of self that is fragmented and unintegrated (Winnicott 1965: 58), which can lead to a premature and isolating self-sufficiency. To use Winnicott's words, the adaptation need not be perfect but only 'good-enough'.

In terms of our work, we regularly come into contact with men, women, and children who have been neglected and uncared for in childhood, whose capacity to see their environment and other people as a resource is thus severely limited (Howe *et al.* 1999: 30). In this context, adaptation to need can help to make resources and services more accessible for people who struggle in this way. Examples include tasks commonly undertaken by social workers, such as providing practical help (taxis, child care, bus fares, adjusting our work patterns). The emphasis is on our adapting to the individual, rather than expecting service users to adapt to us or to 'fit in' (Trevithick 1993, 1995, 1998). Adaptation to need is consistent with user-led perspectives and is particularly valuable when working with minority groups, people with low self-esteem or those who feel marginalized and excluded. However, it may be a difficult intervention to implement in terms of agency policy and practice and the limited resources and time that can be made available.

50. Counselling skills

The British Association for Counselling (BAC), the main accreditation body for counselling in the United Kingdom, describes counselling as:

> ... the skilled and principled use of relationships to develop self knowledge, emotional acceptance and growth, and personal resources. The overall aim is to live more fully and satisfyingly. Counselling may be concerned with addressing and resolving specific problems, making decisions, coping with crisis, working through feelings or inner conflict or improving relationships with others. The counsellor's role is to facilitate the client's work in ways that respect the client's values, personal resources and capacity for self determination.
>
> (BAC 1992)

Of the different 'schools of counselling', five are particularly influential within social work:

- client-centred counselling (sometimes called person-centred or humanist counselling)

- feminist counselling
- cognitive-behavioural counselling
- psychodynamic counselling
- eclectic or integrative counselling (adhering to no one single 'school' but instead combining different approaches).

Within social work, humanist approaches have been particularly influential, specifically the work of Egan (2007), Rogers (1961), Truax and Carkhuff (1967), mainly because they promote personal freedom and are consistent with anti-discriminatory and anti-oppressive perspectives. Brown (2002: 146) summarizes Egan's model as having four components: 'exploration, understanding, action and evaluation'. Rogers' 'core conditions' include congruence, unconditional positive regard and empathy, which Carkhuff and others adapted and developed to emphasize honesty and genuineness, warmth, respect, acceptance, and empathetic understanding (Payne 1997: 178).

However, the place of counselling within social work is more confused than it first appears because a differentiation is not always made between the use of counselling skills, counselling, and therapy (e.g. cognitive-behavioural therapy). Epstein illustrates this point: 'the practice of enhancing clients' knowledge and skill is referred to as counselling, or it may be called therapy or casework, depending on the language habits and preferences of a particular branch of the delivery system' (Epstein 1980: 26). Or again, in the past, 'counselling' has been used interchangeably with 'casework' (Pinker 1990: 18), or any form of one-to-one work. Indeed, Parton (1996: 12) argues that, 'In effect, casework has been reconstituted as counselling and a new, diverse and fast-growing occupation has developed'. This shift has been aided by the development of care managers.

For England (1986: 14), a social worker's role becomes that of a counsellor when 'he [sic] is concerned with improving his client's capacity'. However, social work 'usually exceeds counselling' because it emphasizes problem-solving and help that is 'concrete, specific and focused' (England 1986: 26). This distinction is important because it differentiates between counselling skills focused on addressing the emotional life of an individual and counselling skills focused on more problem-solving and practical aspects. A distinction that I draw between counselling and social work is that I consider a counselling relationship to be a contract between the client and counsellor where permission has been given to explore the emotional life of the client. In social work, we do not have that permission or contract *in the same way* because this kind of emotional exploration is not normally our primary role or purpose. However, we can easily find ourselves listening to people's feelings because all problems have an emotional component. Where this is the case, it is important to draw this difference to the attention of the service user and to check that he or she feels okay to pursue this more emotional focus. I consider it important for qualified social workers to leave their social work course feeling confident to use basic counselling skills, but this makes it essential for us to be clear about our purpose, professional boundaries, and the implications of our work in relation to confidentiality (Seden 2005: 15). Where we find ourselves having to deal with emotional issues on a regular basis, it is advisable to seek additional training in counselling.

Aims of counselling

Depending on the needs of the 'client' and the different practice orientation adopted, McLeod suggests the following aims of counselling:

- *Insight.* The acquisition of an understanding of the origins and development of emotional difficulties, leading to an increased capacity to take rational control over feelings and actions.
- *Relating to others.* Becoming better able to form and maintain meaningful and satisfying relationships with other people, for example within the family or workplace.
- *Self-awareness.* Becoming more aware of thoughts and feelings that had been blocked off or denied, or developing a more accurate sense of how self is perceived by others.
- *Self-acceptance.* The development of a positive attitude towards self, marked by an ability to acknowledge areas of experience that had been the subject of self-criticism and rejection.
- *Self-actualization or individuation.* Moving in the direction of fulfilling potential or achieving an integration of previously conflicting parts of self.
- *Enlightenment.* Assisting the client to arrive at a higher state of spiritual awakening.
- *Problem-solving.* Finding a solution to a specific problem that the client had not been able to resolve alone. Acquiring a general competence in problem-solving.
- *Psychological education.* Enabling the client to acquire ideas and techniques with which to understand and control behaviour.
- *Acquisition of social skills.* Learning and mastering social and interpersonal skills such as maintenance of eye contact, turn-taking in conversations, assertiveness, or anger control.
- *Cognitive change.* The modification or replacement of irrational beliefs or maladaptive thought patterns associated with self-destructive behaviour.
- *Behaviour change.* The modification or replacement of maladaptive or self-destructive patterns of behaviour.
- *Systemic change.* Introducing change to the way in which social systems (e.g. families) operate.
- *Empowerment.* Working on skills, awareness, and knowledge to enable the client to confront social inequalities.
- *Restitution.* Helping the client to make amends for previous destructive behaviour.

- *Generativity and social action.* Inspiring in the person a desire and capacity to care for others and pass on knowledge (generativity) and to
contribute to the collective good through political engagement and community work.

(McLeod 2009: 16–17)

These aims are illuminating because they cover many areas of interest to
social workers. Research also indicates that counselling and casework approaches are highly rated by service users (Hardiker and Barker 1994: 34)
but while counselling is likely to flourish in the voluntary sector, its future
in relation to statutory services remains unclear.

51. Containing anxiety

'Anxiety . . . is a constant feature of our work with clients' (Sheldon 1995:
108), and many of the practice approaches used within social work acknowledge this fact and the distorting and debilitating impact that anxiety
can have. The causes of anxiety are unique to each individual, and dependent on different past and present experiences. However, one of the primary
causes of anxiety is conflict, both internal and external (Howe 1987: 71). It
is helpful to differentiate between fear and anxiety because they are different
on two accounts and require different interventions. *Fear* is used to describe
a reaction to present dangers, specific objects, or events, where the object of
the fear is known and, therefore, can be identified and talked about. *Anxiety*
is used to describe a more generalized emotional state, where the sense of
threat or danger does not have an object and, therefore, cannot be identified
but is instead anticipated or imagined (Reber *et al.* 2009: 48).

Common fears that service users describe include feeling ashamed about
having to seek help, frightened that their children will be removed, and
worried that they will be criticized (Lishman 2009a: 10–11). Often, offering reassurance can help to allay fears but the skill is not to minimize the pain or confusion being experienced or to be overly reassuring
unless we are confident about what we are saying. Being patient, kind,
caring, understanding, non-judgemental, and non-intrusive are important
attributes.

Anxieties, on the other hand, are more likely to be experienced as states
of agitation, nervousness, and panic, where service users find themselves
forgetting things that they would normally remember, including the fact
that they are anxious. Often, fear and anxiety accompany one another.
For example, a person may be frightened to go to the housing department
because they remember previous visits that were unpleasant (fear), yet also
find themselves being unable to get out of the house, losing their house keys,
unable to find a relevant letter, unable to remember the reason for their visit
once they arrive, and so on (anxiety). This kind of amnesia is very common

in anxiety states and something that militates against people being able to see things through and to effect change.

In these situations, containing anxiety involves being open and receptive to the thoughts and feelings of others – becoming a 'container' – so that these feelings can be transformed into something more manageable. This is often achieved through the process of talking to someone who has the ability to listen, to empathize, to take in and to bear the worries being expressed, and the ability to come alongside the individual in ways that communicate an understanding and provide a sense that the person is not alone. The final stage of this process involves offering back the concerns to the anxious person but in a modified form, where the major anguish is acknowledged but also altered so that it no longer carries the same 'sting' or sense of agitation or anguish. In situations of mild anxiety, helping a service user to contain these feelings may not be a time-consuming activity (Trevithick 2011a). Often our openness, communicated by a few well thought out words or gestures, can be sufficient to help people cope with mildly difficult emotions. In more intractable anxiety states, anxieties can feel like an oil slick that keeps on spreading, contaminating almost everything we see and do. In such cases, greater resilience is called for on our part if we are to help service users to deal with these difficult feelings. One way to do this may be to 'meet' the concerns by asking service users to describe in detail the thoughts, feelings, and worries that they have. In doing so, our purpose is to try to break the hold that these anxieties are having on the individual concerned.

Conclusion

As human beings we are greatly relieved by the knowledge that others are prepared to help bear the load we carry. The above skills demonstrate the importance of being able to embrace a range of different interventions, depending on the dilemmas being presented. However, the use of these interventions also involves building on the strengths and abilities that service users bring to an encounter. These may take different forms – for example, they may involve our acknowledging the courageous and honest way that service users explore what empowerment means to them, or the way they square up to the part they played in a particular dilemma. The ability to tell ourselves that truth can be a painful experience but one that can be deeply healing and reparative. For these reasons, it is important to remember that none of the interventions described in this and other chapters can be successfully undertaken without the active cooperation of the individuals involved, because this is central to the reciprocal relationship that lies at the heart of effective and reflective practice. In the past, we have not always created this participative and collaborative framework and this has, as a result, limited our effectiveness (Everitt and Hardiker 1996; Shaw and Shaw 1997).

9 EMPOWERMENT, NEGOTIATION, AND PARTNERSHIP SKILLS

Introduction

Many of the skills I describe in this chapter relate to working with a third party. I take as my starting point the importance of acknowledging and respecting other people's points of view and the need to establish a common purpose in relation to our work. This requires a degree of 'give and take', and the ability to compromise and the capacity to be flexible are essential qualities when attempting to work alongside others.

Specific skills

Skills: Empowerment, negotiation, and partnership skills
52 Empowerment and enabling skills
53 Negotiating skills
54 Contracting skills
55 Networking skills
56 Working in partnership
57 Mediation skills
58 Advocacy skills
59 Assertiveness skills
60 Challenging skills
61 Confronting
62 Dealing with hostility, aggression, and violence

Some skills belong to the same 'family' of negotiation skills but each carry important differences. Some skills are built on other skills. For example, advocacy carries with it the ability to negotiate. Most are finely balanced between the conflicting responsibilities of care and control, yet their overall purpose is to address the concerns of those individuals who seek, or are required to have, a social work service.

52. Empowerment and enabling skills

Considerable controversy surrounds the concept of empowerment: what is meant by the term; whether it is possible for us to empower others and, if so, how this is achieved in terms of the skills and resources required; and whether this falls within our role and agency expectations. Stevenson and Parsloe (1993: 6) use the term to denote both 'process and goal', but empowerment is more commonly used to describe service users being given 'meaningful choice' and 'valuable options' (Clark 2000a: 57) in ways that enable them to gain greater control over their lives and their circumstances. For some, this process involves addressing the impact of inequalities, oppression, and discrimination (O'Sullivan 1999: 27).

In most social work texts enabling is not referred to as a specific skill and, when it is, the reference tends to be quite general (Payne 2005; Seden 2005). One reason for this may be that enabling is not seen to embody distinct characteristics or, more importantly, to address the issue of power and power imbalances in ways embraced by concepts such as 'empowerment' (Braye and Preston-Shoot 1995: 102), 'normalization' (Ramon 1991) or 'user-led' initiatives or movements (Croft and Beresford 2008: 397–8). Braye and Preston-Shoot, drawing on user-led literature, write in detail about 'the key characteristics and qualities required' in relation to empowerment. These include:

- clarity about what involvement is being offered, and what its limits are;
- involvement from the beginning in ways which are central to agency structures and processes but which are also flexible;
- tangible goals for involvement;
- involvement by choice, not compulsion;
- involvement of black and minority perspectives;
- individual and collective perspectives;
- provision of time, information, resources and training;
- openness to advocacy;
- clear channels of representation and complaint;
- involvement of key participants, not just some;
- open agendas;
- facilitation of attendance;
- emphasis on channels, particularly when rights are at risk and the agency's perspective is backed by the statutory power to impose it.

(Braye and Preston-Shoot 1995: 118)

This account highlights important organizational and practical issues and attitudes. The use of advocacy, self-advocacy, users' rights, and the development of user-led services and agendas is obviously important to this process (Braye and Preston-Shoot 1995: 102–18), but how effective these interventions are in practice – in relation to clients' capacity to direct the course of their lives and to improve their lives and situation – is not always clear.

This has led to the criticism that empowerment has limited application in practice and that it is a term that 'is often invoked without being explained' (Wise 1995: 108). Part of the difficulty that the term empowerment causes relates to the context within which social work is located. As practitioners, we do not have unlimited choices. We are bound by the law and agency expectations, as well as the needs of service users. Social work agencies are also constrained by legal requirements, financial limitations, and the expectations of government, other professions, and the public at large.

Yet despite these constraints, the concept of empowerment is important because it attempts to identify particular purposes and how these might be achieved; namely, how to help service users to take their lives forward. One account of this process is described in the work of Lorraine Gutiérrez, an African-American feminist, who identifies the changes sought through the process of empowerment as occurring 'on the individual, interpersonal, and institutional levels, where the person develops a sense of personal power, an ability to affect others, and an ability to work with others to change social institutions' (Gutiérrez 1990: 150). For Gutiérrez, empowerment provides a way to describe the transition from apathy and despair towards a sense of personal power. This involves four psychological changes:

• Increasing self-efficacy (moving from reacting to events to taking action)
• Developing group consciousness
• Reducing self-blame
• Assuming personal responsibility for change.

In this framework, to achieve this transition or change, practitioners need to be able to embrace five 'techniques' or interventions (Gutiérrez 1990: 151–2), which include providing practical assistance:

• Accepting the client's definition of the problem
• Identifying and building upon existing strengths
• Engaging in a power analysis of the client's situation
• Teaching specific skills
• Mobilizing resources and advocating for clients.

This account is helpful because it identifies in greater detail the specific skills involved in empowerment. However, some writers in this field would be uncomfortable with this perspective because of its emphasis on the individual and on looking at psychological processes. It is these differences of opinion that make concepts like empowerment and partnership 'a minefield of ethical issues and dilemmas' (Stevenson and Parsloe 1993: 15). These dilemmas are not confined to direct work with service users because the concept of empowerment can be extended to include the empowerment of social workers, groups of people, organizations, and agencies (Clark 2000a: 29).

Internalized oppression

It is important to recognize that it takes time to help people to empower themselves, and to find ways to move their lives forward, not least because the very nature of oppression means that, for some, the confidence and courage to explore new areas and to take risks feels beyond their reach. When we encounter this sense of impossibility, hopelessness, and defeat, the notion of 'internalized oppression' can give us a language that we can use to help people to understand and to talk about how they came to believe negative statements about themselves and to view these negative personal characteristics are seen as fixed and part of their personality. Negative beliefs of this kind can sometimes be addressed by tracking their origins. Many stem from hurtful comments made by parents, but in my experience an alarming number can be traced back to teachers. For some years I ran workshops for working-class women at the London Women's Therapy Centre (Trevithick 1988). Much of our work involved helping women put words to negative beliefs that they had about themselves, locating the painful experiences that surrounded this process of internalization, and helping them to see how untrue, unfair, and unkind many of these comments were. They served to keep these women 'in their place' and to hold them hostage to these untruths.

People who come to believe, through the process of internalized oppression, that they are worthless, 'stupid', 'no good', or that they 'don't count', find it very difficult to stand up to others, to protect themselves or their loved ones from further oppression, or to take risks without help. The way that help is offered is important: compassion, concern, and the fact that we 'care' form an important value perspective we bring to our work but, in my experience, we are more likely to be successful and resilient in our efforts if our approach has a theoretical underpinning. In addition to Gutiérrez's work, quoted above, I have gained a great deal from the writings of Jean Baker Miller, particularly her concept of 'temporary inequality' (Miller 1986b: 4–5). This describes how we can use the inequality that exists between social workers and service users to name, analyse, and address differences, including difficult feelings located in the present, as well as painful memories from the past. These difficulties are always present yet are rarely acknowledged when people of unequal status, authority, and power encounter one another. (See Chapter 5 for a further account of the work of Jean Baker Miller and the Stone Center in Boston, Massachusetts.)

53. Negotiating skills

Negotiating skills tend to be well covered in social work texts (Coulshed and Orme 2006: 60–2; Lishman 2009a: 151–3; O'Sullivan 1999: 48), some of them concentrating on specific areas, such as negotiating the focus of the work (Trower *et al.* 1988: 34–6) or setting up contracts (Sheldon 1995: 185–7). The following is a summary of the main considerations and skills involved in negotiating.

Negotiation is primarily directed at achieving some form of agreement or understanding. It is important in two ways. First, in relation to direct work with service users, negotiation skills are the tools that establish the climate of shared decision-making and collaboration that lies at the heart of the concept of partnership. It is through negotiation that we arrive at a common agreement across different parties in terms of how problems are understood and how these might be overcome. Negotiation skills are also important in situations of disagreement. There may be no obvious way to overcome underlying differences but where a degree of flexibility and compromise exists, this can be a foundation on which to negotiate. One way to achieve this would be to explore with service users – and other parties involved – their perception of events, particularly how they arrived at the particular position, or belief, they are holding, and what was their starting point (Lishman 2009a: 152). Entering into a dialogue about how an individual arrived at a particular view or position can reveal how painful certain experiences have been and how much their stance is designed to protect them from further pain. Part of our task may involve negotiating a shift in the balance, based on an understanding, respect, and acceptance of people's perception of events even if we are not in agreement. Since our position and starting point is likely to be different, it may be essential to point this out in a sensitive way as part of the negotiation.

Case example: Tim

I once worked with a family where one of their five children, Tim, was constantly being scapegoated and marginalized within the family. A common phrase his parents used was 'He's always been like that, ever since a baby. When he's being like that, we ignore him'. 'Like that' was the shorthand way the parents communicated and justified their lack of empathy and tolerance for this child. As a result Tim was neglected within the family and showed his distress through stealing. The work we contracted to do involved helping Tim's parents to identify at what point they joined forces in the view that Tim was a difficult child and that the best course of action was to ignore him. This work took several months but eventually it transpired that his mother had had an affair and both parents believed Tim to be the child of a different father. A DNA test proved their 'belief' to be wrong, which meant we were then in a position to work on his mother's guilt and his father's rage about the affair and to negotiate a different place for Tim within the family. This negotiation took the form of revising the original contract, unpacking the 'beliefs' that Tim's parents had, some of which Tim had internalized, and carefully negotiating a new place for him in his family.

The second area where negotiation skills are important is in relation to services. It is estimated that about one-third of our work involves face-to-face contact with service users (Coulshed and Orme 2006: 60). The remaining time is spent on indirect service provision, such as negotiating with our own agency and other organizations, or other parties who hold key resources or positions. This figure is likely to be higher where resources are scarce and/or the demands for professional accountability excessive, or for practitioners employed in certain settings, such as community work. For example, as a field worker arguing for resources, I have spent many hours trying to negotiate residential placements, both for children and for older people. It took me some time to realize that I was more likely to be successful in my negotiations if I made sure there was a correct 'fit' between the resources being sought and the needs of the service user. This is very important. Where resources seemed to be withheld for no apparent reason, it can sometimes help to address the reservations of those individuals responsible for resource allocation. For example, many managers worry that once a place has been allocated the social worker will 'disappear' from the life of the child, young person or older person and fail to maintain links with their family and other significant contacts. Although residential care is now a less favoured option in relation to children and young people, these concerns about maintaining links remain (Aldgate 2002: 23–4).

The time and effort involved in mobilizing resources is considerable and can require us having to use collaborative, competitive, or combative tactics depending on the situation and our response (Coulshed 1991: 62–4). In recent years, mobilizing resources has been orientated to 'commissioning services for care management or negotiating packages of care' (Coulshed and Orme 2006: 60). Combative skills are particularly important when we are dealing with injustice or inequalities in resource provision, and one way to see campaigning is as a form of political negotiation. However, our success in these and other endeavours is more likely to depend on how well we prepare and present our case, particularly factual information, and how carefully we have thought through where key figures in the negotiation are coming from. It may also be necessary to enlist further support or leverage so that the same negotiation is being played from several sides. In addition, it is essential to be in a position to highlight the advantages that a negotiated decision could bring to those who would normally be uninterested. One way to achieve this involves appealing to a person's sense of fairness. According to Jordan (1990: 178), social work is 'crucially concerned with fairness, both in redistributing resources to people in need ... and in negotiations over problems in relationships in families, neighbourhoods and communities'. To enlist people's sympathy or sense of fairness – perhaps by asking them to imagine how they might feel in the same situation – can come across as manipulative and the line between being strategic, determined, and manipulative can be difficult to draw. Honesty is an important safeguard. So too is the ability to acknowledge a respect for the other person's point of view, whilst at the same time believing that we can 'change their mind', and do so in a way that retains a sense of personal integrity for all parties concerned.

Finally, it can be easy to give up in our efforts to negotiate if we are immediately unsuccessful, yet our success may depend on our being able to withstand rejection and failure. Resilience, determination, and the skills of persuasion are the hallmarks of a successful negotiator.

54. Contracting skills

Drawing up contracts provides an opportunity to formalize and structure the nature of the contact between ourselves and service users in relation to the purpose of the work and the roles, responsibilities, and expectations of those concerned. The process involved in arriving at this working agreement is as important as the task itself and acts as 'a tangible manifestation of working in partnership' (Aldgate 2002: 24). The contract must be based on the needs of the service user and, for this reason, may be agreed verbally or in writing, sometimes in the form of a letter. Failing to keep a written record of agreements reached is dangerous; reliance on memory alone can be highly problematic, not least because we all hear through our histories and, as the game Chinese Whispers reveals, we can hear the same information quite differently. In some situations, however, perhaps where literacy is a problem, written agreements or contracts may not be appropriate.

Whatever the format, care should be taken to ensure that a shared understanding has been reached, and in a language that is clear, explicit, and accessible, with sufficient information for the task at hand. Confusion and anxiety act as barriers to effective action. For example, contracts may specify the time, length, location, and duration of sessions, together with ground rules, confidentiality and recording procedures. They can also state who is invited to attend, a summary of the major concerns, the purpose of the work in terms of objectives and the approaches to be used, emergency cover arrangements, and how any breakdown of the agreement might be dealt with. It helps to build in some flexibility so that the contract can be revised if required.

Drawing up an action plan is an example of how a contract or working agreement might be used in practice (Payne 2005). Action plans can take different forms. For example, I once ran a group for severely depressed women where suicidal thoughts and intentions were very much in evidence. To address the anxieties that this threat posed to the individuals in question, the workers and other women in the group, we drafted a plan of action in the event of accident or crisis, self-inflicted or not. When drafting individual plans, everyone in the group was asked to lay down in detail what steps we had to take, and in what order, should a crisis occur. We even included details of next-of-kin. Fortunately, these plans never needed to be put into action.

Contracts provide the opportunity to formalize the relationship and the purpose of the work in ways that can bring people together to work in partnership. This structured approach towards a common purpose enables sensitive issues to be addressed at the outset, such as differences in status, authority, knowledge, and experience that we, and service users, bring to the partnership and how these will be worked with. This can demystify the helping process, ensuring that as practitioners we are open about how much power service users and others have, and where our accountability lies (Preston-Shoot 1994: 185). It also provides an opportunity to build on service users' strengths and to provide help when needed.

In contrast, some writers believe that drawing up contracts or written agreements can be oppressive because they assume a freedom of choice that has little bearing on service users' everyday experiences of social inequalities and injustices (Rojek and Collins 1988: 205). Are they contracts or 'con tricks' (Corden and Preston-Shoot 1987)? Similarly, our choices as practitioners are limited by agency policy, our legal responsibilities, and a scarcity of resources and services. To enable 'mutuality and exchange' (Smale et al. 2000) between service users and practitioners, with 'users as equal partners in problem definition and negotiation about solutions' (Braye and Preston-Shoot 1995: 116), a fundamental shift is needed in the extent to which service users' views are allowed to define the problem and seek solutions.

Finally, the term 'contract culture' describes the introduction of internal markets into health and social services in the 1990s and the commissioning of services by a purchaser from a provider. This approach to service delivery has been severely criticized, particularly for failing to increase user choice and involvement (Braye and Preston-Shoot 1995: 22).

55. Networking skills

> Networks operate on the basis of informal connections rather than formal roles, and membership tends to be voluntary and participative. The existence and vitality of the linkages are determined by personal choices, circumstance or occasionally sheer coincidence. Cooperation between members relies on persuasion and reciprocity rather than co-ercion or contracts ... The most important and useful aspect of a network is its patterns of connections, which often reflects an underlying value basis, a shared interest or simply the geography of overlapping lives.
>
> (Gilchrist 2004: 30)

In general, networks can be seen to fall into two categories: formal networks, such as planned and structured support groups, and informal networks, sometimes described in terms of natural networks. These can be made up of carers, family members, friends, and neighbours.

In its recommendation for decentralized community-based services, the Barclay Report (1982: xiii) recognized the importance of 'local networks of formal and informal relationships' and their 'capacity to mobilize individual and collective responses to adversity'. Also, the importance of informal networks and caring resources was acknowledged in the Griffiths Report

(1988) and built into the NHS and Community Care Act 1990, but in ways that were felt by many to be an appropriation by government of 'natural' support systems (Gilchrist 2004). Whereas it is appropriate for statutory services to support existing 'natural' networks, 'attempting to replace formal provision with informal care or to change the existing patterns of informal care is likely to be unsuccessful' (Payne 1997: 152).

According to Coulshed and Orme (2006: 277), networking can involve three 'strategies':

- *Network therapy* uses groupwork skills to help families in crisis by bringing together their network to act as the 'change agents' (e.g. Family Group Conferences used in child protection work)
- *Problem-solving network meetings* bring together formal and informal carers, often to unravel who is doing what
- *Network construction* is how to build new networks and sustain or change existing networks.

All of these involve mediating, advocating, and organizing skills, as well as the ability to assess the capabilities of the individual in question and of the social networks available and what these can sustain. The importance of networking in social work is to strengthen the links and connections that exist for people within a particular community or geographical area. This support is particularly important where there is a danger of people becoming isolated. For example, research indicates that people discharged from psychiatric hospital who have social support are less likely to be readmitted (Huxley 2008: 59; Sheppard 1997: 214). The debilitating impact of isolation is also felt by people with learning disabilities (Booth 2002: 74) and the older people (Phillipson 2008: 51–2). However, it is important to see social support networks as complementing other services, and not replacing the obligations of the state and social services to provide key services. Other forms of support, such as a 'close personal working relationship . . . to sustain community living' (Huxley 2008: 60), are also crucial for individuals who have difficulty relating or whose situation leaves them vulnerable to stigma and social exclusion.

Within this work, our knowledge of black networks may not be built on a 'proper understanding' of black people's experience and, as a result, we may fail to help black people to link to the networks that exist. The dangers here are many. For example, our failure to understand the complex nature of African-Caribbean and Asian cultures can mean that we focus on the problems or 'defects' rather than their resilient and supportive characteristics (Robinson 2007). Although it is always important to locate people within their cultural context, there can be a pull to rely on cultural explanations at the expense of exploring other relevant factors, particularly structural influences and limitations. What is described as 'normal' and, therefore, acceptable for any culture, including aspects of working-class culture, needs to be analysed carefully. For example, it can be thought of as 'normal' and acceptable for working-class people to use physical force, or the threat of violence, to restrain and control their children. These assumptions need to be challenged and so-called 'normal' behaviour carefully scrutinized.

56. Working in partnership

Partnership, and the principles of participation and 'user involvement', inform current legislation in relation to health and social care, having found favour with both the political left and right, but for different reasons. 'Where the left saw empowerment of the poor and disadvantaged, the right saw growth in personal responsibility, independence and individual choice' (Howe 1996: 84). Similarly, it is possible for both left and right to share a commitment to empowerment and its emphasis on 'people taking control of their own lives and having the power to shape their own future' (Shardlow 2007: 46). This joint ownership might help to explain why partnership is considered to be 'very misleading without qualification' (Stevenson and Parsloe 1993: 6) and 'used to describe anything from token consultation to a total devolution of power and control' (Braye and Preston-Shoot 1995: 102).

The point to be stressed is that positive practice must involve service users if it is to achieve agreed objectives (empowerment and personal responsibility), and that within this process service users must be seen not only in terms of the 'problems' they bring, but as 'whole people' and 'full citizens' (Dalrymple and Burke 2006) who have an important contribution to make in terms of their knowledge and perception of the situation, personal qualities, and problem-solving capabilities. This differs from those approaches where there is a 'top-down hierarchical bureaucracy' (Braye and Preston-Shoot 1995: 116), dominated by agency policies and procedures, or an approach where the practitioner is seen to be the expert who diagnoses the problem and prescribes a cure.

One of the most helpful accounts of the principles and skills involved in working in partnership can be found in *The Challenge of Partnership in Child Protection: Practice Guide* (Department of Health 1995). Under four headings, this publication identifies the reasons for working in partnership with parents. These headings have been adapted to include other service user groups:

- *Effectiveness.* More is likely to be achieved through an approach that is co-operative and collaborative (Howe 1987: 7; Sheldon 1995: 126; Thoburn *et al.* 1995).
- *Clients as a source of information.* It is important to build on the detailed knowledge and understanding that service users have of their situation and the problems they face (Sheldon 1995: 125), and to take as our starting point the priorities that they consider most urgent (Lishman 2009a: 152).

- *Citizens' rights.* Service users should have the right to know what is being said about them and to contribute to decisions that affect their lives.
- *Empowering parents.* Involving service users in decision-making helps to build self-esteem and confidence, and to enable clients to feel more in control of their lives (Department of Health 1995: 9–10).

The knowledge, values, and skills required for working in partnership are summarized in this publication under the heading 'Fifteen essential principles for working in partnership' (Department of Health 1995: 14). Many of the values and skills included in that list are described in this text, such as the importance of good communication, listening skills, and observation skills; being respectful, caring, and competent in our approach; being clear in our purpose and intentions, our professional boundaries and responsibilities, including the language we use; being sensitive to the issue of power and power imbalances; being mindful of the importance of the strengths and potential that service users possess, as well as addressing weaknesses, problems, and limitations; being aware of our own personal feelings, values, prejudices, and beliefs; being able to acknowledge our mistakes and to use supervision to ensure the quality of our work and its effectiveness (Department of Health 1995: 14).

This summary serves as a reminder that we have still much to learn about how to work in partnership in ways that enhance service users' capacity to consolidate and extend their self-knowledge, decision-making and problem-solving abilities. This work is much more complex than is sometimes described, particularly where this involves working across differences (Smale *et al.* 2000) and trying to understand the power differentials that exist between practitioners and service users from different cultural, ethnic, and racial groups (Department of Health 1995: 24). For example, the contribution that service users feel they can give – and the knowledge they can actually access and communicate – may, in fact, be quite limited. Some may feel too depleted or have too little confidence to take on the responsibilities implied within the concept of partnership. This can result in an imbalance that must be worked through if service users are to continue to feel engaged and their contribution valued, no matter how limited this might be.

Case example

I recall working with a family where the children, aged two, three, and five years respectively, were severely neglected. Both parents had been diagnosed as having learning difficulties, although what part this played in their ability to parent their children was never clear, because both were known to have had impoverished childhoods, moving in and out of care. Their deep sense of mistrust and fear of social workers made any attempt to find a common purpose a seemingly impossible task. For a long time, a stultifying silence and apparent lack of interest dominated the communication. In desperation, I took the issue to supervision and set about the task of analysing the blocks to communication and to establishing a rapport. One of the problems identified by my supervisor was that my agenda – the protection of the children – was getting in the way of establishing a rapport. I had failed to ask these parents what help they felt they most needed from social services and, in particular, from me. When I did ask this question, I found they wanted my help to press the housing department to mend their leaking roof. The other mistake I had made was that I had failed to reframe their actions and behaviour in positive terms. For example, they were always in when I visited and always allowed me to have contact with the children. They were also committed parents, determined not to see their children 'dumped into care' as they themselves had been. I had not seen their commitment: only their mistrust and lack of cooperation.

By reframing their actions in this way, new possibilities emerged (Watzlawick *et al.* 1974: 115; see also the section on 'reframing' on pp. 242–4). We were able to find 'mutual agreement' (Lishman 2009a: 142): a common purpose. Together, our purpose was to ensure that they did not lose custody of their children. With this aim in mind, we negotiated different tasks, where control of the decision-making process was more equitable (O'Sullivan 1999: 49). I agreed to address the problem about the housing repairs, thereby hoping to bring about some improvement in the quality of their lives and, in this process, to gain some trust, but on condition that both parents attended parenting classes at the local health centre. In other words, I attended to their primary concern and, in return, they attended to mine.

This example highlights the fact that the partnerships created can take many forms. It can be helpful to stress this at the beginning of the contact. Also, partnership does 'not imply an equality of power, or an equality of work' (Marsh 2008: 126). Addressing issues of this kind is a complex activity, requiring sophisticated communication skills. This is particularly true in the area of child protection where research findings indicate that greater parental involvement has been linked to better outcomes (Thoburn *et al.* 1995; Waterhouse and McGhee 2002: 278). The ability to create a climate of inclusion and collaboration, based on a recognition of the importance of everyone's contribution to the partnership process, is a key skill within this process.

The main concern that critics highlight in relation to the notion of partnership centres on the inequalities that exist in terms of power and control. This has been described as 'conflicting imperatives' with regard to 'rights versus risks, care versus control, needs versus resources, professionalism versus partnership with users, professional versus agency agendas' (Braye and Preston-Shoot 1995: 63). Where these conflicts and tensions are not addressed honestly and openly, the partnership or the experience of user involvement can feel hollow. As a result service users can feel their involvement as 'stressful, diversionary and unproductive' (Croft and Beresford 2008: 396). This is particularly the case where service users are invited to 'participate in decisions over which they have no control' (Langan 2002: 215), thereby being rendered powerless. Equally, unless adequate resources are made available for the objectives being pursued, partnerships can become strained and vulnerable to being overtaken by events and the unwelcome intrusion of bigger problems and desperate solutions (Howe 1996: 96). A final concern relates to where our professional responsibilities lie as practitioners in relation to working in partnership. If we are to act as gatekeepers to resources (Phillips 1996: 141), our power and authority need to be made explicit. But if our role is, as Jordan (1990: 4) suggests, to exercise 'moral reasoning' and to use our 'judgement, discretion and skill' to highlight choice and resource inequalities, then this too needs to be made clear, and little progress will be possible without this kind of agitation. How much service users feel able to become involved in this form of political negotiation should be discussed as part of the partnership agreement.

Despite these concerns, working in partnership can provide an important framework for us to work closely with service users. This is likely to involve the skills of working across differences, including cultural and racial differences:

> In order to achieve successful partnerships with families in child protection work, professionals must give special consideration to the different cultural, ethnic and racial origins of families and their different religious beliefs and languages. The many different ethnic and cultural variations in our society require all professionals to develop a personal and organisational commitment to equality and to meeting the needs of families and children as well as understanding the effects of racial discrimination, and cultural misunderstanding or misinterpretation.
> (Department of Health 1995: 24)

From this place, we can learn a great deal about the hardships experienced by service users and encounter first-hand the barriers and obstacles that block the way forward. This may require extending the remit of our role, and the objectives of the partnership, to include working with social or environmental factors that hinder progress, drawing on skills described in this and other chapters, such as negotiating skills, advocacy, and so forth.

57. Mediation skills

> Mediation aims to assist people to articulate their concerns, suggest solutions, discuss areas for compromise and try to reach an agreement ... The benefits of mediation can include favourable agreement, satisfaction, improved relationships, procedural justice and improved problem solving.
> (Hughes and Wearing 2007: 107)

Ensuring that different parties communicate with one another is an important skill in social work. Within this process, mediation skills have a particular part to play 'in disputes between parties to help them reconcile differences, find compromises, or reach mutually satisfactory agreements' (Barker 2003: 266). Although often grouped with advocacy skills, where our role is to represent, defend or to speak for another person, mediation involves taking up a neutral role between two opposing individuals or groups of people rather than pressing for the interests of one person or group against another. Common situations where mediation skills may be called for are disputes between neighbours in conflict or between divorcing parents. One approach to mediation would be to try to find some common ground. In the case of neighbours at 'war', what they might share could be the desire to live in peace. For parents in dispute, the common ground may be their desires for their children's future: to want the best for them and to protect them from harm. To be a successful 'go-between' involves being able to gain a degree of trust from all parties to represent their point of view. This may or may not involve bringing people together into one setting. Mediation, conciliation, and arbitration skills all belong to the same negotiating skills 'family'. To define these terms may be important if it helps to identify the focus of our work. For example, conciliation skills can involve attempting to pacify, whereas in some situations, to act as a mediator may appear more like being a referee.

This neutrality required of a mediator can be a difficult role to sustain in situations where one party is more articulate and powerful than the other. It can feel as if we are condoning the browbeating or bullying of another person.

However, to be drawn outside the role, most commonly into the role of advocate, can have disastrous consequences because, once lost, neutrality may never be regained. One way to avoid this danger is to stay active. For example, we may ask both parties to direct their comments to one another through us, perhaps in the first instance suggesting or insisting they discuss issues likely to be less contentious and more amenable to agreement. Our role is then to address the comments of one party to the other and to feed replies back in the same way and to do so until it seems possible for both parties to speak directly. Within this process it may be helpful to reframe some comments, to keep the same 'frame' but to take some of the 'sting' out of what is being said. This is only possible where people feel comfortable about having the sense of what they are saying reframed in this way. If these efforts fail and we still feel we are being drawn out of role, it is wise to call the session to a halt so that we can reflect on events, seek help if necessary, and review what other steps we (or others) need to take to move the situation forward to a satisfactory resolution. As these examples indicate, mediation is a skilled activity.

Mediation is a term used in other situations. For example, mediators play an important role within cognitive-behavioural approaches as 'people in the client's surroundings who can record, prompt and reinforce appropriate behaviour' (Hudson and MacDonald 1986: 69; Sheldon 1995: 127). In this context, mediators may be family members, friends, or volunteers. Mediation can also be found in divorce court welfare services where its role is to reduce conflict and to work with parents to agree the arrangements for the upbringing of their children (James 2008: 231). Whereas conciliation was once the term used in divorce court proceedings, mediation is now the preferred term. The fact that these terms are sometimes used interchangeably highlights the importance of being clear ourselves in relation to our purpose and role in different situations.

58. Advocacy skills

Advocacy is an important skill in social work, and one that links to other human and civil rights issues such as citizens' charters, empowerment, partnership, collaboration, and participation. Advocacy involves representing the interests of others when they are unable to do so themselves. Central to this work is an acknowledgement of differences in power that disadvantage certain groups of people, denying access to certain resources or opportunities, including the right to participate as full members of society (Townsend 1993: 36). Advocacy aims to ensure that the voices and interests of service users are heard and responded to in ways that affect attitudes, policy, practice, and service delivery. The mandate for this undertaking can be found in the objectives of the NHS and Community Care Act 1990, which is 'to give people a greater say in how they live their lives and the services they need to help them to do so' (Department of Health 1989).

A key concept within advocacy is that of representation, which can involve:

- supporting clients to represent themselves
- arguing clients' views and needs
- interpreting or representing the views, needs, concerns, and interests of clients to others
- developing appropriate skills for undertaking these different tasks such as listening and negotiating skills, empathy, assertiveness skills, being clear and focused, and so on.

Advocacy can involve speaking, writing, acting, or arguing on behalf of others. According to Payne (1997: 269), this representation can take different forms:

- *Case advocacy.* Advocating on behalf of another person for resources, services, or opportunities. This may be undertaken by a professional, volunteer, or peer.
- *Cause advocacy.* Arguing for changes in policies or procedures and other forms of reform (e.g. entitlement to health services or welfare benefits).

- *Self-advocacy.* People finding ways to speak for themselves to protect their rights and to advance their own interests. This links to self-help, group, and peer advocacy. This type of advocacy is used by 'mental health system survivors' and people with learning disabilities.
- *Peer advocacy.* This describes people working together to represent each other's needs. Many self-help groups undertake this kind of advocacy and some are also actively involved in campaigning to influence public opinion and government policies.
- *Citizen advocacy.* This 'involves volunteers in developing relationships with potentially isolated clients, understanding and representing their needs'.

For advocacy to be seen as a legitimate element of the social work role, it is essential that adequate training, supervision, and support are provided. To act as an advocate for another person requires considerable professional confidence and standing on the part of practitioners, particularly when confronted with officialdom and authority figures. Some practitioners have neither the confidence nor the body of knowledge needed to be an effective advocate. This knowledge includes how to use the law, government guidance and regulations, agency policy and practices to act as an advocate for the rights and needs of service users (Braye and Preston-Shoot 1995: 65).

For example, many years ago I was involved in advocating on behalf of a service user and her two children who were homeless and 'squatting' and had been threatened with eviction by the local authority. A telephone call to a squatter's rights organization in London revealed that the local authority had failed to provide three days' notice, which was then required for an eviction order. I passed this information on to the barrister representing this family, who duly presented this information in court. The case was adjourned, with the judge chastising the local authority for failing to prepare their case properly and requiring them to offer alternative accommodation before the next hearing. This example highlights the fact that we are more likely to be successful in our role as advocate where we have gathered accurate, detailed, and relevant facts, including those relating to the law or legal expectations.

As a final point, an important concept within advocacy work relates to the concept of normalization. This is often used to describe a commitment to provide an environment that gives people with disabilities the kind of social roles and lifestyle that other citizens enjoy. Another way to see the concept of normalization would be to see it as a description of what all human beings need: 'It contains, in prototype, a framework of minimum requirements for the good life' (Clark 2000a: 130). We may be called to act as an advocate in relation to any of the five interdependent needs identified by Clark (2000a: 130–1), which are similar to those identified by Maslow (1954), described in Chapter 2. They include:

- safety and psychological security (physical care, security, and safety)
- means of life (basic needs such as food and shelter)

- opportunity for creativity (rewarding work, personal growth)
- social participation and status (recognition and respect)
- power and choice (to participate in society, to make choices).

Describing the different forms of advocacy is relatively straightforward. However, advocacy is a subject that remains bound by qualification and, sometimes, a mistrust about the intentions of practitioners and their skills to undertake this task well. Some writers express the danger of professionals taking over in such a way that service users' ability to represent themselves – or to learn to represent themselves – is undermined or disempowered through pressurizing or persuading (Dalrymple and Burke 2006). Others state that focusing solely on equalizing power imbalances between service users and others more powerful is not enough, and that some would state that it is a requirement for practitioners to challenge inequalities within a given system. However, it is not clear how this can be achieved and whether this form of advocacy is likely to be a priority for social work agencies constrained by other imperatives. Certainly, there is a need for some form of advocacy in areas where our involvement is both sanctioned and greatly needed, namely in relation to welfare rights, but this is an area increasingly neglected by social workers, partly due to the development of specialist welfare rights agencies, and partly because addressing the issue of poverty and difficulties in the area of welfare rights is not considered a priority for some social workers (Walker and Walker 2009: 76).

59. Assertiveness skills

Ongoing experiences of defeat, oppression, and exploitation can leave people feeling powerless and unable to protect themselves properly. This inability can include being unable to protect others in their care. Social workers, as well as service users, can find it difficult to be assertive, particularly when dealing with higher status professionals, such as psychiatrists, solicitors, or senior management. One way to understand the lack of assertiveness is to analyse the issue of powerlessness, defined as 'the inability to manage emotions, skills, knowledge and/or material resources in a way that effective performance of valued social roles will lead to personal gratification' (Solomon 1976: 16), and to link this to concepts such as learned helplessness (Seligman 1975) and locus of control (Cigno 2009; Lefcourt 1976). These concepts help us to map the degree to which people feel in charge of their lives and able to influence their circumstances and future.

Passivity is seen to be the opposite of assertiveness or self-efficacy (Egan 2007: 414), and can lead to worrying consequences: 'Failure to act assertively often results in submission, exploitation and resentment or in aggression, misunderstanding and negative consequences' (Feltham and Dryden 2004: 14). Yet it can be very difficult for people to risk exploring other options, mainly because their view of themselves – their sense of worth as a human being – has taken too many blows and they cannot sustain the confidence or belief in themselves necessary to begin to effect change. Assertiveness skills can be an important starting point and are recognized as crucial in relation to concepts of empowerment, partnership, and participation. Where service users lack the necessary skills and confidence, one option should be that practitioners offer to help service users to acquire these skills (Croft and Beresford 2008: 393–401).

This transition can be difficult to achieve. Central to the task is encouraging service users to challenge self-defeating statements and helping them to substitute these with more positive and hopeful viewpoints. These self-defeating statements can be in the form of attitudes or beliefs, about themselves, other people, or future possibilities and opportunities likely to improve their situation. It also involves helping to address and contain the fears and anxieties that are holding service users back, and encouraging and supporting them to risk taking small steps forward (Egan 2007: 58). This focus on the importance of assertiveness skills is one that has been used a great deal in the United States, particularly in relation to women (Gilligan 1993) but also as a key empowerment strategy for other oppressed groups.

Assertiveness training

There may be times where a more formal teaching approach to assertiveness skills is required. Assertiveness training involves teaching people how to stand up for themselves without being aggressive, threatening, punishing, manipulative, or over-controlling, and without demeaning other people. Drawing on learning theory and other cognitive-behaviourist approaches, including modelling, rehearsal, and operant reinforcement (Sheldon 1995: 202), assertiveness training is designed to identify and replace submissive and self-denying messages with statements that more accurately reflect what the individual feels, needs, or wants. Assertiveness training encourages people to learn to say 'no', to defend themselves, and to complain in ways that are likely to be beneficial and successful in terms of outcomes. Sheldon (1995: 203) identifies a range of skills and tasks associated with assertiveness training:

- *assessment* to gain an understanding of the extent of the problem;
- *discrimination training procedures* to help clients to learn the difference between assertiveness, false or compulsive compliance and aggression;
- *a modelling and rehearsal component* to show the client, step-by-step, the degree of assertiveness appropriate in different circumstances and to encourage the skills to be rehearsed, offering encouragement and validation;
- *a desensitization component* to help to remove the fears by exposing clients to frightening situations; and
- *generalization* to ensure that the skills learned can be generalized to everyday experiences and problems by relating them to real situations.

The importance of people being able to assert their thoughts, feelings, choices, or needs openly and directly cannot be overstated, but its importance is not confined to service users. As practitioners, we too need to be able to assert and represent the needs and rights of others and also our own views and perspectives, personal and professional needs.

60. Challenging Skills

There are times when it is important to challenge or confront certain kinds of behaviour. This includes being able to manage conflict and confrontations (O'Sullivan 1999: 78). It also includes the right to be allowed to challenge our own agency policies and practices without the fear of reprisal. The skill is to know when and how to do this in ways that help to move the situation forward. Some authors view 'challenging as partly synonymous with confrontation' (Feltham and Dryden 2004: 33), whereas Lishman (2009a: 47) emphasizes the fact that challenging can involve 'correcting misinformation'. According to Lishman:

> In . . . confronting and challenging we are facing users with contradictions, distortions, inconsistencies or discrepancies and inviting or stimulating them to reconsider and resolve the contradictions. While such a reconsideration does not in itself change behaviour, the readjustment of interpretations and attitudes involved can lead to behaviour change. The ultimate goal of challenging, however, is problem reformulation, action and change.
>
> (Lishman 2009a: 178)

The timing of challenges, and how they are undertaken, can be as important as what is actually said because a challenge should be made at a point when it is clear that the service user is unlikely to pick up on the 'lack of fit', and needs us to intervene to move the situation forward. For example, some service users do not understand how they come across – the extent to which some of their behaviours are off-putting or set people against them. Millar et al. (1992) see challenging as a form of feedback and stress the tentative nature of the communication as a means of aiding further self-reflection and understanding: 'What interviewees need is a chance to consider what behaviours they display, how they "come across". What appear to be less helpful are attempts to present analyses of underlying meanings, interpretations or evaluative statements' (Millar et al. 1992: 97). A well-timed challenge should strengthen our relationship, whereas one that is premature or inopportune, perhaps because it is too forceful, persistent, or moves too far ahead of a service user, could damage the relationship and threaten progress, sometimes irreparably.

61. Confronting

Kadushin and Kadushin (1997: 183) write of confrontation as 'pulling the interviewee up short ... By acting contrary to the usual social expectation that they will ignore inconsistencies, interviewers set up a new situation that requires resolution'. Part of this task is to help service users to take responsibility and to own their part of whatever problems they have because, without this ownership, they cannot own the solutions. Defining problems in terms of the past means that they cannot be solved because the past cannot be changed. The purpose of confrontation is not to break down people's defences, which would leave them vulnerable because defences are needed for survival, 'but to help people to address concerns and develop new strategies'.

The ability to confront people without making them more defensive and guarded is a skilled activity, involving the qualities of tolerance, patience, and acceptance, remembering that the ultimate goal 'is action and change' (Lishman 2009a: 178). Nelson-Jones (1990: 135–6) offers the following practice guidelines:

- start with reflective responding
- where possible, help speakers to confront themselves
- do not talk down
- use the minimum amount of 'muscle'
- avoid threatening voice and body language
- leave the ultimate responsibility with the speaker
- do not overdo it.

It is important that we think beforehand about the kind of reaction that our challenge is likely to produce and what our response might be. Reactions can range from anger, rage, and pain to a sense of relief. Also, challenging others can be a stressful undertaking, which may call for additional peer and supervisor support.

As a final point, a word of warning is needed in relation to being challenging or confrontational. People who have experienced too many 'put-downs' or too much humiliation in their lives can be extremely sensitive to challenges of any kind, and can experience the mildest rebuke as quite devastating. Sometimes merely asking a particular kind of question can be construed as a form of criticism. This can be expressed in different ways. Some people may become more withdrawn and silent, while others may become agitated or even aggressive. It is not easy to guess the kind of reaction criticism will elicit and even if it does bring about some kind of positive outcome, the ends never justify the means. It is possible that the same outcome could have been achieved by adopting a more caring and sensitive intervention. Also, some people can easily turn criticism against themselves or against others. In my experience, bullying and self-harm among young people can be triggered by criticism, or other 'put-downs', as can aggressive behaviour (Howe *et al.* 1999: 138).

This is not to ignore the importance of being able to challenge the difficult and sometimes abusive behaviour that some people demonstrate, particularly when we are being targeted. It is not possible to avoid feeling critical of some kinds of behaviour: it is part of being human. Some people justify unacceptable behaviour as being natural to a particular culture or group. This may be true but it can leave us feeling unable to challenge certain behaviours. In relation to child abuse, this can have serious consequences (Corby 2006). Where the unacceptable behaviour is extreme, the law should be our 'defining mandate' (Blom-Cooper 1985). Before these extremes are reached, it is important to use our interpersonal skills to help people to find appropriate ways to give vent to feelings of upset, anger, and frustration that are not harmful to themselves or others.

62. Dealing with hostility, aggression, and violence

Violence against social workers is increasing (Littlechild 2005). For example, research indicates that 25–30 per cent of social workers have been physically assaulted at some point in their careers (Rey 1996). Clearly, it is important that we avoid hostile situations as much as possible and minimize the likelihood of being the victims of violence. This section explores the skills involved in dealing with aggressive and violent behaviour.

Sound organizational arrangements can help to keep our fears in check and avoid violent confrontations. The ideal location should be a room that cannot be locked from the inside, which has an alarm/panic button, is within easy reach of others, and has a window for colleagues to keep an unobtrusive yet watchful eye. The seating should be arranged so that it is easy for us or the service user to get to the door and leave. If a service user is known to be violent, it is important to work out a contingency plan beforehand. Our attempts to minimize the risk of violence need to be undertaken in ways that do not exacerbate the situation. Some practitioners easily fall into a 'siege mentality'. Visible protection devices, such as closed-circuit television, buzzers, and combination locks are important but it is essential to remember that most service users are not violent (Lishman 2009a: 28) and that excessive preoccupation with self-protection among practitioners can interfere with our ability to establish a trusting rapport with service users. Clearly, we must protect ourselves, but our best protection is our skill and capacity to avoid or to deal with aggressive and potentially violent encounters because, once we have acquired these skills, they accompany us in all situations.

For example, situations that involve depriving people of their liberty are the most likely to produce aggressive and violent reactions. Given this fact, we need to reflect beforehand whether our intervention is justified when the service user may be a danger to themselves (suicide or deliberate self-harm) or to others (child abuse, domestic violence, or attacks on others). We then need to consider what the person's reaction might be and to prepare our response (Lishman 2009a: 93). For example, we might decide not to undertake a home visit or, if this is essential, take a colleague with us (although to outnumber the service user may be counter-productive). We may also need to be clear how we intend to deal with violent attacks perpetrated against us or others. In my opinion, all violent attacks have to involve the police because, despite convincing justifications, violence goes beyond the realms of acceptable behaviour. If it is known that all attacks will be reported to the police, then this boundary is clear. People who choose violence know the consequences and that it will lead to police involvement. If we feel we played some part in provoking the attack, this too needs to be brought out into the open and our actions need to be seen in context. Some people are very frightening and this can affect our capacity to read situations accurately – our skills can become lost because much of our thinking is taken up working out how to protect ourselves. If the threat is this serious, we need to find ways to leave or, if that is not possible, to ensure that the person in question can leave. Barring the door is unwise.

One of the best ways to defuse a situation is to try to engage the person in a dialogue. This cannot be forced but most people want to be understood. Many have serious grievances about the unfair way they have been treated, and their current behaviour may be some form of retaliation. It is important to listen to their story and to allow ourselves to be influenced by this, but not to the point where we make inappropriate promises. It also helps to remember that most people who are threatening or violent are frightened of themselves and of their own reactions. Many have suffered terrible experiences of violence and know what it is like to be terrified. To reveal how frightened we feel – and the fact that we mean them no harm – can sometimes help to establish a point of contact and help to defuse the situation (Jordan 1990: 185). We may also need to offer a gentle reminder that their current behaviour is unlikely to bring about the outcome they most desire and, indeed, can lead to negative consequences – but caution is needed. To stress negative consequences too much can be experienced as a threat and escalate the situation. To find a way for an individual to back down, but with honour and self-respect, is essential.

10 PROFESSIONAL COMPETENCE AND ACCOUNTABILITY

Introduction

This chapter looks at professional competence and accountability and how this has been conceptualized and represented in social work. The first section of this chapter addresses what is meant by the term *professional*, and how this links to the introduction of a competency-based approach in social work. It then looks at the multiple accountabilities expected of social workers, the significance of multi-disciplinary and multi-agency work, and the importance of developing our own philosophy of practice that includes a cultural sensitivity. The second section looks at the skills that could be considered central to professional competence and accountability. The skills covered in this chapter include:

Professional competence and accountability
63 Managing professional boundaries
64 Respecting confidentiality
65 Record-keeping skills
66 Form filling
67 Case notes
68 Minute-taking skills
69 Report writing skills
70 Using supervision creatively
71 Organizational and administrative skills
72 Letter writing skills
73 The skilled use of emails
74 Telephone contact
75 Mobile phones and text messaging
76 Presentation skills
77 Chairing meetings
78 Coordinating case conferences and reviews
79 Presenting evidence in court
80 Using humour

Professional competence

The term professional can be used in two ways: (1) to describe the extent to which the activities of a particular occupation can claim the status of a profession, and (2) to describe the extent to which a particular occupation can claim a 'distinct knowledge base, and is the possessor of unique sets of skills' (Wilson *et al.* 2008: 696). Barker takes up the latter definition as follows:

> Professional: The degree to which an individual possesses and uses the knowledge, skills, and qualification of a profession and adheres to its values and ethics when serving the client.
>
> (Barker 2003: 342)

When attempting to identify the second feature, namely the characteristics of a profession, seven features have been proposed:

- control over its membership
- self-regulation of members
- distinct knowledge base
- authority that cannot be easily challenged by an 'uninformed public'
- state-licensed monopoly of provision
- regulatory code of ethics
- professional culture.

(Alcock *et al.* 2008: 88)

What is clear from this account, is that social work is precariously positioned in relation to several features identified. It is not possible to explore this subject of professionalism in depth but it is important to identify a number of issues that impact on professional competence and accountability. On the one hand, having professional qualifications 'should increase an individual's potential to exercise skills, criticality and professional autonomy in ways that effectively support service users, facilitate their search for excellence in what they do, and acquire employment in a global market' (Dominelli 2009: 22). On the other hand, for some commentators, 'professionalization' can easily lead to the 'control of knowledge' (Payne 1997: 30) and restrictions being placed on the kind of activities that social workers can undertake, resulting in a loss of professional autonomy, discretion, and sense of identity as social workers. This danger can be seen very clearly with the introduction of a managerialist culture in social work and the development of a rationalist, 'technicist', and one-size-fits-all solution to complex problems. It is a subject that links to the coverage of the *role and task of social work* in Chapter 2, and highlights the fact that considerable disagreement exists about what the role of social work should be. Some of the criticisms and concerns about the particular way that professionalization has developed in social work were summarized as follows:

Commentators have been critical of the self-serving nature of professions and the social work profession in particular. It is argued that professionalization encouraged social workers to give up their claims to change society (Hugman, 1991), led to a diminishing of the authority of women's voices in social work (Dominelli, 1997), and an abandonment of social work's traditional commitment to the poor (Jones, 1997).

(Cree 2008: 297)

An underpinning concern in the above quotation is the extent to which professionalization benefits service users and it is in this arena that some disagreement can be found. What may be the most important issue is not whether social work should be professionalized, but what kind of professionalism should we be involved in promoting and whether it is possible to take up a position where, as social workers, we shape the nature and future of social work. Unless and until we are able to direct – or at the very least to influence – the provision of services and the future of social work, it would seem to be the case that the government of the day will continue to do this for us – and badly.

An example of how the professional practice of social work has been changed – without adequate consultation – can be seen in the relation to the imposition of competences in social work. This is more accurately described in terms of a competency-based approach (Coulshed and Orme 2006: 8–9). To fully understand the impact of this system in social work, it is important to appreciate some of the issues that underpinned its introduction and why it was – and is – unsuitable for social work.

A competency-based approach in social work

Competences became prominent in the USA in the 1960s. They were introduced into the United Kingdom in the 1980s as part of a strategy to develop a skilled workforce and to standardize national and vocational qualifications. Prior to their introduction, numerous awarding bodies were in operation – some in the same or a similar occupational area (Jessup 1991). It was a situation that called for a system to be introduced that could assess and measure occupational capability with a degree of consistency, and in ways that could ensure that standards could be applied across different work settings and broad occupational areas (Lawler 1994). It was a development that was welcomed in some circles as an approach that could improve vocational training in Britain (Clark 1995) and as a way to remove the at times artificial division that existed between vocational and non-vocational qualifications. As such, the introduction of competences opened up new possibilities, particularly for people with limited educational and professional qualifications. However, at the same time it produced a situation whereby jobs that were previously held by professionally qualified and trained individuals, whose training in the helping professions included a theoretical and practical understanding of human behaviour, could be filled by applicants whose abilities were assessed on whether they could meet specified competences, such as those associated with the new job title of 'broker' or 'navigator'.

It is argued that the impact of competences in relation to education resulted in the influence of educators being reduced – a shift that 'employers in the driving seat' (Kelly and Horder 2001: 691). This meant that there was a shift from a learning environment to a task environment, with the role of education and training being shaped to meet requirements set by employers and 'the needs of the market' (Issitt and Woodward 1992: 43). For example, one local authority representative in the Midlands proposed that groupwork skills should be dropped from the teaching offered on social work education and training courses on the basis that social workers no longer offer groupwork as a practice approach (personal communication). Such short sightedness ignores the potential that groupwork approaches can offer, but it also ignores the fact that groupwork skills are regularly used in other contexts, such as teamwork and in work involving service users and carers (Trevithick 2012b).

Limitations of a competency-based approach within social work

In relation to social work, competences were first introduced in 1989 by the Central Council for Education and Training in Social Work (CCETSW), when the new two-year Diploma in Social Work was launched. In a later publication, CCETSW defined competence in social work as:

> Competence in social work is the product of knowledge, skills and values. In order to provide evidence that they have achieved the six core competences students will have to demonstrate that they have: met practice requirements; integrated social work values; acquired and applied knowledge; reflected upon and critically analysed their practice; and transferred knowledge, skills and values in practice.
>
> (CCETSW 1996: 17)

This unproblematic definition of competence suggests that a certain 'minimally adequate level of performance' is being tested (Clark 1995: 568), with a more holistic or integrated appraisal of ability being implied. However, this definition needs to be differentiated from a *competency-based approach*, which describes the fragmentation of tasks and performance, such as the 77 performance indicators in the National Occupational Standards (TOPPS 2002) for social work.

The introduction of a competency-based approach met with considerable opposition and criticism within social work but this was largely ignored due, in part, to the importance placed on competences in the government's 'modernization' of public services. A snapshot of these criticisms include a concern that the complexity of social work activity is being fragmented and reduced to following procedures in ways that are being driven by the requirement 'to act as desired and defined by others' (Barnett 1994: 81). In this process, it is argued that action is being 'shorn of reflection' and 'reduced to mere technique' (Barnett 1994: 149), thereby leading to a tick-box mentality. Also, the emphasis placed on observable performance fails to encompass the 'entirety of what a social worker is required to do' (Lymbery 2003: 104), particularly the quality of the interaction.

In relation to the extent to which performance or actions can be measured, it is important to note that no standardized outcome measures for assessing students' and practitioners' competence have been introduced (Bogo *et al.* 2002), and even if such measures were to be introduced, it is unclear whether a 'small sample of directly observed performances' can be representative of a general 'capability' to determine 'the candidate's potential to perform in the future' (Eraut 1994: 200). The result is 'an inadequate governing framework' that fails to 'properly recognize the constant need for creative solutions to poorly understood problems' (Clark 1995: 563). Clark concludes that a competency-based approach in social work 'has certainly not been demonstrated to be superior, or even workable in practice' (Clark 1995: 579). Howe succinctly summarizes its limitations:

> Such an outlook seeks to establish routines, standardized practices and predictable task environments. It is antithetical to depth explanations, professional integrity, creative practice, and tolerance of complexity and uncertainty.
>
> (Howe 1996: 92)

I share these concerns. It seems to me to be a fundamentally flawed approach to reduce a series of actions to simple sequences and then to attempt to apply these sequences in ways that cannot fully embrace the multifaceted, intricate, and interrelated nature of many of the situations encountered in social work. Many of the essential capacities, interpersonal skills, and personal qualities that we bring to our work – such as our humanity, compassion, concern, and care for others – are integral to the interaction and the quality of service provided. But these essential attributes can be overlooked, and our autonomy in decision-making denied, where the focus is on a superficial conceptualization of behaviour and where the intricacies of practice are reduced to merely following procedures. It is in the quality of the interaction with services users – wrapped in a blanket that embodies knowledge, skills, and values – that is of central importance and these attributes are not 'measurable' in a competency-based approach.

The UK Social Work Reform Board has proposed 'an overarching standards framework', a *Professional Capabilities Framework for Social Workers in England*, to support and inform recommendations relating to a national career structure (SWRB 2010: 6). This framework is designed to integrate 'knowledge, skills, personal qualities and understanding' (Stephenson 1998: 2), and to overcome the fragmentation that is considered to be a feature of a competency-based approach. If adopted, a national social work career structure in the form of a capacities framework could lead to considerable improvement and greater coherence in relation to 'what should be required of social workers at each stage of their career' (SWRB 2010: 6). This task may be difficult to achieve within a culture in health and social care where a more competency-based approach still dominates.

Multiple accountabilities

One reason why a competency-based approach has been so problematic in social work relates to the fact that people are social beings, living in social situations where a variety of factors and influences impact on their lives, and at many different levels – both conscious and unconscious. This means that any attempt to understand the complex interplay of diverse influences necessarily requires a complex and in-depth understanding if progress is to be made and 'unintended consequences' (Laming 2003: 252) to be avoided. A feature of this complicated picture, and of our professional responsibilities within this context, is the 'multiple accountabilities' that social workers are expected to balance (Dominelli and Holloway 2008). This includes being accountable to society at large, the government of the day, employers, colleagues, to our professional values, to ourselves, and also to service users and carers. In relation to service users, Dominelli and Holloway (2008: 1018) note that 'the interweaving of multiple accountabilities amongst a range of stakeholders has been barely addressed', especially – in cases of multiple accountabilities – whether any one should be considered more important.

This can lead to conflicting demands as we attempt to balance the best interests of one group against those of another. For example, in children's services this can lead to tensions as we attempt to balance children's needs and the requirement to protect parents' rights (Hollis and Howe 1990: 549). In adult care, balance may be needed when addressing the needs of a service user against those of their carers/relatives. These themes are linked because the central task of social work involves problem-solving across these conflicting interests and competing needs. In this work, it is probably true to say that social work is 'crucially concerned with fairness' (Jordan 1990: 178) but the extent to which the pursuit of 'fairness' – or, more particularly, redressing injustices – is considered to be a legitimate part of our social work role is a controversial issue. Again, we are caught in a double-bind: we are being asked to be 'empowering' yet not political, and to demonstrate 'accurate empathy, warmth and genuineness which have long been known to be associated with effective social work practice' (Thoburn 2008: 220) yet adhere to targets. It may not always be possible, or effective, to separate these competing accountabilities.

A sense of balance is clearly evident in the requirement for social workers to provide care, protection, and control. The capacity to care for others can sometimes be in conflict with our role as 'agents of social control' (Coulshed and Orme 2006: 125). It is difficult to generalize about how practitioners conceptualize and use the concepts of care, protection, and control powers – not least because practitioners and agencies can exercise a certain degree of discretion in how legislative and policy requirements are interpreted and put into practice. However, I have argued in this text that the use of discretionary powers has become increasingly bound in the imperatives of 'managerialism', as well as the increased emphasis on statutory or legal framings (Clarke 1993). This theme relates to the role and task of social work. Of particular concern in the area of protection and control is the extent to which practitioners can and should intervene. In this area, the concept of *minimum intervention* can be important, that is, the principle that we should intervene only to the extent that our actions are designed to promote the safety and welfare of service users. As stated earlier, where possible this should include eliciting the views and wishes of the individuals involved, and other significant others, using a range of different communication approaches in this consultative process. The use of different modes of communication is particularly important when working with children and with individuals whose comprehension and understanding may be limited. Often, *early intervention* can mean that we are able to avoid having to use statutory powers but so much depends on the situation and the different factors and individuals involved. Early intervention is described as:

A principle now widely informing service delivery in health and social care that emphasizes the importance of intervening positively at an early point in the development of social, psychological, interpersonal or social difficulties. Early intervention services in adult mental health have been a particular focus of recent policy development. Early intervention has to some extent replaced the concept of 'prevention'.
(Wilson *et al.* 2008: 693).

Practitioners who see their professional competence and accountability primarily in terms of their accountability to service users are likely to view their work and priorities differently from those who place agency accountability at the forefront. On the one hand, it is argued that addressing underlying causes, such as poverty and discrimination, cannot be the main priority of social work. The pressure of other demands dominate: 'social workers and their agencies are already very over-pressed with current commitments, many of them statutory, and cannot afford the resources for excursions into areas outside social work proper' (Clark 2000a: 198). On the other hand, Clark puts a counter-argument – namely, that problems cannot be addressed effectively, 'even at the individual level, unless their origin in broader social processes is properly understood. A key example is poverty' . . . [also] 'focusing intervention on individual cases is very inefficient' (Clark 2000a: 198).

Similarly, other authors agree and argue that the way social work is organized and managed is itself problematic and potentially oppressive (Perrott 2009: 104). If professional competence means the ability to 'do the job', this raises the question, what is the 'job'? What is the role or task of social work and social workers and how can effectiveness be measured? In this regard, Munro (2011b: 22) suggests that the government should provide 'clarity around roles, responsibilities, values and accountabilities' while at the same time allowing 'professionals greater flexibility and autonomy to judge *how* best to achieve these goals and protect children and young people'. Whatever our views, social work accountability, competence, and effectiveness are likely to remain centre stage and a feature of our accountability is likely to be demonstrated in our capacity to work with others, to which I now turn.

Multi-disciplinary and inter-agency approaches in social work

One of the areas where social workers are accountable is in relation to multi-disciplinary and inter-agency ways of working. One difficulty is the variety of terms used to describe an integrated approach to service delivery. The following are definitions used in this text:

> *Multi-disciplinary*: A term used when representatives of different disciplines and agencies are brought together, for example in community mental health or learning disability teams. A *multi-disciplinary* approach should foster *inter-professional* working, but cannot guarantee it. Multi-disciplinary working can be seen, for example, when representatives of various agencies work together – social services, health, housing, the independent sector, etc. (Wilson *et al.* 2008: 695).

> *Inter-agency* (or *multi-agency*): describes two or more agencies working together towards an agreed objective or outcome. This term is focused on the contribution of organizations or agencies, rather than the contribution of other practitioners or professionals.

An early account of the importance of different professional bodies and agencies working together can be found in the *Framework for the Assessment of Children in Need and their Families* (Department of Health 2000a). Although the following quotation was drafted in relation to children, where inter-disciplinary approaches were first developed in detail, the principles that it describes are relevant in other areas of health and welfare provision:

> Inter-agency, inter-disciplinary assessment practice requires an additional set of knowledge and skills to that required for working within a single agency or independently. It requires that all staff understand the roles and responsibilities of staff working in contexts different

to their own. Having an understanding of the perspectives, language and culture of other professionals can inform how communication is conducted. This prevents professionals from misunderstanding one another because they use different language to describe similar concepts or because they are influenced by stereotypical perceptions of the other discipline.

(Department of Health 2000a: 63)

What is interesting is the acknowledgement that practitioners will need to acquire 'an additional set of knowledge and skills' to be able to embrace a multi-professional approach and to move away from single-agency or independent working. Examples of the changes initiated include the Common Assessment Framework (CAF), which was introduced to standardize multi-agency working and information sharing, and the Integrated Children's System (ICS), designed to provide information considered to be essential for effective multi-agency practice with children and families in relation to assessment, planning, intervention, and review. The extent to which these policy changes have provided a more integrated service and helped 'people move across professional boundaries' (Department for Education and Skills 2003: 92) has been quite variable. For example, the failures of inter-professional working were highlighted in the Laming Report (2009).

Despite considerable progress in interagency working, often driven by Local Safeguarding Children Boards and multi-agency teams who strive to help children and young people, there remain significant problems in the day-to-day reality of working across organisational boundaries and cultures, sharing information to protect children and a lack of feedback when professionals raise concerns about a child. Joint working between children's social workers, youth workers, schools, early years, police and health too often depends on the commitment of individual staff and sometimes this happens despite, rather than because of, the organisational arrangements. This must be addressed by senior management in every service.

(Laming 2009: 10–11)

In response to these criticisms, an updated version of *Working Together to Safeguard Children* was produced, incorporating new guidelines to promote better inter-agency working (DCSF 2010). It is interesting to note that in *Working Together*, a child is defined as anyone 'who has not yet reached their 18th birthday' (DSCF 2010: 34).

As already noted, early policy and legislation in the area of vulnerability tended to be focused mainly on children's services. However, in 2000 the Department of Health published *No Secrets: Guidance on Developing and Implementing Multi-Agency Policies and Procedures to Protect*

Vulnerable Adults from Abuse (Department of Health 2000b). Its aims involved 'creating a framework for action within which all agencies work together to ensure a consistent and effective response to all concerns' (Wilson *et al.* 2008: 561). As a result, all local authorities are required to initiate procedures for protecting vulnerable adults from abuse, where abuse is defined as:

> Abuse may consist of a single act or repeated acts. It may be physical, verbal or psychological, it may be an act of neglect or an omission to act, or it may occur when a vulnerable person is persuaded to enter into a financial or sexual transaction to which he or she has not consented, or cannot consent. Abuse can occur in any relationship and may result in significant harm to, or exploitation of, the person subjected to it.
>
> (Department of Health 2000b: 9)

An example of an integrated approach in adult care was the introduction of the Single Assessment Process (SAP), designed to integrate the assessment process through the use of shared tools and procedures. It has been suggested that in relation to work with older people, inter-professional working has been relatively successful and evident in the use of shared protocols (Abendstern *et al.* 2011: 481). However, in other areas similar difficulties have been encountered to those found in children's services. For example, the findings of one study 'suggest that some aspects of the [SAP] policy have been taken up more than others and that whilst there is commitment to an integrated approach, this has been hampered by disjointed information sharing initiatives and by lack of involvement from some sectors' (Abendstern *et al.* 2011: 467).

The advantage that multi-disciplinary and inter-agency approaches provide is that they combine the expertise and resources that different disciplines and agencies bring. This approach is also designed to address fragmentation, duplication, delay, and inequitable access. Some excellent examples of multi-disciplinary partnership arrangements can be found in the Local Safeguarding Children Boards (LSCBs) and Adult Safeguarding Boards (ASBs) where representatives from social work, social care, education, health, housing, police, and the independent sector work together to protect vulnerable children and adults. In general, multi-disciplinary and multi-agency approaches work well when there is a shared commitment and a respect for the contribution that different individuals provide. However, not all individuals or professionals command the same status, which means that problems can emerge. This is particularly evident in relation to social workers since in some contexts, the contribution that practitioners can offer, particularly in the area of social factors that impact on the problem presented, is not given the status and importance it deserves. Inequalities of this kind are often at the heart of poor decision-making.

Philosophy of practice

A different way to approach the issue of professional competence and accountability involves focusing on the moral principles and ethical practices that underpin our work. I covered this subject in Chapter 1 when I described the perspectives that inform this text. This focus is described by Gambrill (2006: 12) in terms of a 'philosophy of practice', which is designed to ensure 'the likelihood that clients receive effective service and are not harmed'. The features of this philosophy include (Gambrill 2006: 12–15):

- professionals are responsible for the decisions they make
- services help clients and their significant others to attain outcomes they value
- clients are not harmed
- the least restrictive methods are used
- clients (or their representatives) are fully informed and involved in decisions
- professionals have problem-related knowledge and skills as well as self-directed learning skills to keep them up-to-date
- practice decisions are well reasoned
- critical discussion and testing of claims is valued
- decisions are data based as well as theory based
- individual differences are considered
- self-knowledge that contributes to well-reasoned decisions is sought and used
- words correspond to actions.

I now wish to focus a little more on professional ethics before looking at professional competence and accountability in terms of our ability to evaluate our effectiveness. In a helpful definition, Clark defines professional ethics as follows:

> *Professional ethics* comprise the more or less formalized principles, rules, conventions and customary practices that inform professionals' treatment of their clients, each other, and their relations with society at large ... Professional ethics may be prescribed in written codes, which the individual professional may be required to adhere to upon penalty of disciplinary action or disqualification.
>
> (Clark 2000b: 272)

In essence, this describes the extent to which we adopt a principled position in the respect, honesty, truthfulness, appropriate authority, and accountability we communicate and how these principles inform our work and contact with others.

Evaluating our effectiveness

A feature of professional accountability is the ability to evaluate our effectiveness. According to Shaw (1996: 166), 'social work works'. Similarly, Cheetham *et al.* (1992: 4) state that in some areas 'social work can now claim to be cost effective'. However, these statements call for us to define what effectiveness means and how we measure success. One answer could be to say that 'social work is effective in so far as it achieves intended aims' (Cheetham *et al.* 1992: 10). However, we then must question whether these aims are too high, too low, or appropriate to the situation, given the existence of other constraints and variables operating at the time. These variables over which we may have little or no control – together with the fact that we often encounter problems that are complex, multidimensional, and intractable – make the task of evaluating our effectiveness a difficult and fraught task. This difficulty is made worse by the fact that we know very little about what actually happens in practice in terms of the impact of particular interventions or the extent to which the services provided met desired or agreed outcomes. Evidence of positive or beneficial outcomes is not enough to tell us what factors did or did not play a part in bringing about a particular outcome.

Yet despite these difficulties, it is important that we provide quality services and find ways that can demonstrate the effectiveness of our work (Macdonald and Macdonald 1995). This is demanded of us in a climate where in terms of government policy, 'what works is what counts'. 'Professionals must seek to ensure that their interventions are not only carried out with due competence and in good faith, but are effective in the sense that they lead to the desired outcomes' (Clark 2000a: 56). It is also essential because mistakes can be very costly in terms of human lives, as the errors in child abuse cases and public inquiries reveal. Reflective practice provides an opportunity to review our decisions and decision-making processes, and to learn from the lessons of the past. As well as arriving at decisions based on 'best evidence', reflective practice provides a vital link between theory and practice. (For a fuller account of the importance of reflective practice, see Chapter 4.)

Cultural sensitivity

A feature of this principled position – and the attributes I have just described – can be seen in the extent to which we work from a culturally sensitive perspective. Giddens defines *culture* in terms of:

> The values, ceremonies and ways of life characteristic of a given group. Like the concept of society, the notion of culture is very widely used in sociology, as well as in the other social sciences (particularly anthropology). Culture is one of the most distinctive properties of human social organisation.
>
> (Giddens 2001: 686)

This definition sees culture in its widest form – emphasizing the multi-cultural nature of human society of which ethnicity is one feature. It is important to note that the terms *culture* and *ethnicity* are sometimes used synonymously but they are different (Owusu-Bempah 2008: 318). Similarly, in the United States, ethnicity can be used as a euphemism for *race* or *people of colour* (Robinson 2007: 4). There are a number of different definitions of the term *ethnicity* but it is generally used to describe a group of people who consider themselves – or are considered by others – to have common ties because of their nationality, race, culture, language, religion, or other characteristics that they demonstrate.

This subject is important in a skills text because our culture, our identity, and personal beliefs shape our communication. For example, when people from different cultural backgrounds communicate, their assumptions about the nature, content, and even the purpose of their communication may be different. This means that inter-cultural communication can be both a fascinating and enriching experience but also an area where it is easy for misunderstandings to arise. For example, a person who is reticent in relation to eye contact in British culture may be interpreted as being untrustworthy, guilt-ridden, shifty, uncomfortable, or lacking in self-esteem. In other parts of the world, not making eye contact may indicate respect or sexual modesty (Lishman 2009a: 37). What must be borne in mind is that in terms of how we express the six basic emotions that are consistently referred to – namely, sadness, anger, disgust, fear, surprise, and happiness – all are likely to be influenced by individual and cultural differences. This makes it important to ensure that any assumptions we make are checked out for their factual accuracy.

Cultural sensitivity is also sometimes described in terms of *cultural knowledge*. This focuses on the understanding that underpins the cultural context where people are located and belong, and the shared meaning, values, and worldview that they use to make sense of their experiences at a given point in time. Cultural knowledge can be extended to include what we know – be it tentatively – about groups of people from certain communities and neighbourhood groups. For example, an account of work undertaken in Tower Hamlets highlights the importance of cultural and gender sensitivity, and the extent to which practitioners adopted 'interventions that were sensitive to the cultural beliefs and the views of families' (Gray 2009: 998). For people who come from disadvantaged sectors of the population, the opportunity to share their knowledge and experiences with others can build strong ties and lead to the creation of systems of support, resistance, and empowerment (Graham 2002).

Legislation

Below we look at a number of skills that are associated with professional competence and accountability. Once again, to differentiate between a personal attribute and a social work skill is not always possible. Before addressing the specific skills involved in professional competence and accountability, I want to cover three areas of legislation that are central to the skills described.

Data Protection Act (DPA) 1998

In relation to personal information that is held by other bodies, the Data Protection Act (DPA) 1998 applies. This Act came into force on 1 March 2000 and applies to all bodies within the UK that hold personal information, whether held manually or electronically. It is intended to protect people's privacy, to encourage good practice in the handling of personal information, and to give individuals the right of access to information recorded about them, such as health records or information help by credit reference agencies. Notice must be given to the relevant organization, which is allowed 40 days to respond: a fee may be charged. However, care must be taken 'not to release personal data that may relate to another individual, and in some circumstances the request may be refused if a disclosure would cause damage or distress to the data subject' (Brammer 2007: 115).

Freedom of Information Act (FOIA) 2000

Access to other sorts of information held by public authorities are dealt with according to the rules laid down in the Freedom of Information Act (FOIA) 2000, which came into force on 1 January 2005 to complement the DPA 1998. FOIA, which applies to England, Wales, and Northern Ireland, gives people the right of access to information held by, or on behalf of, public authorities (Scotland has its own Act, passed in 2002). This Act is intended to promote a culture of openness and accountability within the public sector by giving the public greater access to information about how decisions are taken in government and how public services are developed and delivered. Between April and June 2005, a total of 8400 requests for information were made to the government (Brammer 2007: 116). It is now a criminal offence to tamper with or destroy records that have been requested (further information is available on www.foi.gov.uk). (Further information on the above two Acts can be found in Brammer 2007.)

Human Rights Act 1998

The Human Rights Act (HRA) 1998 was described by Jack Straw, the then Home Secretary, as the 'most significant statement of human rights since the 1689 Bill of Rights' (Straw cited in Brammer 2007: 124). The Act 'gives further effect in the UK to the fundamental rights and freedoms in the European Convention on Human Rights' (Human Rights Act 1998: 1). It states that everyone in the UK has fundamental human rights that governments and public authorities are legally obliged to respect. These rights state the following:

- Article 1 – is introductory
- Article 2 – the right to life
- Article 3 – freedom from torture and degrading treatment
- Article 4 – freedom from slavery and forced labour
- Article 5 – the right to liberty and security
- Article 6 – the right to a fair trial
- Article 7 – the right not to be found guilty of an offence that was not a crime when committed
- Article 8 – the right to respect for private and family life
- Article 9 – freedom of thought, conscience and religion, and freedom to express your beliefs
- Article 10 – freedom of expression
- Article 11 – freedom of assembly and association

(Human Rights Act 1998: 3–7)

Qualified Rights. The rights in Articles 8–11 may be qualified where it is necessary to achieve an important objective.

- Article 12 – the right to marry and to start a family
- Article 13 – the right not to be discriminated against in respect of these rights and freedoms
- Article 1 of Protocol 1 – the right to peaceful enjoyment of your property
- Article 2 of Protocol 1 – the right to an education
- Article 3 of Protocol 1 – the right to participate in free elections
- Protocol 6/Article 1 of Protocol 13 – the right not to be subjected to the death penalty

Article 8 is the section of the Act that is often cited in social work, which refers to the right to respect for private and family life, that is, 'you have the right to respect for your private and family life, your home and your correspondence. This right can only be restricted in specified circumstances' (Human Rights Act 1998: 4).

We now turn to look at the specific skills covered in this chapter.

Specific skills

63. Managing professional boundaries

Boundaries are important in social work, as in all other areas of professional activity, because they are a way of marking the responsibilities that lie within a particular role or task, and differentiating these from other activities or aspects of social work. The notion of boundaries can include work with individuals, groups, families, communities, and organizations:

> This concept helps us to look at ways of marking off and establishing the identity of something, by differentiating it from other entities and from its surroundings. It is also concerned with setting limits, as we do in everyday life, for example whenever we delineate what is acceptable from what is not. Boundary definition gives enhanced understanding of the types of relationship and interchange that occur between one entity and another.
>
> (Brearley 1995: 49)

For example, an interview kept within clear boundaries will start and end on time. This clarity allows us to measure whether the service user is late or not. Similarly, we can learn a great deal about service users' capacity to let go – to leave one experience and move on to another – if we set a time for the appointment or session to end and they try to extend this on a regular basis, perhaps with 'doorknob revelations'. Without these boundaries, which act as markers, we can fail to pick up on a range of behaviours that may be relevant. For example, service users who are trying to find employment but are always late for appointments with us may be at risk of losing any job they apply for due to poor timekeeping. To be able to help service users, we have to know what they find difficult.

If we were to meet this same service user away from our agency, say at the local shops, our conversation would not need to be bound by time or other constraints because we would be in a different context but not necessarily in a different role. This means that any conversation we have should be warm and friendly but, at the same time, should not refer to issues of a professional or confidential nature. In social contact of this kind, it is important to strike the right balance between being spontaneous and relaxed yet remaining within professional parameters. Too loose a boundary, such as being overly friendly, can lead to confusion and uncertainty, whereas too rigid a boundary can feel unnecessarily authoritarian and withholding. These concerns do not apply in the same way if we have had contact with an individual, as a friend or neighbour, prior to becoming a client – although some discussion about how to balance these overlapping areas of contact and the different roles they entail is likely to be beneficial.

Thus within any discussion of boundaries, there are areas of overlap. For this reason, Brearley suggests that it is better to think in terms of boundary regions rather than boundary lines. This helps to avoid taking up rigid inflexible positions but instead allows us to explore this overlap based on an acknowledgement of 'common ground and shared territory and concerns between one group or activity and another' (Brearley 1995: 49).

There are several advantages for establishing and working within clear boundaries:

- Boundaries ensure that we keep to the task and roles designated and agreed, thereby ensuring that we are not drawn into other areas or issues. For example, some service users may like to become our friends (or we may want to become their friend). In work settings, this may contravene agency policy, as well as blurring professional boundaries. Even if a particular case were to be closed and contact brought to an end, we have to entertain the possibility that this same individual may want to return for help and support at a later point. If boundaries are blurred, this might make it difficult for this individual to return. Again, it is likely that addressing these concerns will lead to an elegant solution.
- Boundaries ensure the economic use of time and resources. For example, if an interviewing room has been booked for an hour, it can disrupt and frustrate other practitioners if the session is allowed to extend beyond the allocated time in ways that encroach on their work.
- Practical arrangements can be formalized and the contact put on a professional footing. Some practical negotiations are similar to ground rules and can include identifying the purpose of the work or the nature of the task and contract (written or otherwise); the frequency and location of the sessions; who is eligible to attend; agreement about record-keeping; transport/child-care arrangements; expectations about punctuality; smoking prohibitions; how crises or emergencies will be dealt with; behaviour expectations (no alcohol, drug-taking, spitting or violence); communication rules (no swearing or interrupting); and so on.

The above categories are sometimes summarized as the three 'Ts': time, territory, and task. It is normally the responsibility of the practitioner to ensure that these three elements or other boundary issues are adhered to.

64. Respecting confidentiality

One of the most problematic boundary problems in social work is the issue of confidentiality. Confidentiality is essential to create a climate of trust and to protect service users' rights. The general rule is that no information should be disclosed without the service users' consent. Barker differentiates between two types of confidentiality:

- *absolute confidentiality*, where no information is disclosed regardless of circumstances without consent (Barker 2003: 2);
- *relative confidentiality*, indicating the circumstances where it is our ethical or professional responsibility to disclose information (Barker 2003: 365).

These two types of confidentiality appear relatively straightforward but, as we shall see, the picture is more complex.

Agency responsibilities

Most agencies have policies on confidentiality. Where the principles of good practice are in operation, agencies make their confidentiality policy available, in written form, as a guide for practitioners and service users. Some include the agency's record-keeping policy and, as indicated earlier, these record-keeping policies have become more significant with the emphasis placed on inter-disciplinary and inter-agency approaches within social work. In keeping with requirements indicated in the Data Protection Act 1998, it is important for service users to know what information is being passed between one agency and another and, in this process, who has access to their records and under what circumstances (typists, supervisors, line managers, colleagues, other outside agencies, or professional contacts).

What happens in practice?

The extent to which workers read and adhere to these policies, and inform service users of their content, is not clear. In my experience, policies relating to confidentiality – like those relating to health and safety, and similar policy documents – can be easily ignored and left unread on the shelf. Yet it is vital for service users to know what procedures are in place and how these procedures are being rigorously adhered to. Clark takes up this issue and suggests that in everyday experience, the following poor practice and shortcomings are likely to be seen in practice:

- clients ... do not clearly understand what information about them will be communicated and to whom;
- workers discuss identifiable clients' affairs with colleagues in their own agency who are not directly involved with the case as co-workers or supervisors;
- workers fail to ensure that properly informed consent has been given to both the seeking of client information from, and its disclosure to, colleagues in other agencies and/or other professions;
- identifiable information about clients is readily available to large numbers of professional and non-professional agency staff who have no direct legitimate interest in the case;
- agencies do not provide working conditions that enable staff to properly protect clients' privacy;
- files and records are not consistently stored under safe and secure conditions;
- workers often have to make difficult decisions about the communication of sensitive information, especially within families, without the benefit of authoritative guidance.

(Clark 2006b: 119–20)

I have included Clark's comments to highlight the complex issues involved. There are no easy answers to the points raised but one suggestion put forward is that we should share the dilemma with service users – to invite their thinking:

> The job of professionals is therefore not to proclaim their own determination of confidentiality from behind closed doors, as the conventional professional ethics often seem to imply. Rather, the role of professionals is to lead the public debate about where exactly the lines between privacy and the public good are to be drawn.
>
> (Clark 2006b: 134)

This suggestion could have important implications. For example, we may find that people within a particular community who share similar concerns feel that an agency's confidentiality policy works against being able to share these concerns – and instead leaves them isolated from one another and unable to act with a common voice.

Communicating the importance of confidentiality

It is essential for the agency's confidentiality policy to be discussed with service users, and that this information is explained in a manner that ensures that it is 'appropriate to the client's understanding, ability and emotional capacity' to deal with information of this kind (Clark 2000a: 192). However, there are times when confidentiality has to be breached, for example if a person is being abused or likely to be harmed in some way. For this reason, it is unhelpful to state, as I have often heard, that everything that is said will remain confidential. This may be promising more than we can deliver. Instead, it is important to say that any information disclosed will remain confidential unless there are good reasons to break this rule and that where this is the situation, the person involved will be informed beforehand. This information needs to be put forward in a sensitive and thoughtful way so as not to alarm the person involved – it can be helpful to stress that it has to be in the service user's best interest for confidentiality to be breached.

65. Record-keeping skills

Record keeping is an essential skill within social work and can be an intervention in its own right. However, Munro (2011b: 160) notes that 'keeping records to demonstrate compliance has become too dominant', which undervalues the importance of robust record-keeping systems, of which there are many. Yet efficient and effective record-keeping skills are essential to the social work task. Their primary purpose is to enhance service delivery in relation to effectiveness, accountability, and confidentiality. However, such skills can also be a crucial learning tool because record keeping provides an opportunity for analytical reflection and evaluation, particularly in relation to decision-making, formulating hypotheses, and evolving collaborative ways of working. Record keeping provides an opportunity to step back and to think things through. The following is a helpful summary of the multi-purpose nature of record keeping, which can be used:

- as learning and teaching material
- for supervision purposes
- for administrative purposes, e.g. budgeting
- to ensure accountability
- for research and evaluation
- to illustrate shortfalls or absence of services
- to 'cover' the worker for work done
- to provide continuity when workers change
- to aid planning and decision-making
- to monitor progress
- as an *aide mémoire*
- to facilitate client participation, as indicated.

(Coulshed 1991: 41–2)

One of the main tensions within record keeping is how much information to record and how best to do this in ways that are accurate, objectively critical, and sufficiently detailed yet also succinct. Clearly, this decision depends on how the records might be used. Lishman (2009a: 60–2) identifies a range of purposes that records can serve. These include:

- *Legal records*: some legislation requires agencies to keep records, such as keeping a register of people with visual impairment and legal proceedings in relation to complaints or child care legal proceedings.
- *Financial records*: the entitlement to service for some people may need to be assessed and records kept.
- *Management control*: some records are kept to monitor workers' performance and to indicate that employees are complying with legal and agency requirements. The introduction of a managerialist culture has led to a greater emphasis being placed on worker accountability.
- *Accountability*: this involves workers having to 'account for decisions, assessments and work done' (Lishman 2009a: 61).
- *Information storage*: some information is stored in case this is needed at some later point to indicate, for example, the take up of services.
- *Agency evaluation*: some information may be kept for research and evaluation purposes. 'Clear, comprehensive, focused agency recording can contribute to the necessary evaluation of how effective we are' (Lishman 2009a: 62).

In recent years, more structured, proforma-based, and computerized forms of recording, such as the Integrated Children's System (ICS), have been encouraged as a way to standardize and order information, check its validity, draw up and test hypotheses, ensure that facts can be differentiated from opinion or hearsay, relate information to a knowledge base, and to inform future practice. This involves recording significant facts, baseline data collected, decisions made, actions taken, what was agreed when planning, monitoring, and reviewing the work, partnership arrangements, information relating to relevant financial costs, and how the work was evaluated in terms of its effectiveness. However, it is important to note that structuring information does not in itself ensure good practice or effectiveness. Also, it is helpful to consider agency policy in relation to service users' access to their records and in this regard, it can be empowering – where possible – for service users to play an active part in the recording process and for this to be seen as an integral part of the work.

The following provides a snapshot of some points to consider in relation to the different types of record-keeping systems used in social work.

66. Form filling

Two types of forms are commonly used within social work/social care, namely, electronic forms (e-forms) and paper-based, handwritten forms. The skills involved in form filling are:

- If unfamiliar with the form, read the form carefully beforehand and plan your answers.
- Answer all questions. Some forms will not go through, or will be returned, if all questions are not completed.
- Allow some time to check through what you have written.
- Some forms will cut off any words beyond a particular word count. This makes it important to plan your response to keep your comments succinct and to find other ways to convey other vital information.
- Most handwritten forms require black ink to be used.

67. Case notes

Case notes are an important source of information about service users, services, the assessment process and agreed courses of action, intervention strategies and outcomes. They can also communicate a great deal about the quality of your work because they provide essential information about events that have informed decision-making and action.

With the introduction of computer-based systems, there is a danger that practitioners neglect to update other systems for recording events and progress. Case notes can include:

- vital information for reports in relation to case conferences, reviews, tribunals, and for the courts
- evidence of professional accountability

- evidence of a commitment to service user and carer participation
- details for supervision purposes
- continuity between practitioners when workers leave and for work in interdisciplinary contexts
- information for planning and administrative purposes
- data to be used in research and evaluation
- details of any shortfall in service provision
- legal safeguard in a climate of increasing litigation
- a memory aid.

68. Minute-taking skills

In professional circles, the minutes taken at meetings constitute a formal record of discussions and decisions, and a check on any progress achieved. As such, they call for good communication skills, particularly the ability to listen and to summarize key points. These should:

- record the composition and structure of the meeting, such as:
  - those present and absent
  - minutes and matters arising from previous meetings
  - the agenda
  - details of the next meeting
- ensure that the contents of the minutes can be understood by people who were not present at the meeting
- ensure that they convey a balanced, accurate, succinct, and unambiguous account of what is said and any decisions taken
- ensure that action points are clearly identified.

If minute taking is rotated, ideally the person chosen should have no major contribution to make on this occasion and should not be expected to participate fully.

Unlike minutes, a *note* of a meeting normally has less detail, often focusing solely on recording action points. They are considered to be a less formal account.

69. Report writing skills

In social work, you may be asked to produce a report that summarizes key issues on a particular topic, such as the need for an after school club or court report. The length, structure, and layout of the report will vary according to the context but is likely to include some of the following headings:

- cover with a title page
- contents, plus page numbers if appropriate
- summary/executive summary, giving the main findings and recommendations, if any

- introduction, giving the purpose of the report, its subject area, and who it is for
- main section of the report, with clear headings
- conclusion (unless covered in the summary)
- appendices/other relevant information
- glossary of terms if a more specialized terminology has been adopted

70. Using supervision creatively

The purpose of supervision within social work is to facilitate the professional development of practitioners to ensure that our work is effective, efficient, accountable, and undertaken in ways that address with sensitivity the needs of service users. For this reason, regular supervision is recognized as an essential feature of social work practice. However, in some contexts the use of supervision as an opportunity for exploration, reflection, and analysis is being replaced by a managerial agenda where the preoccupation is with risk, safety, accountability, financial constraints on service provision, and the importance of performance management and meeting set targets (Beddoe 2010). As Munro notes:

> A common experience amongst social workers is that the few supervision opportunities are dominated by a managerial need to focus on performance, for example, throughput, case closure, adhering to timescales and completion of written records. This leaves little time for thoughtful consideration of what is happening in the lives of children and their families.
>
> (Munro 2011b: 115)

Lishman (2009a: 65) shares this concern and argues that the main purpose of supervision should be 'different from management control and accountability' because it is built on a 'professional-to-professional relationship rather than a superior-to-subordinate one'. The importance of providing support is central but so too is the importance of challenging professional practice where appropriate so as to reduce worker bias (Coulshed and Orme 2006: 48) and to review decisions made (Milner and O'Byrne 2009: 204; Munro 1996: 973). For example, Hollis and Howe (1990: 548–9) remind us that 'good intentions and keeping to the procedures' are not enough and that 'well judged risks sometimes lead to bad outcomes'. Where practitioners encounter this degree of uncertainty, one of the major functions of supervision is to contain or manage anxiety – a reflective space that helps practitioners to cope with the demands that the work entails. Given the lack of uniformity, it is essential that the purpose of the supervision relationship between the practitioner and supervisor is clarified in the early stages of the relationship.

Most supervision takes place on a regular one-to-one basis with a line manager, although other forms can also exist alongside, or instead of, individual supervision, such as peer, group, and team supervision, as well as inter-agency supervision structures. 'Live' supervision, which may involve inviting a manager or colleague to sit in on a session to give their observations, can be particularly valuable to add another dimension to our appraisal. Similarly, the range of information made available for supervision can also vary and include written case notes or reports, tape or video recordings, feedback from colleagues, service users and others who have direct experience of the work at hand, and/or the practitioner's particular strengths and weaknesses. The range of issues that can form a part of the supervision session can also vary and include:

- A critical analysis of a particular case and the different practice choices adopted. In terms of the *Knowledge and Skills Framework* described in this text, this case analysis would include a focus on the following themes:
  - what method of intervention was chosen and to what effect (i.e. work with individuals, families, groups, and communities)
  - what theories underpinned the work
  - what practice approach was chosen and the rationale (task-centred, ecological, etc.)
  - what perspective was adopted (strength based, feminist, etc.)
  - what skills and interventions were used and their impact and overall effectiveness in terms of achieved and desired outcomes (advocacy, confrontation, etc.).
- Exploring the service user–practitioner relationship, its strengths and weaknesses; and how any of the feelings we or others have might enhance/detract from the work.
- Looking at the supervision session and what is happening in the here and now, particularly with a view to seeing if issues in relation to the service user are being replayed in the supervision session (Mattinson 1975: 11).
- Looking at practitioners' professional development, such as training and conference opportunities, and how these can be used to enhance practitioners' knowledge base and practice effectiveness.

The skills involved in using supervision creatively

To use supervision creatively is a skill. For some practitioners, supervision is not a creative or comfortable experience, perhaps due to personality clashes or because exposing our work to scrutiny in this way feels threatening. For supervision to be effective and supportive, it is important that these difficulties are addressed. Where workload pressures are an inhibiting factor, these tensions need to be fed back into the agency or organizational structure so that accountability is not seen as a one-way process (Macdonald 1990: 542). The following can aid supervision:

- Drafting an agenda for your supervisor that covers the main points to be discussed.

- Preparing for the supervision session well ahead of time. This involves reading through the notes/minutes of the previous session to ensure that action points have been addressed and attending to any outstanding issues.
- Locating any paperwork that may be needed for the session (e.g. forms to be signed).
- Arriving and leaving punctually.
- Making a note after the supervision session of the issues discussed and action points (this may be a responsibility that your supervisor takes up). These notes need to be counter-signed by your supervisor.
- Setting aside time after the supervision session to reflect on the issues covered. This also allows for any immediate action agreed to be taken forward.

71. Organizational and administrative skills

In a recent survey, it was estimated that social workers spend 26 per cent of work time on direct contact with clients (Baginsky et al. 2010: 2). This means that roughly three-quarters of the remaining time is spent dealing with 'indirect' tasks, such as liaising with other agencies, mobilizing resources, attending meetings and training events, and so forth. The multiple roles we perform, amid competing pressures, call for sound organization and planning skills if we are to be efficient and effective in our work. Too often, we are not.

By establishing good organizational and administrative systems, we are in a position to ensure that we make the best use of whatever time and resources we have available to us. This involves devising a personalized administrative system for planning, organizing, monitoring, and reviewing our work to ensure that we are keeping to agreed action plans, targets, aims, and objectives and that these are consistent with the expectations of the agency in terms of its policy, practices, and administrative structures. The emphasis is on an administrative system that aids effective practice, but this requires discipline as well as appropriate agency administrative systems being in place. It means that in addition to agency recording systems, it is important that we maintain a system that we have developed ourselves. The following list indicates some of the issues that warrant consideration for our work to be supported by robust organizational and administrative systems:

- listing what work needs to be undertaken
- prioritizing tasks and what has to be done when
- calculating the time involved for each task
- planning work and keeping a diary
- liaising/collaborating with others
- recording progress and tasks achieved
- presenting work to an agreed format

- demonstrating good time-keeping skills, in particular:
  - punctuality
  - presenting work on time.

Choosing effective alternative means of communication

A feature of professional competence and accountability is the ability to choose an effective and appropriate mode of communication for the individual involved and the situation encountered. Here I look at the advantages and limitations of letter writing, as well as contact by telephone, mobile phone, text, and email. At the outset, it is important to note the following:

- Communication that is not in person can easily be misinterpreted because we 'read' a great deal from people's facial expression, body language, and other forms of non-verbal communication.
- Electronic devices can sometimes convey an unintended meaning, so it is important to be thoughtful about our choice of words, tone adopted, and the pace of the communication.
- Before deciding to communicate in writing, you need to be clear that the person involved can manage the communication, remembering that:
  - some people find reading and comprehension difficult, perhaps because English is not their first language, they have learning difficulties, or the opportunity to develop literacy skills has been hindered in some way;
  - putting things in writing can be a worrying experience for the sender and receiver, mainly because writing carries a certain amount of weight and authority that can be difficult to challenge or refute. Also, what is written is open to different interpretations.
- On the other hand, written forms of communication can clarify key issues, be referred to several times, kept for future reference, shared with others, and generally accessed and transported with relative ease.

72. Letter writing skills

Emails have tended to replace some letter writing in professional circles but in other areas, such as appointments, letters continue to be used, which makes it important to remember the following:

- agencies can adopt different procedures, such as requiring all letters to be approved and/or signed by a senior member of staff
- it is important to be courteous, clear, concise, and to think carefully about wording and how the letter might be received
- all standard letters need to be altered and read through carefully to ensure they cover the specific situation
- thoughtful letter writing can be a time-consuming activity.

The advantages of letter writing include:

- letters can be received and accessed by the majority of the population with little effort, whereas an email, text, mobile or telephone is reliant on the ability to access and use those technologies
- some people prefer to receive a letter because it constitutes a more formal and definite mode of communication and something tangible that can be shown to other people
- the permanence of a letter, when compared to email, text, or mobile/telephone phone calls, means that the letter can be referred to time and again. This can be important for people whose memory is poor
- letters can be used as evidence in situations of disagreement or conflict.

The disadvantages of letter writing include:

- thoughtful letter writing can be a time-consuming activity, especially as mistakes cannot be easily amended
- the written word carries a certain weight and authority that can be difficult to challenge (however, this can also be an advantage)
- letters are not an instantaneous form of communication – they will invariably take one or two days to arrive (longer depending on the distance travelled), whereas emails, texts, mobile and telephone calls are immediate
- poor handwriting can result in information-loss or miscommunication
- letters are not always backed-up (unless the writer makes a copy) so that if the letter goes astray, the information will be lost.

73. The skilled use of emails

Communicating by email is increasingly popular, particularly among professionals, and has several advantages:

- flexibility – people can be away from their own computer because email systems can be accessed from different locations
- time saving – one email can reach a wide audience and aid communication across different groups
- record-keeping – emails can be stored easily and used to record events
- ecology – emails can save on paper and printing costs.

However, it is important to remember that:

- emails that are 'fired off' at speed – or read quickly – can lead to careless and inaccurate messages being sent and result in confusion and misunderstanding
- even when internet and email facilities are set up and affordable, some people find emails costly
- email systems can become overloaded and crash, particularly if unsolicited 'spam' advertisements are not removed
- some people do not have good typing skills and, therefore, the use of emails can require considerable time and effort.

74. Telephone contact

Many one-to-one conversations take place using the telephone. The phone is a particularly important means of communication at times of crisis. For example, the Samaritans received 5 million phone calls in 2007.

Skilful use of the telephone has several advantages:

- provides an immediate, quick, easy, and accessible means of communication
- offers a degree of control to both the caller and receiver in terms of how long the communication will last
- anonymity when needed, which can leave people feeling less guarded
- textphones are available for people who are deaf or hard of hearing
- provides the opportunity to communicate personal qualities that are evident in personal contact (warmth, care, concern)
- provides a lifeline for people in crisis: phone calls to the police, fire, ambulance services regularly save lives.

The main disadvantages of contact by telephone include:

- not all people in the UK and in other countries have or can afford a telephone
- telephone vetting or diversion systems in professional organizations can block communication
- unanswered phone calls can lead to a range of difficult feelings and fantasies, including frustration, disappointment, and despair, and can prevent events moving forward
- if the communication is highly personal, it could be distressing
- if reactions need to be observed, telephone contact is not appropriate – unless unavoidable
- some people come across badly on the telephone, which can lead to misunderstandings.

75. Mobile phones and text messaging

The use of a mobile phone and text messaging has several advantages:

- immediate access if the mobile phone is on and within range of a receiver (this is particularly important as a protective measure when doing home visits)
- if the mobile phone is switched off or out of range, a voice or text message can be sent and picked up and responded to later on or stored at the recipient's convenience (this messaging resource is valuable when working with people who are vulnerable and who rely on messages that convey a sense of concern, encouragement and hope)
- phone calls to a mobile and their numbers can be noted, stored, and retrieved at will.

The disadvantages of mobile phones and text messaging include:

- immediate access can intrude into people's lives in ways that feel unpredictable and intrusive
- mobile phones are dependent on satellite reception, so calls can be made difficult or even ended by a poor signal
- limited character space in text messages can cause senders to over-abbreviate their words, which can lead to misunderstanding and even offence
- overuse of abbreviated spelling can lead to confusion and the habitual incorrect spelling of certain words.

76. Presentation skills

Whenever you are presenting information, it is important to consider:

- *Who* is your audience and what is their level of knowledge in relation to the subject presented?
- *What* is the purpose of the presentation and your objective (e.g. to inform, persuade)?
- *Where* is the venue (your agency, someone's home, a court of law) and to what extent this location is likely to influence your presentation?
- *When* is the presentation taking place: date, time, and how long it will last?

To present a talk in a skilful way can be an exciting and rewarding experience. The following is a checklist for presenting a talk:

- prepare the room/presentation setting
- prepare any visual aids (e.g. flip charts, pens, overhead projectors, PowerPoint)
- prepare yourself, ensuring that you know your subject, the content of your presentation, and that you feel comfortable with your appearance
- keep strictly to time, rehearse your presentation preferably with a 'critical friend' who is willing to give honest feedback on your performance
- make necessary changes in response to the feedback received
- if you have time, rehearse the presentation again, particularly the beginning and end.

77. Chairing meetings

Chairing a meeting calls for good communication, observation, and listening skills. The following are some brief tips:

- prepare and plan for the meeting, sending out a call for agenda items beforehand

- at the beginning of the meeting:
  - ensure that minutes or a note is being taken of the discussion and/or action points
  - welcome attendees and note apologies for absence
  - run through the minutes of previous meetings and matters arising – include unresolved or on-going issues to the agenda. If the minutes need to have been approved, they may need to be formally 'signed off' by the Chair
  - ask if additional agenda items need to be added and prioritize the list – the last item on the agenda is normally AOB (any other business)
- throughout, attempt to keep attendees interested and involved
- keep to time
- at the end, set the date and time of the next meeting.

78. Coordinating case conferences and reviews

Case conferences and reviews call for excellent communication skills to ensure that:

- the person at the centre of the conference/review, their family, and other key individuals understand the process and implications and events that led to a conference being convened
- the views of the individual(s) in question and other key individuals are represented
- relevant information is gathered, collated, and evaluated from other agencies involved and organized and presented thoughtfully
- all parties are reminded that case conferences can be a daunting experiences for everyone concerned because of information disclosed and the number in attendance; this is particularly true in relation to child protection conferences.

79. Presenting evidence in court

The nervousness that court appearances often generate can seriously interfere with our capacity to communicate effectively, so it is important to take steps to reduce stress by:

- preparing and rehearsing your evidence, and reading through your court report; this is particularly important if you are presenting evidence in a childcare case
- rehearsing how you might answer challenging questions
- ensuring that you communicate with key legal people involved so that you are well briefed about the procedures followed in different court hearings

- ensuring you tell the truth, even if this may not be consistent with the stance adopted within your agency
- ensuring you adhere to the dress code for court, which requires more formal attire.

The following are some general principles to be adhered to when drafting a court report:

- Basic information should be included on the front page, including the name of the court and the case number; the name and date of birth of the subject; the type of application; and the author's name and professional address.
- Clarity and concise use of language will always help the reader.
- Avoid dense pages of text, and use bullet points.
- Remember who the report is for, and make appropriate adjustments to style and vocabulary.
- Consider the structure and length of the report – there may be guidance to follow.
- Include a chronology of events.
- A genogram may be useful in family cases if there is a complex family make-up.
- Avoid jargon – ask a non-interested person to check this out; you may be surprised by how much jargon slips in!
- Be non-discriminatory in the language used.
- Distinguish between facts and opinion.
- Avoid unnecessary repetition within the report of material that is available to the court in other documents.
- Conclusions should flow logically from the body of the report.
- Where more than one option is available to the court, set out and discuss each in turn, and make a realistic recommendation.
- Objectivity is all; avoid over-personalizing your report, although it is inevitable that you will be drawing upon your experience.
- Increasingly there are strict timetables for filing of evidence, including reports. Failure to adhere to timetables invites criticism: if unavoidable it is important to seek court approval.

(Wilson *et al.* 2008: 205)

Note that *tribunals* tend to be less formal but they also require you to be well prepared in ways that are similar to the approach used in court appearances.

80. Using humour

The sensitive and skilled use of humour can be helpful in a range of situations. However, for the most part it is a subject that is rarely covered in social work texts. When used well, humour can help to address issues that may be potentially awkward, anxiety provoking, or embarrassing. It can enable us to introduce uncomfortable issues in ways that are tentative, and to back off if we encounter difficult reactions. Humour can also place the interaction on a more normal, ordinary footing and help us to reveal our humanness:

> Humour is an equalizer. It deflates pomposity. Workers' capacity to laugh at themselves without embarrassment or shame communicates genuineness in the relationship. It introduces a desirable element of informality and spontaneity into an essentially formal encounter.
> (Kadushin and Kadushin 1997: 225)

Some of the best use of humour focuses on all that is ridiculous about life, and the human condition – the 'trials and tribulations of everyday life' (Foot 1997: 263). From this perspective, it is about being playful in situations that allow this kind of light-hearted and good-natured interaction. However, such playfulness is influenced by important social and cultural differences that need to be acknowledged. Without this knowledge and sensitivity, it can sometimes be difficult to tell whether someone is *laughing with* or *laughing at* another person. When used appropriately, humour can lead to a sense of enjoyment and fun, and can also be an energizing experience. Laughter can be particularly energizing, depending on its function. For example, Foot looks at the social functions of laughter and describes several types: humorous laughter, social laughter, ignorance laughter, evasion laughter, apologetic laughter, anxiety laughter, derision laughter, and joyous laughter (Foot 1997: 271–5).

However, humour can backfire when it is used in ways that are not appropriate to the situation or to the individual in question. Some people can confuse a more playful interaction or the use of humour with humiliation and can become defensive if there is the slightest hint that they are being laughed at or ridiculed. This may not indicate that the individual has a poor sense of humour but that he or she has been wounded or humiliated in the past by the use of humour and is sensitive in this area. Situations that we find amusing may not amuse others – and this is particularly true of people who are caught up in these situations. Where we have misread a person's capacity in this way, the best course of action is to apologize. It is, therefore, important that we are thoughtful about our reasons for using humour to ensure that it is being used appropriately. For example, the use of humour and some jokes can sometimes belittle other people's suffering, hardship, or oppression. A more subtle misuse can occur when humour is used as a way to communicate ambivalent or hostile emotions that we are not prepared to own, such as the fact that we do not like or respect the person in question. These forms of communication can be deeply confusing and disarming, and leave a person feeling that they do not really know what is being said and, therefore, how best to respond.

A sense of humour is an important attribute for professionals, and also for service users and carers. However, just as we may use humour in a range of different ways, so too may service users and carers. For example, some people may use humour against themselves, or against others who share their oppression. This may help them to cope with difficult experiences or it may indicate that they have internalized their oppression, and come to believe negative comments about themselves and others who share their oppression. Similarly, some service users and careers may use humour to express prejudicial views about other groups of people, making it difficult for us to know how to react, particularly when our agreement is sought. As professionals it is important that we do not endorse comments that reinforce negative, stereotypical, or oppressive attitudes but instead think of ways to challenge these comments. However, interventions of this kind need to be undertaken carefully if they are to be effective in helping to change people's beliefs and attitudes, and if we are to avoid defensive reactions, and oppressive attitudes becoming entrenched even further. Therefore, it is important to remember that the use of humour can be a very vital aid to communication but only if used with considerable caution, and in ways that are culturally sensitive and appropriate to the situation and individual in question.

In this final chapter, a number of important themes have been covered that are central to professional competence and accountability – features that indicate the integrity and credibility that we bring to our work. The first section looked at more general issues that highlight the important context within which social work is located, with a second section looking at a number of skills that enhance practice effectiveness. My final task is to steer this book to an end.

Concluding comments . . .

In this text, I have demonstrated that social work is a highly skilled activity. To support this view, I have identified 80 skills and interventions. The focus of this book has centred on a *Knowledge and Skills Framework* that I have developed – a *framework* designed to integrate theory and practice in ways that ensure that interventions are based on knowledge, skills, and values. The importance of interventions runs throughout this text because it is in our direct contact with others that we demonstrate what we bring to the encounter, both personally and professionally. Interventions mark a meeting point – a place where two paths meet – and where our task is to work from our *best selves* to begin to understand the situation being presented and what our next step might be. To work from our *best selves* is to work from a desire to do well – a desire to meet our own and others' expectations in the hope that our efforts will be worthwhile. What we bring to this encounter is the knowledge, skills, and values we have acquired – attributes that we communicate in a variety of different ways – in verbal and non-verbal forms of communications, in the written word, and in the actions we undertake. What we gain from this encounter is the opportunity it provides for us to grow and to be changed by the experience of 'meeting' another human being. It is this – and the benefits that others reap from our best efforts – that is our ultimate reward.

To be able to work from our *best selves*, it is important that we nurture the attributes we bring by keeping abreast of developments and by regularly updating our knowledge and skills. How we present ourselves communicates who we are, both as individuals and as a profession. It involves acknowledging – and having acknowledged – the contribution we make in a given situation. This emphasis is focused on the 'social' aspects of social work – the fact that people are social beings whose lives are mediated through their relationship with themselves, others, and the world around them. This makes it important for people to be understood in their social context and it is the focus placed on this context – and the importance given to addressing the adversity and discrimination experienced by the people we work among – that makes social work's contribution unique within health and welfare settings. If we take the Benchmark Statement for Social Work as an example, no other profession is required to engage in 'promoting social justice and combating processes that lead to discrimination, marginalisation and social exclusion' (QAA 2008: 7).

The extent to which social work is in a position to meet these requirements is hampered by structural and political factors that have been described in detail in this text. The way forward involves social work and social workers, in collaboration with service users, carers, and others, being able to influence events, particularly legislative and policy agendas, and being in a position to shape the future of social work. In the present climate, this constitutes a formidable task but one that I consider to be the only elegant option.

APPENDICES

APPENDIX 1

Behaviourist approaches

Description/definition

Behaviourist approaches focus on 'how behaviours are acquired and how they are maintained (or lost)' (Howe 2009: 149). They emphasize the importance of observable, testable, measurable, reproducible, and objective responses and behaviours, with a limited focus on analysing the underlying conflicts or causes: 'we are as we behave'. Thus, feelings of distress or neurosis come about through *faulty conditioning* and what needs to be changed, therefore, is this *maladaptive behaviour*. Early writers such as Pavlov (1927), Skinner (1938), and Watson (1970), and later ones such as Bandura (1977), stressed the importance of *social learning theory*: that behaviours are learned and, therefore, can be unlearned. As a therapy, it is considered to be particularly effective in relation to fears and phobias, as well as for obsessional states and compulsive behaviours.

There are different types of behaviourism, including *radical behaviourism*, which 'is the philosophy related to applied behaviour analysis', the latter involving 'the application of findings from the experimental analysis of behaviour to concerns of social importance' (Gambrill 1995: 48). In relation to social work, some influential writers in this field originally focused solely on the importance of behavioural approaches, such as Hudson and Macdonald (1986) and Sheldon (1982). However, in later publications, a cognitive-behavioural approach has been promoted (Macdonald 2007; Sheldon 1995) but with a more behavioural than cognitive orientation, hence their inclusion in this section. Gambrill (1995) succinctly highlights the clarity of a behaviourist approach.

Gambrill's 'indicators of behavioural practice'

A. What will be found
   1. A focus on altering complaints of concern to clients and significant others

2. Translation of complaints into specific behaviors (including thoughts and feelings) that if altered would remove complaints
3. Reliance on basic behavioral principles and related learning theory to guide assessment and intervention
4. Descriptive analysis of problems and related circumstances based on observation (i.e. clear description of problem-related behaviors and related setting events, antecedents, and consequences)
5. Functional analysis: identification of factors that influence problem-related behaviors by rearranging environmental factors and observing the effects
6. Identification of client assets that can be put to good use in attaining desired outcomes
7. Involvement of significant others
8. Selection of intervention programs based on what research suggests is effective and what clients find acceptable
9. Ongoing evaluation of progress using both subjective and objective measures; comparison of data gathered during intervention with baseline data when feasible
10. Clear description of assessment, intervention, and evaluation methods
11. A concern for social validity (i.e. outcomes attained are valued by clients and significant others; procedures used are acceptable to clients)
12. Inclusion of procedures designed to enhance generalization and maintenance of positive gains.
B. What will not be found
1. Appeals to thoughts or feelings as sole causes of behavior
2. Appeals to personality dispositions as sole causes of behavior
3. Use of uninformative diagnostic labels (they provide neither information about problem-related causes nor guidelines for selecting intervention plans)
4. Reliance on self-report alone for assessment, evaluation, or both
5. Vague statements of outcome, problems, or progress indicators
6. Claims of success based on questionable criteria such as testimonials, and anecdotal experience.

(Gambrill 1995: 462)

Key terms

Behaviourist approaches primarily involve *behaviour modification techniques*, that is, a method of assessing and altering behaviour based on the methods of applied behaviour analysis. Many techniques are used in this process, although how these techniques are used can differ greatly from therapist to therapist, such as the importance assigned to the therapeutic relationship. Some of the key concepts used in behavioural approaches/therapy include: *classical conditioning, operant conditioning (OC), conditioned stimulus (CS), conditioned response (CR), unconditioned stimulus (US), unconditioned response (UR)*. Some of the main behavioural techniques used include: assertiveness training, aversion therapy/conditioning, extinction, modelling, reinforcement, social skills training, and systematic desensitization. For a fuller account of the meaning and use of these terms, see Sheldon (1995).

Advantages

* Behavioural techniques are relatively easy to understand, to learn, and to use effectively and can be used alongside other interventions and practice approaches.
* Some techniques have proved to be very successful, such as social skills or assertiveness training, and adaptable across different problems, groups of people, and settings.
* Its systematic approach and use of techniques, plus the importance given to baseline data focusing on target behaviours, means that its effectiveness can be demonstrated empirically.
* Behaviourist approaches and techniques are transferable and widely used in a range of multi-disciplinary contexts, such as health and education, making it possible for disciplines to work from a shared conceptual framework.

Limitations

* The terminology used can be experienced as mechanistic and uncaring, and unappealing as a therapy and as a practice approach.
* It is a directive approach with relatively high expectations in terms of the commitment and motivation required of service users.
* Its focus on modifying certain behaviours, and not underlying causes, can mean that more complex and intractable problems are not addressed.
* The research findings tend to be based on discrete problems. Social factors that contribute to certain types of problem behaviour tend to be ignored or considered beyond the remit of this approach.

Further reading

Bandura, A. (1977) *Social Learning Theory*. Englewood Cliffs, NJ: Prentice-Hall.

Gambrill, E.D. (1985) Behavioral approach, in J.B. Turner (ed.) *Encyclopedia of Social Work*, 18th edn., Vol. 1. Washington, DC: National Association of Social Workers.

Gambrill, E.D. (1995) Behavioural theory, in R.L. Edwards (ed.) *Encyclopedia of Social Work*, 19th edn., Vol. 1. Washington, DC: National Association of Social Workers.

Howe, D. (2008b) *The Emotionally Intelligent Social Worker*. Basingstoke: Palgrave Macmillan.

Hudson, B.L. and MacDonald, G. (1986) *Behavioural Social Work: An Introduction*. London: Macmillan.

Macdonald, G. (2007) Cognitive behavioural social work, in J. Lishman (ed.) *Handbook for Practice Learning in Social Work and Social Care*, 2nd edn. London: Jessica Kingsley.

Pavlov, I.P. (1927) *Conditional Reflexes*. London: Oxford University Press.

Sheldon, B. (1982) *Behaviour Modification: Theory, Practice and Philosophy*. London: Tavistock.

Sheldon, B. (1995) *Cognitive-behavioural Therapy: Research, Practice and Philosophy*. London: Routledge.

Skinner, B.F. (1938) *The Behavior of Organisms: An Experimental Analysis*. New York: Appleton-Century-Crofts.

Skinner, B.F. (1974) *About Behaviourism*. London: Jonathan Cape.

Watson, J.B. (1970) *Behaviourism*. New York: Norton.

APPENDIX 2

Cognitive approaches

Description/definition

Alfred Adler is said to have been the major influence in the development of cognitive therapeutic approaches. These include different therapies, such as reality therapy, existential social work, cognitive analytic therapy, Beck's 'cognitive therapy', and Ellis's rational emotive behaviour therapy. 'Whereas behaviour therapy assumes that faulty learning is at the core of problem behaviours and emotions, cognitive therapies assume that the culprit is *faulty thinking*' (Hockenbury and Hockenbury 2002: 636). Cognitive therapies argue that human emotions and behaviours are largely formed by their cognitive processes, that is, what people think, imagine, or believe. It is their interpretation of specific events that can lead to difficulties: cognitive approaches work to help people to change their cognitive thought and feeling processes. The extent to which a cognitive element is more a feature than behavioural aspects is highly variable, which means that:

> ... the lines separating cognitive, cognitive-behavioural, and some be-haviour therapies are blurring ... contemporary behaviour therapy is progressively becoming more cognitive, and practically every cognitive therapy incorporates elements of behaviour therapy.
> (Prochaska and Norcross 2003: 334)

In 1993, Ellis added the word 'behaviour' to rational emotive therapy be-cause he believed that behaviour was receiving too little focus.

Key terms and techniques of cognitive approaches

Cognitions describe the 'mental activities involved in acquiring, retaining, and using knowledge' (Hockenbury and Hockenbury 2002: 280). Thus cog-nitive therapies attempt to identify and challenge specific instances and general patterns of distorted thinking or unrealistic beliefs. In this task, different terms are used to describe irrational thoughts, feelings, and beliefs, such as *cognitive dissonance*, *cognitive dysfunction*, and *cognitive map*, and a range of techniques are adopted, such as *cognitive restructuring*, where the focus is to encourage individuals to think differently about situations they find troubling. Albert Ellis (1977), Ellis *et al.* (1997), and Aaron Beck (1976) are profoundly influential in this field, but with differences: 'Whereas Ellis would actively dispute the rationality of holding an irrational belief, Beck would simply question the client', often using Socratic questions (Howe 2009: 67).

Ronen (2008: 194–5) cites seven basic features of cognitive therapy:

- Therapy as a meaning-making process that helps the client to develop new, and often more complex, meaning systems of what they define as problematic areas.
- Systematic and goal-directed therapy.
- Focusing on practising and experiencing elements rather than on 'talk therapy'.
- Collaboration between client and therapist.
- Focusing on the client rather than on the problem.
- Facilitating change processes by the therapist.
- Empowerment and development of the client's independent functioning.

Ellis's ABCDE theory of emotions

A central element of rational emotive behaviour therapy, and one that is often cited as a key technique of cognitive-behavioural approaches, is Ellis's ABCDE theory of emotions. Some writers tend to focus on the ABC section only but Ellis considers all stages to be important to avoid 'backsliding' or the possibility of relapse (Ellis *et al.* 1997: 67):

A *Activating* event or situation

(Case example: Mr. Radley's wife died suddenly)

B *Beliefs* (self-defeating beliefs)

iB – irrational belief (*Had I called the doctor earlier, my wife would not have died. It's all my fault*)

C *Consequences* (the emotional/behavioural consequences of these thoughts, feelings, beliefs)

iC – irrational emotional/behavioural consequence (*I deserve to suffer for what I have done. I don't deserve to be helped*)

D *Disputation*

Through exploring the implicit thoughts and dysfunctional emotions and/or behaviours with the guidance of the practitioner, the service user or carer is taught to replace irrational beliefs (iB) with rational beliefs (rB)

rB – rational belief (*I don't have the power to give life to another human being, or to take life away*)

E *Evaluation* **(new effective approach to the problem)**

The process of disputation **(D)** should produce an evaluation of the activating **(A)** event or situation and the emotional/behavioural consequences **(C)** that this event produced

Full sequence A → B → C → D → E

Advantages

- Cognitive approaches tend to be time-limited (1–20 weeks), relatively inexpensive, and applicable across a range of different emotional problems.
- The directive, active, focused, and 'no-nonsense' nature of the approaches adopted makes it possible to address distorted perceptions or unrealistic beliefs within a short time. The use of homework can place the 'client' at the centre of the recovery process.
- Beck's work has been shown to be particularly effective in the field of depression. His instruments, such as the Beck Depression Inventory (Beck and Steer 1987) and Beck Anxiety Inventory, are widely used in health contexts.
- Ellis's ABCDE intervention can be taught and learned easily and can be adapted to different situations and contexts.

Limitations

- This highly individualized approach is not appropriate for some people or situations. Some irrational emotions may be an appropriate response to events such as bereavement, violent attacks, or adversity caused by discrimination and oppression.
- The language used within cognitive therapies, such as distorted cognitions, dysfunctional, irrational, and immature behaviour, can be off-putting both to service users and to practitioners.
- Individuals who are more articulate and in touch with their thoughts, feelings, and beliefs are likely to be able to use this approach more effectively.

Work with more complex or enduring emotional problems, such as severe depression or schizophrenia, has been found to be less successful.

• Although Ellis is said to have published hundreds of articles, there is very limited data on outcome studies (Prochaska and Norcross 2003: 364). Beck's approach has more research data but limited analysis on how people develop 'distorted cognitions'.

Further reading

Beck, A. (1976) *Cognitive Therapy and the Emotional Disorders*. New York: International University Press.

Beck, A. and Steer, R. (1987) *Beck Depression Inventory: Manual*. San Antonio, TX: Psychological Corporation.

Ellis, A. (1977) The basic clinical theory of rational-emotive therapy, in A.A. Ellis and R. Greiger (eds.) *Handbook of Rational-Emotive Therapy*, Vol. 1. New York: Springer.

Ellis, A., Gordon, J., Neenan, M. and Palmer, S. (1997) *Stress Counselling: A Rational Emotive Behaviour Approach*. London: Cassell.

Hockenbury, D.H. and Hockenbury, S.E. (2002) *Psychology*, 3rd edn. New York: Worth Publishers.

Prochaska, J.O. and Norcross, J.C. (2003) *Systems of Psychotherapy: A Transtheoretical Analysis*. Pacific Grove, CA: Brooks/Cole.

Ronen, T. (2008) Cognitive-behavioural therapy, in M. Davies (ed.) *The Blackwell Companion to Social Work*, 3rd edn. Oxford: Blackwell Publishing.

APPENDIX 3

Crisis intervention

Description/definition

For understandable reasons, crisis intervention is often confused with crises that require an immediate response. This means that its distinct theoretical and practice features are often misrepresented. Also, this confusion is compounded because there are very few examples of the use of crisis intervention in UK social work today. However, similar, intense forms of support continue to be developed, such as assertive outreach used in the field of mental health (McCulloch 2000; Ryan and Morgan 2004). In the USA, crisis intervention is used with older people with dementia, people who are bereaved, terminally ill, or suicidal, in the aftermath of a disaster, and in cases involving domestic violence (Roberts 2005). Also, as a time-limited approach, it shares some similarities with brief therapy and other types of focused approaches. However, these do not share the same theoretical framework, a feature that distinguishes crisis intervention as a practice approach.

Crises can be conceptualized in different ways and are sometimes linked to the concept of stress. In western culture, the term is often used to suggest a negative or fraught experience, but in different cultures, a *crisis* can be seen as:

- a hazardous event (UK)
- decision-making (Greece)
- danger and opportunity (Chinese), represented in two Chinese characters, *Wei* and *Chi*.

Caplan (1964), Parad (1965), and Rapoport (1967) led the development of crisis intervention in the USA. A crisis is defined as a 'breakdown of *homeostasis* or psychological equilibrium' (O'Hagan 2000: 79), meaning that for a time an individual is thrown into 'an upset in a steady state' (Rapoport 1967), and unable to benefit from their normal methods of coping. 'What happens in a crisis is that our habitual strengths and ways of coping do not work; we fail to adjust either because the situation is new to us, or it has not been anticipated, or a series of events become too overwhelming' (Coulshed and Orme 2006: 134). Crises do not have to be urgent situations: an admission to hospital could lead to a crisis. Hence the importance of recognizing how different people react to external events and crises.

Key concepts

Caplan (1964) described a three-stage model, based on the view that people act as self-regulating systems to try to maintain an internal state of equilibrium. These stages of a crisis are:

- *Impact* – this stage is characterized by disbelief and unreality, where the sense of equilibrium feels threatened or lost. 'I can't take it in … this can't be happening to me'.
- *Recoil* – attempting to restore the equilibrium but being unable to do so, leaving the individual physically or psychologically exhausted, defeated and showing signs of stress, such as simultaneous feelings of anger and guilt.
- *Adjustment/adaptation* or *breakdown* – where the individual begins to move towards a higher level of functioning. If the adjustment is successful, the progress made can often be detected within 4–6 weeks.

The approach is based on the perspective that crises are time-limited and usually last no longer than 6 weeks. It draws from psychoanalytic theory, particularly ego psychology, and emphasizes that people's capacity to deal with problems – to be able to return to a steady state – is based on three factors:

- people's internal psychological strengths and weaknesses (ego strength)
- the nature of the problem faced
- the quality of help provided.

Advantages

- As a time-limited (1–6 weeks) and focused approach, it can be considered highly effective in terms of effort and resources.
- It can be adapted to practice in a number of different contexts. People who are helped and supported to develop new adaptive ways of coping can sometimes function at a higher level, such as people who work through bereavement.
- Its sound theoretical and practice framework provides an analysis of both internal and external factors, providing a way to understand the link between internal crises and external changes.

- It is relevant and useful across a range of short-term crises, particularly experiences of bereavement and loss, depression, traumatic experiences such as accidents, and other situations where people feel 'thrown' and unable to cope.

Limitations

- The most serious and common limitation is the fact that the term *crisis intervention* is too often used incorrectly, mainly because the words *crisis* and *intervention* are regularly used in social work to denote the need to intervene immediately and purposefully in response to a general emergency or catastrophe of some kind. A response to a crisis is not *crisis intervention*.
- Specific training is required for this approach to be used effectively. Such training is not widely available in the UK.
- It may not be possible, because of limited resources, funding, or time, to assemble all the elements necessary for positive change to occur. As a result, unless fundamental changes are introduced, this approach will not be seen as a viable option, particularly in funded statutory social work contexts.
- It can involve workers being highly intrusive and directive, which can raise important ethical issues. This makes it essential to ensure that service users' rights and choices remain at the centre of the decision-making process.

Further reading

Caplan, G. (1964) *Principles of Preventative Psychiatry*. New York: Basic Books.

Coulshed, V. and Orme, J. (2006) *Social Work Practice: An Introduction*, 4th edn. Basingstoke: Macmillan/BASW.

McCulloch, A. (2000) Assertive outreach, in M. Davies (ed.) *Blackwell Encyclopaedia of Social Work*. Oxford: Oxford University Press.

O'Hagan, K. (2000) Crisis intervention, in M. Davies (ed.) *Blackwell Encyclopaedia of Social Work*. Oxford: Oxford University Press.

Parad, H.J. (1965) *Crisis Intervention: Selected Readings*. New York: Family Service Association of America.

Rapoport, L. (1967) Crisis-orientated short term casework, *Social Services Review*, 41: 31–44.

Roberts, A.R. (1990) *Crisis Intervention Handbook: Assessment, Treatment and Research*. Belmont, CA: Wadsworth.

Roberts, A.R. (ed.) (2005) *Crisis Intervention Handbook: Assessment, Treatment and Research*, 3rd edn. Oxford: Oxford University Press.

Ryan, P. and Morgan, S. (2004) *Assertive Outreach: A Strengths Approach to Policy and Practice*. Edinburgh: Churchill Livingstone.

APPENDIX 4

Ecological approach in

social work

Description/definition

An ecological perspective
An orientation in social work and other professions that emphasizes understanding people and their environment and the nature of their transactions.

(Barker 2003: 136)

Key points

An ecological approach draws heavily on systems theory, a framework that analyses the complex reciprocal connections and interrelationships that exist between elements that make up the whole *system*, and other mutually influencing factors in the social setting and wider environment, known as the *subsystems*. Munro highlights the importance of systems theory in social work:

Systems theory
A system is a collection of parts (or subsystems) that interact to accomplish an overall goal. Systems have inputs, processes, outputs and outcomes, with ongoing feedback among these various parts. If one part of the system is removed, the nature of the system is changed. Complex systems, such as social systems, comprise numerous subsystems as well. These subsystems are arranged in hierarchies and integrated to accomplish the overall goal of the overall system. Each subsystem has its own boundaries of sorts and includes various inputs, processes, outputs and outcomes geared to accomplish an overall goal for the subsystem.

(Munro 2010a: 1137)

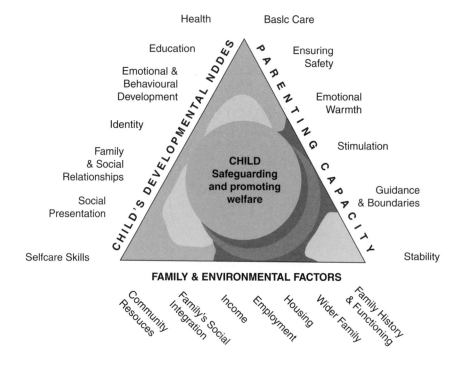

Figure A1 Framework for the Assessment of Children in Need and their Families

The ecological model proposed by Bronfenbrenner (1979) has been highly influential in the field of human development. For example, his model is a central feature of the *Framework for the Assessment of Children in Need and their Families* (Department of Health 2000), a framework that is used in many countries outside the UK because of the focus placed on analysing both formal and informal sources of support that may be available to the child, family, group, or community (see Figure A1). Within this context, an ecological approach is influential in the area of child abuse, where social support networks indicate a protective factor (Garbarino and Kostelny 1992).

The work of Bronfenbrenner is also central to the work of Germain and Gitterman in their conceptualization of a 'life model' approach in social work practice, who state: 'Ecological thinking is less concerned with cause and more concerned with the consequences of exchanges between A and B, and how to help modify maladaptive exchanges' (Germain and Gitterman 1995: 817). Their 'life model' approach focuses on:

1. people's strengths, their innate push toward health, continued growth, and release of potential;

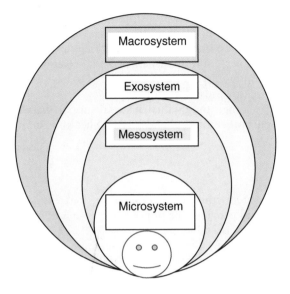

Figure A2   Bronfenbrenner's ecological model

2. modification of the environment, as needed, so that they sustain and promote well-being to the maximum degree possible; and
3. raising the level of person-environment fit for individuals, families, groups and communities.

(Germain and Gitterman 1995: 817)

Other writers in this field emphasize the radical potential of this perspective and the links that can be made between structural disadvantage and life chances (Jack 2011). This is a focus that is consistent with practice perspectives and interventions that embrace an anti-oppressive and empowerment perspective.

Key concepts (see Figure A2)

- *Collective efficacy* – seen as a measure of social capital. High levels of unemployment and poverty can undermine collective efficacy.
- *Exosystems* – settings that do not directly influence individual development yet play a part, such as parental income.
- *Macrosystems* – all other systems, such as the cultural and societal context or environment.
- *Mesosystems* – interactions between microsystems, where interactions take place that influence individual development.
- *Microsystems* – the context that individuals create around them.

- *Social capital* – includes the relationships and exchanges between all members of a neighbourhood, community, or a society. The level of social capital links to the notion of *human capital*, which describes the knowledge, skills, resourcefulness, and quality of personal relationships and connections within a community. Both are considered to have a significant impact on individual health and behaviour.
- *Social support* – range and quality of social support networks or systems that have important emotional and physical health benefits.

Advantages

- It is built on systems theory and, therefore, locates individuals in their wider context and provides the opportunity to incorporate a sociological perspective into an assessment.
- Its broader social and cultural analysis enables us to see the impact of government policy on everyday life – an important perspective for people living in poverty or with adversity.
- It resists the temptation to individualize problems and solutions, and enables us to see the complex way that different factors interweave.
- It encourages the development of an equal, non-authoritarian relationship where both service user and social worker can work together to establish a significant and meaningful relationship.

Limitations

- Complex familial, social, cultural, and environmental factors, and their interconnections, can be difficult to identify and to unravel, making it difficult to know where to intervene – if at all.
- Different perspectives adopted, which can range from support for radical change to those designed to reinforce the status quo, can lead to uncertainty.
- Most social workers have not had the training required to apply this perspective. In particular, most social workers are not trained – or encouraged – to develop the skills necessary to intervene effectively in ways that influence wider social factors and organizational and political systems.
- Unless additional resources are made available, social workers attempting to apply this perspective can be set up to fail (Jack and Gill 2003).

Further reading

Barker, R.L. (2003) *The Social Work Dictionary*, 5th edn. Silver Spring, MD: NASW Press.

Bronfenbrenner, U. (1979) *The Ecology of Human Development: Experiments by Nature and Design*. Cambridge, MA: Harvard University Press.

Department of Health (DH) (2000) *Framework for the Assessment of Children in Need and their Families*. London: Department of Health.

Garbarino, J. and Kostelny, K. (1992) Child maltreatment as a community problem, *Child Abuse and Neglect*, 16: 455–64.

Germain, C.B. and Gitterman, A. (1995) *Ecological perspective*, in R.L. Edwards (ed.) *Encyclopedia of Social Work*, 19th edn., Vol. 1. Washington, DC: National Association of Social Workers.

Jack, G. (2011) Ecological perspective, in M. Gray, J. Midgley and S. Webb (eds.) *Social Work Handbook*. London: Sage.

Jack, G. and Gill, O. (2003) *The Missing Side of the Triangle: Assessing the Importance of Family and Environmental Factors in the Lives of Children*. Ilford: Barnardo's.

Munro, E. (2010a) Learning to reduce risk in child protection, *British Journal of Social Work*, 40: 1135–51.

APPENDIX 5

Feminist perspectives in

social work

Description/definition

... feminist social work [is] a form of social work practice which
takes gendered inequality and its elimination as the starting point for
working with women, whether as individuals, in groups or within
organisations, and seeks to promote women's well-being as women
define it.

(Dominelli 2008: 111)

Focus of feminist social work

Social work is very much a women's issue. The majority of social workers
are women, who are often working with female clients and also with women
employed in the sphere of health and social care. Feminist analysis attempts
to define – and to redefine – women's roles and responsibilities and how
oppression and disadvantage impact on women as service users, carers, and
practitioners. This is sometimes called a *woman-centred practice* (Orme
2009: 203), where the 'commonalities' that women share as women are
incorporated 'as visible parts of our practice' (Hamner and Statham 1999:
21). This perspective suggests that because men lack the experience of being
a woman, they can develop a 'gender perspective' but not a 'woman-centred
perspective' (Hamner and Statham 1999: 21). This is an important, complex,
and controversial issue.

The feminist phrase, *the personal is political*, has been enormously influential worldwide and has enabled women, through the process of *consciousness raising*, to analyse their experiences of inequality and oppression and to politicize these experiences in campaigns designed to challenge

government policy and patriarchal ideology (Hartman 1981; White 2006). It was feminists who first threw light on sexual abuse, domestic violence, rape, and other important issues once thought to belong to the private sphere of the family and beyond public scrutiny (Hester *et al.* 2006). Different schools of thought exist, but a feminist perspective usually embraces certain principles:

1. A recognition of the inequalities that exist between men and women, and a belief that patriarchal assumptions inhibit women's opportunities and life chances.
2. A commitment to explore ways to circumvent – or overcome – sexist barriers that assail women's sense of confidence, self-esteem, and status. These barriers may be kept in place by *internalized oppression*, that is, by the way that women have come to accept negative beliefs about themselves and other women.
3. An emphasis on women putting themselves – and their interests, needs, and concerns – at the centre of their thinking and decision-making. This may involve redefining the roles they have been ascribed, or adopted, and supporting women in ways that enable them to find their voice, personal power, and autonomy.
4. A way of working that acknowledges power and status differences (Wise 1995: 113) yet works to establish egalitarian, honest, and open relationships between female social workers and service users/carers.
5. A perspective that links 'personal' and 'political' issues in ways that enhance awareness and that seek collective solutions to individual problems, based on a recognition of women's contribution and the diversity of women's experience, knowledge, and strengths.

Advantages

- Feminism draws on a rich theoretical framework that is capable of providing in-depth analyses of women's experiences, both within and outside social work. It can also analyse the impact of sexism on men and boys and apply feminist principles in relation to work with men.
- Feminism has had a profound impact on social work. The most striking example is evident in the area of domestic/family violence where feminist activists and researchers have indicated the scale of women's suffering. In statistics available from Women's Aid (UK):
  - on average, two women a week are killed by a current or former male partner
  - one in four women will be a victim of domestic violence in their lifetime
  - one incident of domestic violence is reported to the police every minute
  - over a third of women will experience violence on a number of occasions within the same year (Office for National Statistics 2010: 125).

• Linking 'the personal and the political' is an accessible perspective, and one that speaks to the experiences of women from different disadvantaged groups. Feminism has shown that oppressed people, in this case women, can change the course of history through collective action.
• A feminist analysis can mean that areas of women's lives that may have been previously ignored can be brought into the frame and included as a focus of the work to be undertaken, such as inequalities in income (equal pay), housing provision, employment, and educational opportunities.

Limitations

• Most women experience additional oppressions, such as discrimination in relation to class, race, age, disabilities, sexual orientation, culture, and religious beliefs. These additional oppressions are not always given sufficient weight.
• Applying a feminist perspective is not easy (Trevithick 1998; Wise 1995). Many of the same inequalities and barriers that exist for women as service users and carers also exist for feminist practitioners. Like other organizations, the hierarchy of social work is male dominated and located within patriarchal assumptions (Dominelli 2002: 43).
• There is no clear or agreed position among feminists about the negative impact of sexism on men and male children. Some argue that feminism should embrace the whole of humanity.
• Some women (and men) see feminism as divisive and do not want to explore differences between men and women, or issues of inequality and discrimination.

Further reading

Dominelli, L. (1997) *Sociology for Social Work*. Basingstoke: Macmillan.
Dominelli, L. (2002) *Feminist Social Work: Theory and Practice*. Basingstoke: Palgrave.
Dominelli, L. (2008) Feminist theory, in M. Davis (ed.) *The Blackwell Companion to Social Work*, 3rd edn. Oxford: Blackwell Publishing.
Hamner, J. and Statham, D. (1999) *Women and Social Work: Towards a Woman-Centred Practice*, 2nd edn. Basingstoke: Macmillan/BASW.
Hartman, H. (1981) The unhappy marriage of Marxism and feminism: towards a more progressive union, in L. Sargent (ed.) *Women and Revolution*. Boston, MA: South End.
Hester, M., Pearson, C., Harwin, N. and Abrahams, H. (2006) *Making an Impact – Children and Domestic Violence: A Reader*, 2nd edn. London: Jessica Kingsley.

Orme, J. (2009) Feminist social work, in R. Adams, L. Dominelli and M. Payne (eds.) *Critical Practice in Social Work*, 2nd edn. Basingstoke: Palgrave Macmillan.

Trevithick, P. (1998) Psychotherapy and working class women, in I.B. Seu and M.C. Heenan (eds.) *Feminism and Psychotherapy: Reflections on Contemporary Theories and Practices*. London: Sage.

White, V. (2006) *The State of Feminist Social Work*. London: Routledge.

Wise, S. (1995) Feminist ethics in practice, in R. Hugman and D. Smith (eds.) *Ethical Issues in Social Work*. London: Routledge.

APPENDIX 6

Motivational interviewing

Miller and Rollnick (2002: 25) define motivational interviewing as 'a client-centred, directive method for enhancing intrinsic motivation to change by exploring and resolving ambivalence'. One of the most important interventions to emerge in recent years, motivational interviewing was developed by William Miller in the USA, who began his career as a therapist using behavioural, self-control techniques with 'problem drinkers'. He developed this approach when his work and research revealed greater success when adopting this method. It is an approach that is 'built on a fundamental objection to the traditional disease-oriented model of motivation' (Barber 2002: 92) in relation to addictive behaviour. A disease model dominates many medical treatments and can also be found in the work of organizations such as Alcoholics Anonymous: 'one does not become an alcoholic, one is born an alcoholic'. This view sees alcoholism is an incurable, irreversible condition, where change is more likely to happen when people's lives have reached 'rock bottom' – which is said to be the point at which denial and resistance break down. A different but related interpretation states that addiction indicates a weak or 'deficient personality'. These explanations are wholly inadequate not least because people who are struggling with a 'physiological and psychological dependence on a behaviour or substance' (Barker 2003: 7) can be found to respond to the right kind of help.

Motivational interviewing stands in opposition to the *disease* or *deficiency* model, and instead offers 'a client-centred and empathic counselling style' (Miller and Rollnick 2002: 37) that incorporates some features of psychosocial and cognitive-behavioural approaches within its framework. Miller describes five features of this approach. First, it is 'an evolution of the client-centred approach' put forward by Carl Rogers; second, it differs from Rogers' work because it is 'consciously directive'; third, it is viewed as a 'method of communicating rather than a set of techniques'; fourth, 'the focus of motivational interviewing is on eliciting the person's intrinsic motivation for change'; and fifth, 'the method focuses on exploring and resolving ambivalence as a key in eliciting change' (Miller and Rollnick 2002: 25–6).

In particular, motivational interviewing is based on four general principles:

- *Express empathy* – this stresses the underlying principle of a client-centred approach, which is that acceptance facilitates change. It is therefore important to understand where the service user is coming from and to do this by 'skilful reflective listening' (Miller and Rollnick 2002: 37). This perspective sees ambivalence – that is, the reluctance to change – as normal.
- *Develop discrepancy* – this principle departs from a rigorous use of a client-centred approach, which is non-directive, because motivational interviewing is directive. Its intention is to help resolve ambivalence so that change can occur. This principle stresses that it is the service user, and not the practitioner, who needs to present the argument for change and that change becomes possible when the service user recognizes a discrepancy between what is actually happening and what the person wants to happen.
- *Roll with resistance* – this principle stresses that the 'Resistance that a person offers can be turned or reframed slightly to create a new momentum' (Miller and Rollnick 2002: 40). Practitioners should avoid persuasion or the desire to highlight the benefits that change could bring. Instead, the emphasis is on drawing out a service user's resistance and encouraging them to find their own answers and solutions.
- *Support self-efficacy* – 'the concept of *self-efficacy* . . . refers to a person's belief in his or her ability to carry out and succeed with a specific task. Self-efficacy is a key element in motivation to change and is a reasonably good predictor of treatment outcome' (Miller and Rollnick 2002: 40). This principle emphasizes the importance of faith and hope as central elements in the process of change, including the practitioner's belief that change is possible. It is the individual in question who is responsible for initiating and implementing the changes that they wish to embrace.

Advantages

- It deliberately avoids labelling or stereotyping service users, or using 'enlightenment, confrontation, punishment' to change behaviour. In the area of substance abuse, Miller and Rollnick (2002: 14) notes that 'knowledge-focused education and insight-oriented persuasion have been spectacularly unsuccessful in changing substance abuse'.
- It places responsibility for change with the service user but considerable focus is also placed on the skills and attributes of the practitioner – 'often one of the strongest predictors of client motivation (retention, adherence,

behaviour change) is the counsellor to who they were assigned' (Miller 2006: 137).
• Wider social issues are recognized as important: 'Environmental considerations, developmental transitions, associated problems, access to resources, and resolution of associated problems seem particularly important for promoting or hindering self-change' (DiClemente 2006: 95).
• As an approach, motivational interviewing can be adapted for use with a range of different problems involving denial and resistance and its success is supported by research (Rollnick *et al.* 2008).

Limitations

• Motivational interviewing is sometimes offered in ways that do not adhere to the principles and specific approach it embodies. Additional training is needed in its effective use, plus access to ongoing supervision. However, further research is needed to identify its specific benefits for social work (Forrester *et al.* 2007).
• It can be difficult to work with ambivalence and resistance in a working environment that does not support and endorse this approach.
• It can be hard to avoid falling into a number of 'traps', such as taking sides, labelling, or blaming service users, adopting the role of expert, or steering the focus in a direction that is different from the one presented by the service user (Miller and Rollnick 2002: 57–63).
• It is possible to underestimate the signs of ambivalence, which can lead practitioners to be too prescriptive or to offer insufficient direction when this is required (Miller and Rollnick 2002: 128–9).

Further reading

Barber, J.G. (2002) *Social Work with Addictions*, 2nd edn. Basingstoke: Palgrave Macmillan.
Barker, R.L. (2003) *The Social Work Dictionary*, 5th edn. Silver Spring, MD: NASW Press.
DiClemente, C.C. (2006) Natural change and the troublesome use of substances, in W.R. Miller and K.M. Carroll (eds.) *Rethinking Substance Abuse: What the Science Shows, and What We Should Do About it*. London: Guilford Press.
Forrester, D., McCambridge, J., Waissbein, C., Emlyn-Jones, R. and Rollnick, S. (2008) Child risk and parental resistance: can *motivational interviewing* improve the practice of child and family social workers in working with parental alcohol misuse, *British Journal of Social Work*, 38: 1302–19.

Miller, W.R. (2006) Motivational factors in addictive behaviours, in W.R. Miller and K.M. Carroll (eds.) *Rethinking Substance Abuse: What the Science Shows, and What We Should Do About it*. London: Guilford Press.

Miller, W.R. and Rollnick, S. (2002) *Motivational Interviewing: Preparing People for Change*, 2nd edn. London: Guilford Press.

APPENDIX 7

Person-centred approaches

Considerable confusion exists in social work about the difference between a more general 'client-centred' perspective and Rogers' client-centred approach. To address this confusion, the term *person-centred* approach is used in this text to describe the work of Carl Rogers.

Description/definition

A person-centred approach is usually attributed to the work of Carl Rogers. It was developed for counselling, rather than social work, where it is best used (Thorne 2002: 175). Rogers based his work on the humanist belief that human beings have an innate motivation to grow, develop, and change, that is, to self-actualize (see Maslow's Triangle in Chapter 5):

> One of the most revolutionary concepts to grow out of our clinical experience is the growing recognition that the innermost core of a man's [*sic*] nature, the deepest layers of his personality, the base of his 'animal nature' is positive in nature – is basically socialized, forward-moving, rational and realistic.
>
> (Rogers 1961: 90–1)

Key concepts

For people to move forward, Rogers argued that they need a non-directive stance, where their thoughts, feelings, and actions are not subject to advice, interpretation, criticism, confrontation, or challenge beyond encouraging people to clarify what they see to be happening. To steer the counselling session or discussion in a particular direction would be seen to contravene a person's innate ability to be his or her own change agent. This non-directive, non-judgemental, accepting, warm, and caring stance forms part of the 'facilitative conditions', which Rogers summarized as involving empathy, unconditional positive regard, and congruence:

- *Empathy* – caring, warmth. 'It means entering the private perceptual world of the other and becoming thoroughly at home in it' (Rogers 1975: 2).
- *Unconditional positive regard* – respect, non-possessive warmth, acceptance, and non-judgementality even if the individual's actions are not approved of or condoned.
- *Congruence* – genuineness, authenticity, acting in a human way as a real person and not hiding behind a mask or professional role.

This is one of the most popular approaches among social work practitioners because of its hopefulness, accessibility, and flexibility. It has also given rise to other developments and research (Truax and Carkhuff 1967). However, the distinct features of this approach can be misunderstood or denied. For example, treating people with warmth, respect, and dignity – or 'centring' our focus on service users and their concerns – does not indicate that a person/client-centred approach is being adopted. This approach was designed for counselling, where the opportunity to demonstrate its distinct features and the importance of self-actualization is possible. In social work, it is our professional responsibility to contradict the principle of self-determination where serious risk is involved.

Rogers' 'seven stages of progress'

Rogers provides a framework for understanding personal change in terms of seven 'stages of progress' (Rogers 1961: 132–59). Within this framework, his 'necessary and sufficient conditions of therapeutic personality change' (Rogers 1957) are located in the client–therapist therapeutic relationship, with the process of change leading not only to changes in behaviour but also to a fundamental shift in self-perception and how individuals relate to themselves. The changes identified involve moving away from the past and blaming external causes (parents, partners, employers, school) to a more balanced perspective, embracing greater personal responsibility. McLeod summarizes these seven stages:

- *Communication is about external events.* Feelings and personal meanings are not 'owned'. Close relationships are construed as dangerous. Rigidity in thinking. Impersonal, detached. Does not use first-person pronouns.
- *Expression begins to flow more freely in respect of non-self topics.* Feelings may be described but not owned. Intellectualization. Describes behaviour rather than inner feelings. May show more interest and participation in therapy.

- *Describes personal reactions to external events.* Limited amount of self-description. Communication about past feelings. Beginning to recognize contradictions in experience.
- *Descriptions of feelings and personal experiences.* Beginning to experience current feelings, but fear and distrust of this when it happens. The 'inner life' is presented and listed or described, but not purposefully explored.
- *Present feelings are expressed.* Increasing ownership of feelings. More exactness in the differentiation of feelings and meanings. Intentional exploration of problems in a personal way, based on processing of feelings rather than reasoning.
- *Sense of an 'inner referent', or flow of feeling that has a life of its own.* 'Physiological loosening', such as moistness in the eyes, tears, sighs, or muscular relaxation, accompanies the open expression of feelings. Speaks in present tense or offers vivid representation of past.
- *A series of felt senses connecting the different aspects of an issue.* Basic trust in own inner processes. Feelings experienced with immediacy and richness of detail. Speaks fluently in present tense.

(McLeod 2009: 191)

Advantages

- It is an accessible approach that is easy to understand (but not always easy to achieve).
- All forms of experience are valued. People are encouraged to find their own way in their own time.
- It resists the temptation to criticize or to see events in a negative light.
- It encourages the development of an equal, non-authoritarian, significant, and meaningful relationship between the service user and social worker.

Limitations

- It is difficult for social workers to demonstrate empathy, unconditional positive regard, and congruence in their everyday work: to adapt this approach may be inconsistent with its philosophy.
- The considerable motivation and cooperation required can make this approach inappropriate when working with people who are resistant, 'involuntary', destructive, or dangerous.
- Its focus on individual change tends to ignore the importance of changing external constraints that impact on people's well-being and life chances.
- There are doubts whether it can be used with problems that are severe or where the individual does not have the capacity for reflection (McLeod 2009: 90).

Further reading

McLeod, J. (2009) *An Introduction to Counselling*, 4th edn. Maidenhead: Open University Press.

Mearns, D. and Thorne, D. (2000) *Person-centred Therapy Today: New Frontiers in Theory and Practice*. London: Sage.

Rogers, C.R. (1951) *Client-Centred Therapy*. Boston, MA: Houghton Mifflin.

Rogers, C.R. (1957) The necessary and sufficient conditions of therapeutic personality change, *Journal of Consulting Psychology*, 21: 95–103.

Rogers, C.R. (1961) *On Becoming a Person*. Boston, MA: Houghton Mifflin.

Rogers, C.R. (1975) Empathic: an unappreciated way of being, *Counseling Psychologist*, 5: 2–10.

Thorne, B. (2002) Person-centred counselling, in M. Davies (ed.) *The Blackwell Companion to Social Work*, 2nd edn. Oxford: Blackwell Publishing.

Truax, C.B. and Carkhuff, R.R. (1967) *Towards Effective Counselling and Psychotherapy*. Chicago, IL: Aldine.

APPENDIX 8

Psychosocial approaches

Description/definition

Psychosocial approaches within social work draw on psychoanalytic theory and practice derived from the work of Freud and his followers. Florence Hollis, an important writer in this field, summarizes the main elements of the psychosocial approach as follows:

> It is . . . an attempt to mobilize the strengths of the personality and the resources of the environment at strategic points to improve the opportunities available to the individual and to develop more effective personal and interpersonal functioning.
>
> (Hollis 1977: 1308)

This definition stresses the importance of both internal and external factors in relation to people's capacity to cope with the everyday stresses of modern living. As such, it contradicts the myth that psychosocial approaches are only concerned with people's inner, emotional life: the external world is also an important area of analysis and concern. It is important to note that psychoanalysis has been influential in the development of a range of different theories and therapeutic approaches that are relevant to social work, including: ego psychology; crisis intervention; attachment theory; Erikson's conceptualization of the 'eight stages of man'; transactional analysis; group therapy, particularly group analysis; and psychoanalytic perspectives developed in relation to systems theory, ecological perspectives, and family therapy. In the past, a psychosocial approach has been linked to the term 'casework' or 'social casework' (Howe 2002: 171). At the heart of casework – and a psychosocial approach – lies the relationship created between the service user and social worker. 'The social worker shows human concern for clients but disciplines his or her use of the relationship in keeping with the assessment of the client's needs and interventive goals' (Goldstein 1995a: 1950).

Key concepts

What differentiates psychoanalytic perspectives from other schools of thought is the concept of the unconscious. Other concepts are also central, the most relevant for social work being the defences (or defence mechanism), resistance, repression, regression, splitting, transference, and counter-transference (Brearley 2007: 89–90; Trevithick 2011a), some of which are defined below:

- *Conscious* – the *conscious* was described by Freud as 'immediate data' and refers to all thoughts, feelings, and sensations that we are aware of at a given moment. However, what we know consciously is more complex than it first appears.
- *Preconscious* – thoughts, images, and perceptions that are not in one's immediate awareness but that can be recalled with relative ease (Barker 2003: 334).
- *Unconscious* – central to the concepts of transference and resistance is the notion of the unconscious, that is, 'mental processes of which the subject is not aware' (Rycroft 1968: 172).
- *Defence mechanism* – in psychoanalytic theory, defences seen as strategies that a person employs, either knowingly or unknowingly, to avoid facing aspects of the self that are felt to be threatening (Jacobs 2010: 110).
- *Transference* – 'As we relate with others, we often have thoughts and feelings about them that are actually based on our relationship experiences with someone else, particularly our parents. We therefore feel about or react to them inappropriately. This is the phenomenon of *transference*' (Howe 2008b: 167).
- *Counter-transference* – can describe the reactions that arise from being open and receptive to the transferred feelings of others. It can also describe our own unresolved feelings from the past. These can blur reality.

Transference occurs in every human relationship in that it involves passing on or 'transferring' an emotion or pattern of relating from one person to another person. Feelings of mistrust, dislike, love, and care can arise in response to the practitioner's particular qualities but can also be a reflection of earlier feelings, fears, and anxieties being activated. In this situation, it is important not to collude or to allow ourselves to be manipulated by these aspects of *positive* and negative *transference* feelings, but instead to help the individual to understand what these feelings represent and *what we have become for them*. For example, a female pupil who is refusing to attend school may experience her social worker as blaming her, or as judging her critically, when the social worker has neither felt nor indicated such unsympathetic reactions. The practitioner might pick up these feelings through her recognition of counter-transference reactions (John and Trevithick 2012).

Advantages

- Concepts such as the unconscious, transference, counter-transference, and defences illuminate our understanding of human beings in ways that are central to judicious decision-making and action (Howe 2009).
- It is a discipline that can explain almost all human aspects of behaviour, including complex and destructive behaviour. An important feature involves identifying the meaning individuals place on events.
- Its recognition of good and bad elements within human nature, and neutrality about emotions, avoids the danger of judging people.
- It has inspired the development of many other theories and practices and continues to do so, such as some relationship-based perspectives in social work.

Limitations

- Some of the concepts that are central to psychosocial approaches can be difficult to understand and to apply without good instruction and supervision.
- It can also lead to service users' thoughts, feelings, and actions being pathologized and can run the risk of creating an unhealthy dependency.
- External factors, such as social causes and cultural influences, can be neglected. Also, a political perspective is often lacking, leading to the criticism that practitioners working from a psychosocial approach are out of touch with 'bread and butter' issues.
- The benefits and outcomes of a psychosocial approach can be hard to evaluate in terms of effectiveness because of the emphasis placed on quality of life issues, such as the capacity to cope and to relate to oneself and to others in ways that feel satisfying.

Further reading

Barker, R.L. (2003) *The Social Work Dictionary*, 5th edn. Silver Spring, MD: NASW Press.

Brearley, J. (2007) A psychoanalytic approach to social work, in J. Lishman (ed.) *Handbook of Theory for Practice Teachers*, 2nd edn. London: Jessica Kingsley.

Goldstein, E.G. (1995a) Psychosocial approach, in R.L. Edwards (ed.) *Encyclopedia of Social Work*, 19th edn., Vol. 1. Washington, DC: National Association of Social Workers.

Hollis, F. (1977) Social casework: the psychosocial approach, in J.B. Turner (ed.) *Encyclopedia of Social Work*, 17th edn. Washington, DC: National Association of Social Workers.

Howe, D. (2002) Psychosocial work, in R. Adams, L. Dominelli and M. Payne (eds.) *Social Work: Themes, Issues and Critical Debates*, 2nd edn. Basingstoke: Macmillan.

Howe, D. (2008b) *The Emotionally Intelligent Social Worker*. Basingstoke: Palgrave Macmillan.

Howe, D. (2009) *A Brief Introduction to Social Work Theory*. Basingtoke: Palgrave Macmillan.

Jacobs, M. (2010) *Psychodynamic Counselling in Action*, 4th edn. London: Sage.

John, M. and Trevithick, P. (2012) Psychosocial practice in social work, in P. Stepney and D. Ford (eds.) *Social Work Models, Methods and Theories*, 2nd edn. Lyme Regis: Russell House (forthcoming).

Rycroft, C. (1968) *A Critical Dictionary of Psychoanalysis*. Harmondsworth: Penguin.

Trevithick, P. (2011a) Understanding defences and defensive behaviour in social work, *Journal of Social Work Practice*, Vol. 25, No. 4, December 2011: 389–412.

APPENDIX 9

Radical and activist perspectives

in social work

Description/definition

Aspects of radical social work are described in different ways: as *activist* (Healy 2000), as *critical social work practice* (Fook 2002; Mullaly 2002; Pease 2002), as *emancipatory approaches* (Dominelli 2009: 51) and as *radical social work* (Ferguson 2008; Ferguson and Woodward 2009; Lavalette 2011). All these perspectives stress the connection between 'personal troubles' and 'public issues' (Mills 1959: 130), or the feminist notion that the *personal is political*. Their starting point is the view that social inequalities are built into the fabric of most western capitalist societies and that within this unjust and unfair system, the poorest and most vulnerable groups suffer. Where problems – their causes and solutions – are individualized, people can become divided and isolated from those who share similar experiences.

Radical social work was most prominent in Great Britain in the 1970s, in the wake of the civil rights/black movement, feminist and anti-war movements. Social workers interested in radical reform drew their inspiration from *Case Con* – a 'revolutionary magazine for social workers', published from 1970 to 1977 – and other important texts (Bailey and Brake 1975; Langan and Lee 1989). Similar developments occurred in the USA, Canada, and Australia, but with the political shift away from progressive politics in the 1980s, the voice of radical, activist, and feminist perspectives in social work became less directly influential.

Focus of radical social work

Practitioners who work from a radical activist perspective are involved in a range of issues relevant to social justice and the 'rights of clients'. The UK

Social Work Action Network (SWAN) is made up of social work practitioners, service users, academics, and students who work together on a range of issues, including:

Social, economic, and political solutions

This emphasizes the importance of social, economic, and political solutions to 'social problems', thereby shifting the onus of blame from the individual, without denying the importance of individual responsibility. It involves campaigning for alternatives that address the underlying causes of social and health inequalities, and related issues such as poverty, violence, crime, and how these impact on people's sense of well-being and life chances. Particular criticism is levelled at the limitations of neo-liberal policies and practices, particularly managerialism.

Collective action

A radical/ activist social work perspective stresses the importance of bringing people together to ensure, through collective action, that the voice of disadvantaged people can be heard. Groupwork skills are particularly important in this regard. So too is *consciousness raising*, which involves becoming aware – and helping others to become aware – of the way that issues of power and domination, and social and economic inequalities, impact on the lives of people who are disadvantaged.

Taking action can be inspiring and unifying. For example, in the mid-1970s, myself and other 'members' of *Case Con* initiated a meeting at which we challenged psychiatrists about treatment of patients, particularly the use of ECT (electric shock treatment). Similar actions involved campaigning and agitating about homelessness, the 'cohabitation rule', the inadequate services for women experiencing domestic/family violence, and so forth.

Influencing social work practice

Concerns were voiced in the 1970s about the allocation of resources, and how inequalities and discriminatory practices impacted on the availability and quality of service provided. These concerns continue today in the way that social work services are fragmented, 'bureaucratized', restricted, and under-resourced, a situation that has led to the call for collective action.

Advantages

- Practitioners who work from a radical or activist perspective are passionately committed to the issue of social justice and to working alongside people from disadvantaged groups so as to initiate change.

- It is a perspective that is centrally involved in bringing social workers – and service users – together so that their collective voice can be heard.
- This perspective has the potential to form alliances with other progressive groups/organizations, such as trade unions and those involved with social justice and anti-poverty, both at home and abroad.
- The influence of radical or activist perspectives has been far reaching and evident in perspectives that embrace anti-oppressive, anti-racist, and empowerment approaches.

Limitations

- Encouraging people to come together can be difficult because the benefits of collective action may not always be evident and agitating for change can be frightening.
- Activism takes courage, as well as time and effort, and it can be particularly difficult to keep issues alive when progress is blocked and other pressures mount.
- Activism is more likely to be successful where practitioners have a good knowledge of key issues – poverty, take up of benefits, housing policy – and how these issues impact on specific communities, but acquiring this knowledge takes time and skill.
- The absence of success can leave people demoralized and defeated and vested interests have been known to intimidate or threaten people who are involved in pressing for change – both situations can result in membership falling off.

Further reading

Bailey, R. and Brake, M. (1975) *Radical Social Work*. London: Edward Arnold.
Dominelli, L. (2009) Anti-oppressive practice: the challenges in the twenty-first century, in R. Adams, L. Dominelli and M. Payne (eds.) *Social Work: Themes, Issues and Critical Debates*, 3rd edn. Basingstoke: Palgrave Macmillan.
Ferguson, I. (2008) *Reclaiming Social Work: Challenging Neo-Liberalism and Promoting Social Justice*. London: Sage.
Ferguson, I. and Woodward, R. (2009) *Radical Social Work in Practice: Making a Difference*. Bristol: Policy Press.
Fook, J. (2002) *Social Work: Critical Theory and Practice*. London: Sage.
Healy, K. (2000) *Social Work Practices: Contemporary Perspectives on Change*. London: Sage.
Langan, M. (2002) The legacy of radical social work, in R. Adams, L. Dominelli and M. Payne (eds.) *Social Work: Themes, Issues and Critical Debates*, 2nd edn. Basingstoke: Macmillan.

Langan, M. and Lee, P. (eds.) (1989) *Radical Social Work Today*. London: Unwin Hyman.

Lavalette, M. (2011) *Radical Social Work Today: Social Work at the Crossroads*. Bristol: Policy Press.

Mills, C.W. (1959) *The Sociological Imagination*. Oxford: Oxford University Press.

Mullaly, R. (2002) *Challenging Oppression: A Critical Social Work Approach*. Oxford: Oxford University Press.

Pease, B. (2009) From radical to critical social work: progressive transformation or mainstream incorporation?, in R. Adams, L. Dominelli and M. Payne (eds.) *Critical Practice in Social Work*, 2nd edn. Basingstoke: Palgrave Macmillan.

Social Work Action Network (SWAN) Website available at: http://www.social workfuture.org/

APPENDIX 10

Strengths perspectives

Strengths perspective

An orientation in social work and other professional practices that emphasizes the clients' resources, capabilities, support systems, and motivations to meet challenges and overcome adversity. This approach does not ignore the existence of social problems, individual disease, or family dysfunction; it emphasizes the client's assets that are used to achieve and maintain individual and social well-being.

(Barker 2003: 420)

One of the approaches indicated in the Department of Health's *Framework for the Assessment of Children in Need and their Families* (see Appendix 4) is the importance of practitioners 'building on strengths as well as identifying difficulties' (Department of Health 2000: 13). It is a perspective that acknowledges the inherent capacity to adapt, learn, grow, change, and use their inner resources to confront and respond to daily challenges in their lives (Kisthardt 2009: 54). Like motivational interviewing and solution-focused approaches (de Shazer 1985), a strengths perspective runs counter to a *deficit perspective*, that is, 'the supposition that clients become clients because they have deficits, problems, pathologies and diseases: that they are, in some critical way, flawed and weak' (Saleebey 1992: 3). As a perspective, rather than a theory or model, it is a lens that provides 'a slant on the world, built of words and principles ... [that] are tentative, still evolving and subject to revision' (Saleebey 2009: 15), and a lens that can be incorporated alongside other approaches, such as task-centred work. Saleebey highlights six principles that underpin a strengths perspective:

- every individual, group, family, and community has strengths
- trauma and abuse, illness and struggle may be injurious, but they may also be sources of challenge and opportunity
- assume that you do not know the upper limits of the capacity to grow and change and take individual, group, and community aspirations seriously

- we best serve clients by collaborating with them
- every environment is full of resources
- caring, caretaking, and context: 'In one sense, social work is about care and caretaking' (Saleebey 2009: 18).

As is evident, this perspective recognizes the importance of resilience, that is, the ability of individuals to keep going in ways that enable them to overcome hazards, and to deal with risk and other forms of adversity. Howe takes up the point about the healing capacity of human beings:

> Minds, as well as bodies, have a remarkable capacity to self-heal. Personal resilience can be bolstered by recognizing personal strengths but it can also be enhanced by working together with others who share the same needs and experiences. Not only does meeting others generate ideas, it helps people to believe in themselves.
>
> (Howe 2009: 106)

A central feature is the ability to ask good questions, but questions of a particular kind. This might involve asking:

- *Survival questions* – what has helped you in the past – how have you managed to keep going, to rise to challenges, what qualities can you rely on in yourself?
- *Support questions* – which people have given you 'special understanding, support, and guidance' (Saleebey 2009: 102)? Where did you find these individuals?
- *Exception questions* – what was happening when things went well and what was different at that time?
- *Possibility questions* – what vision do you have for the future? What hope and aspirations do you have for yourself and others?
- *Esteem questions* – 'When people say good things about you, what are they likely to say' (Saleebey 2009: 102)? What are you proud of, in terms of your accomplishments?
- *Perspective questions* – what ideas, thoughts, and theories do you have about your current situation? What sense do you make of what's happened to you?
- *Change questions* – what would you most like to change about your life? How can I help you to achieve this change?
- *Meaning questions* – what gives your life meaning? If you have a belief, what is it? What do you value most in life?

Advantages

- Unlike many of the practice approaches, this perspective was developed in social work for social work, although its impact has been felt in other disciplines. The focus placed on people's strengths has constituted an important paradigm shift in social work.

- A strengths perspective, as opposed to a deficit model, can put individuals in touch with the more resilient characteristics that they may have lost touch with. This perspective is consistent with anti-oppressive, empowerment, culturally sensitive, and emancipatory approaches within social work because the work is built on the service users' interpretation of events and the importance of validating the meaning they give to experience (Houston 2010).
- It is a perspective that can work alongside other practice approaches and in ways that cover different fields of practice, such as work involving individuals, families, groups, and communities.
- People who believe in themselves and can act on their own behalf, and who also feel cared for and supported by others, are much more likely to achieve their goals and to have a better quality of life.

Limitations

- Unless skilfully undertaken, attempting to put people in touch with their strengths can be experienced as irrelevant and come across as failing to understand or dismissing the severity of the problems being experienced.
- This perspective is most often used when working with individuals, which means that other areas where it could be applied, such as work with families, groups, and communities tend to be ignored.
- This perspective is based on establishing a collaborative relationship, where the notion of the practitioner as an 'expert' is not appropriate. Some practitioners may find it difficult to come alongside service users in this way.
- The skilled use of this approach is dependent on good training and appropriate supervision, but both can be difficult to access.

Further reading

Barker, R.L. (2003) *The Social Work Dictionary*, 3rd edn. Silver Spring, MD: NASW Press.

de Shazer, S. (1985) *Keys to Solution in Brief Therapy*. London: W.W. Norton.

Department of Health (DH) (2000) *Framework for the Assessment of Children in Need and their Families*. London: Department of Health.

Houston, S. (2010) Beyond *homo economicus*: recognition, self-realization and social work, *British Journal of Social Work*, 40: 841–57.

Howe, D. (2009) *A Brief Introduction to Social Work Theory*. Basingstoke: Palgrave Macmillan.

Kisthardt, W.E. (2009) A strengths model of case management: the principles and functions of a helping partnership with persons with persistent mental illness, in D. Saleebey (ed.) *The Strengths Perspective in Social Work Practice*. London: Longman.

Saleebey, D. (ed.) (1992) *The Strengths Perspective in Social Work Practice*. London: Longman.

Saleebey, D. (ed.) (2009) *The Strengths Perspective in Social Work Practice*, 5th edn. London: Allyn & Bacon.

APPENDIX 11

Task-centred approaches

Description/definition

Task-centred practice is a technology for alleviating specific target problems perceived by clients, that is, particular problems clients recognize, understand, acknowledge, and want to attend to ... Task-centred practice has a particular way of unfolding. It consists of a start-up and four sequential but overlapping steps. The regularity of the steps is important because orderly, systematic processes are most likely to result in good outcomes. Under the pressure of problem-solving, these steps tend to occur out of sequence; nonetheless, the practitioner should return to the normal procedure as soon as possible.

(Epstein and Brown 2002: 93)

Basic map in task-centred work (Epstein and Brown 2002: 93)

Start up: Client referred by an agency
    or   Client applies independently and voluntarily
      ↓
Step 1:   Client target problems identified (three maximum)
      ↓
Step 2:   Contract: plans, target problem priorities, goals, practitioner tasks, duration, schedule, and participants
      ↓
Step 3:   Problem-solving
      ↓
Step 4:   Termination

All approaches involve undertaking a range of activities, or tasks, but these are not always performed in a systematic way – which is central to task-centred work or practice. The activities associated with this area of practice are not considered to constitute a theoretical approach because task-centred practice does not have a distinct theory base (Marsh 2008: 121). This point is important because working from distinct theories and concepts enables us to engage in theory and skill development – because we are engaged in testing out the relevance of theories – and, where appropriate, adapt these theories to meet new situations.

Task-centred practice emerged from the research undertaken by Reid and Shyne (1969) and Reid and Epstein (1972) in the United States, who found that short-term interventions were as effective as long-term work. The basis on which these findings were made has been questioned because the research sample was small and there were some methodological limitations in relation to the study design (Wilson et al. 2008: 367). Nevertheless, the impact of this research study was profound because the findings challenged the ideas dominant at that time, particularly the principles that underpinned long-term work:

> In doing this, it recognized that the person with the problems also had the means to resolve them, and that social work intervention should become more of a partnership. In this way, task-centred casework can be seen to be at the beginning of attempts to empower users of social work services.
>
> (Coulshed and Orme 2006: 157)

This strategy involves working in close collaboration with service users – and others – to agree specific goals or outcomes and to identify what steps, tasks, or 'building blocks' need to be undertaken to achieve those goals. Focusing on tasks in this way is one of the best ways we have of identifying whether an individual is motivated and whether he or she has the necessary skills, knowledge, confidence, and resources to undertake and complete a particular task or to achieve a specific goal or outcome. This helps us to see what role we might need to play in this collaborative endeavour. This may involve teaching specific skills, such as how to make a telephone call, or providing vital information, such as where to go for help. It may also involve our taking responsibility for specific tasks appropriate to our professional role, such as liaising with agencies. At the heart of task-centred work lies the importance of utilizing, extending, and consolidating service users' strengths and abilities to address key issues in ways that 'reflect the actual reality of the users' relationships and lives' (Marsh 2008: 125).

Advantages

- Tasks and goals are discreet and chosen because they are achievable. This enhances the likelihood of success and builds confidence because its focus is on enhancing people's capacities and strengths.

- Task-centred work is time-limited, usually spanning three months. Its outcomes and effectiveness are easy to evaluate and to research (Epstein and Brown 2002: 92).
- It is based on an approach that is highly collaborative in character, where service users are central to all decision-making. The importance of service user self-determination is central to the work undertaken.
- Practitioners can learn this strategy relatively easily. It is also adaptable. For example, identifying target problems and specific tasks in this systematic way can be used as part of other practice approaches.

Limitations

- Despite claims to the contrary, this may be a difficult strategy to use when working with reluctant or 'involuntary' service users who may not be prepared to collaborate.
- More difficult, underlying problems may never be identified to be worked on. Also, the work can result in despondency and loss of confidence if tasks are not achieved.
- Some people are overwhelmed by the problems they face and may not have the energy to work on the tasks they have agreed to take on.
- There may be too much focus on service users adjusting to difficult situations, as opposed to looking for more creative solutions further afield: 'At worst – when a genuinely necessary resource is unavailable and no satisfactory substitute is possible – the practitioner should help the client relinquish the expectations that the resource can be obtained' (Epstein 1995: 321).

Further reading

Coulshed, V. and Orme, J. (2006) *Social Work Practice: An Introduction*, 4th edn. Basingstoke: Macmillan/BASW.

Epstein, L. (1995) Brief task-centered social work, in R.L. Edwards (ed.) *Encyclopedia of Social Work*, 19th edn., Vol. 1. Washington, DC: National Association of Social Workers.

Epstein, L. and Brown, L.B. (2002) *Brief Treatment and a New Look at the Task-centered Approach*. London: Allyn & Bacon.

Marsh, P. (2008) Task-centred work, in M. Davies (ed.) *The Blackwell Companion to Social Work*, 3rd edn. Oxford: Blackwell Publishing.

Marsh, P. and Doel, M. (2005) *The Task-Centred Book*. London: Routledge/Community Care.

Reid, W.J. and Epstein, L. (1972) *Task-Centered Casework*. New York: Columbia University Press.

Reid, W.J. and Shyne, A. (1969) *Brief and Extended Casework*. New York: Columbia University Press.

Wilson, K., Ruch, G., Lymbery, M. and Cooper, A. (2008) *Social Work: An Introduction to Contemporary Practice*. Harlow: Pearson Education.

APPENDIX 12

Stages of change

(or cycle of change)

Description/definition

The *Stages of Change*, also known as the *Cycle of Change*, is a central concept within the trans-theoretical model of psychotherapy. This approach is committed to integrating different models of psychotherapy and behaviour change, thereby drawing 'from the entire spectrum of the major theories – hence the name *trans-theoretical*' (Prochaska and Norcross 2003: 516). The model covers three dimensions: (1) processes, (2) stages, and (3) levels of change.

Here I focus on five *stages of change* – namely, precontemplation, contemplation, preparation, action, and maintenance – that describe the stages that people go through during the change process. Change is not conceptualized as a linear process but as a spiral, where individuals progress through the stages haphazardly, although no stage can be skipped. Relapse can happen at any stage and, at this point, the individual regresses to an earlier stage. Since people who are not ready for change set themselves up (or are set up) for failure, it is important to know at what stage an individual is located, so that problem-solving efforts can be maximized (Prochaska *et al.* 1994: 39). The five stages are:

1. *Precontemplation.* People at this stage cannot see the problem, although this may be clearly visible to others, such as their family, friends, doctor, or social worker. Therefore, 'there is no intention to change behaviour now or in the future' (Prochaska and Norcross 2003: 519). Some may make the right noises, complain that they are being coerced, or locate the problem in others. The reality is that they may be too well defended, or too hopeless or demoralized, to try to effect change.

2. *Contemplation.* People at this stage have acknowledged that there is a problem but are 'not quite ready to go yet' (Prochaska *et al.* 1994: 42). Readiness for change is an important issue in this approach. People can remain stuck in 'chronic contemplations' for long periods, where the attempt to understand the problem, its cause, and possible solutions is at the expense of moving forward. As a result, thinking can become a substitute for action (Prochaska and Norcross 2003: 520).

3. *Preparation.* 'Individuals in this stage are intending to take action immediately and report some small behavioural changes' (Prochaska and Norcross 2003: 520). However, although they appear committed and ready for action, some ambivalence may be evident about the prospect of change, perhaps expressed in an undue concern about the best course of action, a desire to move too quickly, an inability to set clear targets or 'a clear criterion for success' (Barber 2002: 26).

4. *Action.* 'In this stage, individuals modify their behaviour, experiences, and/or environment in order to overcome their problems' (Prochaska and Norcross 2003: 521). This stage involves energy and commitment and changes initiated are likely to be quite visible and given the greatest recognition by others. This last point is important. The danger at this stage is that people, including professionals, may confuse action with change, that is, superficial action may be taken but fundamental change has not occurred. This may eventually lead to failure.

5. *Maintenance/termination.* 'In this final stage, people work to prevent relapse and consolidate the gains attained during action. Traditionally, maintenance has been viewed as a static stage. However, maintenance is a continuation, not an absence, of change' (Prochaska and Norcross 2003: 522). The changes achieved need to be recognized and celebrated, particularly when the maintenance is spread over a long period.

Termination is sometimes cited as *relapse* whereas Prochaska and Norcross (2003) and DiClemente (2006) use the term *maintenance*. Termination occurs when temptation has abated and the individual does not have to struggle to avoid relapse. Alcoholics Anonymous and some workers in the field of addiction believe that some maintenance will always be required. A great deal depends on the individual and, more importantly, the external support for change.

The stages of change are shown in Figure A3.

Advantages

- This approach has been adopted in a wide range of different health and welfare contexts – for drug addiction, smoking cessation, eating disorders, domestic/family violence, etc.

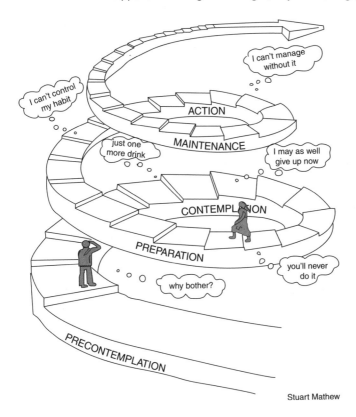

Stuart Mathew

Figure A3   The stages of change

- It provides an accessible framework from which to analyse change, and the change process, making it possible to identify appropriate strategies (Barber 2002: 29).
- This approach is compatible with other approaches, such as motivational interviewing (DiClemente and Velasquez 2002), cognitive interventions in the early stages, and behavioural/task-centred approaches in the later stages.
- Considerable research evidence supports the view that people pass through the stages identified (Prochaska and Norcross 2003: 536).

Limitations

- This approach does not provide a coherent theory/practice about how to bring about change. It is 'more successful as a description *of* change than as a prescription *for* change' (Barber 2002: 33).

- Its individualistic focus, dominant in the United States, can place too much weight on individual effort and not enough on environmental causation and support structures. Thus, the link between addictive behaviour and social inequalities warrants further emphasis (Prochaska and Norcross 2010).
- Treatment methods used at different stages tend to be vague and largely untested. Some authors question the research findings (Barber 2002: 33).
- This approach has been applied and adapted in ways that are not always appropriate and do not strictly adhere to the original theory and concepts put forward (Corden and Somerton 2004).

Further reading

Barber, J.G. (2002) *Social Work with Addictions*, 2nd edn. Basingstoke: Palgrave Macmillan.

Corden, J. and Somerton, J. (2004) The transtheoretical model of change: a reliable blueprint for assessment in work with children and families?, *British Journal of Social Work*, 34: 1025–44.

DiClemente, C.C. (2006) Natural change and the troublesome use of substances, in W.R. Miller and K.M. Carroll (eds.) *Rethinking Substance Abuse: What the Science Shows, and What We Should Do About it*. London: Guilford Press.

DiClemente, C.C. and Velasquez, M.M. (2002) Motivational interviewing and the stages of change, in W.R. Miller and S. Rollnick (eds.) *Motivational Interviewing: Preparing People for Change*, 2nd edn. London: Guilford Press.

Miller, W.R. and Rollnick, S. (eds.) (2002) *Motivational Interviewing: Preparing People for Change*, 2nd edn. London: Guilford Press.

Prochaska, J.O. and Norcross, J.C. (2003) *Systems of Psychotherapy: A Transtheoretical Analysis*, 5th edn. Pacific Grove, CA: Brooks/Cole.

Prochaska, J.O. and Norcross, J.C. (2010) *Systems of Psychotherapy: A Transtheoretical Analysis*, 7th edn. Belmont, CA: Wadsworth Cengage Learning.

Prochaska, J.O., Norcross, J.C. and DiClemente, C.C. (1994) *Changing for Good*. New York: Avon.

REFERENCES

Abercrombie, N., Hill, S. and Turner, B.S. (2006) *Penguin Dictionary of Sociology*, 5th edn. London: Penguin Books.

Abendstern, M., Hughes, J., Clarkson, P., Sutcliffe, C. and Challis, D. (2011) The pursuit of integration in the assessment of older people with health and social care needs, *British Journal of Social Work*, 41: 467–85.

Acheson, D. (1998) *Inequalities in Health: Report of an Independent Inquiry*. London: HMSO.

Adams, R. (2009) Advocacy and empowerment, in R. Adams, L. Dominelli and M. Payne (eds.) *Critical Practice in Social Work*, 2nd edn. Basingstoke: Palgrave Macmillan.

Ainsworth, M.D.S., Blehar, M., Walters, E. and Wall, S. (1978) *Patterns of Attachment: A Psychological Study of the Strange Situation*. Hillsdale, NJ: Lawrence Erlbaum Associates.

Alcock, C., Daly, G. and Griggs, E. (2008) *Introducing Social Policy*, 2nd edn. London: Longman Pearson.

Alcock, C., Erskine, A. and May, M. (eds.) (2002) *The Blackwell Dictionary of Social Policy*. Oxford: Blackwell Publishing.

Aldgate, J. (2002) Family breakdown, in M. Davies (ed.) *The Blackwell Companion to Social Work*, 2nd edn. Oxford: Blackwell Publishing.

Angelou, M. (1994) *Wouldn't Take Nothing for My Journey Now*. London: Virago.

Applegate, J.S. and Bonovitz, J.M. (1995) *The Facilitating Partnership: A Winnicottian Approach for Social Workers and other Helping Professionals*. Northvale, NJ: Jason Aronson.

Asquith, S., Clark, C. and Waterhouse, L. (2005) *The Role of the Social Worker in the 21st Century: A Literature Review*. Edinburgh: Scottish Executive Education Department.

Audit Commission (1983) *Performance Review in Local Government: A Handbook for Auditors and Local Authorities*. London: Audit Commission.

Audit Commission (1992) *Community Care: Managing the Cascade of Change*. London: HMSO.

Aymer, C. and Okitikpi, T. (2000) Epistemology, ontology and methodology: what's that got to do with social work?, *Social Work Education*, 19(1): 67–75.

Baginsky, M., Moriarty, J., Manthorpe, J., Stevens, M., MacInnes, T. and Nagendran, T. (2010) *Social Workers' Workload Survey: Messages from the Frontline – 2010. Findings from the 2009 Survey and Interviews with Senior Managers*. Available at: http://www.info4local.gov.uk/documents/publications/1505411 [accessed 1 June 2011].

Bailey, R. and Brake, M. (1975) *Radical Social Work*. London: Edward Arnold.

Bandura, A. (1969) *Principles of Behavior Modification*. New York: Holt, Rinehart & Winston.

Bandura, A. (1977) *Social Learning Theory*. Englewood Cliffs, NJ: Prentice-Hall.

Banks, S. (2006) *Ethics and Values in Social Work*, 3rd edn. Basingstoke: Palgrave Macmillan.

Bannock, G., Baxter, R.E. and Davis, E. (2003) *The Penguin Dictionary of Economics*, 7th edn. London: Penguin.

Barber, J.G. (2002) *Social Work with Addictions*, 2nd edn. Basingstoke: Palgrave Macmillan.

Barclay Report (1982) *Social Workers: Their Roles and Task*. London: Bedford Square Press.

Barker, R.L. (2003) *The Social Work Dictionary*, 5th edn. Washington, DC: National Association of Social Work Press.

Barnett, R. (1994) *The Limits of Competence: Knowledge, Higher Education and Society*. Buckingham: Open University Press.

Barton, R. (2008) The carer's perspective, in M. Davies (ed.) *The Blackwell Companion to Social Work*, 3rd edn. Oxford: Blackwell Publishing.

Bateman, N. (2008) Welfare rights practice, in M. Davies (ed.) *The Blackwell Companion to Social Work*, 3rd edn. Oxford: Blackwell Publishing.

Beck, A. (1976) *Cognitive Therapy and the Emotional Disorders*. New York: International University Press.

Beck, A. and Steer, R. (1987) *Beck Depression Inventory: Manual*. San Antonia, TX: Psychological Corporation.

Beddoe, L. (2010) Surveillance or reflection: professional supervision in 'the risk society', *British Journal of Social Work*, 40: 1279–96.

Beech, C. and Ray, M. (2009) Older people, in R. Adams, L. Dominelli and M. Payne (eds.) *Critical Practice in Social Work*, 2nd edn. Basingstoke: Palgrave Macmillan.

Benjamin, J. (1998) *Shadow of the Other: Intersubjectivity and Gender in Psychoanalysis*. London: Routledge.

Benner, P. (1984) *From Novice to Expert: Excellence and Power in Clinical Nursing Practice*. Menlo Park, CA: Addison Wesley.

Beresford, P. and Croft, S. (2000) User participation, in M. Davies (ed.) *The Blackwell Encyclopaedia of Social Work*. Oxford: Blackwell Publishing.

Beresford, P., Croft, S. and Adshead, L. (2008) 'We don't see her as a social worker': a service user case study of the importance of the social worker's relationship and humanity, *British Journal of Social Work*, 38(7): 1388–1407.

Beresford, P., Shamash, O., Forrest, V., Turner, M. and Branfield, F. (2005) *Developing Social Care: Service Users' Vision for Adult Support. Report of a Consultation on the Future of Adult Social Care*. Adult Services Report #07. London: SCIE in association with Shaping Our Lives.

Berger, R. (2010) EBP: practitioners on search of evidence, *Journal of Social Work*, 10(2): 175–91.

Biestek, F.P. (1961) *The Casework Relationship*. London: Allen & Unwin.

Birdwhistell, R. (1970) *Kinesics and Context*. Philadelphia, PA: University of Pennsylvania Press.

Bisman, L. (2004) Social work values: the moral core of the profession, *British Journal of Social Work*, 34: 109–23.

Blakemore, K. and Griggs, E. (2007) *Social Policy: An Introduction*, 3rd edn. Maidenhead: Open University Press.

Blewett, J., Lewis, J. and Tunstill, J. (2007) *The Changing Roles and Tasks of Social Work: A Literature Informed Discussion Paper*. London: General Social Care Council.

Blom-Cooper, L. (1985) *A Child in Trust: A Report of the Panel of Inquiry into Circumstances Surrounding the Death of Jasmine Beckford*. London: London Borough of Brent.

Bogo, M. (2006) *Social Work Practice: Concepts, Processes, and Interviewing*. New York: Columbia University Press.

Bogo, M., Regehr, C., Hughes, J., Power, R. and Globerman, J. (2002) Evaluating a measure of student field performance in direct service: testing reliability and validity of explicit criteria, *Journal of Social Work Education*, 38(3): 385–401.

Bogo, M., Regehr, C., Power, R., Hughes, J., Woodford, M. and Regehr, G. (2004) Toward new approaches for evaluating student field performance: tapping the implicit criteria used by experienced field instructors, *Journal of Social Work Education*, 40(3): 417–26.

Booth, T. (2002) Learning difficulties, in M. Davies (ed.) *The Blackwell Companion to Social Work*, 2nd edn. Oxford: Blackwell Publishing.

Boseley, S. (2004) Big rise in the number of children given mind-altering drugs, *Guardian*, 18 November.

Bowlby, J. (1951) *Maternal Care and Mental Health: A Report Prepared on Behalf of the World Health Organization*. Geneva: World Health Organization.

Bowlby, J. (1979) *The Making and Breaking of Affectional Bonds*. London: Tavistock.

Bowlby, J. (1980) *Attachment and Loss, Vol. III: Loss, Sadness, and Depression*. London: Hogarth.

Bowlby, J. (1988) *A Secure Base: Clinical Applications of Attachment Theory*. London: Routledge.

Brammer, A. (2007) *Social Work Law*, 2nd edn. Harlow: Pearson Education.

Brandon, M., Belderson, P., Warren, C., Howe, D., Gardner, R., Dodsworth, J. and Black, J. (2008) *Analysing Child Deaths and Serious Injury Through Abuse and Neglect: What Can We Learn? A Biennial Analysis of Serious Case Reviews 2003–2005*. London: Department for Children, Schools and Families.

Braye, S. and Preston-Shoot, M. (1995) *Empowering Practice in Social Care*. Buckingham: Open University Press.

Braye, S. and Preston-Shoot, M. (2006) The role of law in welfare reform: critical perspectives on the relationship between law and social work practice, *International Journal of Social Welfare*, 15: 19–26.

Brayne, H. and Carr, H. (2008) *Law for Social Workers*, 10th edn. Oxford: Oxford University Press.

Brearley, J. (1995) *Counselling and Social Work*. Buckingham: Open University Press.

Brearley, J. (2007) A psychoanalytic approach to social work, in J. Lishman (ed.) *Handbook of Theory for Practice Teachers*, 2nd edn. London: Jessica Kingsley.

Brennan, Z. (2007) Dave Cameron says he's in touch with reality ... but with so much wealth and blue blood you have to wonder, *Daily Mail*, 15 June.

Breuer, J. and Freud, S. (1893/1955) *Studies on Hysteria*. London: Hogarth Press.

Bricker-Jenkins, M. (1990) Another approach to practice and training, *Public Welfare*, 48(2): 11–16.

Brindle, D. (2009) Taking the long view. An interview with Lord Sutherland, Chair of the Royal Commission on the Long Term Care (of older people). *Guardian*, 25 February.

British Association for Counselling (BAC) (1992) *16th Annual Report 1991/92*. Rugby: BAC.

British Association of Social Workers (BASW) (2002) *The Code of Ethics for Social Work*. Birmingham: BASW. Available at: http://www.basw.co.uk/about/code-of-ethics/ [accessed 6 June 2011].

Broadhurst, K., Hall, C., Wastell, D., White, S. and Pithouse, A. (2010) Risk, instrumentalism and the humane project in social work: identifying the informal logics of risk management in children's statutory services, *British Journal of Social Work*, 40: 1046–64.

Bronfenbrenner, U. (1979) *The Ecology of Human Development Experiments by Nature and Design*. Cambridge, MA: Harvard University Press.

Broudy, H.S., Smith, B.D. and Burnett, J. (1964) *Democracy and Excellence in American Secondary Education*. Chicago, IL: Rand McNally.

Brown, G. and Atkins, M. (1997) Explaining, in O. Hargie (ed.) *A Handbook of Communication Skills*, 2nd edn. London: Routledge.

Brown, H.C. (1998) *Social Work and Sexuality: Working with Lesbians and Gay Men*. Basingstoke: Macmillan.

Brown, H.C. (2002) Counselling, in R. Adams, L. Dominelli and M. Payne (eds.) *Social Work: Themes, Issues and Debates*, 2nd edn. Basingstoke: Macmillan.

Brown, M. (ed.) (1983) *The Structure of Disadvantage*. London: Heinemann.

Bullock, A. and Trombley, S. (eds.) (1999) *The New Fontana Dictionary of Modern Thought*, 3rd edn. Hammersmith: HarperCollins.

Burke, B. and Harrison, P. (2009) Anti-oppressive approaches, in R. Adams, L. Dominelli and M. Payne (eds.) *Critical Practice in Social Work*. Basingstoke: Palgrave Macmillan.

Bywaters, P., McLeod, E. and Napier, L. (2009) *Social Work and Global Health Inequalities: Practice and Policy Developments*. Bristol: Policy Press.

Caplan, G. (1964) *Principles of Preventative Psychiatry*. New York: Basic Books.

Carey, M. (2008) Everything must go? The privatization of state social work, *British Journal of Social Work*, 38: 918–35.

Central Council for Education and Training in Social Work (CCETSW) (1996) *Assuring Quality in the Diploma in Social Work – 1: Rules and Requirements for the DipSW*, 2nd revision. London: CCETSW.

Centre for Reviews and Dissemination (CRD) (undated) *Glossary of Research Terms*. Available at: http://www.york.ac.uk/inst/crd/index_guidance.htm [accessed 7 June 2010].

Charity Commission (2007) *Stand and Deliver: The Future for Charities Providing Public Services*. London: Charities Commission. Available at: http://www.charity-commission.gov.uk/library/guidance/rs15text.pdf [accessed 3 September 2010].

Cheetham, J., Fuller, R., McIvor, G. and Petch, A. (1992) *Evaluating Social Work Effectiveness*. Buckingham: Open University Press.

Chenoweth, L. and McAuliffe, D. (2008) *The Road to Social Work and Human Service Practice: An Introductory Text*, 2nd edn. Melbourne, VIC: Cengage Learning.

Chesler, P. (1974) *Women and Madness*. London: Allen Lane.

Child Poverty Action Group (CPAG) (2010) *Poverty in the UK: A Summary of Facts and Figures*. London: CPAG. Available at: http://www.cpag.org.uk/povertyfacts [accessed 9 September 2010].

Chodorow, N.J. (1978) *The Reproduction of Mothering: Psychoanalysis and the Sociology of Gender.* Berkeley, CA: University of California Press.

Cigno, K. (2009) Cognitive behavioural practice, in R. Adams, L. Dominelli and M. Payne (eds.) *Critical Practice in Social Work*, 2nd edn. Basingstoke: Palgrave Macmillan.

Citizens Advice Bureau (CAB) (2010) *Charities Challenge Government over £16bn Unclaimed Benefits.* London: CAB. Available at: http://www.citizensadvice.org.uk/press_office201022 [accessed 8 July 2011].

Clark, C. (1995) Competence and discipline in professional formation, *British Journal of Social Work*, 25: 563–80.

Clark, C. (2000a) *Social Work Ethics: Politics, Principles and Practice.* Basingstoke: Macmillan.

Clark, C. (2000b) Professional ethics, in M. Davies (ed.) *The Blackwell Encyclopaedia of Social Work.* Oxford: Blackwell Publishing.

Clark, C. (2006a) Moral character in social work, *British Journal of Social Work*, 36: 75–89.

Clark, C. (2006b) Against confidentiality? Privacy, safety and the public good in professional communications, *Journal of Social Work*, 6(2): 117–36.

Clarke, J. (ed.) (1993) *A Crisis in Care: Challenges to Social Work.* London: Sage.

Coates, J., Gray, M. and Hetherington, T. (2006) An 'ecospiritual' perspective: Finally, a place for indigenous approaches, *British Journal of Social Work*, 36: 381–99.

Cochrane Collaboration (undated) *Cochrane Collaboration Glossary of Research Terms.* Available at: http://www.cochrane.org/glossary/5 [accessed 1 June 2011].

Collins, J. and Collins, M. (1981) *Achieving Change in Social Work.* London: Heinemann.

Collins, S., Coffey, M. and Morris, L. (2010) Social work students: stress, support and well-being, *British Journal of Social Work*, 40: 963–82.

Colman, A.M. (2009) *A Dictionary of Psychology*, 3rd edn. Oxford: Oxford University Press.

Corby, B. (2006) *Child Abuse: Towards a Knowledge Base*, 3rd edn. Maidenhead: Open University Press.

Corden, J. and Preston-Shoot, M. (1987) Contract or con trick? A reply to Rojek and Collins, *British Journal of Social Work*, 17: 535–43.

Corden, J. and Somerton, J. (2004) The transtheoretical model of change: a reliable blueprint for assessment in work with children and families?, *British Journal of Social Work*, 34: 1025–44.

Coulshed, V. (1991) *Social Work Practice: An Introduction*, 2nd edn. Basingstoke: Macmillan/BASW.

Coulshed, V. and Orme, J. (2006) *Social Work Practice: An Introduction*, 4th edn. Basingstoke: Macmillan/BASW.

Coulter, S. (2010) Systemic family therapy for families who have experienced trauma: a randomised controlled trial, *British Journal of Social Work* (DOI: 10.1093/bjsw/bcq132).

Cree, V.E. (2008) Social work and society, in M. Davies (ed.) *The Blackwell Companion to Social Work*, 3rd edn. Oxford: Blackwell Publishing.

Crisp, B.R., Anderson, M.R., Orme, J. and Lister, P.L. (2003) *Learning and Teaching in Social Work Education: Assessment*. Bristol: Policy Press.

Croft, S. and Beresford, P. (2008) Service users' perspectives, in M. Davies (ed.) *The Blackwell Companion to Social Work*, 3rd edn. Oxford: Blackwell Publishing.

Cunningham, J. and Cunningham, S. (2008) *Sociology and Social Work*. Exeter: Learning Matters.

Dalrymple, J. and Burke, B. (2006) *Anti-oppressive Practice: Social Care and the Law*, 2nd edn. Maidenhead: Open University Press.

Daniel, B. (2008) Psychology and social work, in M. Davies (ed.) *The Blackwell Companion to Social Work*, 3rd edn. Oxford: Blackwell Publishing.

Daniel, B. and Bowes, A. (2010) Re-thinking harm and abuse: insights from a lifespan perspective, *British Journal of Social Work* (DOI: 10.1093/bjsw/bcq116).

Daniel, B., Wassell, S. and Gilligan, R. (1999) *Child Development for Child Care and Child Protection Workers*. London: Jessica Kingsley.

Dartington Social Research Unit (DSRU) (1995) *Child Protection and Child Abuse: Messages from Research*. London: HMSO.

Davies, M. (1981) *The Essential Social Worker: A Guide to Positive Practice*. Aldershot: Arena.

Davis, A. and Ellis, K. (1995) Enforced altruism in community care, in R. Hugman and D. Smith (eds.) *Ethical Issues in Social Work*. London: Routledge.

Davis, A. and Garrett, P.M. (2004) Progressive practice in tough times: social work, poverty and division in the 21st century, in M. Lymbery and S. Butler (eds.) *Social Work Ideals and Practice Realities*. Basingstoke: Palgrave Macmillan.

de Shazer, S. (1985) *Keys to Solution in Brief Therapy*. London: W.W. Norton.

Department for Communities and Local Government (2011) *Travellers*. Available at: http://www.communities.gov.uk/documents/statistics/pdf/1932949.pdf [accessed 10 September 2011].

Department for Education and Skills (2003) *Every Child Matters*. London: The Stationery Office.

Department for Works and Pensions (2009) *Income Related Benefits Estimates of Take-Up in 2007–08*. Available at: http://www.dwp.gov.uk/docs/ifd250609benefits.pdf [accessed 9 July 2011].

Department of Health (1989) *The Care of Children: Principles and Practice in Regulations and Guidance*. London: HMSO.

Department of Health (1999) *Royal Commission on Long Term Care: NHS Plan*. London: Department of Health.

Department of Health (2000) *Framework for the Assessment of Children in Need and their Families*. London: Department of Health.

Department of Health (2001) *National Framework for Older People*. London: Department of Health.

Department of Health (2002) *Guidance on the Single Assessment Process for Older People*, HSC 2002/001: LAC (2002) 1. London: Department of Health.

Department of Health (2003) *Fair Access to Care Services: Guidance on Eligibility Criteria for Adult Social Care*. London: Department of Health.

Department of Health (2005) *Adult Social Care*. London: Department of Health.

Department of Health (2008a) *Transforming Social Care*, LAC (DH) 1. London: Department of Health. Available from: http://www.dh.gov.uk/en/Publicationsandstatistics/Lettersandcirculars/LocalAuthorityCirculars/DH_081934 [accessed 19 April 2009].

Department of Health (2008b) *Putting People First – Working to Make it Happen: Adult Social Care Workforce Strategy – Interim Statement*. London: Department of Health.

Department of Health and Department for Education and Skills (2006) *Options for Excellence: Building the Social Care Workforce of the Future*. London: Department of Health.

Department of Health and Social Security (1980) *Inequalities in Health* (The Black Report). London: HMSO.

Devaney, J., Lazenbatt, A. and Bunting, L. (2011) Inquiring into non-accidental child deaths: reviewing the review process, *British Journal of Social Work*, 41: 242–60.

Dickson, D. and Bamford, D. (1995) Improving the inter-personal skills of social work students – the problem of transfer of learning and what to do about it, *British Journal of Social Work*, 25: 85–105.

DiClemente, C.C. (2006) Natural change and the troublesome use of substances, in W.R. Miller and K.M. Carroll (eds.) *Rethinking Substance Abuse: What the Science Shows, and What We Should Do About it*. London: Guilford Press.

DiClemente, C.C. and Velasquez, M.M. (2002) Motivational interviewing and the stages of change, in W.R. Miller and S. Rollnick (eds.) *Motivational Interviewing: Preparing People for Change*, 2nd edn. London: Guilford Press.

Dinnerstein, D. (1978) *The Rocking of the Cradle*. London: Souvenir Press.

Dominelli, L. (1997) *Sociology for Social Work*. Basingstoke: Macmillan.

Dominelli, L. (2002) *Feminist Social Work Theory and Practice*. Basingstoke: Palgrave.

Dominelli, L. (2008) Feminist theory, in M. Davis (ed.) *The Blackwell Companion to Social Work*, 3rd edn. Oxford: Blackwell Publishing.

Dominelli, L. (2009) Anti-oppressive practice: the challenges in the twenty-first century, in R. Adams, L. Dominelli and M. Payne (eds.) *Social Work: Themes, Issues and Critical Debates*, 3rd edn. Basingstoke: Palgrave Macmillan.

Dominelli, L. and Holloway, M. (2008) Ethics and governance in social work research in the UK, *British Journal of Social Work*, 38: 1009–24.

Dorling, D. (2010) *Injustice: Why Social Inequality Persists*. Bristol: Policy Press.

Doyle, C. (2006) *Working with Abused Children*, 3rd edn. Basingstoke: Macmillan.

Drakeford, M. (2008) Social work and politics, in M. Davies (ed.) *The Blackwell Companion to Social Work*, 3rd edn. Oxford: Blackwell Publishing.

Dreyfus, H.L. and Dreyfus, S.E. (1986) *Mind over Machine: The Power of Human Intuition and Expertise in the Age of the Computer*. Oxford: Blackwell Publishing.

Drury Hudson, J. (1997) A model of professional knowledge for social work, *Australian Social Work*, 50(3): 35–44.

Drury Hudson, J. (1999) Decision making in child protection: the use of theoretical, empirical and procedural knowledge by novices and experts and implications for fieldwork placement, *British Journal of Social Work*, 29: 147–69.

Dustin, D. (2007) *The Mcdonaldization of Social Work*. Aldershot: Ashgate.

Eagleton, T. (2007) *The Meaning of Life*. Oxford: Oxford University Press.

Edwards, J.B. and Richards, A. (2002) Relational teaching: a view of relational teaching in social work education, *Journal of Teaching in Social Work*, 22(1/2): 33–48.

Egan, G. (2002) *The Skilled Helper: A Systematic Approach to Effective Helping*, 7th edn. Pacific Grove, CA: Brooks/Cole.

Egan, G. (2007) The Skilled Helper: A Problem-Management and Opportunity Development Approach to Helping, 9th edn. Belmont, CA: Brooks/Cole, Cengage Learning.

Eichenbaum, L. and Orbach, S. (1982) *Outside In: Inside Out. Women's Psychology: A Feminist Psychoanalytic Approach*. Harmondsworth: Penguin.

Eichenbaum, L. and Orbach, S. (1984) *What do Women Want?* London: Fontana.

Elliott, N. (2008) The global vortex: social welfare in a networked world, *Journal of Social Work Practice*, 22(3): 269–87.

Ellis, A. (1977) The basic clinical theory of rational-emotive therapy, in A.A. Ellis and R. Greiger (eds.) *Handbook of Rational-Emotive Therapy*, Vol. 1. New York: Springer.

Ellis, A., Gordon, J., Neenan, M. and Palmer, S. (1997) *Stress Counselling: A Rational Emotive Behaviour Approach*. London: Cassell.

England, H. (1986) *Social Work as Art: Making Sense of Good Practice*. London: Allen & Unwin.

Epstein, L. (1980) *Helping People: The Task-centered Approach*. St. Louis, MO: Mosby.

Epstein, L. (1995) Brief task-centered social work, in R.L. Edwards (ed.) *Encyclopedia of Social Work*, 19th edn., Vol. 1. Washington, DC: National Association of Social Workers.

Epstein, L. and Brown, L.B. (2002) *Brief Treatment and a New Look at the Task-centered Approach*. London: Allyn & Bacon.

Eraut, M. (1985) Knowledge creation and knowledge use in professional contexts, *Studies in Higher Education*, 10(2): 117–33.

Eraut, M. (1994) *Developing Professional Knowledge and Competence*. London: Falmer Press.

Eraut, M. (2008) How professionals learn through work. Unpublished paper from SCEPTrE, University of Sussex.

Erikson, E. (1965) *Childhood and Society*, 2nd edn. Harmondsworth: Penguin.

Ernst, S. and Maguire, M. (eds.) (1987) *Living With the Sphinx: Papers from the London Women's Therapy Centre*. London: Women's Press.

Erskine, A. (2003) The approaches and methods of social policy, in P. Alcock, A. Erskine and M. May (eds.) *The Student's Companion to Social Policy*, 2nd edn. Oxford: Blackwell Publishing.

Evans, O. (2010) Two children in care cost Buckinghamshire County Council £750k, *This is Local London*, 8 June. Available at: http://www.thisislocallondon.co.uk/news/8207200.print [accessed 6 August 2010].

Evans, T. (2011) Professionals, managers and discretion: critiquing street-level bureaucracy, *British Journal of Social Work*, 41: 368–86.

Everitt, A. and Hardiker, P. (1996) *Evaluating Good Practice*. Basingstoke: Macmillan/BASW.

Fairbairn, W.R. (1952) *Psychoanalytic Studies of the Personality*. London: Routledge & Kegan Paul.

Feltham, C. and Dryden, W. (2004) *Dictionary of Counselling*, 2nd edn. London: Whurr.

Ferguson, I. (2008) *Reclaiming Social Work: Challenging Neo-Liberalism and Promoting Social Justice*. London: Sage.

Ferguson, I. and Woodward, R. (2009) *Radical Social Work in Practice: Making a Difference*. Bristol: Policy Press.

Fisher, M. (ed.) (1983) *Speaking of Clients*. Sheffield: Social Services Research.

Fisher, M. (1998) Research, knowledge and practice in community care, *Issues in Social Work Education*, 17(2): 1–14.

Fisher, M. (2002) The Social Care Institute for Excellence, the role of a national institute in developing knowledge and practice in social care, *Social Work and Social Sciences Review*, 10(1): 36–64.

Fisher, M. (2003) Preface, in R. Pawson, A. Boaz, L. Grayson, A. Long and C. Barnes, *Types and Quality of Knowledge in Social Care*. SCIE Knowledge Review #7. Bristol: Policy Press.

Fiske, S.T. and Taylor, S.E. (1991) *Social Cognition*, 2nd edn. London: McGraw-Hill.

Flax, J. (1981) The conflict between nurturance and autonomy in mother–daughter relationships and within feminism, in E. Howell and M. Bayes (eds.) *Women and Mental Health*. New York: Basic Books.

Folgheraiter, F. (2004) *Relational Social Work: Toward Networking and Societal Practices*. London: Jessica Kingsley.

Fonagy, P., Steele, H., Higgitt, A. and Target, M. (1994) The Emmanuel Miller Memorial Lecture 1992: 'The theory and practice of resilience', *Journal of Child Psychology and Psychiatry*, 35(2): 231–57.

Fook, J. (2002) *Social Work, Critical Theory and Practice*. London: Sage.

Fook, J., Ryan, M. and Hawkins, L. (2000) *Professional Expertise: Practice, Theory and Education for Working in Uncertainty*. London: Whiting & Birch.

Foot, H.C. (1997) Humour and laughter, in O.D.W. Hargie (ed.) *The Handbook of Communication Skills*, 2nd edn. London: Routledge.

Forrester, D., Kershaw, S., Moss, H. and Hughes, L. (2007) Communication skills in child protection: how do social workers talk to parents?, *Child and Family Social Work*, 13: 41–51.

Forrester, D., McCambridge, J., Waissbein, C., Emlyn-Jones, R. and Rollnick, S. (2008) Child risk and parental resistance: can *motivational interviewing* improve the practice of child and family social workers in working with parental alcohol misuse, *British Journal of Social Work*, 38: 1302–19.

Foucault, M. (1984) *The Foucault Reader*, edited by P. Rabinow. New York: Pantheon Books.

Fraser, M.W., Richman, J.M., Galisnsky, M.J. and Day, S.H. (2009) *Intervention Research: Developing Social Programs*. Oxford: Oxford University Press.

French, R. (1999) The importance of capacities in psychoanalysis and the language of human development, *International Journal of Psychoanalysis*, 80: 1215–25.

French, S. and Swain, J. (2008) The perspective of the Disabled People's Movement, in M. Davies (ed.) *The Blackwell Companion to Social Work*, 3rd edn. Oxford: Blackwell Publishing.

Freud, S. (1919/1924) Turnings in the way of psycho-analytic therapy, *Collected Papers (Vol II). Clinical Papers: Papers on Technique*, 4th edn. London: Hogarth Press.

Frost, L. (2008) Why teach social work students psychosocial studies?, *Social Work Education*, 27(3): 243–61.

Gambrill, E. (1985) Behavioural approach, in J.B. Turner (ed.) *Encyclopedia of Social Work*, 18th edn., Vol. 1. Washington, DC: National Association of Social Workers.

Gambrill, E. (1995) Behavioural theory, in R.L. Edwards (ed.) *Encyclopedia of Social Work*, 19th edn., Vol. 1. Washington, DC: National Association of Social Workers.

Gambrill, E. (1997) *Social Work Practice: A Critical Thinker's Guide*. Oxford: Oxford University Press.

Gambrill, E. (2006) *Social Work Practice: A Critical Thinker's Guide*, 2nd edn. Oxford: Oxford University Press.

Gambrill, E. (2010) Evidence-informed practice: antidote to propaganda in the helping professions?, *Research on Social Work Practice*, 20: 302–20.

Garbarino, J. and Kostelny, K. (1992) Child maltreatment as a community problem, *Child Abuse and Neglect*, 16: 455–64.

Garrett, P.M. (2007) Making 'anti-social behaviour': a fragment on the evolution of 'ASBO politics' in Britain, *British Journal of Social Work*, 37: 839–56.

Gender Identity Research and Education Society (GIRES) (2009) Gender variance in the UK: prevalence, incidence, growth and distribution. Available at: http://www.gires.org.uk/assets/Medpro-Assets/GenderVarianceUKreport.pdf [accessed 10 September 2011].

General Social Care Council (GSCC) (2002) Codes of Practice for Social Care Workers and Employers. London: GSCC. Available at: http://www.gscc.org.uk.

General Social Care Council (GSCC) (2008) *Social Work at its Best: A Statement of Social Work Roles and Tasks for the 21st Century*. London: GSCC.

Gentleman, A. and Mulholland, H. (2010) Unequal Britain: richest 10% are now 100 times better off than the poorest, *Guardian*, 19 September.

Gerdes, K.E., Segal, E.A. and Lietz, C.A. (2010) Conceptualising and measuring empathy, *British Journal of Social Work*, 40(7): 2326–43.

Germain, C. (1983) *Handbook of Clinical Social Work*. San Francisco, CA: Jossey-Bass.

Germain, C.B. and Gitterman, A. (1995) Ecological perspective, in R.L. Edwards (ed.) *Encyclopedia of Social Work*, 19th edn., Vol. 1. Washington, DC: National Association of Social Workers.

Gibbs, L. and Gambrill, E. (1996) *Critical Thinking for Social Workers: Exercises for the Helping Profession*. Thousand Oaks, CA: Pine Forge Press.

Gibson, A. (2007) Erikson's life cycle approach to development, in J. Lishman (ed.) *Handbook for Practice Learning in Social Work and Social Care: Knowledge and Theory*. London: Jessica Kingsley.

Giddens, A. (2001) *Sociology*, 4th edn. Cambridge: Polity Press.

Gilchrist, A. (2004) *The Well-Connected Community*. Bristol: Polity Press.

Gill, O. and Jack, G. (2007) *The Child and Family in Context: Developing Ecological Practice in Disadvantaged Communities.* Lyme Regis: Russell House.

Gilligan, C. (1993) *In a Different Voice: Psychological Theory and Women's Development*, 2nd edn. Cambridge, MA: Harvard University Press.

Gilligan, J. (2001) *Preventing Violence.* London: Thames & Hudson.

Gilligan, R. (1997) Beyond permanence? The importance of resilience in child placement practice and planning, *Adoption and Fostering*, 21(1): 12–20.

Gitterman, C.B. and Germaine, A. (2008) *The Life Model of Social Work Practice: Advances in Theory and Practice*, 3rd edn. New York: Columbia University Press.

Goldstein, B.P. (2008) Black perspectives, in M. Davies (ed.) *The Blackwell Companion to Social Work*, 3rd edn. Oxford: Blackwell Publishing.

Goldstein, E.G. (1995a) Psychosocial approach, in R.L. Edwards (ed.) *Encyclopedia of Social Work*, 19th edn., Vol. 1. Washington, DC: National Association of Social Workers.

Goldstein, E.G. (1995b) *Ego Psychology and Social Work Practice*, 2nd edn. London: Free Press.

Goleman, D. (1996) *Emotional Intelligence: Why it can matter more than IQ.* London: Bloomsbury.

Goodman, A. (2009) *Social Work with Drug and Substance Misusers.* Exeter: Learning Matters.

Gough, D. (1993) *Child Abuse Investigations: A Review of the Research Literature.* London: HMSO.

Gould, N. (2000) Becoming a learning organisation: a social work example, *Social Work Education*, 19(6): 585–96.

Gould, N. (2006) An inclusive approach to knowledge for mental health social work practice and policy, *British Journal of Social Work*, 36(1): 109–25.

Gould, N. and Kendall, T. (2007) Developing the NICE–SCIE Guidelines for Dementia Care: The challenges of enhancing the evidence base for social and health care, *British Journal of Social Work*, 37(3): 475–90.

Graham, M. (2002) Creating spaces: exploring the role of cultural knowledge as a source of empowerment in models of social welfare in Black Communities, *British Journal of Social Work*, 32: 35–49.

Gray, B. (2009) Befriending excluded families in Tower Hamlets: the emotional labour of family support workers in cases of child protection and family support, *British Journal of Social Work*, 39: 990–1007.

Gray, M. (2010) Theories of social work practice, in L. Nicholas, J. Rautenbach and M. Maistry (eds.) *Introduction to Social Work.* Cape Town: Juta.

Gray, M. and Schubert, L. (2010) Turning base metal into gold: transmuting art, practice, research and experience into knowledge, *British Journal of Social Work*, 40: 2308–25.

Gray, M. and Webb, S.A. (eds.) (2009) *Social Work Theories and Methods*. London: Sage.

Griffiths, R. (1988) *Community Care: Agenda for Action*. London: HMSO.

Guntrip, H. (1977) *Psychoanalytic Theory, Therapy and the Self*. London: Hogarth.

Gutiérrez, L.M. (1990) Working with women of color: an empowerment perspective, *Social Work*, 35(2): 149–53.

Habermas, J. (1968) *Knowledge and Human Interests*. London: Heinemann.

Hafford-Letchfield, T. (2010) The age of opportunity? Revisiting assumptions about the life-long learning opportunities of older people using social care services, *British Journal of Social Work*, 40: 496–512.

Hague, G. and Malos, E. (2005) *Domestic Violence: Action for Change*. Cheltenham: New Clarion.

Halpern, D. and Bates, C. (with G. Beales and A. Heathfield) (2004) *Personal Responsibility and Changing Behaviour: The State of Knowledge and its Implications for Public Policy*. Discussion paper. Cabinet Office: Prime Minister's Strategy Unit.

Hamner, J. and Statham, D. (1999) *Women and Social Work: Towards a Woman-Centred Practice*, 2nd edn. Basingstoke: Macmillan/BASW.

Hardiker, P. and Barker, M. (1994) *The 1989 Children Act – Significant Harm: The Experience of Social Workers Implementing New Legislation*. Leicester: University of Leicester School of Social Work.

Hargie, O. and Dickson, D. (2004) *Skilled Interpersonal Communication: Research, Theory and Practice*, 4th edn. Hove: Routledge.

Harne, L. and Radford, J. (2008) *Tackling Domestic Violence: Theories, Policies and Practice*. Maidenhead: Open University Press.

Harris, J. (2003) Let's talk business, *Community Care*, 21 August, pp. 36–7.

Harris, J. and White, V. (eds.) (2009) *Modernising Social Work: Critical Considerations*. Bristol: Policy Press.

Hart, J.T. (2004) Inverse and positive care laws, *British Journal of General Practice*, 54(509): 890.

Hartman, A. (1992) In search of subjugated knowledge, *Social Work*, 37(6): 483–4.

Hartman, H. (1981) The unhappy marriage of Marxism and feminism: towards a more progressive union, in L. Sargent (ed.) *Women and Revolution*. Boston, MA: South End.

Hatcher, S. and Arroll, B. (2008) Assessment and management of medically unexplained symptoms, *British Medical Journal*, 336: 1124–8.

Hayes, D. and Houston, S. (2007) 'Lifeworld', 'system' and family group conferences: Habermas's contribution to discourse in child protection, *British Journal of Social Work*, 37(6): 987–1006.

Healy, K. (2000) *Social Work Practices: Contemporary Perspectives on Change*. London: Sage.

(2005) *An Introduction to Systemic Therapy with Families*. Base: Palgrave Macmillan.

. (2008) Adolescence, in M. Davies (ed.) *The Blackwell Companion al Work*, 3rd edn. Oxford: Blackwell Publishing.

ty's Revenue and Customs (HMRC) (2007) *Child Tax Credit and working Tax Credit: Take-up rates 2006–07*. Available at: http://www.hmrc.gov.uk/stats/personal-tax-credits/cwtc-take-up2006-07.pdf [accessed 9 July 2011].

Her Majesty's Treasury (2004) *The Orange Book Management of Risk – Principles and Concepts*. London: HM Treasury.

Hester, M., Pearson, C., Harwin, N. and Abrahams, H. (2006) *Making an Impact – Children and Domestic Violence: A Reader*, 2nd edn. London: Jessica Kingsley.

Hibbert, J. and van Heeswyk, D. (1988) Black women's workshop, in S. Krzowski and P. Land (eds.) *In Our Experience: Workshops at the Women's Therapy Centre*. London: Women's Press.

Hills, J., Brewer, M., Jenkins, S., Lister, R., Lupton, R., Machin, S., Mills, C., Modood, T., Rees, T. and Riddel, S. (2010) *An Anatomy of Economic Inequality in the UK: Summary*. Report of the National Equality Panel. London: Government Equalities Office.

Hockenbury, D.H. and Hockenbury, S.E. (2002) *Psychology*, 3rd edn. New York: Worth Publishers.

Hoggett, P. (2000) *Emotional Life and the Politics of Welfare*. Basingstoke: Macmillan.

Hollis, F. (1964) *Casework: A Psychosocial Therapy*. New York: Random House.

Hollis, F. (1977) Social casework: the psychosocial approach, in J.B. Turner (ed.) *Encyclopedia of Social Work*, 17th edn. Washington, DC: National Association of Social Workers.

Hollis, M. and Howe, D. (1990) Moral risks in the social work role: a response to Macdonald, *British Journal of Social Work*, 20: 547–52.

Holman, R. (1993) *A New Deal for Social Welfare*. Oxford: Lion.

Horder, W. (2002) Care management, in M. Davies (ed.) *The Blackwell Companion to Social Work*, 2nd edn. Oxford: Blackwell Publishing.

Houston, S. (2010) Beyond *homo economicus*: recognition, self-realization and social work, *British Journal of Social Work*, 40: 841–57.

Howarth, J. and Shardlow, S.M. (2003) *Making Links across Specialisms: Understanding Modern Social Work Practice*. Exeter: Russell House.

Howe, D. (1987) *An Introduction to Social Work Theory*. Aldershot: Gower.

Howe, D. (1994) Modernity, post modernity and social work, *British Journal of Social Work*, 24: 513–32.

Howe, D. (1995) *Attachment Theory for Social Work Practice*. Basingstoke: Macmillan.

Howe, D. (1996) Surface and depth in social-work practice, in N. Parton (ed.) *Social Theory, Social Change and Social Work*. London: Routledge.

Howe, D. (1998) Relationship-based thinking and practice in social work, *Journal of Social Work Practice*, 16(2): 45–56.

Howe, D. (2002) Psychosocial work, in R. Adams, L. Dominelli and M. Payne (eds.) *Social Work: Themes, Issues and Critical Debates*, 2nd edn. Basingstoke: Macmillan.

Howe, D. (2006) Disabled children, maltreatment and attachment, *British Journal of Social Work*, 36: 743–60.

Howe, D. (2008a) Relating theory to practice, in M. Davies (ed.) *The Blackwell Companion to Social Work*, 3rd edn. Oxford: Blackwell Publishing.

Howe, D. (2008b) *The Emotionally Intelligent Social Worker*. Basingstoke: Palgrave Macmillan.

Howe, D. (2009) *A Brief Introduction to Social Work Theory*. Basingstoke: Palgrave Macmillan.

Howe, D. (2011) *Attachment across the Lifecourse: A Brief Introduction*. Basingtoke: Palgrave Macmillan.

Howe, D., Brandon, M., Hinings, D. and Schofield, G. (1999) *Attachment Theory, Child Maltreatment and Family Support*. Basingstoke: Macmillan.

Hudson, B.L. and Macdonald, G. (1986) *Behavioural Social Work: An Introduction*. London: Macmillan.

Hudson, B.L. and Sheldon, B. (2000) The cognitive-behavioural approach, in M. Davies (ed.) *The Blackwell Encyclopaedia of Social Work*. Oxford: Blackwell Publishing.

Hughes, M. and Wearing, M. (2007) *Organisations and Management in Social Work*. London: Sage.

Hugman, R. (1991) *Power in Caring Professions*. Basingstoke: Macmillan.

Hugman, R. (2009) But is it social work? Some reflections on mistaken identities, *British Journal of Social Work*, 39: 1138–53.

Humphries, C. (2008) Domestic violence, in M. Davies (ed.) *The Blackwell Companion to Social Work*, 3rd edn. Oxford: Blackwell Publishing.

Huxley, P. (2008) Mental illness, in M. Davies (ed.) *The Blackwell Companion to Social Work*, 3rd edn. Oxford: Blackwell Publishing.

Inman, P. (2010) Pension pots increase by £400,000 in a year for top company directors, *Guardian*, 9 September.

International Federation of Social Workers (IFSW) (2010) *Poverty Eradication: The Role of Social Work*. Available at: http://www.ifsw.org/p38001913.html [accessed 1 June 2011].

International Federation of Social Workers/International Association of Schools of Social Work (IFSW/IASSW) (2000) *Definition of Social Work*. Available at: http://www.ifsw.org/en/p38000208.html [accessed 1 June 2011].

Issitt, M. and Woodward, M. (1992) Competence and contradiction, in P. Carter, T. Jeffs and M.K. Smith (eds.) *Changing Social Work and Welfare*. Buckingham: Open University Press.

Ixer, G. (1999) There's no such thing as reflection, *British Journal of Social Work*, 29: 513–27.

Jack, G. (2000) Ecological influences on parenting and child development, *British Journal of Social Work*, 30: 703–20.

Jack, G. (2012) Ecological perspective, in M. Gray, J. Midgley and S. Webb (eds.) *Social Work Handbook*. London: Sage (forthcoming).

Jack, G. and Gill, O. (2003) *The Missing Side of the Triangle: Assessing the Importance of Family and Environmental Factors in the Lives of Children*. Ilford: Barnardo's.

Jack, G. and Jack, D. (2000) Ecological social work: the application of a systems model of development in context, in P. Stepney and D. Ford (eds.) *Social Work Models, Methods and Theories*. Lyme Regis: Russell House.

Jackson, S. (2000) Children's rights, in M. Davies (ed.) *The Blackwell Encyclopaedia of Social Work*. Oxford: Blackwell Publishing.

Jacobs, M. (2010) *Psychodynamic Counselling in Action*, 4th edn. London: Sage.

James, A.L. (2008) Social work, divorce and the family courts, in M. Davies (ed.) *The Blackwell Companion to Social Work*, 3rd edn. Oxford: Blackwell Publishing.

Janis, I.L. (1982) *Groupthink: Psychological Studies of Policy Decisions and Fiascoes*. Boston, MA: Houghton Mifflin.

Jessup, G. (1991) *Outcomes: NVQs and the Emerging Model of Education and Training*. London: Falmer Press.

Jewett, C. (1997) *Helping Children Cope with Separation and Loss*. London: Free Association Books.

John, M. and Trevithick, P. (2012) Psychosocial practice in social work, in P. Stepney and D. Ford (eds.) *Social Work Models, Methods and Theories*, 2nd edn. Lyme Regis: Russell House (forthcoming).

Jones, C. (1997) British social work and the classless society: the failure of a profession, in H. Jones (ed.) *Towards a Classless Society?* London: Routledge.

Jones, K., Cooper, B. and Ferguson, H. (eds.) (2008) *Best Practice in Social Work: Critical Perspectives*. Basingstoke: Palgrave Macmillan.

Jones, R. (2008) The sixth giant: We need another giant step to tackle care and support, *Guardian*, 1 October 2008.

Jordan, B. (1990) *Social Work in an Unjust Society*. London: Harvester/Wheatsheaf.

Jordan, B. and Parton, N. (2000) Politics and social work, in M. Davies (ed.) *The Blackwell Encyclopaedia of Social Work*. Oxford: Blackwell Publishing.

Jordan, J.V. (1991) Empathy, mutuality, and therapeutic change: clinical implications of a relational model, in J.V. Jordan, A.G. Kaplan, J.B. Miller, I.P. Stiver and J.L. Surrey (eds.) *Women's Growth and Connection: Writings from the Stone Center*. New York: Guilford Press.

Jordan, J.V. (ed.) (1997) *More Writings from the Stone Center*. New York: Guilford Press.

Jordan, J.V. (ed.) (2007) *Women's Growth in Diversity: More Writings from the Stone Center*. New York: Guilford Press.

Jordan, J.V. (2009) *Relational-Cultural Therapy*. Washington, DC: American Psychological Association.

Jordan, J.V., Kaplan, A.G., Miller, J.B., Stiver, I.P. and Surrey, J.L. (eds.) (1991) *Women's Growth and Connection: Writings from the Stone Center*. New York: Guilford Press.

Joseph Rowntree Charitable Trust (2007) *Moving on from Destitution to Contribution: Joseph Rowntree Charitable Trust Inquiry into Destitution among Refused Asylum Seekers. Commissioner's Report*. York: JRCT.

Joseph Rowntree Foundation (2009) *Monitoring Poverty and Social Exclusion*. Available at: http://www.jrf.org.uk/publications/monitoring-poverty-2009 [accessed 1 June 2011].

Kadushin, A. and Kadushin, G. (1997) *The Social Work Interview: A Guide for Human Service Professionals*, 4th edn. New York: Columbia University Press.

Kanter, J.S. (2004) *Face to Face with Children: The Life and Work of Clare Winnicott*. London: Karnac Books.

Karpman, S. (1968) Fairy tales and script drama analysis, *Transactional Analysis Bulletin*, 7: 39–48.

Kelly, J. and Horder, W. (2001) The how and the why: competences and holistic practice, *Social Work Education*, 20(6): 689–99.

Kemshall, H. and Pritchard, J. (1999) *Good Practice in Working with Violence*. London: Jessica Kingsley.

Kennard, D., Roberts, J. and Winter, D.A. (1993) *A Work Book of Group-Analytic Interventions*. London: Routledge.

Kisthardt, W.E. (2009) A strengths model of case management: the principles and functions of a helping partnership with persons with persistent mental illness, in D. Saleebey (ed.) *The Strengths Perspective in Social Work Practice*. London: Longman.

Klein, W.C. and Bloom, M. (1995) Practice wisdom, *Social Work*, 40(6): 799–807.

Kohlberg, L. (1969) *Stages in the Development of Moral Thought and Action*. New York: Holt, Rinehart & Harcourt Brace.

Kolb, D.A. (1984) *Experiential Learning: Experience as the Source of Learning and Development*. London: Prentice-Hall.

Koprowska, J. (2010) *Communication and Interpersonal Skills in Social Work*, 3rd edn. Exeter: Learning Matters.

Kris, E. (1956) The recovery of childhood memories in psychoanalysis, *Psychoanalytic Study of the Child*, 11: 54–88.

Krzowski, S. and Land, P. (1988) *In Our Experience: Running Workshops with Women*. London: The Women's Press.

Kuhn, T.S. (1970) *The Structure of Scientific Revolutions*. Chicago, IL: Chicago University Press (first published 1962).

Laming, H. (2003) *The Victoria Climbié Inquiry: Report of an Inquiry by Lord Laming*. (Cmnd. 5730). London: The Stationery Office.

Laming, H. (2009) *The Protection of Children in England: A Progress Report*. London: The Stationery Office.

Land, H. and Himmelweit, S. (2010) *Who Cares: Who Pays? A Report on Personalisation in Social Care Prepared for UNISON*, March. Available at: http://www.unison.org.uk/acrobat/19020.pdf [accessed 5 September 2010].

Langan, M. (2002) The legacy of radical social work, in R. Adams, L. Dominelli and M. Payne (eds.) *Social Work: Themes, Issues and Critical Debates*, 2nd edn. Basingstoke: Macmillan.

Langan, M. and Lee, P. (eds.) (1989) *Radical Social Work Today*. London: Unwin Hyman.

Lavalette, M. (2011) *Radical Social Work Today: Social Work at the Crossroads*. Bristol: Policy Press.

Lawler, J. (1994) A competence based approach to management education in social work: a discussion of the approach and its relevance, *Social Work Education*, 13(1): 60–82.

Leece, J. and Leece, D. (2011) Personalisation: perceptions of the role of social work in a world of brokers and budgets, *British Journal of Social Work*, 41: 204–23.

Lefcourt, H.M. (1976) *Locus of Control: Current Trends in Theory and Research*. Hillsdale, NJ: Lawrence Erlbaum Associates.

Lefevre, M. (2010) *Communicating with Children and Young People: Making a Difference*. Bristol: Policy Press.

Le Riche, P. and Tanner, K. (2000) Observation in social work, in M. Davies (ed.) *The Blackwell Encyclopaedia of Social Work*. Oxford: Blackwell Publishing.

Lerner, B. (1972) *Therapy in the Ghetto*. Baltimore, MD: Johns Hopkins University Press.

Lesser, Y. (2007) Potential space: knowing and not knowing in the treatment of traumatized children and young people, *British Journal of Social Work*, 37: 23–37.

Lishman, J. (2009a) *Communication in Social Work*, 2nd edn. Basingstoke: Macmillan/BASW.

Lishman, J. (2009b) Personal and professional development, in R. Adams, L. Dominelli and M. Payne (eds.) *Social Work: Themes, Issues and Critical Debates*, 3rd edn. Basingstoke: Palgrave Macmillan.

Littlechild, B. (2005) The nature and effects of violence against child-protection social workers: providing effective support, *British Journal of Social Work*, 35: 387–401.

Local Government Association (LGA) (2010) *The LGA Quick Guide to Local Government*. London: LGA.

Loewenberg, F.M. (1984) Professional ideology, middle range theories and knowledge building for social work practice, *British Journal of Social Work*, 14: 309–22.

Long, A.F., Grayson, L. and Boaz, A. (2006) Assessing the quality of knowledge in social care: exploring the potential of a set of generic standards, *British Journal of Social Work*, 36: 207–26.

Lovat, T. and Gray, M. (2008) Towards a proportionist social work ethics: a Habermasian perspective, *British Journal of Social Work*, 38: 1100–14.

Lukes, S. (1974) *Power: A Radical View*. London: Macmillan.

Lymbery, M.E.F. (2003) Negotiating the contradictions between competence and creativity in social work education, *Journal of Social Work*, 3(1): 99–117.

Macdonald, G. (1990) Allocating blame in social work, *British Journal of Social Work*, 20: 525–46.

Macdonald, G. (2007) Cognitive behavioural social work, in J. Lishman (ed.) *Handbook for Practice Learning in Social Work and Social Care*, 2nd edn. London: Jessica Kingsley.

Macdonald, G. (2008) The evidence-based perspective, in M. Davies (ed.) *The Blackwell Companion to Social Work*, 3rd edn. Oxford: Blackwell Publishing.

Macdonald, G. and Macdonald, K. (1995) Ethical issues in social work research, in R. Hugman and D. Smith (eds.) *Ethical Issues in Social Work*. London: Routledge.

Macdonald, G. and Macdonald, K. (2010) Safeguarding: a case for intelligent risk management, *British Journal of Social Work*, 40: 1174–91.

Main, M. (1995) Recent studies in attachment: overview, with selected implications for clinical work, in S. Goldberg, R. Muir and J. Kerr (eds.) *Attachment Theory: Social, Developmental and Clinical Perspectives*. Hillsdale, NJ: Analytic Press.

Marks, D. (2008) Physical disability, in M. Davies (ed.) *The Blackwell Companion to Social Work*, 3rd edn. Oxford: Blackwell Publishing.

Marmot Review (2010) *Fair Society, Healthy Lives: The Marmot Review*. Available at: http://www.marmot-review.org.uk [accessed 1 June 2011].

Marris, P. (1996) *The Politics of Uncertainty: Attachment in Private and Public Life*. London: Routledge.

Marsh, P. (2008) Task-centred work, in M. Davies (ed.) *The Blackwell Companion to Social Work*, 3rd edn. Oxford: Blackwell Publishing.

Marsh, P. and Doel, M. (2005) *The Task-Centred Book*. London: Routledge/Community Care.

Marsh, P. and Fisher, M. (2005) *Developing the Evidence Base for Social Work and Social Care Practice*. London: Social Care Institute for Excellence.

Marsh, P. and Fisher, M. (2008) The development of problem-solving knowledge for social care practice, *British Journal of Social Work*, 38: 971–87.

Marsh, P. and Triseliotis, J. (1996) *Ready to Practise? Social Workers and Probation Officers: Their Training and First Year at Work*. Aldershot: Avebury.

Maslow, A.H. (1954) *Motivation and Personality*. New York: Harper & Row.

Maslow, A.H. (1968) *Toward a Psychology of Being*, 2nd edn. New York: Van Nostrand.

Maslow, A.H. (1973) *The Farther Reaches of Human Nature*. London: Pelican Books.

Matthews, S., Harvey, A. and Trevithick, P. (2003) Surviving the swamp: using cognitive-behavioural therapy in a social work setting, *Journal of Social Work Practice*, 17(2): 163–72.

Mattinson, J. (1975) *The Reflection Process in Casework Supervision*. London: Institute of Marital Studies.

Mautner, T. (2000) *The Penguin Dictionary of Philosophy*. London: Penguin.

Mayer, J.E. and Timms, N. (1970) *The Client Speaks*. London: Routledge & Kegan Paul.

McBeath, G. and Webb, S.A. (2002) Virtue ethics and social work: being lucky, realistic, and not doing one's duty, *British Journal of Social Work*, 32: 1015–36.

McCluskey, J. (1992) *Where there's a Will: A Guide to Developing Single Homelessness Strategies*. London: Campaign for Homeless and Rootless.

McCulloch, A. (2000) Assertive outreach, in M. Davies (ed.) *The Blackwell Encyclopaedia of Social Work*. Oxford: Blackwell Publishing.

McDonald, A. (2010) *Social Work with Older People*. Cambridge: Polity Press.

McGuire, J. (ed.) (1995) *What Works: Reducing Offending Guidelines from Research and Practice*. Chichester: Wiley.

McLaughlin, H. (2007) *Understanding Social Work Research*. London: Sage.

McLaughlin, H. (2009) What's in a name: 'client', 'patient', 'customer', 'consumer', 'expert by experience', 'service user' – what's next?, *British Journal of Social Work*, 39: 1101–17.

McLaughlin, H. (2010) Keeping service user involvement in research honest, *British Journal of Social Work*, 40: 1591–608.

McLeod, J. (2007) *Counselling Skill*. Maidenhead: Open University Press.

McLeod, J. (2009) *An Introduction to Counselling*, 4th edn. Maidenhead: Open University Press.

Means, R., Richards, S. and Smith, R. (2008) *Community Care: Policy and Practice*, 4th edn. Basingstoke: Palgrave Macmillan.

Mearns, D. and Thorne, D. (2000) *Person-centred Therapy Today: New Frontiers in Theory and Practice*. London: Sage.

Mehrabian, A. (1972) *Nonverbal Communication*. Chicago, IL: Aldine.

Mercer, S.W. and Reynolds, W.J. (2002) Empathy and quality of care, *British Journal of General Practice*, 52(suppl. 1): 9–12.

Mercer, S.W., McConnachie, A., Maxwell, M., Heaney, D. and Watt, G.C.M. (2004) The Consultation and Relational Empathy (CARE) measure: development and preliminary validation and reliability of an empathy-based consultation process measure, *Family Practice*, 21(6): 699–705.

Merton, R.K. (1968) *Social Theory and Social Structure*, enlarged edition. London: Collier-Macmillan.

Miliband, D. (2006) Speech to the National Council for Voluntary Organisations' Annual Conference, *Guardian*, 21 February.

Millar, R., Crute, V. and Hargie, O. (1992) *Professional Interviewing*. London: Routledge.

Miller, J.B. (1986a) *What do we mean by relationships?* Work in Progress #22. Wellesley, MA: Stone Center Publication.

Miller, J.B. (1986b) *Towards a New Psychology of Women*, 2nd edn. Harmondsworth: Penguin.

Miller, J.B. (2003) *Telling the Truth About Power*. Wellesley, MA: Stone Center.

Miller, J.B and Stiver, I.P. (1997) *The Healing Connection: How Women Form Relationships in Therapy and in Life*. Boston, MA: Beacon Press.

Miller, W.R. (2006) Motivational factors in addictive behaviours, in W.R. Miller and K.M. Carroll (eds.) *Rethinking Substance Abuse: What the Science Shows, and what we should do about it*. London: Guilford Press.

Miller, W.R. and Rollnick, S. (2002) *Motivational Interviewing: Preparing People for Change*, 2nd edn. London: Guilford Press.

Mills, C.W. (1959) *The Sociological Imagination*. Oxford: Oxford University Press.

Milner, J. and O'Byrne, P. (2009) *Assessment in Social Work*, 3rd edn. Basingstoke: Palgrave Macmillan.

Mitchell, J. (1974) *Psychoanalysis and Feminism*. Harmondsworth: Penguin Books.

Mitchell, J. (1984) *Women: The Longest Revolution*. London: Virago.

Moss, B. (2008) *Communication Skills for Health and Social Care*. London: Sage.

Mruk, C.J. (1999) *Self-Esteem: Research, Theory and Practice*, 2nd edn. London: Free Association Books.

Mullaly, R. (1997) *Structural Social Work: Ideology, Theory, and Practice*, 2nd edn. Oxford: Oxford University Press.

Mullaly, R. (2002) *Challenging Oppression: A Critical Social Work Approach.* Oxford: Oxford University Press.

Mullaly, R. (2007) *The New Structural Social Work*, 3rd edn. Oxford: Oxford University Press.

Mullender, A. (2008) Gendering the social work agenda, in M. Davies (ed.) *The Blackwell Companion to Social Work*, 3rd edn. Oxford: Blackwell Publishing.

Munby, T. (2008) The legal perspective, in M. Davies (ed.) *The Blackwell Companion to Social Work*, 3rd edn. Oxford: Blackwell Publishing.

Munro, E. (1996) Avoidable and unavoidable mistakes in child protection work, *British Journal of Social Work*, 26: 793–808.

Munro, E. (1998a) Improving social workers' knowledge base in child protection work, *British Journal of Social Work*, 28: 89–105.

Munro, E. (1998b) *Understanding Social Work: An Empirical Approach.* London: Athlone Press.

Munro, E. (2004) State regulation of parenting, *Political Quarterly*, 75(2): 180–4.

Munro, E. (2008) *Effective Child Protection*, 2nd edn. London: Sage.

Munro, E. (2010a) Learning to reduce risk in child protection, *British Journal of Social Work*, 40: 1135–51.

Munro, E. (2010b) *The Munro Review of Child Protection. Part One: A Systems Analysis.* Available at: http://www.education.gov.uk/munroreview/downloads/TheMunroReviewofChildProtection-Part%20one.pdf [accessed 19 November 2010].

Munro, E. (2011a) *The Munro Review of Child Protection Interim Report: The Child's Journey.* Available at: http://www.education.gov.uk/publications/standard/publicationDetail/Page1/DFE-00010-2011 [accessed 19 February 2011].

Munro, E. (2011b) *The Munro Review of Child Protection: Final Report – A Child-Centred System* (Cm 8062). London: The Stationery Office.

Murphy, R. (2010) Let's tackle the tax gap once and for all, *Guardian*, 20 August.

National Equality Panel (2010) Report of the National Equality Panel: Executive Summary. Available at: http://sticerd.lse.ac.uk/dps/case/cr/CASEreport60_executive_summary.pdf [accessed 10 July 2011].

Nelson-Jones, R. (1990) *Human Relationship Skills.* London: Cassell.

Nelson-Jones, R. (2000) *Introduction to Counselling Skills: Text and Activities.* London: Sage.

Nettleton, S. (2006) *The Sociology of Health and Illness*, 2nd edn. Cambridge: Polity Press.

Nevo, I. and Slonim-Nevo, V. (2011) The myth of evidence-based practice: towards evidence-informed practice, *British Journal of Social Work* (DOI: 10.1093/bjsw/bcq149).

Norton-Taylor, R. (2009) Revealed: the £130bn cost of Trident replacement, *Guardian*, 18 September.

Office for National Statistics (2010) *Social Trends*, No. 40. Basingstoke: Palgrave Macmillan.

O'Hagan, K. (2000) Crisis intervention, in M. Davies (ed.) *The Blackwell Encyclopaedia of Social Work*. Oxford: Blackwell Publishing.

Okitikpi, T. and Aymer, C. (2010) Key Concepts in Anti-Discriminatory Social *Work*. London: Sage.

Orme, J. (2009) Feminist social work, in R. Adams, L. Dominelli and M. Payne (eds.) *Critical Practice in Social Work*, 2nd edn. Basingstoke: Palgrave Macmillan.

Osmond, J. (2005) The knowledge spectrum, a framework for teaching knowledge and its use in social work practice, *British Journal of Social Work*, 35: 881–900.

Osmond, J. and O'Connor, I. (2004) Formalizing the unformalized: practitioners' communication of knowledge in practice, *British Journal of Social Work*, 34: 677–92.

O'Sullivan, T. (1999) *Decision-making in Social Work*. Basingstoke: Macmillan.

O'Sullivan, T. (2005) Some theoretical propositions on the nature of practice wisdom, *Journal of Social Work*, 5: 221–42.

Owen, P. (2010) Database closure could put children at serious risk, warns charity, *Guardian*, 6 August.

Owusu-Bempah, K. (2008) Culture, ethnicity and identity, in M. Davies (ed.) *The Blackwell Companion to Social Work*, 3rd edn. Oxford: Blackwell Publishing.

Palmer, G. (2010) *Relative Poverty, Absolute Poverty and Social Exclusion*. York: Joseph Rowntree Foundation. Available at: http://www.poverty. org.uk/summary/social%20exclusion.shtml [accessed 17 September 2010].

Parad, H.J. (1958) *Ego Psychology and Dynamic Casework*. New York: Family Service Association of America.

Parad, H.J. (1965) *Crisis Intervention: Selected Readings*. New York: Family Service Association of America.

Parsloe, P. (1988) Developing interviewing skills, *Social Work Education*, 8(1): 3–9.

Parsloe, P. (2000) Generic and specialist practice, in M. Davies (ed.) *The Blackwell Encyclopaedia of Social Work*. Oxford: Blackwell Publishing.

Parton, N. (ed.) (1996) *Social Theory, Social Change and Social Work*. London: Routledge.

Parton, N. (2000) Some thoughts on the relationship between theory and practice in and for social work, *British Journal of Social Work*, 30: 449–63.

Parton, N. and Kirk, S. (2010) The nature and purposes of social work, in I.F. Shaw, K. Briar-Lawson, J.R. Orme and R. Ruckdeschel (eds.) *The Sage Handbook of Social Work Research*. London: Sage.

Parton, N. and O'Byrne, P. (2000) *Constructive Social Work: Towards a New Practice.* Basingstoke: Macmillan.

Pavlov, I.P. (1927) *Conditional Reflexes.* London: Oxford University Press.

Pawson, R., Boaz, A., Grayson, L., Long, A. and Barnes, C. (2003) *Types and Quality of Knowledge in Social Care.* SCIE Knowledge Review #7. Bristol: Policy Press.

Payne, M. (1997) *Modern Social Work Theory,* 2nd edn. Basingstoke: Macmillan.

Payne, M. (2005) *Modern Social Work Theory,* 3rd edn. Basingstoke: Macmillan.

Pearson, G. (1973) Social work as the privatized solution of public ills, *British Journal of Social Work,* 3: 209–27.

Pease, B. (2009) From radical to critical social work: progressive transformation or mainstream incorporation?, in R. Adams, L. Dominelli and M. Payne (eds.) *Critical Practice in Social Work,* 2nd edn. Basingstoke: Palgrave Macmillan.

Penna, S. (2000) Modernity, in M. Davies (ed.) *The Blackwell Encyclopaedia of Social Work.* Oxford: Blackwell Publishing.

Perrott, S. (2009) Social work and organisations, in R. Adams, L. Dominelli and M. Payne (eds.) *Social Work: Themes, Issues and Critical Debates,* 3rd edn. Basingstoke: Palgrave Macmillan.

Phillips, A. (1988) *Winnicott.* London: Fontana.

Phillips, J. (1996) The future of social work with older people in a changing world, in N. Parton (ed.) *Social Theory, Social Change and Social Work.* London: Routledge.

Phillips, J. (2007) *Care.* Cambridge: Polity Press.

Phillipson, C. (2008) The frailty of old age, in M. Davies (ed.) *The Blackwell Companion to Social Work,* 3rd edn. Oxford: Blackwell Publishing.

Piachaud, D. and Sutherland, H. (2001) Child poverty in Britain and the New Labour Government, *Journal of Social Policy,* 30(1): 95–118.

Piaget, J. (1932) *The Moral Judgement of the Child.* London: Routledge & Kegan Paul.

Pierson, J. (2002) *Tackling Social Exclusion.* London: Routledge.

Pinker, R. (1990) *Social Work in an Enterprise Society.* London: Routledge.

Polanyi, M. (1967) *The Tacit Dimension,* London: Routledge & Kegan Paul.

Popper, K.L. (1994a) *Knowledge and the Body–Mind Problem: In Defence of Interaction* (edited by M.A. Notturno). London: Routledge.

Popper, K.L. (1994b) *The Myth of the Framework: In Defence of Science and Rationality* (edited by M.A. Notturno). London: Routledge.

Preston-Shoot, M. (1994) Written agreements: a contractual approach to social work, in C. Hanvey and T. Philpot (eds.) *Practising Social Work.* London: Routledge.

Prideaux, D. (2002) Researching the outcomes of educational interventions: a matter of design, *British Medical Journal*, 324: 126–7.

Pritchard, C. (2000a) Self-harm, in M. Davies (ed.) *The Blackwell Encylopaedia of Social Work*, 2nd edn. Oxford: Blackwell Publishing.

Pritchard, C. (2000b) Suicide, in M. Davies (ed.) *The Blackwell Encylopaedia of Social Work*, 2nd edn. Oxford: Blackwell Publishing.

Prochaska, J.O. and Norcross, J.C. (2003) *Systems of Psychotherapy: A Transtheoretical Analysis*. Pacific Grove, CA: Brooks/Cole.

Prochaska, J.O. and Norcross, J.C. (2010) *Systems of Psychotherapy: A Transtheoretical Analysis*, 7th edn. Belmont, CA: Wadsworth Cengage Learning.

Prochaska, J.O., Norcross, J.C. and DiClemente, C.C. (1994) *Changing for Good*. New York: Avon.

Pugh, R. and Williams, D. (2006) Language policy and provision in social service organizations, *British Journal of Social Work*, 36: 1227–44.

Quality Assurance Agency for Higher Education (QAAHE) (2008) *Subject Benchmark Statement for Social Work*. Available at: http://www.qaa.ac.uk/academicinfrastructure/benchmark/statements/socialwork08.

Ramon, S. (1991) *Beyond Community Care: Normalization and Integration Work*. London: Macmillan.

Rapoport, L. (1967) Crisis-orientated short term casework, *Social Services Review*, 41: 31–44.

Reason, J. (1997) *Managing the Risks of Organizational Accidents*. Aldershot: Ashgate.

Reber, A.S., Allen, R. and Reber, E.S. (2009) *The Penguin Dictionary of Psychology*, 4th edn. London: Penguin.

Reid, W.J. (1978) *The Task-Centred System*. New York: Columbia University Press.

Reid, W.J. (2002) Knowledge for direct social work practice: an analysis of trends, *Social Service Review*, 76(1): 6–33.

Reid, W.J. and Epstein, L. (1972) *Task-Centered Casework*. New York: Columbia University Press.

Reid, W.J. and Shyne, A. (1969) *Brief and Extended Casework*. New York: Columbia University Press.

Rey, L.D. (1996) What social workers need to know about client violence, *Families in Society*, 77(1): 33–9.

Richards, S., Ruch, G. and Trevithick, P. (2005) Communication skills training for practice, the ethical dilemma for social work education, *Social Work Education*, 24(4): 409–17.

Roberts, A.R. (ed.) (2005) *Crisis Intervention Handbook: Assessment, Treatment and Research*, 3rd edn. Oxford: Oxford University Press.

Roberts, G. and Preston-Shoot, M. (2000) Law and social work, in M. Davies (ed.) *The Blackwell Encyclopaedia of Social Work*. Oxford: Blackwell Publishing.

Robinson, L. (1995) *Psychology for Social Workers: Black Perspective*. London: Routledge.

Robinson, L. (2000) Social work practice in a multi-cultural society, in M. Davies (ed.) *The Blackwell Encyclopaedia of Social Work*. Oxford: Blackwell Publishing.

Robinson, L. (2007) *Cross-Cultural Child Development for Social Workers: An Introduction*. Basingstoke: Palgrave Macmillan.

Robinson, L. (2009) Cross-cultural and black perspectives through the life course, in R. Adams, L. Dominelli and M. Payne (eds) *Critical Practice in Social Work*, 2nd edn. Basingstoke: Palgrave Macmillan.

Rogers, A. and Pilgrim, D. (2010) *A Sociology of Mental Health and Illness*, 4th edn. Maidenhead: Open University Press.

Rogers, C.R. (1951) *Client-Centered Therapy*. Boston, MA: Houghton Mifflin.

Rogers, C.R. (1957) The necessary and sufficient conditions of therapeutic personality change, *Journal of Consulting Psychology*, 21: 95–103.

Rogers, C.R. (1961) *On Becoming a Person*. Boston, MA: Houghton Mifflin.

Rogers, C.R. (1975) Empathic: an unappreciated way of being, *Counseling Psychologist*, 5: 2–10.

Rojek, C. and Collins, S. (1988) Contact or con trick?, *British Journal of Social Work*, 18: 11–22.

Rollnick, S., Miller, W.R. and Butler, C.C. (2008) *Motivational Interviewing in Health Care: Helping Patients Change Behavior*. London: Guilford Press.

Ronen, T. (2008) Cognitive-behavioural therapy, in M. Davies (ed.) *The Blackwell Companion to Social Work*, 3rd edn. Oxford: Blackwell Publishing.

Rothman, D. (2003) Intervention research, in R.L. Edwards (ed.) *Encyclopedia of Social Work*, Vol. 1, 19th edn. Washington, DC: National Association of Social Workers.

Royal Commission on Long Term Care (1999) *With Respect to Old Age: Long Term Care – Rights and Responsibilities*. London: The Stationery Office.

Ruch, G. (2004) From triangle to spiral: reflective practice in social work education, practice and research, *Social Work Education*, 21: 199–216.

Ruch, G., Turney, D. and Ward, A. (eds.) (2010) *Relationship-Based Social Work: Getting to the Heart of Practice*. London: Jessica Kingsley.

Rutter, M. and Rutter, M. (1993) *Developing Minds: Challenge and Continuity Across the Life Span*. Harmondsworth: Penguin.

Ryan, J. and Trevithick, P. (1988) Lesbian workshop, in S. Krzowski and P. Land (eds.) *In Our Experience: Workshops at the Women's Therapy Centre*. London: Women's Press.

Ryan, P. and Morgan, S. (2004) *Assertive Outreach: A Strengths Approach to Policy and Practice*. Edinburgh: Churchill Livingstone.

Rycroft, C. (1972) *A Critical Dictionary of Psychoanalysis*. Harmondsworth: Penguin.

Ryle, G. (1949) *The Concept of Mind.* Chicago, IL: The University of Chicago Press.

Sackett, D.L., Rosenberg, W.M., Jray, J., Haynes, R.B. and Richardson, W.S. (1996) Evidence-based practice: what it is and what it isn't, *British Medical Journal,* 312: 71–3.

Sainsbury, E. (1987) Client studies: their contribution and limitations in influencing social work practice, *British Journal of Social Work,* 17: 635–44.

Sainsbury, E., Nixon, S. and Phillips, D. (1982) *Social Work in Focus: Clients' and Social Workers' Perceptions of Long Term Social Work.* London: Routledge & Kegan Paul.

Saleebey, D. (ed.) (1992) *The Strengths Perspective in Social Work Practice.* London: Longman.

Saleebey, D. (2006) The strengths approach to practice, in D. Saleebey (ed.) *The Strengths Perspective in Social Work Practice,* 4th edn. London: Allyn & Bacon.

Saleebey, D. (ed.) (2009) *The Strengths Perspective in Social Work Practice,* 5th edn. London: Allyn & Bacon.

Salzberger-Wittenberg, I. (1970) *Psycho-analytic Insight, and Relationships.* London: Routledge.

Samaritans (2005) *Summary of Results of Surveys Carried out into Giving Trends.* Available at: http://www.samaritans.org/about_samaritans/facts_and_figures/giving_trends [accessed 1 June 2011].

Samuel, M. (2009) Direct payments, personal budgets and individual budgets, *Community Care,* 8 April.

Schön, D. (1983) *The Reflective Practitioner: How Professionals Think in Action.* New York: Basic Books.

Scott, J. and Marshall, G. (eds.) (2009) *Oxford Dictionary of Sociology,* revised 3rd edn. Oxford: Oxford University Press.

Scourfield, P. (2004) Questions raised for Local Authorities when old people are evicted from their care homes, *British Journal of Social Work,* 34: 501–16.

Seden, J. (2005) *Counselling Skills in Social Work Practice,* 2nd edn. Maidenhead: Open University Press.

Seebohm Report (1968) *Report of the Committee on Local Authority and Allied Personal Social Services* (Cmnd 3703). London: HMSO.

Seligman, M.E.P. (1975) *Helplessness.* San Francisco, CA: Freeman.

Seu, I.B. and Heenan, M.C. (eds.) (1998) *Feminism and Psychotherapy: Reflections on Contemporary Theories and Practices.* London: Sage.

Shackle, S., Hegarty, S. and Eaton, G. (2009) The new ruling class, *New Statesman,* 1 October. Available at: http://www.newstatesman.com/uk-politics/2009/10/oxford-universitywealth-school [accessed 6 June 2011].

Shardlow, S. (2007) The social policy context of practice learning, in J. Lishman (ed.) *A Handbook for Practice Learning in Social Work and Social Care: Knowledge and Theory.* London: Jessica Kingsley.

Shaw, I. (1996) *Evaluating in Practice*. Aldershot: Arena.

Shaw, I. and Shaw, A. (1997) Keeping social work honest: evaluating as profession and practice, *British Journal of Social Work*, 27: 847–69.

Shaw, I., Bell, M., Sinclair, I., Sloper, P., Mitchell, W., Dyson, P., Clayden, J. and Rafferty, J. (2009) An exemplary scheme? An evaluation of the Integrated Children's System, *British Journal of Social Work*, 39: 613–26.

Shaw, I.F. (2007) Is social work research distinctive?, *Social Work Education*, 26(7): 659–69.

Shaw, M. and Dorling, D. (2004) Who cares in England and Wales? The inverse care law: cross-sectional study, *British Journal of General Practice*, 54(509): 899–903.

Sheldon, B. (1982) *Behaviour Modification: Theory, Practice and Philosophy*. London: Tavistock.

Sheldon, B. (1995) *Cognitive-behavioural Therapy: Research, Practice and Philosophy*. London: Routledge.

Sheldon, B. (2000) Cognitive behavioural methods in social care: A look at the evidence, in P. Stepney and D. Ford (eds.) *Social Work Models, Methods and Theories*. Lyme Regis: Russell House.

Sheldon, B. (2001) The validity of evidence-based practice in social work: a reply to Stephen Webb, *British Journal of Social Work*, 31: 801–9.

Sheldon, B. and Macdonald, G. (2009) *A Textbook of Social Work*. London: Routledge.

Sheppard, M. (1994) Childcare, social support and maternal depression: a review and application of findings, *British Journal of Social Work*, 24: 287–310.

Sheppard, M. (1995) Social work, social science and practice wisdom, *British Journal of Social Work*, 25: 265–94.

Sheppard, M. (1997) The psychiatric unit, in M. Davies (ed.) *The Blackwell Companion to Social Work*. Oxford: Blackwell Publishing.

Sheppard, M. (1998) Practice validity, reflexivity and knowledge for social work, *British Journal of Social Work*, 28: 763–81.

Sheppard, M. (2002) Mental health and social justice: gender, race and psychological consequences of unfairness, *British Journal of Social Work*, 32(6): 779–97.

Sheppard, M. (2006) *Social Work and Social Exclusion: The Idea of Practice*. Aldershot: Ashgate.

Sheppard, M. and Crocker, G. (2008) Locus of control, coping and proto prevention in child and family care, *British Journal of Social Work*, 38(2): 308–21.

Sheppard, M. and Ryan, K. (2003) Practitioners as rule using analysts: a further development of process knowledge in social work, *British Journal of Social Work*, 33: 157–76.

Sheppard, M., Newstead, S., DiCaccavo, A. and Ryan, K. (2000) Reflexivity and the development of process knowledge in social work: a classification and empirical study, *British Journal of Social Work*, 30: 465–88.

Sheppard, M., Newstead, S., DiCaccavo, A. and Ryan, K. (2001) Comparative hypothesis assessment and quasi triangulation as process knowledge: assessment strategies in social work practice, *British Journal of Social Work*, 31: 863–85.

Shulman, L. (1999) *The Skills of Helping Individuals, Families, Groups and Communities*, 4th edn. Itasca, IL: Peacock.

Sidebotham, P., Fox, J., Horwath, J., Powell, C. and Perwez, S. (2008) *Preventing Childhood Deaths: An Observational Study of Child Death Overview Panels in England*. London: Department for Children, Schools and Families.

Simon, E. (2010) Cut the cost of nursing home care: the cost of a year's stay in a nursing home is now comparable with the cost of a luxury cabin for a year on the Queen Elizabeth liner, *Daily Telegraph*, 7 June.

Skills for Care (2010) Website available at: http://london.skillsforcare.org.uk [accessed 5 September 2010].

Skinner, B.F. (1938) *The Behavior of Organisms: An Experimental Analysis*. New York: Appleton-Century-Crofts.

Skinner, B.F. (1974) *About Behaviourism*. London: Jonathan Cape.

Smale, G. and Tuson, G. (with N. Biehal and D. Statham) (2000) *Social Work and Social Problems*. Basingstoke: Macmillan.

Smith, V. (1986) Listening, in O. Hargie (ed.) *A Handbook of Communication Skills*. London: Routledge.

Soanes, C. and Stevenson, A. (eds.) (2003) *Oxford Dictionary of English*, 2nd edn. Oxford: Oxford University Press.

Social Care Institute for Excellence (SCIE) (undated) Website available at: http://www.scie.org.uk.

Social Services Inspectorate (SSI) (1991) *Getting the Message Across: A Guide to Developing and Communicating Policies, Principles and Procedures on Assessment*. London: HMSO.

Social Work Reform Board (SWRB) (2010) *Building a Safe and Confident Future: One Year On. Detailed Proposals*. Progress Report from the Social Work Reform Board, London, Department of Education. Available at: https://www.education.gov.uk/publications/eOrderingDownload/Building%20a%20safe%20and%20confident%20future%20-%20One%20year%20on.pdf [accessed 1 July 2011].

Social Work Task Force (SWTF) (2009a) *Facing up to the Task: The Interim Report of the Social Work Task Force*. Available at: http://publications.education.gov.uk/default.aspx?PageFunction=productdetails&PageMode=publications&ProductId=DCSF-00752-2009& [accessed 1 June 2011].

Social Work Task Force (SWTF) (2009b) *Building a Safe, Confident Future: The Final Report of the Social Work Task Force*. Available at: https://www.

education.gov.uk/publications/eOrderingDownload/01114-2009DOM-EN.pdf [accessed 1 June 2011].

Solomon, B. (1976) *Black Empowerment*. New York: Columbia University Press.

Spicker, P. (1995) *Social Policy: Themes and Approaches*. Hemel Hempstead: Prentice-Hall/Harvester Wheatsheaf.

Stephenson, J. (1998) The concept of capability and its importance in higher education, in J. Stephenson and M. Yorke (eds.) *Capability and Quality in Higher Education*. London: Kogan Page.

Stepney, P. (2000) The theory to practice debate revised, in P. Stepney and D. Ford (eds.) *Social Work Models, Methods and Theories*, 2nd edn. Lyme Regis: Russell House.

Stepney, P. and Ford, D. (eds.) (2000) *Social Work Models, Methods and Theories*, 2nd edn. Lyme Regis: Russell House.

Stevenson, O. (1998) *Neglected Children: Issues and Dilemmas*. Oxford: Blackwell Science.

Stevenson, O. (2005) Genericism and specialization: the story since 1970, *British Journal of Social Work*, 35: 569–86.

Stevenson, O. and Parsloe, P. (1993) *Community Care and Empowerment*. York: Joseph Rowntree Foundation.

Sullivan, D.P. (2012) Strengths perspective, in M. Gray, J. Midgley and S. Webb (eds.) *Social Work Handbook*. London: Sage (forthcoming).

Surrey, J.L. (1991) Relationships and empowerment, in J.V. Jordan, A.G. Kaplan, J.B. Miller, I.P. Stiver and J.L. Surrey (eds.) *Women's Growth and Connection: Writings from the Stone Center*. New York: Guilford Press.

Social Work Action Network (SWAN) (undated) Website available at: http://www.socialworkfuture.org/

Tashakkori, A. and Teddlie, C. (eds.) (2003) *Handbook of Mixed Methods in Social and Behavioral Research*. Thousand Oaks, CA: Sage.

Taylor, C. and White, S. (2006) Knowledge and reasoning in social work, educating for humane judgement, *British Journal of Social Work*, 36: 937–54.

Thoburn, J. (2008) The community child care team, in M. Davies (ed.) *The Blackwell Companion to Social Work*, 3rd edn. Oxford: Blackwell Publishing.

Thoburn, J., Lewis, A. and Shemmings, D. (1995) *Paternalism or Partnership? Family Involvement in the Child Protection Process*. London: HMSO.

Thompson, N. (2009) *People Skills*, 3rd edn. Basingstoke: Palgrave Macmillan.

Thorne, B. (2002) Person-centred counselling, in M. Davies (ed.) *The Blackwell Companion to Social Work*, 2nd edn. Oxford: Blackwell Publishing.

Thornicroft, G. (2006) *Shunned: Discrimination against People with Mental Illness*. Oxford: Oxford University Press.

Thyer, B.A. and Myers, L.L. (2011) The quest for evidence-based practice: a view from the United States, *Journal of Social Work*, 11: 8.

TOPSS (2002) *The National Occupational Standards and Key Skills for Social Work*. Leeds: TOPSS UK Partnership.

Townsend, P. (1979) *Poverty in the United Kingdom*. Harmondsworth: Penguin.

Townsend, P. (1993) *The International Analysis of Poverty*. Hemel Hempstead: Harvester Wheatsheaf.

Trevithick, P. (1988) Unconsciousness raising with working class women, in S. Krzowski and P. Land (eds.) *In Our Experience: Workshops at the Women's Therapy Centre*. London: Women's Press.

Trevithick, P. (1993) Surviving childhood sexual and physical abuse: the experience of two women of mixed Irish-English parentage, in H. Ferguson, R. Gilligan and R. Torode (eds.) *Surviving Childhood Adversity: Issues for Policy and Practice*. Dublin: Social Studies Press.

Trevithick, P. (1995) 'Cycling over Everest': groupwork with depressed women, *Groupwork*, 8(1): 5–33.

Trevithick, P. (1998) Psychotherapy and working class women, in I.B. Seu and M. Colleen Heenan (eds.) *Feminism and Psychotherapy: Reflections on Contemporary Theories and Practices*. London: Sage.

Trevithick, P. (2000) *Social Work Skills: A Practice Handbook*, 3rd edn. Maidenhead: Open University Press.

Trevithick, P. (2003) Effective relationship-based practice: a theoretical exploration, *Journal of Social Work Practice*, 17(2): 173–86.

Trevithick, P. (2005) *Social Work Skills: A Practice Handbook*, 2nd edn. Maidenhead: Open University Press.

Trevithick, P. (2008) Revisiting the knowledge base of social work: a framework for practice, *British Journal of Social Work*, 38: 1212–37.

Trevithick, P. (2011a) Understanding defences and defensiveness in social work, *Journal of Social Work Practice*, 25(4):389–412.

Trevithick, P. (2011b) The generalist versus specialist debate in social work education in the UK, in J. Lishman (ed.) *Research Highlights: Volume on Social Work Education*. London: Jessica Kingsley, pp. 233–54.

Trevithick, P. (2012a) Practice perspectives, in M. Gray, J. Midgley and S.A. Webb (eds.) *Social Work Handbook*. London: Sage (forthcoming).

Trevithick, P. (2012b) Groupwork theory and practice, in P. Stepney and D. Ford (eds.) *Social Work Models, Methods and Theories*, 2nd edn. Lyme Regis: Russell House (forthcoming).

Trevithick, P., Richards, S., Ruch, G. and Moss, B. (2004) *Knowledge Review: Teaching and Learning Communication Skills in Social Work Education*. Bristol: Policy Press.

Trotter, C. (2006) *Working with Involuntary Clients: A Guide to Practice*, 2nd edn. London: Sage.

Trower, P., Casey, A. and Dryden, W. (1988) *Cognitive-Behavioural Counselling in Action*. London: Sage.

Truax, C.B. and Carkhuff, R.R. (1967) *Towards Effective Counselling and Psychotherapy*. Chicago, IL: Aldine.

Tsang, N.M. (2007) Reflection as dialogue, *British Journal of Social Work*, 37(4): 681–94.

Turner, F.J. (1974) *Social Work Treatment: Interlocking Theoretical Approaches*, 1st edn. London: Collier Macmillan.

UK Parliament website. Available at: http://www.parliament.uk/about/how/laws/flash-passage-bill/ [accessed 1 June 2011].

Ungar, M. (2004) A constructionist discourse on resilience: multiple contexts, multiple realities among at-risk children and youth, *Youth and Society*, 35(3): 341–65.

Wade, D.T. and Halligan, P.W. (2004) Do biomedical models of illness make for good healthcare systems, *British Medical Journal*, 329: 1398–401.

Walker, C. and Walker, A. (2009) Social policy and social work, in R. Adams, L. Dominelli and M. Payne (eds.) *Social Work: Themes, Issues and Critical Debates*, 3rd edn. Basingstoke: Palgrave Macmillan.

Walter, I., Nutley, S.M. and Davies, H.T.O. (2003) *Research Impact: A Cross Sector Review*. St. Andrews: RURU, University of St. Andrews.

Walter, I., Nutley, S., Percy-Smith, J., McNeish, D. and Frost, S. (2004) *SCIE Knowledge Review 7: Improving the Use of Research in Social Care Practice*. London: Social Care Institute for Excellence.

Watzlawick, P., Weakland, J. and Risch, R. (1974) *Change: Principles of Problem Formation and Problem Resolution*. London: Norton.

Waterhouse, L. (2008) Child abuse, in M. Davies (ed.) *The Blackwell Companion to Social Work*, 3rd edn. Oxford: Blackwell Publishing.

Waterhouse, L. and McGhee, J. (2002) Social work with children and families, in R. Adams, L. Dominelli and M. Payne (eds.) *Social Work: Themes, Issues and Critical Debates*, 2nd edn. Basingstoke: Palgrave Macmillan.

Watson, J.B. (1970) *Behaviourism*. New York: Norton.

Webb, S.A. (2001) Some considerations on the validity of evidence-based practice in social work, *British Journal of Social Work*, 31: 57–79.

Webb, S.A. (2006) *Social Work in a Risk Society: Social and Political Perspectives*. Basingstoke: Palgrave Macmillan.

Webb, S.A. (2010) (Re)assembling the left: the politics of redistribution and recognition in social work, *British Journal of Social Work*, 40: 2364–79.

Weick, A. (1983) A growth-task model of human development, *Social Casework*, 64(3): 131–7.

Welford, A.T. (1958) *Ageing and Human Skill*. London: Oxford University Press.

Wenger, E. (1998) *Communities of Practice: Learning, Meaning, and Identity*. Cambridge: Cambridge University Press.

White, S., Hall, C. and Peckover, S. (2009) The descriptive tyranny of the Common Assessment Framework: technologies of categorization and professional practice in child welfare, *British Journal of Social Work*, 39: 1197–217.

White, V. (2006). *The State of Feminist Social Work*. London: Routledge.

Whitttaker, A. (2009) *Research Skills for Social Work*. Exeter: Learning Matters.

Wilkinson, R. and Pickett, K. (2009) *The Spirit Level: Why More Equal Societies Almost Always do Better*. London: Allen Lane.

Williams, J. (2001) 1998 Human Rights Act: social work's new benchmark, *British Journal of Social Work*, 31: 831–44.

Williams, J. (2004) Social work, liberty and the law, *British Journal of Social Work*, 34: 37–52.

Wilson, K. (2000) Therapeutic intervention, in M. Davies (ed.) *The Blackwell Encyclopaedia of Social Work*. Oxford: Blackwell.

Wilson, K., Ruch, G., Lymbery, M. and Cooper, A. (2008) *Social Work: An Introduction to Contemporary Practice*. Harlow: Pearson Education.

Winnicott, D.W. (1958) *Collected Papers: Through Paediatrics to Psycho-Analysis*. London: Tavistock (reprinted 1992 by Karnac Books).

Winnicott, D.W. (1965) *The Maturational Process and the Facilitating Environment: Studies in the Theory of Emotional Development*. London: Hogarth (published 1990 by Karnac Books).

Winnicott, D.W. (1986) *Home is Where We Start From*. Harmondsworth: Penguin.

Wise, S. (1995) Feminist ethics in practice, in R. Hugman and D. Smith (eds.) *Ethical Issues in Social Work*. London: Routledge.

World Heath Organization (WHO) (undated) Social determinants of health. Available at: http://www.who.int/social_determinants/en/ [accessed 10 September 2011].

INDEX

A

abandonment, impact of, 104, 218, 219
abuse, 81, 111, 170, 175, 181, 192, 199,
    284, 330, 349
  abuse defined, 284
  abuse of social workers, 273
  alcohol abuse/misuse, 120, 129, 154,
    175, 23, 291, 333, 335, 358
  children/young people abuse of, 75,
    175, 188, 244, 273, 24, 286, 324
  defined, 284
  disabled people, vulnerability to
    abuse/neglect, 81, 283–4
  domestic violence/family abuse, 45, 48,
    75, 181, 274, 319, 330, 331, 346,
    358
  drug abuse/misuse, 50, 75, 120, 154,
    175, 243, 291, 358
  emotional abuse, 81, 181
  mental health, vulnerability to abuse,
    81, 283–4
  neglect, as a form of abuse, 11, 25, 75,
    138, 141, 143, 181, 247, 257,
    263, 284, 327
  older people, abuse/vulnerability of, 81,
    283–4
  physical abuse, 114, 181
  sexual abuse, 114, 145, 146, 181, 217,
    244, 245, 330. *See also* rape
  substance abuse/misuse, 75, 175, 334,
    335, 336, 360
  unacceptable behaviour, abuse as, 273
  vulnerable adults, working with, 170,
    283–4, 293
  working with children who have been
    abused, 170, 192, 204, 217, 245,
    274, 293, 339
academic curriculum/subjects taught, 25,
    34, 38, 44, 116

academics, 51, 53, 55, 57, 95, 100, 160
acceptance, 126, 128, 233, 239, 247, 248,
    249, 257, 272, 334, 338
access to files, 288, 292, 295, 202, 212
access to resources/rationing services, 64,
    68, 76, 88, 179, 183, 236, 267,
    335
access to knowledge/research findings, 48,
    58, 93
accountability, 6, 38, 55, 63, 65, 66, 71,
    225, 228, 258, 260
  see Chapter Ten on Professional
    Competence and Accountability,
    275–308
achievements, importance of recognizing,
    104, 126, 142, 156, 234, 354,
    355, 358
action plans, 176, 180, 259, 299
action, linked to understanding, 4, 13, 31,
    32, 45, 95, 101, 117, 153, 162,
    182, 259
  effective action, as knowledge, skills and
    values in action, 5, 32, 33, 45,
    121, 153, 159
  see social action
Acts of Parliament, *see legislation*
active listening responses, *see* social work
    skills/no. 26
actualizing tendency/self-actualizing,
    110, 124, 125, 126, 127, 249,
    338
adaptation/adapting to need, 46, 139,
    157, 226, 245, 246, 247, 320
  see social work skills/no. 49
addiction, 75, 81, 154, 243, 334, 334,
    358, 360
  see alcohol abuse/misuse
  see drug abuse/misuse
adolescents, *see* young people

administrative skills, *see* social work
    skills/no. 71
adoption, 181, 189, 199
adult social care, 68
    Adult Safeguarding Boards (ASBs), 284
    adult social care departments, creation
        of, 69
        see also social care
    assessment, 6, 67, 69, 74, 100, 129,
        175, 179, 182, 183, 185, 213
    assessment, 174–182, 198
    carers, *see careers*.
    Carers (Recognition and Services) Act
        (1995), 179, 180
    charities, 71, 72–3, 75, 79, 83, 110,
        365, 366
        Joseph Rowntree Charitable
            Trust/Rowntree Foundation, 53,
            75, 78, 81, 378, 384, 391
    community care, 63, 69, 179, 185, 238
        see also National Health Service
            (NHS) and Community Care Act
            (1990)
    Community Care (Direct Payments)
        Act (1996), 63, 179
    direct payments, 63, 68, 69, 179
    Directors of Adult Social Services
        (DASS), 69
    Fair Access to Care Services (2003), 68,
        268
    generativity versus stagnation
        (Erikson), 135
    health care, 68, 87, 88, 176
        see also health
    individual budgets, 68, 69
    integrity versus despair/disgust
        (Erikson), 135
    knowledge-base, 28, 51, 55, 58, 280
    managerialism/'marketization', 38, 55,
        67, 70
    mental capacity/Mental Capacity Act
        2005, 180
    National Framework for Older People
        (2001), 181, 368
    National Health Service (NHS) and
        Community Care Act (1990),
        67–9, 71, 73, 179, 182, 261, 267
    personal budgets, 68, 69
    personalization, 68, 69, 246, 299
    provision and cost of social care, 72,
        73, 183

Putting People First (2008), 40, 68, 181
    Royal Commission on Long Term Care
        (1999), 70
    separation of adult and children's
        services, 68
    Single Assessment Process (SAP), 284
    Skills for Care, 6, 23, 72
    social care and social work, 5–6
    social care defined, 6
    Transforming Social Care (2008), 68,
        181
    *Types and Quality of Knowledge in
        Social Care*, 28
    vulnerable adults and abuse/*No Secrets*
        guidance (2000), 283–4
    workforce, statistics for social care, 72
adversity, 11, 49, 86, 106, 108, 113, 124,
    127, 131, 139, 142, 143, 147,
    154, 183, 260, 308, 317, 326, 350
    hardship, 75, 111, 154, 161, 194, 265,
        306
    see also poverty and disadvantage
    see also health/health inequalities
advice, *see* social work skills/no. 36
    Citizens Advice Bureau, 79, 80, 366
advocacy, *see* social work skills/no. 58
agency/agencies, 11, 21, 33, 61–2, 63,
    65–6, 70–4, 80–1, 89, 159–60,
    180, 188, 200, 260, 291, 295
    agency policy and practice/procedures,
        178, 181, 247, 268
    local authority, 39, 54, 55, 68, 69,
        71–2, 86, 179, 268, 278
    private, voluntary, and independent
        sector (PVI), 71
    separation of adult and children's
        services, 68
    social services, 38, 39, 63, 65, 68, 72,
        106, 162, 164, 165, 191, 205,
        230, 238, 260, 261, 264, 282
    third sector, 71
    voluntary sector, 70, 72, 250
    inter-agency cooperation, 171, 181,
        282–4, 292, 298
    financial constraints/under-resourcing,
        7, 12, 41, 64, 68, 71, 77, 105,
        176, 222, 225, 236, 247, 297,
        321, 346
    multi-disciplinary/inter-disciplinary
        approaches, 275, 282–4, 292, 313
    see also charities

agreements/working agreements, 259,
260, 266, 385
see contracts, 46, 69, 213, 248, 253,
256, 257, 259–60, 291, 353
see also action plans
aggressive, hostile and violent behaviour
patterns
aggression/aggressive, 46, 117, 178,
181, 253, 269, 272, 273–4
hostility/hostile reactions, 46, 99, 113,
136, 138, 197, 253, 273–4
violence/violent behaviour, 45, 46, 48,
75, 114, 145, 181, 182, 253, 262,
273–4, 291, 371, 319, 330, 346
alcohol addiction/alcohol abuse/misuse,
120, 129, 154, 175, 23, 291, 333,
335, 358
Alcoholics Anonymous, 333, 358
see motivational interviewing, 333–336
see Cycle of Change, 357–360
see also drug addiction/abuse
analysis and synthesis, 92, 96, 99–102,
181
see also critical thinking,
see also critical reflection/reflexivity,
anger, 136, 183, 219, 149, 272, 273, 287,
320
anti-depressant prescriptions, 50
prescriptionsanti-discriminatory
perspectives/practice, 48, 201,
248, 340
anti-oppressive perspectives/practice, 47,
48, 110, 180, 248, 325, 347, 351
anti-racist perspectives/practice, 47, 347
anti-social behaviour, 41, 372
anxiety/anxious states, 9, 11, 129, 136,
140, 200, 210, 215, 227, 241,
250–1, 270, 294, 306, 31, 342
anxiety in social workers, 98, 197, 228,
233, 297
causes of anxiety, 138, 144, 191, 193,
235, 259
defined, 250
differentiated from fear, 250
impact of anxiety, loss of
memory/concentration, 197, 230
triggers defences/defensiveness, 133
see also containing anxiety, social work
skills/no. 51
approach, *see* practice approach(es)
see also skills

approval, 115, 126, 233
assertive/assertiveness, *see* social work
skills/no. 59
assertive outreach, 319, 321
assessment, *see* social work skills/no. 6
assumptions, and the assessment process,
17–20, 22, 26, 38, 82, 106, 167
196, 170, 214, 287, 330
ideological assumption, 48–50
Eurocentric assumptions, 146–149
asylum seekers/refugees, 75, 83, 181, 230
attachment/attachment theory, 36, 136–9,
143, 195, 246, 341
adulthood, continues in, 137
affectional bonds, 136
Bowlby, 124, 125, 136, 139, 246
defined, 136
impact throughout the lifespan, 124,
137
protective factors, identification of,
124, 324, (added later
See also lifespan
separation reactions, *protest, despair,
detachment*, 137
strange situation test (Ainsworth), 137
types of attachment, *secure, insecure
avoidant, insecure ambivalent,
insecure, disorganised*, 138
attributes/qualities, personal, 10, 11–2,
13, 111, 118, 187, 195, 262, 279,
280, 288, 302
audit culture, 41, 67
Audit Commission, 67, 239
authentic, 338
authority
see also professional boundaries
see also roles and responsibilities
autonomy, 71, 73, 74, 135, 143, 340,
279, 282, 380, 371
personal autonomy, 326, 328
professional autonomy, 97, 99, 276
avoidance, 18, 29, 106, 130, 133, 208,
210, 342
defined, 133
tax avoidance, 80

B
Baby P tragedy, 12
see also Laming inquiries
Bandura, 129, 241, 311
Barclay Report, 39, 260

baseline data, importance of, 176, 177,
178, 295, 312, 313
BASW see British Association of Social
Workers, 3, 7, 64, 89
behavior
behaviour as clues, 113, 114, 154, 157
behaviour change, 5, 129, 161, 249,
271, 335, 357
behaviour modification, 312
patterns of behaviour, 31, 119–120,
122, 169, 174, 199, 249,136
pattern recognition, 119–120
personal responsibility for behaviour,
255, 262, 338
see also Chapter Five: Understand
Human Beings
behaviourism
behaviourist approaches, 311–4
Gambrill, 129–30
see cognitive approaches
see cognitive-behavioural approaches
beliefs, importance of, 130, 148, 256,
257, 263, 270, 287, 289, 307,
330, 331
defined, 28
irrational/negative beliefs, 249, 316–7
benefits, see welfare rights/benefits
bereavement and loss, 88, 136, 141, 142,
143, 181, 194, 222, 229
best evidence, 54, 55, 286
see evidence-based practice
best self, working from, 227
bias, 55, 101, 106, 107, 129, 145, 172,
233, 297
Biestek, 13, 228
Bills/Acts of Parliament, 64
black/ethnic minority groups, 48, 146,
147–8, 254, 206, 261
statistics on numbers of, 83
see anti-racist perspectives/practice
Eurocentric bias,
see racism. 29, 36, 143, 147, 180
blame culture, 57, 108, 110, 132, 187,
232, 346
self-blame, 217, 243, 255
Blom Cooper, 272, 363
biology, 37, 124, 134
body language, 133, 166–7, 172, 196,
272, 300
bonds/bonding, see Bowlby and
attachment theory,

boundaries/maintaining professional
boundaries, see social work
skills/no. 63
Bowlby, 124, 125, 136, 139, 246
breaking bad news, see social work
skills/no. 45
brief therapy, 202, 219
time-limited work, 317, 319, 320, 355
British Association for Counselling and
Psychotherapy (BACP), 247
British Association of Social Workers
(BASW), 3, 7, 64, 89
brokering, 278
building blocks, see task-centred
approaches
bullying behaviour, 101, 222, 266, 273
bureaucracy/'bureaucratized' approaches
to service delivery, 39, 40, 41,
262, 246
burn-out, 228

C
CAF, see Framework for the Assessment
of Children in Need and their
Families.
capacity
capacity building and social work, 4,
9–13
capacity to grow and change, 18, 350
coping capacity, 10, 237
defined, 9
care and control, 33, 41, 238, 253
care management, 238, 258
care/caring, 178, 193, 226, 238–9, 243,
250, 263, 338, 350
caring tone of voice, 203, 212
ethics of care/caring, central in social
work, 42
quality of care, 87
pitfalls in caring/dependency, 239–240
see also social care
see also social work values
carers, 7, 10, 13, 23, 27, 48, 54, 63, 74,
83, 114, 137, 138, 139, 179
Carers (Recognition and Services) Act
(1995), 179, 180
carers, 7, 10, 13, 23, 27, 48, 54, 63, 74,
114, 137, 138, 139, 179, 184,
239, 362
conflicting needs, 280
formal and informal carers, 261

foster carers/fostering, 139, 167, 181, 189, 208, 211, 373
  participation in decision-making, 296
  recognition, of importance, 181
  rewards, 239
  statistics on the number of carers, 83
  strain on carers, 238
case conferences, 275, 295, 304
  see also coordinating case conferences and reviews, social work skills/no. 78
case closure/termination skills, 218, 221, 297, 354, 358
case law, 63
case records, *see* social work skills/no. 67
  see also record keeping skills, social work skills/no. 65
case study, defined, 54
casework/social casework, 6, 13, 43, 112, 248, 250, 341, 354
CCETSW (Central Council for Education and Training in Social Work), 39, 278
challenging, *see* social work skills/no. 60
change
  behaviour change, 5, 129, 161, 249, 271, 335, 357
  changed by the encounter with others, 45, 94, 111, 168, 184, 308
  levels of change, 357
  personal change, tendency to individualized, 15, 103, 161, 338–9, 345
  process of change, 123, 130, 334, 338
  social action/social change,, 3, 6, 20, 161, 250, 345–348, 376
chairing events, *see* social work skills/no. 77
charities, 71, 72–3, 75, 79, 83, 110, 365, 366
  Joseph Rowntree Charitable Trust/Rowntree Foundation, 53, 75, 78, 81, 378, 384, 391
child abuse, *see* abuse
child deaths and inquiries, 25,-6, 52, 69, 97, 106, 133, 162, 188, 286
  see Laming reports/inquiries
child neglect, 11, 25, 75, 138, 141, 143, 181, 247, 257, 263
  linked to abuse, 284
Children Act, England (1989), 189

Children Act (2004), 65, 69
children and young people
  abuse of, 75, 175, 188, 244, 273, 24, 286, 324
  adolescence, *see* young people
  care order, 238
  emotional development, 139, 142, 247
  child protection conferences, 304
  child protection, 70, 71, 106, 182, 185, 261, 262, 264, 265
  children and families, 23, 72, 283
  Children's Plan, 40
  children's rights, 48, 66
  children's services, 69, 72, 74, 175, 280, 283, 284
  communicating with children, 171
  Every Child Matters, 65, 69, 70, 181
  family work, 43
  Framework for the Assessment of Children in Need and their Families (CAF), 74, 139, 282, 283, 324, 349, 368
  in care/children 'looked after', 238, 218
  Integrated Children's System (ICS), 74, 107, 283, 294
  Laming, reports/inquiries, 12, 25–6, 69, 74, 106, 107, 133, 183, 280, 283
  Local Safeguarding Children Boards (LSCB), 284
  neglect, *see* child neglect
  risk, children placed at, 40, 162
  safeguarding children, 283, 284, 324
  significant harm, 284
  resilience/survival skills, 142–145, 148
  UN Convention on the Rights of the Child (UNCRC), 66
  working with children who have been abused, 170, 192, 204, 217, 245, 274, 293, 339
  see also young people/adolescents
Children's Trusts, 70
Chronically Sick and Disabled Persons Act (1970), 179
chronomics, 167
circular questions, *see* social work skills/no. 21
Citizens Advice Bureau, 79, 80, 366
clarifying, *see* social work skills/no. 24
class
  middle class, 75, 83, 110, 147, 148

class (*Continued*)
Registrar General's classification, 82,
84, 86
National Statistics Socio-Economic
Classification (NS-SEC), 82, 84,
85
socio-economic classification/social
class, 82
upper class, 83, 86
working class, 19, 75, 83–5, 86, 256,
261, 22
see also health inequalities
see also inverse care law
see also income inequalities
see also poverty
client, *see* service user
Client/person-centred approaches, 47,
236, 247, 333–4, 338–40
Climbé, Victoria, *see* Laming
reports/inquiries
closed questions, *see* social work skills/no.
18
closure/case closure/termination skills,
218, 221, 297, 354, 358
endings, importance of, 218–223
codes
BASW's Code of Ethics, 3, 7
policy, codes defined, 65
GSCC codes of practice, 7
cognitive approaches, 315–318
cognitive development, 123
cognitive behavioural approaches, 45, 47,
117, 125, 130, 131, 160, 178,
197, 234, 236, 241, 242, 248,
266, 311
collaboration, importance of, 11, 181,
257, 264, 267, 308, 316
collective action, 161, 169, 331, 346, 347
commissioning care services, 68, 69, 71,
73, 258, 260
common purpose, importance of
identifying, 165, 203, 253, 259,
263, 264
common sense, 30, 92–3, 166, 169
communication
artificial communication, 167
central importance in social work, 4,
8–9, 32, 154–5
central to effective practice, 8
communication of meaning, 154, 155,
157, 164, 166, 168, 171, 172, 184

Braille, 166, 231
British Sign Language (BAL), 165
cultural differences, 148, 166, 287, 306
defences, as a barrier to
communication, 133, 210, 272
dress as communication, 168
jargon, 31, 58, 205, 305
Makaton, 166
physical contact/touching, 8, 113, 167,
191, 192, 195
questions, *see also* social work skills
relationship-based, importance of,
14–17
respect, important to communicate,
118, 161, 195, 135, 241, 147,
248, 257, 258, 285, 289, 338
termination, *see* ending an interview,
social work skills/no. 33
closing the case and ending the
relationship, social work skills/no.
34
tone, importance of, 142, 167, 169,
173, 208, 211, 212, 233, 239, 300
tone and timing, 202, 203, 241
see verbal communication skills, social
work skills/no. 2
see non-verbal communication skills,
social work skills/no. 3
see Chapter Six
communicating with children/young
people, 171
communities of practice, 38
community care, 69, 186, 238
see National Health Service (NHS) and
Community Care Act (1990),
67–9, 71, 73, 179, 182, 261, 267
see also adult care
community work, 43, 160, 250, 258
community/ies, 7, 9, 12, 39, 47, 100, 143,
159, 106, 189, 228, 260, 261,
287, 293, 324, 345, 347
Community Care (Direct Payments) Act
(1996), 63, 179
competency-based approach, 156, 275,
277–80
professional competence, 96, 118, 135,
144, 155, 164, 167, 229, 276–80,
281, 282, 285, 287, 288, 300
complaint/s, 65, 179, 254, 294, 312
complexity, inherent in social work, 4, 5,
20, 27, 40, 98, 107, 120, 279

computer/information technology skills (ICT skills), 74, 164, 294, 295
see also emails, *see* social work skills/no. 73
concept, defined, 29
conditioning, 124, 128, 129, 312, 313
confidentiality, *see* social work skills/no. 64
conflict, 11, 15, 18, 37. 124, 176, 243, 264, 270, 301
confrontation/being confrontative, *see* social work skills/no. 61
congruence, 128, 178, 248, 338, 339
consent, 284, 291, 292
Conservative Government (1979–97), 67–8
containing anxiety, *see* social work skills/no. 51
see also anxiety
continuing professional development (CPD), 103, 297, 298
contracting skills, *see* social work skills/no. 54
contracts 46, 69, 213, 248, 253, 256, 257, 259–60, 291, 353
see also written agreement/s
control, *see* care and control
coping skills/capacity, 10, 237
corrective feedback, 209
Coulshed, 3, 13, 32, 258, 294
Coulshed and Orme, 43, 110, 160, 174, 246, 256, 257, 258, 261, 277, 281, 297, 320, 354
counselling, *see* social work skills/no. 50
counter-transference, 112, 134, 342, 343
courage, 11, 75, 183, 198, 244, 251, 256, 347
court, 37, 63, 65, 242, 267, 268, 276, 295, 296, 303
see presenting evidence in court, social work skills/no. 79
creativity, 92, 97, 109–110, 111, 126, 269
crime/offending behaviour, 59, 75, 86, 129,175, 289, 330, 346
criminal justice system, 58, 70, 175, 180, 228
young offenders, 41, 49
Criminal Justice Act (1991), 180
crisis intervention, 319–321
confused with crisis work, 319, 321

assertive outreach, 319, 321
crisis emergencies, 40, 73, 135, 237, 247, 259, 261, 291, 302, 321
critical social work/critical best practice, 57, 345
critical thinking, 28, 33, 61, 91, 96, 102–103, 105, 106, 120, 181
Gambrill, 11, 102–3
culture, 15, 36, 38, 39, 127, 166, 168, 214, 231, 273
anti-dependency culture, 49
audit culture, 47, 67, 71
Cultural sensitivity, 286–287
Eurocentric culture, 148, 242, 261, 319
managerialist culture, 97, 276, 294
meaning of culture, 48, 97, 98, 101, 107, 112
organizational culture, 10, 12, 97, 98, 107–108, 112, 113, 118, 260, 280, 283, 288, 294
curiosity, importance of, 18, 204
Cycle of Change, see *Stages of Change*, 357–360

D
data/baseline data, importance of, 176, 177, 178, 295, 312, 313
Data Protection Act (DPA)(1998), 288, 291
death of children, inquiries into, 25, 6, 52, 69, 97, 106, 133, 162, 188, 286
decision-making,
judicious decision-making, 54, 92, 96, 105, 107, 112, 120, 181, 183, 228, 236, 243
service user involvement in, 33, 100, 106, 127, 160, 236, 257, 262, 263, 264, 321, 330, 343, 355
see also judgements
defence budget, 79–80
defences/defence mechanism, 13, 18, 131, 142, 343
avoidance, 133–134, 210, 272, 342
defined, 132, 342
denial, 133
dementia, 391, 373
demonstration skills, 157, 232, 242
see also presentation skills, social work skills/no. 76
desensitization, 129, 270, 313

Department of Health (DoH), 6, 8, 23, 65, 68, 69, 181, 183, 262, 263, 265, 267, 282, 283, 284, 324, 349
dependence/dependency, 124, 127, 138, 139–141, 226, 247, 333
independence, 124, 127, 138, 139, 140, 141, 226, 247, 262
interdependence, 139–141, 247
unhealthy dependency, 104, 221, 228, 343
see also Winnicott
depression, 27, 117, 136, 176, 218, 317, 318, 321
deprivation, 3, 75, 76, 81, 88
defined, 88
see also poverty
despair, 16, 134, 135, 137, 183, 198, 255, 302
developmental delay, 142
developmental process, see Chapter Six: Human Growth and Development
DiClemente, 335, 358, 359
difference, working with, 9, 13, 145, 148, 160, 207, 230, 242, 259, 263, 265, 285, 287, 306, 330
difficulties' becoming 'problems' (Watzlawick et al. 1974), 175–6
Diploma in Social Work, 278
directive/non-directive interventions, 160, 171, 172, 210, 236, 334, 337
see social work skills/no. 41
Directors of Adult Social Services (DASS), 69
disability/people with disabilities
abuse, vulnerability to, 170, 283–4, 293
access, 165, 193, 230
British Sign Language (BAL), 165
children, disabled, 143, 144, 199, 376
Chronically Sick and Disabled Persons Act (1970), 179
communication, key considerations, 165–6, 181, 230–1
Community Care (Direct Payments) Act (1996), 63, 179
direct payments, 63, 68, 69, 179
disability benefits, 80
disability movement, importance of user led policies, 240
disability statistics, 78, 79, 80, 83, 87
disabled people, vulnerability to abuse/neglect, 81, 283–4

Disabled Persons Act (1971)/(1986), 179, 231
impairment, defined, 104, 165, 230, 294
independent living, 68
loop systems, 165
Makaton, 166
medical/biomedical model and disability, 43
social model of disability, 43
working with, 47, 81, 87, 166, 181, 229, 230, 231, 240, 261, 268, 282, 371, 380
disadvantage, 7, 47, 75, 81, 82, 86, 89, 160, 161, 167, 201, 262, 267, 287, 325, 329, 346
defined, 88
discrimination, 15, 22, 24, 77, 88, 118, 147, 254, 265, 281, 308, 317, 331
see also anti-discrimination/ anti-oppressive practice
see also poverty
distractions, see sticking to the point and purpose of the interview, social work skills/no. 28
distress, 42, 111, 114, 124, 128, 136, 138, 141, 144, 167, 168, 170, 175, 176, 196, 203, 211, 217, 221, 244, 257, 288, 311
Dockar-Drysdale, 117
doctors, 49, 69, 84, 106, 154, 201
see also medicine
domestic violence/family abuse, 45, 48, 75, 181, 274, 319, 330, 331, 346, 358
murder of women, statistics, 330
doorknob revelations, 219–221
double-loop learning, 107–108
Dreyfus and Dreyfus, 120, 157, 158
drug addiction/drug use/misuse, 50, 75, 120, 154, 175, 243, 291, 358
see also alcohol abuse
see also Cycle of Change
see also motivational interviewing
drug companies, 49, 50, 56, 175
duty
duties placed on local authorities, 65, 231
duties as a professional, 49, 161

E

eclectic approaches/theories, 45, 248
ecological theory/perspectives, 12, 43, 47,
    100, 159, 176, 180, 298, 323,
    327, 341
economy, efficiency and effectiveness
    (three E's), 38, 67
economics, relevance to social work, 37, 38
education and training, *see* social work
    education and training
effective action, 259
    see action, linked to understanding
effectiveness, *see* evidence
ego, 131, 132, 134, 320, 341
ego psychology, 131, 320, 341
Erikson's *Eight Stages of Development*,
    18, 123, 124, 125, 134–136, 341
emails, *see* social work skills/no. 73
emancipatory practice/perspectives, 41,
    98, 106, 345, 351
emotional abuse, 81, 181
emotional development, 18, 123, 124,
    131, 139, 142, 145, 247
emotional energy, 141, 230
emotional support, 10, 127, 226, 237
empathy, *see* social work skills/no. 13
empowerment, *see* social work skills/no.
    52
enabling, 93, 182, 200, 205, 239, 243,
    249, 254–255
encouragement, *see* social work skills/no.
    39
endings an interview, *see* social work
    skills/no. 33
    see closing the case/ending the
    relationship, social work skills/no.
    34
engaging/engagement skills, *see* social
    work skills/no. 7
England, H., 10, 30, 97, 109, 110, 112,
    124, 153, 226, 248
England, population, 83
environmental/social factors, 27, 112,
    124, 144, 174, 176, 265, 284,
    312, 313, 324, 326, 327, 377
environmental capacities, 4, 10, 12
    personal change, facilitating, 161,
    338–9
epistemology, 38, 97
Eraut, 10, 32, 62, 91, 94, 95, 97, 99, 101,
    103, 105, 108, 109, 115, 116,
    119, 279

ethics/ethical practice
    professional ethics, 55, 56, 285, 293,
        15, 23, 49, 56, 106, 118 130,
        234, 255, 285, 291, 321
    ethical practice, 7, 15, 23, 38, 49
    See BASW'S Code of Ethics, 3, 7
ethnicity, 81, 181, 287
Eurocentric bias, 36, 48, 146–149
European Convention on Human Rights,
    288
European legislation and international
    law, 66
European Union (EU) legislation, 66
evaluation of information received, 26,
    53, 102
Every Child Matters, 65, 69, 70, 181
evidence
    barriers to the take up of research,
        157–159
    baseline data, importance of, 176, 177,
        178, 295, 312, 313
    best evidence, 54, 55, 286
    case study, 53
    evaluation of effectiveness, 177, 181,
        294, 312, 317
    evidence based practice (EBP), 52,
        54–7
    evidence based/actions backed by
        evidence, 16, 26, 101, 107, 120
    financial constraints/under-resourcing,
        41,64, 68, 71, 77, 105, 176, 222,
        225, 236, 247, 297, 321, 346
    meta analysis, 53
    randomized control trials (RCT),
        53–54, 55, 62
    review, 53
    Sackett, 54
    single case design/evaluation/N = 1, 54
    systematic reviews, 53, 58, 59
    variables, impact of, 55, 57, 117, 120,
        167, 218, 286
    see research and social work
evidence/testimony, *see* presenting
    evidence in court, social work
    skills/no. 79
excluded/social exclusion, 17, 77, 242,
    247, 261, 264, 308
exosystem 325
expert knowledge, skills and experience,
    23, 27, 120, 157, 158, 204, 228,
    262, 335, 351
eye contact, 172, 190, 249, 287

experiential knowledge and experience,
170
experiences positive and negative, 10, 11,
15, 16, 18, 223
explanations, see social work skills/no. 38

F
facilitating environment, 9, 18, 338
facilitating relationship, 13, 14
facilitative skills, 199, 208, 254, 316
  see also empowerment
family therapy, 45, 47, 56, 57, 202, 204,
242, 342
family work, 43
Fair Access to Care Services (2003), 68,
268
fear, differentiated from anxiety, 250
feedback/giving and receiving feedback,
  see social work skills/no. 27
feminist perspectives in social work, 239,
329–332
feminist therapy, 145,146
  Stone Center (Boston, USA), 14, 145,
  256
  Women's Therapy Centre, 146, 256
feminization of poverty, 76
fields of practice (4), work with
  individuals, families, groups or
  groupwork, communities, 47
files, access to, see confidentiality
financial constraints/under-resourcing, 7,
  12, 41,64, 68, 71, 77, 105, 176,
  222, 225, 236, 247, 297, 321,
  346
financial problems/hardships, see poverty
forms/form filling, see social work
  skills/no. 66
Fook, 29, 30, 36, 48, 49, 62, 98, 99, 103,
  116, 157, 345
foster carers/fostering, 139, 167, 181,
  189, 208, 211, 373
Foucault, 98
fragmentation, 36, 39, 278, 280, 284
*Framework for the Assessment of
  Children in Need & their Families*
  (CAF), 74, 139, 282, 283, 324,
  349, 368
Freedom of Information Act (2000), 288
Freud, 18, 19, 123, 124, 131, 134, 136,
  144, 145, 341, 342
  psychosocial approaches, 341–344
functionalism, 37

G
Gambrill, 30, 54, 61, 62, 106, 169, 171,
  178, 199
  behaviourist , importance of, 129–30,
  311–2
  critical thinking, 11, 102–3
  philosophy of practice, 17, 285
gatekeeping, 265
gender
  feminism, 14, 30, 36, 47, 124, 145,
    146, 180, 248, 255, 298, 345
  feminist perspectives in social work,
    239, 329–332
  patriarchy, 36, 145, 330, 331
  poverty, feminization of, 76
  statistics on female and male
    population, 83
General Social Care Council (GSCC),
  Codes of Practice, 7
generalist skills, 3, 22, 33, 44, 45, 161,
  180
  specialist skills, 22, 45, 180
  see also lexicon of social work skills
genogram, 305
gesture/s, 8, 19, 75, 164, 166, 167, 169,
  171, 172, 195, 208, 209, 231,
  240, 251
'Gloucester Judgement', 63
government policy, Conservative/
  Labour/Coalition, 21, 66, 68, 69,
  70, 73, 85, 262, 385
  'modernization agenda', 68, 279, 374
  see also law/legislation
Green papers, 64
groupthink, 106, 170
giving and receiving feedback, see social
  work skills/no. 27
groupwork skills, 261, 278, 346
guidance, 31, 156, 222
  guidance documents, their status, 64,
    65, 116, 189
  giving advice, see social work skills/no.
    36

H
Habermas, 98
hardship/adversity, see adversity
health
  health care, 58, 68, 87, 88, 176
  health inequalities, 15, 21, 86–88, 346
  illness/ill health, 38, 75, 83, 86, 87,
    181, 237, 350

inverse care law, 87–8
life expectancy, 86, 87
Marmot Review (2010), 15, 80, 87
medical/biomedical model, 38
model, mental health/illness, 27, 48,
    69, 70, 72, 75, 80, 136, 145, 175,
    181, 186, 238, 268, 281, 319
see disability/people with disabilities
healthy sense of outrage, 49, 80, 111, 245
Hierarchy of Needs (Maslow), 124,
    125–7
hierarchy of research methods, 55
helping/providing help, *see* social work
    skills/no. 35
heuristics, 93
Hollis, 13, 43, 341
home visits, 7, 190, 197, 274, 302
homelessness, 75, 120, 181, 237, 268, 346
honest/honesty, 15, 156, 164, 183, 209,
    228, 234, 248, 251, 258, 264,
    285, 303, 330
hope, 16, 17, 42, 125, 135, 164, 171, 204,
    227, 235, 243, 270, 302, 307
hostility/hostile reactions, 46, 99, 113,
    136, 138, 197, 253, 273–4
heterosexism/heteronormalism, 48
hospitals, location of interview, 189
housing, 37, 67, 71, 77, 79, 86, 88, 109,
    161, 165, 229, 250, 282, 284,
    324, 331, 347
hostility/hostile reactions, *see* social work
    skills/no. 62
Howe, 13, 16, 17, 21, 28, 30, 41, 42, 48,
    73, 74, 110, 114, 117, 137, 138,
    139, 144, 199, 243, 250, 262,
    265, 279, 280, 311, 316, 341,
    342, 343, 350
human growth and development, *see*
    Chapter Six: Understanding
    Human Beings
Human Rights Act (1998), 66, 288–9
humanism/humanist approaches, 37, 124,
    125–8, 180, 247, 248, 338
see also client/person-centred
    approaches
humour, *see* social work skills/no. 80
hunches, *see* intuition
hypotheses, 28, 29, 91, 96, 97, 100–102,
    105, 106, 113, 120, 132, 162,
    168, 170, 184, 204, 245
hypothetical questions, *see* social work
    skills/no. 22

I
id, 131, 132
identity, 134, 287
ideology, 28, 36
    dominant ideology, 28, 36, 82, 93,
        242
    impact on social work, 25, 68, 102
    role of ideology, 48–50, 175
income inequality, 87
independence, *see* dependence/dependency
individual budgets, 68, 69
individualizing problems, 15, 37, 103,
    161, 317, 326, 346, 360
    public issues seen as *personal troubles*
        (Mills), 15, 103, 346
inequality
    see social inequalities
    see health inequalities
infancy/childhood, 17, 42, 108, 111, 131,
    134, 135, 136, 141, 145, 232,
    233, 246, 247
    see attachment
    see Winnicott
informal carers, 261
informal opening conversations, ('social
    chat'), *see* social work skills/no. 11
information gathering, *see* social work
    skills/no. 16
information, providing, *see* social work
    skills/no. 37
information technology/computer skills,
    74, 164, 294, 295
injustice, defined, 7, 15, 18, 111, 118,
    258, 260, 280
interdependence, *see* dependence/
    dependency
internalized oppression/internalization,
    256, 330
internet, 301
interpersonal skills, *see* social work
    skills/no. 1
interpretations/offering interpretations,
    see social work skills/no. 48
inter-professional collaboration/contexts
    collaboration, importance of, 11, 181,
        257, 264, 267, 308, 316
    differences in status, 106, 284
    information sharing, 283, 284
    inter-agency cooperation, 171, 181,
        282–4, 292, 298
    multi-disciplinary/inter-disciplinary
        approaches, 275, 282–4, 292, 313

interventions
  defined, 45, 157
  directive interventions, 160
  Dreyfus and Dreyfus levels of skill,
    158–159
  focus of interventions, 160–162
  generalist skills/interventions, 45
  knowledge skills and values in action,
    153
  micro, mezzo and macro skills and
    interventions, 159
  non-directive interventions, 160
  specialist skills/interventions, 45
  when and how to intervene, 162–163
  see social work skills for a lexicon of 80
    skills and interventions
interviews/interviewing skills
  interviewing skills
  see Chapter Seven: interviewing skills
  intuition, *see* social work skills, *see* social
    work skills/no. 15
  inverse care law, 87
  involuntary clients, 339, 335
  isolation, impact of, 75, 135, 238, 261

J
judgements
  common errors when observing others,
    169–171
  individual errors and omissions, 106–7
  judicious decision-making, 54, 92, 96,
    105, 107, 112, 120, 181, 183,
    228, 236, 243
  organizational errors, 107–8
  see assumptions
  justice/social justice, 3, 7, 15, 49, 88, 106,
    161, 164, 308, 345, 346, 347

K
Kadushin and Kadushin, 13, 166, 167,
    173, 185, 188, 190, 192, 195,
    204, 209, 214, 215, 218, 221,
    233, 235, 227, 306
kinesics, 167
knowing how, 26, 91, 174
knowing that, 26, 91
knowledge base of social work
  adapted/borrowed from other
    disciplines, 35–39
  uneasy marriage between theory and
    practice, 50–51

  knowledge defined, 26
  indigenous' knowledge, defined, 27
  knowledge and skills framework,
    32–34
  proof, 28
  research, importance of, 51–59
  science/empirical knowledge, 30, 37
  social sciences, importance of, 6, 37,
    57, 119, 286
  subjugated knowledge, 27
  tacit knowledge, 33, 93, 108, 115–116,
    120, 169, 181
  theory defined, 29–30
  truth or reality, 26
  see also Chapter Two: Theoretical
    Knowledge
  see also Chapter Three: Factual
    Knowledge
  see also Chapter Four: Practice
    Knowledge
Koprowska, 8, 14, 112, 156, 163

L
labeling/stereotyping, 27, 75, 137, 170,
    172, 173, 189, 226, 243, 261,
    283, 307, 334, 335. 27, 243, 261
Laming, reports/inquiries, 12, 25–6, 69,
    74, 106, 107, 133, 183, 280, 283
  'Baby P', Protection of Children in
    England ('Baby P' Inquiry)
    (2008), 12
  Victoria Climbé Inquiry (2003), 12, 25,
    69, 133
language, 20, 24, 38, 43, 58, 95, 112,
    173, 207, 227, 230, 256, 259,
    263, 283, 305, 317
  choice of words, 164, 202, 206, 211,
    239, 300
  speech, 166, 214, 215
  see verbal communication skills, social
    work skills/no. 2
law/legislation/policy influences
  Acts of Parliament
  Carers (Recognition and Services) Act
    (1995), 179, 180
  Children Act (2004), 65, 69, 180
  Children Act, England (1989), 189
  Chronically Sick and Diabled Persons
    Act (1970) 179
  Community Care (Direct Payments)
    Act (1996), 63, 179

Criminal Justice Act (2002), 180
Data Protection Act (DPA)(1998), 288, 291
Freedom of Information Act (FOIA) (2000), 288
Human Rights Act (HRA), 66, 288–9
Local Authority Social Services Act (1970), 65
Mental Capacity Act (2005), 180
Mental Health Act (2007), 180
National Health Service (NHS) and Community Care Act (1990), 67–9, 71, 73, 179, 182, 261, 267
case law, 63
Children's Plan, 40
codes, defined, 65
command papers, 64
consultation process, for new legislation
court work/giving evidence,
discretionary powers of local authorities, 71
duties, defined, 65
European Union (EU) legislation, 66
Every Child Matters, 65, 69, 70, 181
Fair Access to Care Services (2003), 68, 268
Gloucester Judgement, 63
Green papers, 64
guidance documents, their status, 64
how laws are made/progress of a Bill to an Act , 64
legal mandate of social workers, 41, 63, 162, 267, 273
mandatory powers of local authorities, 71
Ombudsman, 65
powers, defined, 65
principles underpinning the UK legal system, 63–4
Putting People First, 40, 68, 181
Royal Commission on Long Term Care, 70
secondary legislation, 65
United Nations Convention on the Rights of the Child, (adopted 1989), 66
White papers, 64
see social policy
leaflets/written information, 230–1
learned helplessness, 104, 130, 269

learning difficulties/disabilities, 72, 113, 114, 166, 181, 240, 261, 268, 282, 300
learning theory/social learning theory,124, 130, 270, 311, 312
legislation, *see law*
letter writing, *see* social work skills/no. 72
lexicon of 80 skills and interventions, *see* social work skills
lifespan, 117, 123, 124, 134
life story work, 201, 269
Lishman, 8, 14, 103, 112, 160, 161, 167, 168, 172, 188, 189, 191, 194, 199, 202, 203, 217, 226, 228, 229, 230, 233, 235, 236, 245, 250, 256, 257, 262, 264, 271, 272, 273, 274, 287, 294, 297
listening, importance of, *see* social work skills/no. 5
see social work skills/no. 26. active listening responses ('minimum encouragers')
Local Authorities Social Services Act, (1970), 65
locus of control, 130–1
loop learning, single and double, 107–108
loop system/hearing impairments, 165
loss, *see* bereavement and loss, 88, 136, 141, 142, 143, 181, 194, 222, 229

M
macro skills and interventions, 159
macrosystem, 325
managerialism, culture in social work, 55, 67, 70
bureaucratic approaches to service delivery, 39, 40, 41, 262, 246
managerialism, 38, 41, 67, 68, 71, 97, 98, 276, 281, 294, 297, 346
marketization/market force mechanisms, 67–68
New Public Management, 67–68
marginalized groups/marginalization, 81, 148, 247, 257
Marx/Marxism, 30, 37, 84, 93
Maslow, 18, 110, 123, 124, 125–127
material assistance, *see* social work skills/no. 42
meaning/communication of meaning, 154, 155, 157, 164, 166, 168, 171, 172, 184, 287

mediation skills, *see* social work skills/no. 57

medication, 49, 50, 56, 175, 201–2

medical/biomedical model, 38, 43, 49

children prescribed mind-altering drugs, 50

medicalization of behaviour, 49

Mehrabian, 166

men/males, 19, 38, 78, 83, 87, 145, 147, 330, 331

mental health/mental illness, 69, 70, 72, 81, 136, 145, 175, 181, 186, 281, 282, 319, 363

anxiety states, 251

assertive outreach, 319, 321

depression, 27, 117, 136, 176, 218, 317, 318, 321

early intervention, 281

isolation and social exclusion, impact of, 75, 135, 238, 261

medical/biomedical model, 38, 43, 49

Mental Health Act (2007), 180

mental health/vulnerability of people with, 81, 283–4

mental/emotional distress, 136, 176

survivors/service user movement, 48, 238, 268

vulnerability to abuse/neglect, 81, 283–4

mesosystem, 325

methodology, 27, 54

mezzo skills and interventions, 159

micro skills and interventions, 159

microsystem, 325

middle class, 75, 83, 110, 147, 148

minute taking, *see* social work skills/no. 68

mobile phones and texts, *see* social work skills/no. 75

modelling and social skills training, *see* social work skills/no. 46

model, defined, 43

modernization agenda, 68, 279

monitoring, 174, 177, 294, 295, 299

motivational interviewing, 22, 127, 174, 243

see Appendix Six: Motivational Interviewing 333–336

multi-disciplinary/inter-disciplinary approaches, 275, 282–4, 292, 313

Munro, 112, 134, 157, 158, 171, 172, 188, 190, 191, 192, 195

mutuality, 111, 128, 146, 191, 227, 239, 260

N

narrative approaches, 177, 233

National Framework for Older People (2001), 181, 368

National Health Service (NHS) and Community Care Act (1990), 67–9, 71, 73, 179, 182, 261, 267

National Health Service (NHS),

National Institute for Health and Clinical Excellence (NICE), 50, 58

National Occupational Standards (NOS), 3, 278

National Statistics Socio-Economic Classification (NS-SEC), 82, 84, 85

needs-led versus resource-led, 179

need, children in, *see* children and young people

neglect, child, 11, 25, 75, 138, 141, 143, 181, 247, 257, 263

as a form of abuse, 284

negotiation skills, *see* social work skills/no. 53

networks/social network, 12, 14, 77, 119, 229, 261

support network, 13, 238, 261, 324, 326

networking, *see* social work skills/no. 55

neuroscience, 195

New Labour, 68–70

New Public Management/managerialism, 67–68

non-directive/directive interventions, *see* interventions

non-verbal communication, *see* social work skills/no. 3

see body language

see verbal communication skills, social work skills/no. 2

normative, normalization, 124, 146–147, 254, 268

notes/taking notes, 296

Northern Ireland, 66, 288

population, 83

NOS (National Occupational Standards),
   3, 278
numeracy skills, 164

O
observation, *see* social work skills/no. 4
offence, confrontation work,
offenders/crime, *see* crime/offending
   behaviour
offending behaviour, dealing with,
older people, 67, 68, 79, 83, 181, 193, 27,
   258, 261, 284, 319, 362
   Adult Safeguarding Boards (ASBs), 284
   Community Care (Direct Payments)
      Act (1996), 63, 179
   direct payments, 63, 68, 69, 179
   eligibility criteria for service provision,
   generativity versus stagnation
      (Erikson), 135
   health care, 68, 87, 88, 176
   individual budgets, 68, 69
   integrity versus despair/disgust
      (Erikson), 135
   Mental Capacity Act (2005), 180
   Single Assessment Process for older
      people (SAP), 284
   statistics, people of pensionable age, 83
   vulnerability to abuse/neglect, 81,
      283–4
   see also adult social care
   see also health
open questions, *see* social work skills/no.
   17
oppression, 3, 19, 24, 30, 47, 111, 123,
   124, 146, 254, 269, 306, 307,
   317, 329, 331
internalized oppression/internalization,
   defined, 256, 330
   see discrimination
   see social inequalities
   see social injustice
   see poverty
Options for Excellence (2006), 6, 368
organizational skills, *see* social work
   skills/no. 71
Organizations
   see agencies
   see private voluntary and independent
      sector
   see statutory sector
outcomes, desired, 100, 129, 286, 298,
   312

P
paradigm, defined, 100, 351
paralinguistics, 167
paraphrasing, *see* social work skill/no. 23
parent theories/theoretical offspring', 59
parents, 143, 168, 241, 256, 263, 264,
   266, 280, 324, 325
parent-child relationship, 136, 137,
   138, 139, 140, 227
parents in poverty, 77–78
partnership working, 40, 153, 181, 186,
   227, 253, 255, 257, 259, 260,
   270, 284, 295, 354
   see working in partnership, social work
      skills/no. 56
participation/service user participation,
   77, 106, 262, 269, 294, 296, 338
past on present, impact of, 11, 92, 124,
   137, 141
   pitfalls of search for past causes, 177,
      188, 202, 204, 209, 218, 226,
      233, 245, 250, 272, 306, 338–9
pathologising, 27, 343, 349
patriarchy, 36
patronizing, dangers of being
patterns of behaviour, 31, 119–120, 122,
   169, 174, 199, 249, 136
   pattern recognition, 119–120
payments, (direct payments). 63, 68, 69,
   179
Putting People First, 40, 68, 181
personal change, tendency to
      individualized, 15, 103, 161,
      338–9, 345
personal responsibility for behaviour, 255,
   262, 338
personal is political, 330, 345
personal budgets, 68, 69
personal social services budget, 72
personalization, 68, 69, 246, 299
person-centred (client-centred) approaches
   see Appendix Seven: Person-Centred
      Approaches 337–340
   see Roger's client centred approach,
      127–128
person-in-the situation, 42
perspectives that inform this text
   importance of knowledge and skills,
      4–7
   importance of communication skills in
      social work, 8–9
   social work as capacity building, 9–13

perspectives that inform this text
(*Continued*)
relationship-based perspective, 13–17
personal perspectives and assumptions,
17–20
persuasion/being directive, *see* social work
skills/no. 51
philosophy of practice, 17, 285
philosophy, relevance in social work, 17,
36, 37, 38, 59, 71, 96, 109, 196,
241, 275, 311
phobias, 129, 131
physical abuse, 114, 181
physical contact/touching, 8, 113, 167,
191, 192, 195
physical/therapeutic restraint, 8
placements, 72, 95, 189
planning and preparation, *see* social work
skills/no. 8
play, 10
points of failure/failure situations, 139,
141–142
police, and violent attacks, 69, 274, 283,
284, 330
policy
agency policy and practice/procedures,
178, 181, 247, 268
social policy, 21, 33, 37, 40, 66–70,
181
Social Work and Social Policy Subject
Centre (SWAP), 21, 51
politics, 15, 22, 49 38, 67, 77, 102, 104,
146, 159, 250, 258, 262, 265,
280, 308, 326, 329, 331, 343
speaking out about *social ills/social
evils* 19, 161
personal is political, 330, 345
front-line perspectives, importance of,
278, 346
see Appendix 9: Radical and Activist
Perspectives in Social Work,
345–348
see radical social work,
Popper, 26, 28, 29, 38
postmodernism, 30, 31, 98
poverty
absolute poverty, 76
deprivation, 88
disadvantage, 88–89
people on benefit 78–79
poverty line, how its calculated, 77–78
relative poverty, 76–77

measures of poverty, 77–78
tax loopholes, 80
unclaimed benefits, 79
central concern in social work, 15, 21,
75, 76–78
see also class
see also discrimination
see also health inequalities
see also social inequalities
see also social isolation
positivism, 37, 96, 102
presenting information, *see* social work
skills/no. 76
protective factors, identification of, 124,
324
power, 98, 254, 263, 264, 269, 334
power, linked to differences in status,
27, 106, 265, 330
powerless/powerlessness, 130, 265,
269
practical help/practical and material
assistance, *see* social work
skills/no. 42
practice
(a) skills and interventions/lexicon of
80 skills, 45–6
(b) fields of practice, 47
(c) practice approaches, 47
(d) values-based perspectives, 47–48
difficulty bringing about change, 5
knowledge and skills framework,33
practice wisdom, 92, 108, 118–19,
120, 181
practice approaches, growth in number
of, 44
different directive and non-directive
emphasis, 160, 178, 180
practice approaches
Appendix 1: Behaviourist approaches,
311–314
Appendix 2: Cognitive approaches,
315–318
Appendix 3: Crisis Intervention,
319–321
Appendix 4: Ecological approach in
social work, 323–327
Appendix 5: Feminist perspectives in
social work, 329–332
Appendix 6: Motivational Interviewing,
333–336
Appendix 7: Person-centred
approaches, 337–340

Appendix 8: Psychological approaches, 341–344
Appendix 9: Radical and activist perspectives in social work, 345–348
Appendix 10: Strengths perspectives, 349–352
Appendix 11: Task-centred approaches, 353–356
Appendix 12: Stages of Change (or Cycle of Change), 357–360
other perspectives, 48
practice, values-based perspectives
anti-discriminatory perspectives/practice, 48, 201, 248, 340
anti-oppressive perspectives/practice, 47, 48, 110, 180, 248, 325, 347, 351
anti-racist perspectives/practice, 47, 48, 347
private, voluntary, and independent sector (PVI), 71
privatization, withdrawal and increased cost of services, 72
probation, 49 191, 193
probing, *see* social work skills/no. 30
problems
as *unsatisfied wants*, 175
problems differentiated from difficulties, 175
social problems, 37, 67, 75, 103, 175, 346, 350
public issues seen as *personal troubles* (Mills), 15, 103, 346
problem-solving, 3, 5, 93, 100, 103–105, 181, 229, 248, 249, 261, 280, 353, 359
see social work skills/no. 63. managing professional boundaries
professional boundaries, *see* social work skills/no. 63
professional development, 103, 297, 298
professional use of self, *see* social work skills/no. 14
prompting, *see* social work skills/no. 29
projection, 41, 66, 134
protection, 133, 190, 273, 281
child protection, 70, 71, 106, 182, 185, 261, 262, 264, 265
safeguarding, 283, 284, 324
protective factors, 124, 324
resilience/survival skills, 142–145, 148

providing information, *see* social work skills/no. 37
proxemics, 167
psychiatric admissions, reduced with support, 238, 261
psychoanalytic concepts, 341–344
anxiety, importance of containing, 48, 46, 225, 250–1, 212, 234, 242
avoidance, 133–134, 210, 272, 342
conscious, 342
counter-transference, 112, 134, 342, 343
defences/defence mechanism, 13, 18, 131, 142, 342
defined, 132, 342
denial, 133
preconscious, 342
psychoanalytic influence in social work, 341–344
transference, 342
unconscious, 342
psychology
and importance in social work, 37
behaviourism, 128–131
biological factors, 37, 123, 134
cognitive-behavioural therapy (CBT),45, 47, 117, 125, 130, 131, 160, 178, 197, 234, 236, 241, 242, 248, 266, 311
Eurocentric bias, 146–8
feminist, 145–6
humanism, 125–8
psychoanalysis, 131–145
psychotherapy, *see* therapy
psychotropic drugs, issued to children, 50
drugs*public issues* seen as *personal troubles* (Mills), 15, 103, 346
child deaths and inquiries, 25,-6, 52, 69, 97, 106, 133, 162, 188, 286
see Laming reports/inquiries
punctuality, as demonstrating reliability, 167, 291, 299, 300
purchaser/provider split, 67, 260
Putting People First (2008), 40, 68, 181
PVI, 71

Q
quality assurance, 38
quality control, 53
quality of life, 88, 161, 238, 343, 351
questions
asking good questions, 199

questions (*Continued*)
    asking questions, common errors when
        questioning, 199–200
    circular, *see* social work skills/no. 21
    closed, *see* social work skills/no. 18
    hypothetical, *see* social work skills/no.
        22
    open, *see* social work skills/no. 17
    what, *see* social work skills/no. 19
    why, *see* social work skills/no. 20

R
race/racism, 29, 36, 143, 147, 180
    anti-racist perspectives/practice, 47, 48,
        347
    ethnicity, 287
radical social work, 43, 345–348
randomized control trials (RTCs) 53–54,
        55, 62
rape, 146, 330
rapport, *see* social work skills/no. 9
rational-technical, 41, 180
rationing resources, 64, 68, 183
reassurance, *see* social work skills/no. 40
reciprocal/reciprocity, 16, 41, 111, 136,
        140, 227, 239, 251, 260, 343
recording/record keeping skills, *see* social
        work skills/no. 65
    Data Protection Act (DPA)(1998), 288,
        291
    Freedom of Information Act (FOIA)
        (2000), 288
recognition, pattern, 119–120
referral, 100, 101, 176, 12, 202, 229
reflective practice, 97, 98–99, 115, 251,
        286
reflexivity, 28, 33, 91, 92, 97–99, 105,
        143, 181
    use of self, *see* social work skills/no. 14.
        professional use of self
    see also critical thinking
    see also critical reflection
    see also evidence based practice
reframing, *see* social work skills/no. 47
Registrar General's classification, 82, 84,
        86
relationship building, 14, 15
relationships based approach, central
        importance in social work, 13–17,
        36, 89, 343
eliability and consistency, 112, 139, 167,
        168

religious/spiritual beliefs, 15
reluctant/involuntary service users, 339,
        335
reports/report writing, *see* social work
        skills/no. 69
research and social work
    barriers to the take up of research,
        157–159
    baseline data, importance of, 176, 177,
        178, 295, 312, 313
    best evidence, 54, 55, 286
    case study, 53
    *critical best practice perspective,
        research informed practice,*
        57
    evaluation of effectiveness, 177, 181,
        294, 312, 317
    evidence based practice (EBP), 52,
        54–7
    evidence based/actions backed by
        evidence, 16, 26, 101, 107, 120
    evidence-based policy and practice, 57
    hierarchy of research methods, 55
    knowledge-based practice, 57
    literature reviews, 53, 58
    meta analysis, 53
    methodology, 27, 54
    multi-method research, 52
    qualitative methods, 52, 56
    quantitative methods, 52, 54
    randomized control trials (RCT),
        53–54, 55, 62
    research-based knowledge, 57
    research-informed practice, 57
    review, 53
    Sackett, 54
    single case design/evaluation/N=1, 54
    systematic reviews, 53, 58, 59
    variables, impact of, 55, 57, 117, 120,
        167, 218, 286
    what works approach, 56, 286
residential care, escalating costs of, 67–68,
        70, 72
residential workers/working from their
        best selves, 190
resilience/survival skills
    in children, 142–145, 148
    practitioner resilience, 183, 251, 256,
        259
    service user resilience, 261, 350, 351
resources, *see* financial resources
respectful uncertainty, 106

responses/active listening responses
('minimum encouragers'), *see*
social work skills/no. 26
restraint, 8
reviews/coordinating case conferences and
reviews, *see* social work skills/no.
78
rights
human rights, 3, 7, 37, 49, 63, 66,
106
Human Rights Act (1998), 288–9
welfare rights/benefits, 48, 80, 79, 81,
161, 228, 229, 269
risk, 16, 27, 72, 77, 88, 142, 162
linked to danger, 40, 160, 176, 236,
273, 274, 297, 338
rights vs risks, 264
risk assessment, 6, 179–183, 213
risk defined, 182
safety, 114, 125, 126, 133, 138, 176,
268, 281, 292, 342
child protection/safeguarding, *see* child
protection
complexity and uncertainty, 279
risk management, 38, 40, 41, 56, 107,
177, 182
Rogers', 13, 18, 94, 101, 124, 110, 124,
195, 233, 248, 333, 337–338
Seven Stages of Progress, 338–339
Rogers' client-centred approach
127–128
roles and responsibilities, professional, 50,
282, 329
Rowntree/Joseph Rowntree Charitable
Trust/Foundation, 53, 75, 78, 81,
378, 384, 391
Royal Commission on Long Term Care
(1999), 70
Ruch, 13, 43, 98
rule based knowledge/behaviour, 62, 73,
102, 107, 108, 156, 181
rural neglect, 16

S
Sackett, 54
SAP (Single Assessment Process),
284
Schön, 20, 30, 94, 95, 96–98, 101, 108,
115
SCIE, (Social Care Institute for
Excellence), 8, 21, 28
scientific/empirical knowledge/methods,

Scotland, 66
population, 83
secondary legislation, 65–6
secure base, 136, 144
Seebohm Report, 39, 69
self-actualization/actualizing tendency/self
determination, 110, 124, 125,
126, 127, 200, 228, 240, 249,
355, 337, 338
self-awareness/self-knowledge, 33, 97, 99,
110, 111, 112, , 192, 195, 196,
197, 217, 227, 249, 263, 285
self-advocacy, 254, 268
self-disclosure, *see* social work skills/no.
32
self-blame, 217, 243, 255
self-esteem/self-worth/self image , 9, 14,
135, 136, 137, 143, 178, 234,
236, 243, 247, 263, 287, 330
self harm, 273, 274
self-help, 39, 229, 268
self-sufficiency, 127, 140, 228, 247
sense of self, 109, 144, 187, 247
separation, reactions in children, 136,
137, 222
service provision, 7, 39, 40, 67, 71, 73,
107, 257, 296, 297
service user/s
as, *clients, customers (cus), consumers,
recipients of services,
PWUCS/C,*.23
capacities that service users bring to the
encounter, 10–11
central importance in assessment, 16,
27, 31, 32, 33, 69, 74, 100, 107,
153, 165, 174–84, 198, 213,
295
coping skills/capacity, 10, 237
inverse care law, 87–8
involvement in decision-making, 66,
100, 127–8, 160, 236, 257, 263,
279
involvement in social work education
and training, 51
knowledge, skills and values,
user involvement, 262, 264
user-led policies, 240, 254
value given to helping and caring,
238–9
see adult social care
see children and young people
see disability/people who are disabled

service user/s (*Continued*)
    see disability/people with disabilities
    see older people
    see mental health/mental illness
    settings/practice location, 7, 50, 56, 57,
        117, 139, 189–190, 273, 277,
        291, 301, 303
sexism/sexist assumptions, 145, 330, 331
sexual abuse, 114, 145, 146, 181, 217,
        244, 245, 330. *See also* rape
    see also abuse
sexual orientation/preference, 15, 81, 83,
        148, 331
shaking hands, 191–192
shame/shameful feelings, 17, 110, 135,
        217, 226, 243, 250, 306
shared meanings, 287
Sheppard, 5, 10, 31, 48, 56, 62, 88, 92,
        94, 99, 100, 101, 102, 119, 147,
        237, 238, 261
signposting, *see* referrals
silence/allowing and using silences, *see*
        social skills/no. 31
Single Assessment Process (SAP), 284
single loop learning, 107–108
Skills for Care, 6, 23
    workforce, statistics for social care,
        72
smell, 167
social action/social change, 3, 6, 20, 161,
        250, 345–348, 376
social beings, 17, 124, 280, 308
social capital, 12, 325, 326
social care defined, 6
    workforce, statistics, 72
    social care and social work, 5–6
social Care Institute for Excellence (SCIE),
        see SCIE, 8, 21, 28
social casework, 6, 13, 43, 112, 248, 250,
        341, 354
social chat/informal opening
        conversations, *see* social work
        skills/no. 11
social class, *see* class
social control, 240, 281
social exclusion, 17, 77, 242, 247, 261,
        264, 308
    see also disadvantage
    see also discrimination
    see also poverty
    see also social justice

social factors, importance of, 27, 124,
        144, 284, 313, 326
    see also environmental factors
social ills/social evils 19, 161
social inequalities, 30, 76, 77, 80, 82, 87,
        88, 118, 146, 147, 249, 260, 345,
        360
social justice, 3, 7, 15, 49, 88, 106, 161,
        164, 308, 345, 346, 347
social learning theory/learning theory 124,
        130, 270, 311, 312
social model of disability, 43
social network, 12, 14, 77, 119, 229, 261
Social Policy and Social Work Subject
        Centre *(SWAP)*, 21, 51
social policy, 21, 33, 37, 40, 66–70, 181
social problems, 37, 67, 75, 103, 175,
        346, 350
Social Services Inspectorate, 164–5
social services, 38, 39, 63, 65, 68, 72,
        106, 162, 164, 165, 191, 205,
        230, 238, 260, 261, 264, 282
    financial constraints/under-resourcing,
        7, 12, 41, 64, 68, 71, 77, 105,
        176, 222, 225, 236, 247, 297,
        321, 346
    National Health Service (NHS) and
        Community Care Act (1990),
        67–9, 71, 73, 179, 182, 261, 267
    separation of adult and children's
        services, 68
    see also agency/agencies
social support, 13, 237, 238, 261, 324,
        326
    see also caring
Social Work Benchmark Statement
        (2008), 7, 100, 118, 159
social work education and training,
    academics, 51, 53, 55, 57, 95, 100, 160
    academic curriculum/subjects taught,
        25, 34, 38, 44, 116
    access to knowledge/research findings,
        48, 58, 93
    continuing professional development
        (CPD) 103, 297, 298
    generalist skills confused with generic
        theory-base, 45
    neglect of skills teaching and research,
        8, 44, 45
    placements, 72, 95, 189
    service user involvement, 51

social work skills
advanced skills, 45, 156
basic skills, 156, 172
professional competence, 96, 118, 135,
144, 155, 164, 167, 229, 276–80,
281, 282, 285, 287, 288, 300
directive/non-directive interventions,
160, 171, 172, 210, 236, 334, 337
generalist skills, 45, 248
evaluation of effectiveness, 177, 181,
294, 312, 317
interventions, defined, 45, 157
levels of skill, Dreyfus and Dreyfus,
158–159
focus of interventions, 160–162
generalist skills, 45
knowledge skills and values in action,
153
micro, mezzo and macro skills and
interventions, 159
non-directive interventions, 160
when and how to intervene, 162–163
specialist skills, defined, 159
skill, definition of, 155
terminology, lack of conceptual rigour,
43
transferability of knowledge and skills,
22, 23, 31, 32, 36, 45, 57, 108,
120, 161, 181, 313
see also knowledge-base of social work
**social work skills/a lexicon of 80
generalist skills/interventions, 46**
1. interpersonal skills, 97, 115, *163–164,*
176, 249, 255, 273, 279, 281, 341
2. verbal communication skills, 8, *164–6,*
95, 111, 159, 171, 195, 230, 232,
241, 259, 284, 308
ability to articulate, 48, 50, 89, 101,
112, 116, 119, 195, 226, 265,
266, 317
choice of words, 164, 202, 206, 211,
239, 300
language, 20, 24, 38, 43, 58, 95,
112, 173, 207, 227, 230, 256,
259, 263, 283, 305, 317
speech, 166, 214, 215
3. non-verbal communication skills, 8,
111, 115, 154, 164, *166–168,*
172, 195, 300, 308
body language, 133, 172, 196, 272,
300

4. observation/observation skills, 29, 31,
46, 52, 54, 94–5, 115, 129, 137,
154, 166, *168–171,* 205, 241,
263, 298, 303, 312
and interpretation, 169
common errors when observing
others, 169–171
5. listening skills, 112, 164, *171–174,*
263, 303
active listening, 171, 172
active listening responses, 26
incredulous listening, 171–172
hearing versus listening, 173
non-selective 171–172
limited listeners, 173
pretend listeners, 173
self centred listeners, 173
see social work skills/no. 26. active
listening responses ('minimum
encouragers')
6. assessment skills, 153, 154, *174–184,*
186, 213, 270, 282, 283, 284,
294, 295, 324, 326, 342, 350
assessments based on the *Knowledge
and Skills Framework,* 180–1
assessments, different approaches,
178–9
baseline data, importance of, 176,
177, 178, 295, 312, 313
best evidence, 54, 55, 286. added
later)
common purpose, importance of
identifying, 165, 203, 253, 259,
263, 264
difficulties' becoming 'problems',
175–6
eligibility criteria, 68, 368
environmental/social factors,
importance of in assessment
process, 27, 174, 184, 312, 313,
324, 326
evidence-based, 30, 52, 54–7, 101,
107, 120
*Framework for the Assessment of
Children in Need and their
Families* (CAF), 74, 139, 282,
283, 324, 349, 368
genogram, 305
group or team assessments, 179
home visits, 7, 190, 197, 274,
302

social work skills/a lexicon of 80 generalist skills/interventions, (*Continued***)**
information gathering skills, 198–200
service users, central importance, 16, 27, 31, 32, 33, 69, 74, 100, 107, 153, 165, 174–84, 198, 213, 295
joint assessments, 178
judgements, judicious decision-making, 54, 92, 96, 105, 107, 112, 120, 181, 183, 228, 236, 243
individual errors and omissions, 106–7
common errors when observing others, 169–171
organizational errors, 107–8
multi-disciplinary assessments, 179
needs-led versus resource-led, 179
observation skills, importance in assessment process, 31, 154, 168–171, 174–184, 312
see also observation
outcomes, desired, 100, 129, 286, 298, 312
planning, importance of, 169, 174, 185
power, impact of differences on assessment process, 27, 56, 98, 106, 130, 235, 236
see also power
practice emphasis in assessment, 178
protective factors, identification of, 124, 324
referrals, 100, 101, 176, 12, 202, 229
risk assessment, 6, 179–183, 213
Single Assessment Framework (SAP), 284
six main tasks involved in an assessment, 176–7
variables, impact of, 55, 57, 117, 120, 167, 218, 286
see also critical thinking and analysis
see also demonstrating and evaluating effectiveness
see also reflective practice
7. engaging with the task, *187–188*, 197, 214

8. planning and preparing for the interview, *188–190*
planning, 74, 169, 174, 185, 218, 238, 283, 294, 295, 296, 299
preparation, 185, 218, 257, 258, 259
9. creating a rapport, 32, 33, 163, 189, *190–191*, 210, 235, 239
10. welcoming skills, 190, *191–192*, 193, 194, 304
shaking hands, 191–2
see warm/warmth, importance of
11. informal opening conversations ('social chat'), *192–194*
12. sympathy, 134, *194*, 196, 237, 258
13. empathy, 111, 112, 128, 143, 146, 164, 171, 191, *194–196*, 248, 267, 277, 280, 334, 388, 389
14. professional use of self/use of self, 32, 33, 46, 108, 110–12, 120, 181, 186, *196–197*
15. use of intuition, 92, 93, 96, 97, 108, 110, 111, 112–114, 115, 120, *197–198*, 244
intuitive reasoning, 114, 134, 118, 195
Munro, 112, 114, 134, 188
see also tacit knowledge
16. information gathering, 176, 180, 193, *198–200*
17. open questions, *200–201*
18. closed questions, 46, 186, 196, 200, *201–202*
19. *what* questions, *202–203*
20. *why* questions, *203–204*
21. circular questions, *204*
22. hypothetical questions, 102, *204–205*
23. paraphrasing, *205–206*, 207, 212
24. clarifying, 186, 202, 205, *206–7*
25. summarizing, 187, 205, *207–208*
26. active listening responses ('minimum encouragers'), *208–209*
27. giving and receiving feedback, 156, 170, 205, *209–210*
28. sticking to the point and purpose of the interview, *210–212*
29. prompting, *212–213*
30. probing, *213–214*
31. allowing and using silences, 170, 172, 199, *214–217*
32. using self-disclosure, 112, *217–219*
33. ending an interview, *219–221*

34. closing the case and ending the relationship, *221–226*
35. providing help, 6, 41, 103–4, 131, 134, 155, 160, 222, *226–228*, 232, 239, 249
36. giving advice, 46, *228–229*, 230, 231, 237, 337
37. providing information, 51, 160, 213, *229–231*, 239
38. providing explanations, 29, 229, 230, *231–233*
39. offering encouragement and validation, 208, *233–234*, 237, 270, 302
40. providing reassurance, 133, 138, 192, 210, *234–235*, 250
41. using persuasion and being directive, 160, *235–236*, 240, 259, 260, 334
42. providing practical and material assistance, 6, 11, 13, 39, 41, 105, 127, 226, 227, 229, *236–237*
43. providing support, 6, 13, 143, 226, *237–238*, 261, 297, 320
44. providing care, *238–240*
care/caring, 178, 193, 226, 238–9, 243, 250, 263, 338, 350
caring tone of voice, 203, 212
ethics of care/caring, central in social work, 42
quality of care, 87
pitfalls in caring/dependency, 239–240
45. breaking *bad news*, 225, 230, *240–1*
46. modelling and social skills training, 129, *241–242*, 270, *313*
47. reframing, *242–244*
48. offering interpretations, 133, *244–245*
49. adapting to need, *245–247*
50. counselling skills, 13, 36, 39, 46, 47, 127, 160, 164, 187, 225, 226, 237, *247–250*
aims of counselling, 249–250
change process/Rogers' Seven Stages of Progress, 338–339
client/person centred approaches, 337–340
defined, 247
51. containing anxiety, 48, 46, 225, 212, 234, 242, *250–254*
52. empowerment and enabling skills, 3, 6, 14, 48, 249, *254–256*, 262, 270, 287, 316, 347, 351

enabling, 93, 182, 200, 205, 239, 243
53. negotiating skills, 159, *256–259*, 265, 266, 267
54. contracting skills, *259–260*, 256
contracts 46, 69, 213, 248, 253, 256, 257, 291, 353
written agreement/s, 259, 260
55. networking skills, *260–262*
56. working in partnership, 40, 153, 186, 259, 255, 259, 260, 265, 270, 284, 354, *262–265*
57. mediation skills, *265–267*
58. advocacy skills, 6, 43, 46, 47, 88, 161, 165, 236, 240, 253, 254, 261, 265, 266, *267–9*, 298
59. assertiveness skills, 46, 242, 249, 253, 267, *269–271*
assertiveness training, 146, 270–1, 313
60. being challenging/challenging skills, 102, 103, 133, 254, 271, 272, 304
61. being confrontative, 80, 99, 133, 134, 170, 203, 240, 249, 271, *272–3*, 298, 334, 337
62. dealing with hostility, aggression, and violence, 46, 99, 113, 136, 138, 197, 253, *273–4*
63. managing professional boundaries, 16, 46, 112, 190, 193, 193, 245, 249, 263, 275, 283, *289–291*
roles and responsibilities, 50, 282, 329
64. respecting confidentiality, 46, 162, 189, 193, 249, 259, 275, 290, *291–293*
Data Protection Act (DPA)(1998), 288, 291
Freedom of Information Act (FOIA) (2000), 288
Human Rights Act (HRA), 66, *288–9*
65. record-keeping skills, 291, 292, *293–295*, 301
66. form filling, *295*
67. updating case notes, *295–296*
68. minute-taking skills, *296*, 299, 304
69. report writing skills, *296–297*
70. using supervision creatively, 15, 45, 95, 97, 103, 112, 113, 116, 134, 162, 168, 169, 171, 221, 238, 263, 243, *297–299*, 351

social work skills/a lexicon of 80
    generalist skills/interventions,
    (Continued)
71. organizational and administrative
    skills, 46, 107, 276, 294, 296,
    299–300
72. letter writing skills, 300–301
73. skilled use of emails, 300, 301–302
74. telephone contact/skills, 167, 300,
    301, 302, 354
75. using mobile phones and text
    messaging, 302–303
76. presentation skills, 303
77. chairing meetings, 303–304
78. coordinating case conferences and
    reviews, 259, 304
79. presenting evidence in court,
    304–305
80.-using humour, 305–307
social work theory
    uneasy marriage between theory and
        practice, 50–51
    knowledge defined, 26
    theory defined, 29–30
    see knowledge
    see also Chapter Two: Theoretical
        Knowledge
    see also Chapter Three: Factual
        Knowledge
    see also Chapter Four: Practice
        Knowledge
social work/social workers
    a skilled and knowledgeable activity, 3,
        307
    abuse of, 273
    action, linked to understanding, 4, 13,
        31, 32, 45, 95, 101, 117, 153,
        162, 182, 259
    British Association of Social Workers
        (BASW), 3, 7, 64, 89
    capacities social workers bring to the
        encounter, 11–12
    continuing professional development
        (CPD), 103, 297, 298
    evidence based practice (EBP), 52, 54–7
    evidence based/actions backed by
        evidence, 16, 26, 101, 107, 120
    knowledge and skills framework,
        32–34
    partnership working, 40, 153, 181,
        186, 227, 253, 255, 257, 259,
        260, 262–265, 270, 284, 295, 354

professional boundaries, 16, 46, 112,
    190, 193, 193, 245, 249, 263,
    275, 283, 289–91
research, barriers to the take up of,
    157–159
research, importance of, 51–59
roles and responsibilities, 50, 282,
    329
tacit knowledge, 33, 93, 108, 115–116,
    120, 169, 181
title of social work protected, 6
uneasy marriage between theory and
    practice, 50–51
see knowledge-base of social work
see social work skills and interventions
society, 5, 9, 12, 15, 18, 29, 30, 37, 38,
    41, 50, 71. 111, 118, 119, 140,
    176, 265, 285, 286
audit society, 71, 75, 76, 77, 81, 82,
    86, 88, 111
social workers as change agents, 5, 41,
    81, 277
status of groups in society, 15, 24, 29,
    75, 76–79, 82–89, 161, 226, 267
sociology, 30, 33, 35, 36, 37, 44, 93, 180,
    286, 326
socio-economic classification/social class,
    82
specialization, 39, 229, 297
specialist skills, 22, 45, 157, 180
speech, 166, 214, 215
spiritual dimension, importance of, 15,
    19, 249
stage theory and lifespan development,
    117, 123, 124, 134
Stages of Change see Cycle of Change, see
    Appendix Twelve, 357–360
statutory social work, 70–72, 250, 261,
    321
changing nature of, 69–70, 73–74
privatization, withdrawal and increased
    cost of services, 72
statutory powers/mandate/
    requirements, 36, 37, 56, 63, 65,
    162, 254, 281
stereotyping/labeling, 75, 137, 170,
    •172, 173, 189, 226, 283, 307,
    334, 335
sticking to the point and purpose of the
    interview, see social work
    skills/no. 28
stigma, 27, 243, 261

Stone Center (Boston, USA) 14, 145, 256
strange situation test, 137
stress/stressed 9, 12, 83, 112, 114, 131,
    143, 144, 163, 184, 236, 237,
    238, 264, 272, 304, 319, 320,
    341
strengths-based approaches, *see* Appendix
    Ten, 349–352
substance abuse/misuse, 75, 175, 334,
    335, 336, 360
suicide, 175, 274
summarizing, *see* social work skills/no. 25
superego, 131, 132
supervision, *see* social work skills/no. 70
support, emotional, 10, 127, 226, 237
support, social, 13, 237, 238, 261, 324,
    326
    see also caring
    see providing help, social work
        skills/no. 35
    see proving support, social work
        skill/no. 43
    see proving care, social work skill/no.
        44
support, 13, 237, 238, 261, 324, 326
survivors, see service users
SWAP (Social Policy and Social Work
    Subject Centre), 21, 51
symbolic communication, 167–168
sympathy, *see* social work skills/no. 12
systematic reviews, 53, 58, 59
systems theory/systemic perspectives, 21,
    43, 47, 87, 168, 176, 203, 249,
    323, 326, 341
    loops, learning, 104, 107

T
tacit knowledge, 33, 93, 108, 115–116,
    120, 169, 181
task-centred approaches, *see* Appendix
    Eleven, 353
teams and teamwork, 47, 58, 110, 179,
    278
technicist/technical-rational/rational-
    technical, 41, 96, 97, 98, 102,
    108, 180, 276
technical knowledge, 162
telephone skills, *see* social work skills/no.
    74
termination/disengagement,
    see ending an interview, social work
        skills/no. 33

see closing the case and ending the
    relationship, social work skills/no.
    34
terminology, differences in use of,
    43
testimony/presenting evidence in court, *see*
    social work skills/no. 79
texts/using mobile phones and text
    messaging, *see* social work
    skills/no. 75
theoretical approaches, *see* practice
    approaches
theory/theoretical knowledge,
    uneasy marriage between theory and
        practice, 50–51
    knowledge defined, 26
    theory defined, 29–30
    see knowledge
    see also Chapter Two: Theoretical
        Knowledge
    see also Chapter Three: Factual
        Knowledge
    see also Chapter Four: Practice
        Knowledge
therapy/psychotherapy, 19, 45, 47, 56,
    57, 127, 129, 130, 202, 204, 241,
    242
    CBT, 56, 248
    family therapy, 45, 47
    feminist, 145–146
third sector, 71
time-limited work/brief therapy, 202, 219,
    317, 319, 320, 355
time, territory and task (3 't's),
    291
TOPSS, *see* National Occupational
    Standards
touching/physical contact, 8, 113, 167,
    191, 192, 195
tracking, 205
training, *see* social work education and
    training
transferability 22, 23, 31, 32, 36, 45, 57,
    108, 120, 161, 181, 313
    transferability of knowledge, skills and
        values, 116–8
transference, 342
Transforming Social Care (2008), 68,
    181
transparent/transparency, 193
trans-theoretical model of psychotherapy,
    357

trauma, 9, 45, 57, 75, 113, 138, 140, 141,
144, 170, 177, 187, 201, 218,
229, 245, 321, 349
    defined, 144
Trevithick, 11, 13, 16, 18, 19, 20, 42, 43,
44, 45, 47, 49, 51, 52, 99, 115,
116, 117, 120, 125, 132, 134,
142, 146, 175, 188, 246, 247,
251, 256, 278, 331, 342
truth, 26, 27, 28, 170, 234, 251, 256, 285
    facing the truth, 13, 111, 245, 305
    universal truths, problematic concept,
30, 93

U
unacceptable behaviour, 129, 243, 273
uncertainty, leading to bureaucratic
approaches, 39, 40, 41, 262,
246
unconscious, 342
United Nations Convention on the Rights
of the Child, (adopted 1989), 66
upper class, 83, 86
user involvement, 262, 264
users, *see* service user
use of self/professional use of self, 32, 33,
46, 108, 110–12, 120, 181, 186
    see the professional use of self, social
skills/no. 14
V
validation/offering encouragement and
validation, *see* social work
skills/no. 39
valid/validity, 30, 34, 55, 94, 66, 170,
177, 218, 295, 312
value for money, 67
**values/values-based perspectives in social
work,**
    anti-discriminatory
perspectives/practice, 48, 201,
248, 340
    anti-oppressive perspectives/practice,
47, 48, 110, 180, 248, 325, 347,
351
    anti-racist perspectives/practice, 47, 48,
347
    professional ethics/practice, 3, 7, 15,
23, 38, 49.55, 56, 285, 293, 15,
23, 49, 56, 106, 118 130, 234,
255, 285, 291, 321

variables, 55, 57, 117, 120, 167, 218, 286
verbal ability/verbal communication skills,
    see social work skills/no. 2
victim perspective, 19, 130, 273, 330
Victoria Climbé Inquiry (2003), 12, 25,
69, 133
    see Laming report
violence/violent behaviour, 45, 46, 48, 75,
114, 145, 181, 182, 253, 262,
273–4, 291, 371, 319, 330, 346
voluntary sector, 70, 72, 250
volunteers, 72, 73, 165, 267, 268
vulnerable adults, 283–4, 293
    Adult Safeguarding Boards (ASBs),
284
    vulnerable adults and abuse/*No Secrets*
guidance (2000), 283–4
W
Wales, population, 83
warm/warmth, 14, 112, 139, 172, 178,
190, 191, 192, 193, 194, 195,
238, 248, 280, 290, 302, 342,
337, 338
    see welcoming skills, social skills/no. 10
Watzlawick, 103, 104, 175, 202, 242,
243, 264
welcoming skills, *see* social work skills/no.
10
welfare rights/benefits, 48, 80, 79, 81,
161, 228, 229, 269
welfare state, 38, 41, 68
    see also modernization agenda,
what questions, *see* social work skills/no.
19
what works, 56, 286
White papers, 64
why questions, *see* social work skills/no.
20
Winnicott, 9, 18, 42, 49, 117,
124, 138, 139, 146, 246,
247
    Clare Britton Winnicott, 139
    Winnicott's writing on dependence and
points of failure, 139–142
wisdom, *see also* practice wisdom, 92,
108, 118–19, 105, 120, 135, 181,
219
women, 38, 75, 78, 82, 83, 110, 117, 124,
147, 191, 239, 270, 277, 346

domestic violence, 45, 48, 75, 144, 181, 274, 319, 330, 331, 346, 358
feminist/feminism
feminist perspectives in social work, 239, 329–332
feminization of poverty, 76
feminist therapy 145, 146
Women's Therapy Center (London), 14, 145, 256
working class women, 19, 27, 146, 256
working models, defined, 137
working through feelings and inner conflicts, 247
working with abused children and adults, 170, 192, 204, 217, 245, 274, 293, 339
working class, 19, 75, 83–5, 86, 256, 261, 22
workload, 89, 298
written agreement/s, 259, 260

writing, 154, 206, 236, 259, 267, 275
see report writing skills, social works skills/no. 69
see letter writing skills, social works skills/no. 72

Y
young people/adolescents,
adolescents, 135, 136, 215
identity vs. role confusion (Erikson), 135
anti social behaviour, in young people, 41
youth offending, 41
physical/therapeutic restraint, 8
self-harm, 273, 274, 386
statistics, number of young people, 83
working with, 47, 117, 168, 171, 182, 206, 215, 227, 240, 258, 273, 375, 282, 283, 393, 379